UNIVERSITY OF WOLVERHAMPTON

THE IDEA OF PROSTITUTION

Other books by Sheila Jeffreys

The Spinster and Her Enemies: Feminism and Sexuality, 1880–1930
(1985, 1997)

Anticlimax: A Feminist Perspective on the Sexual Revolution
(1990)

The Lesbian Heresy
(1993)

The Sexuality Debates
(1987), Editor

Not a Passing Phase: Reclaiming Lesbians in History, 1840–1985
(1989), Contributing Editor

THE IDEA OF PROSTITUTION

8-11. sex trafficking
Stigma - 223-231.

SHEILA JEFFREYS

SPINIFEX

Spinifex Press Pty Ltd
504 Queensberry Street
North Melbourne, Vic. 3051
Australia
women@spinifexpress.com.au
http://www.spinifexpress.com.au/~women
Copyright © 1997 Sheila Jeffreys.
First edition published by Spinifex Press, 1997

Edited by Janet Mackenzie
Indexed by Trish Holt
Page design and typesetting in Sabon by Lynne Hamilton
Cover design by Kim Roberts
Made and printed in Australia by Australian Print Group

National Library of Australia
Cataloguing-in-Publication data:
Jeffreys, Sheila.
The idea of prostitution.
Bibliography.
Includes index.
ISBN 1–875559–65–5
1. Prostitution. 2. Sexual ethics. 3. Feminist theory. I.
Title
306.74

CONTENTS

ACKNOWLEDGEMENTS   vii
INTRODUCTION   1

CHAPTER 1   the traffic in women,
             feminism and the league of nations   7

CHAPTER 2   the revolt of the johns:
             prostitution and the sexual revolution   35

CHAPTER 3   normalising prostitution:
             the prostitutes' rights movement   65

CHAPTER 4   homosexuality and prostitution   92

CHAPTER 5   prostitution as "choice"   128

CHAPTER 6   just a job like any other?
             prostitution as "work"   161

CHAPTER 7   'why cars? who's driving?'prostitution
             and the theorising of sexuality   196

CHAPTER 8   prostitution as "sex"   213

CHAPTER 9   prostitution as male sexual violence   242

CHAPTER 10   sexual violence, feminist human rights
             theory and the omission of prostitution   275

CHAPTER 11   trafficking, prostitution and human rights   306

CONCLUSION   universalising prostitution   339

BIBLIOGRAPHY   349
INDEX   373

For Ann Rowett, with love.

ACKNOWLEDGEMENTS

I have been meaning to write at length about prostitution since 1980, when I wrote a brief paper on the topic for the Sexual Violence conference held in Leeds, England, in that year. I have considered for twenty years that men's abuse of women in prostitution lies at the very core of the oppression of women. My ideas here are the result of working in groups with radical feminist activists against pornography and prostitution during all this time. I would like to thank all those feminists who have inspired and shaped my thoughts on the issue in Britain in the London Revolutionary Feminist Anti-Pornography Group, in Women Against Violence Against Women, in the Patriarchy Study Group, in Lesbians against Sadomasochism. In Melbourne, these inspirational sisters in the local branch of the Coalition Against Trafficking in Women are Marilyn Born, Vanessa Born, Jane Guthrey, Bridget Haire, Sam Horsfield, Mary Sullivan, Renate Klein, Carole Moschetti, Rye Senjen, Caroline Spencer, Jill Spencer.

I would like to thank Kathleen Barry, first Director of the Coalition Against Trafficking in Women, for providing the framework of ideas and organisation that has made it possible for me and feminists in many countries to challenge prostitution. The present Directors, Dorchen Leidholdt and Janice Raymond, are enabling this challenge to continue. My thanks to them too.

My thinking on the issue was greatly clarified by the feminist anti-prostitution activists who organised the study tour of sex tourism in the Philippines that I was lucky enough to take part in in 1995, particularly Cecilia Hoffman and Aida Santos. I am grateful for the work of feminists in organisations dedicated to ending men's abuse of women in prostitution, such as WHISPER, the Council for Prostitution Alternatives and SAGE in the United States, and their counterparts everywhere. Their work is the heart of the passionate international struggle to end prostitution to which I hope this book will contribute.

Sheila Jeffreys
Melbourne, August 1997

ABBREVIATIONS

AMSH	Association for Moral and Social Hygiene
ASI	Anti-Slavery International
CATW	Coalition Against Trafficking in Women
CORP	Canadian Organisation for the Rights of Prostitutes
COYOTE	Cast Off Your Old Tired Ethics
ECP	English Collective of Prostitutes
GAATW	Global Alliance Against Trafficking in Women
HIRE	Hooking Is Real Employment
SAGE	Standing Against Global Exploitation
WEDPRO	Women's Education, Development, Productivity and Research Organisation
WHISPER	Women Hurt In Systems of Prostitution Engaged in Revolt

INTRODUCTION

This book is called *The Idea of Prostitution* because it is concerned with ways of thinking about prostitution. The aim is to explain how feminist thinking on prostitution has become so polarised at the end of the twentieth century. Whilst some are defining men's use of women in prostitution as a form of sexual violence, there are others who seek to normalise and legitimise "sex work" as a reasonable job for a woman. Such opposite views, all calling themselves "feminist", did not always exist. In the late nineteenth and early twentieth centuries, feminist attitudes were much more homogeneous. One prominent member of the Ladies' National Association for the Repeal of the Contagious Diseases Acts, Elizabeth Wolstenholme Elmy, expressed the typical feminist perspective of the time well when she wrote of prostitution as the "profanation of the dignity and individuality of women" (quoted in Jeffreys, 1997, p. 34). The feminist determination to end prostitution was strong and internationally united in this period, though there were differences in the analysis of why prostitution must end and how this was to be achieved (see Jeffreys, 1985, ch. 1). In the first chapter of this book, I document the ways in which the feminist anti-prostitution campaigns of the period before World War I went international in the 1920s and 1930s. Feminists from a variety of countries and organisations sought a convention to outlaw the traffic in women, a campaign which resulted in a new Convention Against the Traffic in Persons in 1949. Knowledge of this history, the ideas, the language and tactics of our foresisters, and of the response of male defenders of prostitution, which is examined here in Chapter 2, is crucial to our understanding of the debate around the same issues today. Many of the earlier feminist insights remain directly relevant and we should not have to reinvent the wheel.

Since the late 1960s, radical feminist theorists have analysed prostitution uncompromisingly as the ultimate in the reduction of women to sexual objects which can be bought and sold, to a sexual slavery that lies at the root of marriage and prostitution and forms the foundation of women's oppression (Millett, 1975; Barry, 1979, 1995; Dworkin, 1983). But in the last two decades the ideas of many feminists about prostitution have changed. This book will seek to explain why the strength of that earlier condemnation gave way, and how the very different voices of the 1980s and 1990s came into being. The prostitutes' rights movement of the 1980s proposed that prostitution was a form of work just like any other, freely "chosen" by women (Delacoste and Alexander, 1988; Pheterson, 1989a; Bell, 1987a). Some representatives of prostitutes' rights groups have even argued that prostitution represents sexual liberation for women. The language of work and choice and sex has also been adopted by some feminist theorists and academics who profess to have been convinced by the arguments of pro-prostitution activists (Bell, 1994; Sullivan, 1994).

In the 1990s a new position is gaining ground in the international human rights arena and purporting to be "feminist". It represents prostitution as a form of wonderful beneficence bestowed upon women by free-market capitalism, which will enable women to exercise the agency and free will necessary to their subjecthood, and will assure them of the "right to prostitute" (Klap et al. 1995). Though radical feminists and anti-violence feminists continue to maintain that prostitution is a crime against women and are refining that analysis with insights gained through the anti-violence struggle and the language of international human rights, it has become increasingly difficult to express the view that prostitution must be brought to an end (Barry, 1995; Raymond, 1995).

Another meaning I hope to convey by the title is that an "idea" is a necessary precursor to a man's action in using a woman in prostitution. I want to distinguish my approach to prostitution from any that might see prostitution as natural, biologically driven, or inevitable. Sexological and most other approaches to prostitution start from the premise that men's behaviour in using women in prostitution is simply the acting out of a biological imperative. (Forel, n.d.; Benjamin and Masters, 1965). Men are seen as doing what comes naturally. On the contrary, I consider that men's behaviour in choosing to use women in prostitution is socially constructed out of men's dominance and women's subordination. An "idea of prostitution" needs to exist in the heads of individual men to enable them to conceive of buying women for sex. This is the idea that woman exists to be so used, that it is a possible and appropriate way to use her. A necessary component of this idea is that it will be sexually exciting to so use a woman.

In order to discuss prostitution in a way which highlights the abuse involved, it is necessary to reject the new vocabulary which the prostitutes' rights movement has introduced. In this new vocabulary, prostitution is "sex work" and the men who abuse women in prostitution are called "clients". No effective term is available which can identify the abusive behaviour. What should the perpetrator be called? In the absence of a more felicitous choice of terms, I shall use the term *john* in this book, because it has been invented by women in prostitution and is nicely contemptuous. It implies that the men who use women in prostitution are generic males, indistinguishable one from another. I use it to separate my approach from those seeking to legitimise prostitution as work by using the term *client*. But a term needs to be invented which would be the equivalent of *batterer* or *rapist* and place responsibility for abuse upon the abuser. *Prostitution abuser* is a possibility, but not an elegant one.

Traditional definitions of prostitution by male commentators have seen prostitution as a sexual activity of women. The johns—or perpetrators, if we take an anti-violence perspective—have been omitted from the definition entirely, and thus from any consideration in most research and analysis of prostitution to the present day. I would like to transform the traditional definition to represent a radical feminist approach. Abraham Flexner, whose *Prostitution in Europe* of 1913 is often relied upon as a foundational text in the study of prostitution, defines prostitution as:

> characterised by three elements variously combined: barter, promiscuity, emotional indifference. Any person is a prostitute who habitually or intermittently has sexual relations more or less promiscuously for money or other mercenary considerations. [quoted in Ellis, 1946, pp. 152–3]

This definition is concentrated upon those used and abused in prostitution and fails to mention the abusers. But if the term *prostitution abuser* is inserted into Flexner's definition, then it can be reframed to express the ways in which prostitution is a form of male sexual behaviour. For the purposes of this book, prostitution means:

> Male sexual behaviour characterised by three elements variously combined: barter, promiscuity, emotional indifference. Any man is a prostitution abuser who, for the purposes of his sexual satisfaction, habitually or intermittently reduces another human being to a sexual object by the use of money or other mercenary considerations.

I shall concentrate on the forms of male behaviour in which men use their hands, penises or mouths on or in the bodies of women. Other forms of male sexual behaviour clearly fall within this definition, such as the subordination of women involved in paying to see, in person or in magazine or video form, women naked and humiliated, or to speak to women on the phone to similar effect. These will not be considered in any detail here, but certainly require their own detailed feminist analysis.

Pro-prostitution forces within the prostitutes' rights movement began, in the 1980s, to promote the term *sex work* as an alternative to *prostitution* (Jeness, 1993). This change in terminology is designed to convey a change in status for prostitution, from deviant sexual behaviour to just a job like any other (see Chapter 3). I do not use the term *sex work* because I see it as normalising prostitution. The acceptance of the term makes it difficult to conceptualise prostitution as a form of violence, a crime against women. I will use the term *prostitution* rather than *sex work* to apply to the way in which a woman's body is bought and used by johns. I use the term *prostituted women* rather than *prostitutes* for similar reasons. The advantages offered by this term were pointed out to me by feminist anti-prostitution campaigners in the Philippines when I visited on a study tour of sex tourism in 1995 (see Santos, 1992, 1995). *Prostitutes* are visible in a way that johns are not. *Prostitute* can be seen as an identity in a way that *keyboard operator*, for instance, seldom is. The term *prostituted women* brings the perpetrator into the picture: somebody must be doing something to the woman for her to be "prostituted". The term *sex industry* I will use to refer to the global industrialisation of the many forms of sexual exploitation, from interactive Internet striptease and sex phonelines to old-fashioned ejaculation in a prostituted woman's vagina, from which third parties in the form of sex industrialists and their supporters in governments can make a profit.

The Idea of Prostitution is conceived as a contribution to the process of transforming the way that prostitution is thought about. Presently a massive capitalist industry is being constructed worldwide to exploit women as the "last colony" (Mies, *et al.* 1988). The idea that prostitution is just "work" and "choice" and "sex" directly supports this brutal exploitation. Sexual liberals, queer theorists, pimps and the owners of

brothels quoted on the stock exchange, pro-prostitution
activists and sex tourists, all use the same language and seem
totally united in their determination to resist feminist and
other criticisms of their business and their pleasures. I will
argue that prostitution is a form of male sexual violence
against women, consistent in its effects upon the abused
women with other forms of violence, particularly child sexual
abuse. I will suggest that the most useful way forward to
combat the international industry of sexual exploitation
today is to fight prostitution as a violation of women's human
rights. This approach will target the perpetrators, both the
men who abuse women and those who profit from this abuse,
whilst decriminalising and giving practical support to the
women who have been abused.

Kathleen Barry, whose theory and activism are central to
the feminist struggle against prostitution, says that imagining
a world without prostitution is like imagining a world without slavery in the United States in the 1820s (1995, p. 316).
Slavery is now seen by human rights activists and the vast
majority of political theorists and governments as unacceptable. But in Britain, for instance, in the eighteenth century
many justifications were advanced for this abuse of human
rights (Fryer, 1988). The struggle to change the idea of slavery, to make what seemed unobjectionable into an almost uni-
versally reviled institution, was long and hard. It has been
remarkably successful. Though many forms of slavery do still
exist in different parts of the world, the defence of slavery at
the United Nations would not be treated with complacency.
Feminist anti-prostitution activists and theorists have the
same aim with regard to prostitution. We want to see a situation in which the defence or acceptance of men's use of
women in prostitution in any national or international political forum will be greeted with shock and condemnation, and
it is my hope that this book will contribute to that end.

CHAPTER 1

the traffic in women, feminism and the league of nations

> ... a question which touched the whole position and dignity of women. [Madame Avril de Sainte-Croix, League of Nations Minutes, 1928, p. 27]

In the period between the two world wars, feminists campaigned through the League of Nations against the traffic in women and against prostitution itself. This campaign was extensive, lengthy, international, and surprisingly successful, but is little known amongst contemporary feminists. The ideas and strategy of this earlier campaign are fascinating for the similarities to and differences from the feminist anti-prostitution campaign of groups like the Coalition Against Trafficking in Women today. The distinction currently made by prostitutes' rights groups and many human rights activists between forced and free prostitution, in which "free" prostitution is regarded as the exercise of a reasonable choice, was clearly a problem in this earlier time too. But then, as we shall see, no feminists were making the distinction, only the men who opposed them. These earlier feminist campaigners fought to gain recognition that the cause of prostitution lay not in women, but in men's demand. They wanted campaigns of public education to eliminate the demand. Today feminist anti-prostitution campaigners still seek to gain recognition of men's responsibility for prostitution, still seek to make the abusive men visible. The unity and clarity of

these pre-World War II feminist activists throws into sharp
relief the confusion that has allowed some feminist theorists
and activists at the end of the twentieth century to give support to a pro-prostitution ideology that sees prostitution as
women's choice, work and sexual liberation.

Historians of sexuality have tended to dismiss the late-
nineteenth-century concern with what came to be called the
White Slave Traffic as a "moral panic" because it was
allegedly directed towards a phenomenon so unimportant in
real terms as to indicate a concern with something quite different from its ostensible object. Jeffrey Weeks (1981) suggests that there was, in this period, a transferred panic from
other social anxieties onto sexuality. I suggest here that the
concern about the White Slave Traffic was indeed about more
than the traffic itself. For feminists, campaigning against the
White Slave Traffic was a way of gaining ground in their
struggle against prostitution in general. In the period between
the world wars the traffic was chosen as an issue which would
secure the support of influential men, such as those in the
League of Nations. Progress could be made, through careful
manipulation of the agenda, towards their ultimate aim, the
elimination of men's use of women in prostitution. But the
traffic in women was an important matter of concern in its
own right. The traffic which feminists were concerned with in
the 1920s and 1930s was one in which women were transported to other countries to be prostituted, but not necessarily
or usually by deception or force. The women usually knew, as
we shall see, that they would be prostituted.

In the popular mind, the traffic was understood to involve
force and violence and to be carried out against the victim's
will. There was little established evidence of a traffic exhibit-
ing these characteristics, but much more evidence, as the
League of Nations reports were to show, of a traffic in which
the women involved knew of the use to which they would be
put. The campaign began in 1875 through the work of
Josephine Butler in England, already experienced in campaigning against the *Contagious Diseases Acts*. Butler worked

against state regulation of prostitution in the form of examination of prostituted women for disease or the licensing of brothels. Such abuses, she considered, gave official approval to the double standard of morality and the degradation of women constituted by men's use of them in prostitution. She took up trafficking as a related issue, resulting from and integrally linked to regulation. Trafficking, she asserted, was a "consequence of the still greater evil—official and tolerated vice", so the struggle must continue against "all government and official recognition of the necessity of vice for men, and of the destruction of women for this end" (Butler, 1881, p. 5). The Federation of National Unions for the Protection of Girls was set up on her initiative, with the object of combating the White Slave Traffic by prevention. Before World War I it was responsible for 518 homes accommodating 27,000 travelling girls annually so that they would not fall into the clutches of white slavers.

The campaign was accelerated at the close of 1879 by A. S. Dyer's well-publicised discovery of an English girl, confined against her will in a licensed house of prostitution in Brussels. Josephine Butler, impressed by Dyer's findings, wrote "A Call to Action" to the ladies of Birmingham in 1881. She said that this "modern slave traffic" was worldwide and identified the traffic in women with the traffic in slaves across the Atlantic, quoting a Belgian economist saying, "Wherever there is slavery there must be a slave trade." She claims that the Blue Book of evidence of the House of Lords committee set up to look at the matter "shows that for long years past there has been a systematic slave trade in white women going on—in horror, cruelty, and vileness surpassing all we have read of the negro slave trade" (ibid., p. 9). So far as the evidence available would suggest, the traffic in white women for prostitution, though vile indeed, was on a very different scale from the traffic in black slaves.

In working with men like Dyer, Butler engaged in what Kathleen Barry describes as a "tactical mistake" of "resorting to coalition politics with paternalistic men in order to build her movement" (1995, p. 109). Her support for W. T. Stead in his exposure of child prostitution through the purchase of 13-year-old Eliza Armstrong associated Butler's crusade with some disquieting tactics. Her other tactical mistake, Barry suggests, lay in concentrating on the "forced" prostitution which trafficking was understood to represent, so that "the false distinction between free and forced prostitution" served to "legitimise everyday street and brothel prostitution".

Did the White Slave Traffic exist?

In Britian concern mounted and led to the passing of a bill in 1912 aimed at outlawing the White Slave Traffic. Feminists were involved in the Pass the Bill Committee and became implicated in the extraordinary stories of women being kidnapped in broad daylight in the public street. Teresa Billington-Greig wrote a persuasive article, "The Truth About White Slavery", asserting that the traffic was a myth. She was a suffragist who was critical of the militant tactics of the Women's Social and Political Union, which was particularly prominent in the anti-trafficking campaign. Billington-Greig (1913) was concerned because there had been "so many of these stories, and in nature they have been so disturbing that thousands of simple souls have been filled with alarm and dismay". The stories were contained in books like *Pitfalls for Women*, which gave a few individual case histories in which "English girls are victimised—girls who are as pure as the dew, that sparkles on the grass at the first blush of dawn in the spring" (Anon., n.d., a, p. 5).

The cover of *In the Grip of the White Slave Trader* features an innocent girl in a white dress who, looking distressed and big-eyed, is held fiercely by a massive hand around her torso (Anon., n.d., b). *Pitfalls for Women* asserted that all girls who went missing from home became victims of the traffic. Billington-Greig sought to discover the truth by asking for examples from anti-trafficking organisations and the police of incidents of trafficking. She was unable to confirm a single one, and this does make the depth and fury of the campaign puzzling. She showed that missing girls scarcely outnumbered missing boys, the numbers were small, and most were found. It was ironic that so many feminist energies and sympathies were diverted before 1914 into concern about the White Slave Traffic rather than about the thousands of women routinely used in prostitution by men. The exceptions had become more important than the rule, and did indeed constitute a concentration on "forced" rather than "free" prostitution.

The *Vigilance Record*, journal of the National Vigilance Association which was involved in the Pass the Bill Committee, contains frequent reports of cases of trafficking which reached the courts. An item under the heading "Is It Possible?" in March 1911 discussed the problem that some readers did not believe the reports the journal carried of the White Slave Traffic and wrote in suggesting the stories were exaggerated. This is countered with the story of Anna Solken, eighteen years old, who was brought to London under false pretences and forced onto the street. She ran away and the procurers were prosecuted (*Vigilance Record*, No. 3, p. 18). Several cases of this kind were reported each year. But some of the cases reported under the heading of the White Slave Traffic were ordinary prostitution with no obvious suggestion of trafficking. They covered cases in which, for example, girls of fourteen were imprisoned by pimps and turned out onto the streets by violence. It seems likely that trafficking carried out by deception or force did exist, but on a small scale. The more significant problem was the traffic in women who were willing.

Trafficking and international law up to 1914

The campaign against the traffic became international with the first congress on the White Slave Trade, held in London in 1899. The "shocking revelations" at that congress were that "women, for the most part under age, were engaged for lucrative posts, and then, always in complete ignorance of the abominable lot which awaited them, transported to foreign countries and finally flung penniless into houses of debauchery" (League of Nations, 1921, p. 3).

As a result of the London congress, international committees and an international office were established. Two diplomatic conferences were then held in 1902 and in 1910; they came up with two International Conventions, the first signed in 1904 and the second in 1910. Signatories to the 1904 Convention committed themselves to setting up central authorities in their countries to co-ordinate information concerning the traffic. Ports and stations were to be watched for procurers in charge of women and girls, and competent authorities were to be notified. There was to be voluntary repatriation of girls and women who desired this to their countries of origin, and supervision of employment agencies which found employment for women abroad. The 1910 Convention went considerably further. Signatory countries agreed to punish those who, "to gratify the passions of another person", enticed or procured a woman or girl under the age of twenty, "even with her consent", or a woman or girl over twenty by "violence, threats, fraud or any compulsion". Further congresses were held in 1912 and 1913, before the war closed frontiers and made the traffic difficult.

Trafficking at the League of Nations

It was the strength of the international pre-war campaign by feminists and others which resulted in the explicit condemnation of trafficking in the post-war settlement. Article 23 of the League of Nations Covenant committed the League to action against the traffic in women and children. The League gained the task of supervising the International Conventions. In 1920 the Council agreed to the appointment of an officer attached to the secretariat whose special duty was to "keep in touch with all matters relative to the White Slave Traffic" (*ibid.*, p. 4). This was Rachel Crowdy, a feminist who had, with her friend, Katharine Furse, organised Voluntary Aid Detachments for France in World War I. Feminists in this period had great expectations of the League of Nations, though it was an organisation totally dominated by men. Crowdy was exceptional in being made head of a section, the social section concerned with the traffic in drugs and women. Though progress was likely to be difficult, the existence of an international organisation, dealing not just with peace but with social issues, seemed a golden opportunity to feminists at the time. (For feminist attitudes towards the League, see Miller, 1994.)

In 1921, as symbol of the importance it attributed to the issue, the League held a conference on trafficking at which the third International Convention was drawn up. This confirmed and ratified the provisions of the two earlier Conventions and included "attempts" at procuration as well as actual procuration, the extradition of persons accused or convicted of procuration, and the raising of the age of protection from twenty to twenty-one. There were also articles covering the licensing and supervision of employment agencies, the protection of women and children seeking employment in another country, the protection of women and children travelling on emigrant ships, and the placing of warning notices in stations and ports. The Traffic in Women Committee in the 1920s and 1930s discussed ways to make the Conventions more effective. As a result of these discussions, there was a fourth Convention in 1933. It broadened the offence of procuration to cover women or girls of full age even with consent, but this was limited by the insertion of a clause "in another country" to protect the interests of regulationist countries who feared such an article could affect those recruiting for brothels in their own national traffic in women.

Rachel Crowdy, who ran the Traffic in Women Committee for ten years until 1932, explained that it was necessary in the beginning for business to be restricted to what could be clearly identified as "international" traffic. Many committee members though, particularly those representing the voluntary organisations, were abolitionists and determined to eliminate state regulation of prostitution if not prostitution itself. Crowdy was a convinced feminist and abolitionist herself, and she defined state regulation as the system under which a government "convinced of the need for promiscuous sexual relations" makes it "as easily available as possible for the citizen by tolerating and controlling brothels, making itself responsible for the medical examination of the women inmates, and, if necessary, subsidising these institutions" (International Bureau, 1943, p. 38). Her position required tact. One government representative told her that if the advisory committee discussed "for a single moment the question of licensed houses" then its delegates would be withdrawn once and for all (Crowdy, 1949, p. 19). But over the next two decades feminists and abolitionists won the arguments at the League, at least in part. Abolitionists were constantly pushing the League in the direction of abolition of state regulation, arguing that regulation was the basis of the traffic. Feminists went further and sought to direct the League committee to understand and challenge what they saw as the real cause of prostitution in general—that is, men's demand.

As a result of the two reports from League enquiries into the traffic, published in 1927 and 1933, a draft Convention was prepared by 1937 which provided for punishment of anyone who kept or managed a brothel or in any way exploited the prostitution of another, and thus sounded the death-knell for licensed brothels. In 1938 it was recommended that a conference be called for 1940 to draw up a final Convention from the draft. This became impossible because of the outbreak of World War II. After the war, the International Bureau for the Suppression of the Traffic in Women and Children fought for the Convention to be taken up by the United Nations. It was agreed in slightly amended form in 1949. Abolitionist energies then went into gaining signatures for the Convention. Progress was slow and the number of signatories remained low, perhaps because changes in sexual morality which were to lead to the "sexual revolution" of the 1960s created a less sympathetic climate for curbing men's sexual prerogatives.

What was the traffic in women?

When the issue of trafficking was taken over by the League, changes began to appear in the definition of the problem. At the 1921 conference the expression "White Slave Traffic" was immediately dropped as misleading, and the title "Trafficking in Women and Children" adopted. The League's definition of trafficking swiftly dropped the requirement for force or guile. The League carried out two extensive investigations into trafficking, one into the countries of Europe, South and North America (1927) and one into trafficking in the East (1933). It was understood from the beginning that the object of enquiry was a traffic in which the women would have a reasonable idea of their destination and purpose. The 1927 definition was "direct or indirect procuration and transportation for gain to a foreign country of women and girls for the sexual gratification of one or more other persons" (League of Nations, 1927, p. 9). Mr Sempkins of the International Bureau, when discussing the 1927 report in committee, saw as one of its most useful functions this change in definition. "For the man in the street", he said, "it had dissipated the misunderstanding that this traffic meant traffic in innocent or kidnapped women" (League of Nations Minutes, 1928, p. 22). With this broader definition it was possible to find plentiful examples of the traffic, but the report expressed the difficulty of gaining accurate numbers. It merely said that "a large amount of traffic is being carried on" (League of Nations, 1927, p. 10).

Large numbers of European women were trafficked to the cities of Central and South America, to Egypt, Tunis and Algeria. Most were from Austria, France, Germany, Greece, Hungary, Italy, Poland, Romania, Spain and Turkey. Sometimes foreign women represented 70 to 80 per cent of the total number of prostituted women in a destination city. Buenos Aires was identified as an important destination for the trafficking of women from Europe (Bristow, 1982). The estimate of foreign prostituted women in the city was 4500, of whom 75 per cent were considered to have been trafficked. The women were not "unsuspecting or defenceless". They were not "decoyed" or "in ignorance of the real purpose" of their journey. But, the League report pointed out, they could be said to have been trafficked because they did not travel on their own initiative. They went with or at the behest of their *souteneurs* or pimps. Traffickers suggested the idea, lent the money, and arranged travel and passports. Though the women were not innocent when they started out, they often ended up in bad situations completely in the power of their pimps.

> Once a foreign girl is taken to a distant country where she does not understand the language and customs, and is far from her home and friends, the power of the souteneur is proportionately increased and she is accordingly a better subject for intimidation than local girls. Herein lies the studied cruelty and slavery which inevitably follows the international traffic. [League of Nations, 1927, p. 15]

The 1927 report asserted forcefully that regulation, in the form of licensed brothels, stimulated the traffic. Licensed brothels provided entrepôts in which trafficked women could be stored, and created a demand for constant new recruits which fuelled the trade. This official recognition of the dangers of regulation was a useful weapon for the abolitionists, but the report was geographically limited and there was a call for a similarly detailed report on traffic in the East.

The enquiry in the East, published in 1933, faced particular difficulties. The League committee was now firmly launched on the acquisition of evidence which would allow the outlawing of state regulation, and governments represented on the committee (mainly Western) were gradually being won over to the abolitionist cause. But in order to get governments in the East to agree to co-operate in the enquiry, it was necessary to impress upon them that it was to be "strictly confined to the international aspect of the question" (League of Nations, 1933, p. 14). The investigators were to "avoid going into certain questions which might involve interference in local customs". This euphemism meant in particular the practices of child marriage and the *devadasi* problem in India, where girl children were dedicated to temple prostitution from an early age.

The protection of traditions and customs was taken to some extraordinary lengths. One was the argument that prostitution was somehow different and natural in eastern countries. A. De Graaf explained that this bizarre rationalisation was used at the 1921 League of Nations conference on trafficking. He said that the committee "felt that something had to be done" and consulted experts on the traffic in the East. The experts

> at once denied the existence of such a traffic and said there was no harm in it in the East; that the position of Oriental women was quite different ... that the women submitted themselves of their own free will for gain. [League of Nations, 1921, p. 52]

The argument about local customs was used by the Indian representative in defence of the *devadasi* system. India was not a signatory to the Convention and S. M. Edwardes, the Indian representative, explained that such "local customs" would not allow the established minimum age limit to be raised to twenty as demanded in the Convention. That would be in advance of the general body of orthodox opinion. It would also, he said, be in conflict with "established physical facts", because it was "well known that the climatic conditions of India result in maturity being reached at an earlier age than in Europe" (*ibid.*, pp. 56–7). He thought there should be no "impolitic interference by the state with religions and social customs" such as the "dedication of women to temples", which "date back to immemorial antiquity and had no parallel in the West".

The report found that the traffic in the East consisted of "a certain movement of occidental prostitutes to the Orient" but "hardly any in the other direction" (League of Nations, 1933, p. 21). The most serious problem of occidental women concerned Russian refugee women in North China and Manchuria. Most of the traffic was from one Asian country to another, the largest group being Chinese women, then

Japanese, Koreans, Siamese, Filipino, Indian, Iraqui, Persians and Syrians. These women did not service occidental tourists, as might happen in today's sex tourism, but went to foreign countries "in search of clients among their own countrymen abroad". Nowhere were there found "attempts to provide exotic novelty to brothel clients by offering them women of alien races" (ibid., p. 22). The Russian women in North China formed two distinct groups. One was composed of working-class women fleeing Soviet Russia who fell into difficulties on the refugee route. The women and children might take refuge in small Chinese villages with a Chinese family when the money ran out, and the male breadwinner would go on ahead to make money and come back for the womenfolk. When the man did not reappear, the women would be pressed into service in the local brothel serving Chinese men. The other group served Russians in China, mainly in the Hansen area where Russians had been engaged on building a railway. In this group many women were at work as professional dancing partners.

Chinese women were trafficked in considerable numbers. The numbers officially known to the authorities in 1930–31 were: Indo-China, 50; Siam, 1000; Philippines, a few; Dutch East Indies, not known; British Malaya, 5000–6000; British India, 30; Hong Kong, 4000; Macao, 1000; Japanese leased territory of Kwantung, 800. The reasons for such large numbers of Chinese women, according to the report, were the low status of Chinese girls, population pressures and poverty. The system of informal adoption of Chinese girls was open to abuse. In the mui-tsai system the position of the adopted girl was somewhere between a servant and a modest member of the family (Jaschok, 1988). She was vulnerable to sexual abuse by family members, but not usually sold into prostitution. Other forms of adoption constituted unconditional guardianship, in which families maintained no contact with their girl children. Girls were given to theatrical troupes as actresses, and in some cases sold directly into sexual slavery.

The feminist analysis

The distinctive feminist analysis of prostitution in this period can be gleaned from the disagreements that took place in the Traffic in Women Committee and at conferences of the International Bureau. The International Bureau for the Suppression of the Traffic in Women and Children was a sister organisation of the National Vigilance Association. The latter contained much feminist influence, but had demonstrated before and after World War I that it was prepared to curtail the liberties of prostituted women in order to combat "vice". This brought it into conflict with the feminist organisation in London, the Association for Moral and Social Hygiene (AMSH), which was the British branch of the International Abolitionist Federation and committed to the abolition of state regulation of prostitution (see Jeffreys, 1985). The same sort of conflict over the rights and liberties of women was reproduced in the League committee between representatives of the International Bureau and those speaking for women's organisations, or representing a feminist perspective. The distinctive feminist point of view, which targeted men as the cause of prostitution and sought to protect prostituted women from persecution, can be followed in the pages of *The Shield*, journal of the AMSH. *The Shield* was set up in 1870 by the Ladies' National Association for the Repeal of the Contagious Diseases Acts and represented, from the beginning, the perspective of Josephine Butler and other feminists. Alison Neilans, an ex-suffragist, was the very effective secretary of this organisation. *The Shield* covered and commented upon all the developments in the League on trafficking, and carried details of the response of women's organisations internationally.

Another good source for the feminist perspective is the British Commonwealth League. This organisation was set up in 1925 out of the British Overseas Committee of the International Woman Suffrage Alliance and the British Dominions Women Citizens Union. Its president was Mrs Marjorie Corbett Ashby, who was also in the AMSH. The organiser was Miss M. Chave Collison, also a member of the AMSH, who became secretary of that organisation after the death of Alison Neilans. The AMSH was one of the participating organisations, and many of the same women appear in the pages of *The Shield* and the conference reports of the British Commonwealth League. The latter was set up to promote women's equal rights and interests at Imperial Conferences and on all issues concerning women in the British Empire. It considered, as issues of sex slavery, the phenomena of *mui tsai*, Indian child marriage, "female circumcision", and *devadasi* or temple prostitution.

The feminists involved in seeking to guide the work of the League of Nations committee tried to move it towards the feminist understanding of trafficking in women as slavery. Nina Boyle, who had been a suffragist before World War I, was working for the Save the Children Fund in the 1930s. She expressed rage in *The Shield* in 1931, that the League of Nations was failing to identify the sex slavery of women as slavery. Sex slavery was not mentioned in the anti-slavery Convention of 1925. Boyle explained that the anti-slavery Convention was based upon the principle that "none may own nor dispose of the person of a man, and more particularly of the person of a wage-earner" (1931, p. 136). Women did not have the right not to be slaves because "a woman is not entitled to be a 'person'". Women had "no real right to personal freedom". The Convention skated over "the difficulty of discriminating between slavery [and] 'bona fide marriage customs'". Boyle identified the traffic in women for prostitution, and the selling of girls in marriage or adoption into prostitution, as forms of slavery "of which women alone are victims". People were prepared to be outraged over the *mui-tsai* system in Hong Kong, she suggested, because this was about domestic rather than sexual slavery, but had little interest in the selling of girl children for sexual use. Only forms of slavery which threatened the interests of "workers" were likely to be recognised, and the sexual slaves "do not compete in any labour market; they are not a danger to the industrial organiser" (*ibid.*, p. 137).

Feminists in the British Commonwealth League were determined to make sure that the sex slavery of women sold into marriage was taken seriously as a form of slavery. A resolution of its 1930 conference demanded that the Imperial Conference should support the setting up of a slavery commission by the League of Nations which would have sex slavery on its agenda. "It urges especially that those forms of slavery where the status of women is such that her husband's relatives and other persons exercise over her rights of ownership shall be examined with a view to their ultimate abolition" (British Commonwealth League, 1930, p. 14). Men, it was pointed out, had freed themselves from being sold, and "Women are now intent on doing the same for their fellow women, though in their case sale, barter or inheritance is slavery disguised as family custom." Nina Boyle, in a speech at the same conference, spoke against the situation in South Africa. Fathers there could sell their girl children to men and then, if the full price was not paid in time, reclaim their daughters, even if they had borne children, and resell them. She also drew attention to the slavery of women in prostitution:

> I have not read in any book that has been published yet on Slavery of those terrible women slaves in Japan, kept in padlocked cages for the purpose of public lust, open and public where everyone can see. 3,000 of them were roasted to death in the terrible fire that swept over Tokio, in the wake of the earthquake, abandoned by everybody. No one has spoken of these things. [*ibid.*, p. 40]

Opposition to state regulation was central to feminist campaigns. Madame Avril de Sainte-Croix could always be relied upon to give the feminist point of view on the committee. She represented women's international organisations: the International Council of Women, the International Suffrage Alliance, the YWCA, the Women's International League for Peace and Freedom, the Association of Hindu Women, and the St Joan's Social and Political Alliance. The question of the regulation of prostitution in licensed brothels, she explained, had ceased to be merely a question of public health and public order. It was now "a question which touched the whole position and dignity of women" (League of Nations, 1928, p. 27). Even if the suppression of licensed houses, led to clandestine houses, this would be an advance "as the State would not then seem to be tolerating and sanctioning something which was regarded by all women as abominable". She saw official acceptance of prostitution as educating men to treat women as subordinate.

The women's associations which she represented held that it was useless to instruct youths to respect women whilst, in the neighbourhood of the schools where they received such instruction, there were licensed houses where all such respect was flouted and destroyed (*ibid.*, p. 28). Feminist interests went further than civil libertarian notions of equality of men and women before the law and the iniquity of state violation of individual rights. The concern with trafficking and with regulation were used strategically to approach what was clearly the goal of feminist influence, the elimination of prostitution itself. Miss Blanche Leppington expressed this very well in *The Shield* in 1921. Feminist emphasis on the issue of trafficking arose from the need to, as she put it, "drive a nail where it will go—and where you can find some effectual hammer for driving it in". Trafficking was an issue which could mobilise men who were complacent about the existence of prostitution.

> Many men who would smile contemptuously at the suggestion that prostitution can ever be banished from civilised life would agree that the trapping of innocent girls by fraud or force into a life of vice is a real offence against the community, since it is snatching women from prospective wifehood and motherhood—now of supreme and recognised importance to the state—and forcing them into a mischievous and anti-social career. [*The Shield*, April 1921, p. 139]

It was this paternalistic concern for the protection of woman's sacred separate sphere which constituted "the strength of the now widespread movement for suppressing the White Slave Traffic", and caused it to appeal "to the ordinary conscience and common sense of ordinary men". Men who had accepted that prostitution was inevitable might be persuaded that outlawing trafficking provided "an aim not impossible of fulfilment—the cutting off of one of the most powerful feeders of prostitution" (*ibid.*, p. 140).

Men who considered that "free" prostitution was acceptable could be mobilised around the issue of "force". This was clearly in the mind of the AMSH in 1924, when Dr Snow of the League of Nations committee of experts called at the offices of the AMSH and asked for their views on trafficking. The AMSH sent a letter suggesting why a campaign against forced trafficking was easier but not sufficient. "Most men are willing enough to condemn and legislate against a traffic in young unwilling women which is carried out by means of force, fraud or misrepresentation ..." (*The Shield*, November 1927, p. 34). But the real traffic, the AMSH suggested, was in women who were not physically forced and knew that the traffic was for the purpose of prostitution.

Feminists sought to influence the Traffic in Women Committee against the passing of any resolutions which discriminated against women. One issue which raised the question of discrimination was that of the compulsory repatriation of prostituted women. Proposals were gaining ground in the committee that foreign women engaged in prostitution should be compulsorily repatriated to their countries of origin, and that foreign women should not be allowed to work in tolerated or licensed brothels in countries which had not abolished regulation. The International Bureau for the Suppression of the Trafficking in Women and Children supported compulsory repatriation, and its views were influential. But at its eighth congress in 1930, it was civil libertarian men who fought against discrimination against women. Monsieur Tomorowicz from Poland remonstrated. He said he did not

accept the "mistaken Bureau thesis, that the importance of
attainment and preservation of a high standard of morality
overrides any objection to action being taken against any particular class of either sex", and any repressive policy to prevent entry of prostitutes into foreign countries would lead to
"administrative and police chicanery" (International Bureau,
1930, p. 92). Monsieur Reelfs of Switzerland also objected
because "The prostitute was being considered as a special
class which could be driven from place to place" (ibid., p. 96).

The feminists objected also to the expulsion of foreign
women from licensed houses. They argued that such expulsion could be seen as intervention by the League in regulating,
and therefore condoning, prostitution. S. W. Harris, official
representative of Great Britain on the League committee, was
scathing about feminist objections. He had consulted all the
women's organisations in England, he said, and the great
majority were in favour.

> One or two had been doubtful because they were afraid that,
> if the resolution were adopted, it might mean that the League
> would give some kind of official sanction to the system of
> licensed houses. This argument was ingenious, but perverse.
> Further, some women's organisations desired to have total
> abolition and did not wish to accept any compromise.
> [League of Nations Minutes, 1923, p. 22]

In the event, the resolution on compulsory repatriation
was passed, with four voting yes, two no, two abstentions and
one absence.

The prevention of prostitution

Despite the attempts at its inception to limit discussion to trafficking in women, the considerations of the Traffic in Women
Committee had been pushed, by the 1930s, towards the larger
question of how to prevent prostitution itself. This was an
area on which there was considerable disagreement between
the feminists who blamed men for prostitution and those men

and women who blamed women. Prevention required an analysis of causation. The woman-blamers concentrated on why women entered prostitution; the feminists considered that this tack was unlikely to help much towards ending prostitution, since it was not women who caused prostitution at all, but men's demand. The idea that men's demand caused prostitution was a mainstay of feminist arguments in the late nineteenth century and it united both the christians and the freethinkers, those from a tradition of protecting civil liberties and those involved in social purity (see Jeffreys, 1997). The woman-blaming approach which sought to explain prostitution by pathologising the women became more popular as the sciences of sexology and psychology gained in influence. It was promoted by some anti-trafficking campaigners, such as Sybil Neville Rolfe of the Social Hygiene Council, whose perspective was anti-civil libertarian. It seemed reasonable to those who blamed women to suggest restrictions on women's freedom. These competing explanations, combined with others concentrating on social and economic factors, were discussed in League of Nations publications in the late 1930s and 1940s.

In the late nineteenth century, social purity feminists had been able to combine a belief in men's responsibility for prostitution with a belief in the efficacy of "rescue" work. But rescue work, which entailed the relegation of prostituted women to reform institutions, fell out of favour after World War I. It was recognised as ineffective, and seen to be dependent upon an undesirable ideology of woman-blaming that underlay it. In 1916, an article in *The Shield* by Constance Tite questioned its usefulness. She explained that the idea of rescue work implied that "To men vice is natural, to women it is not", and some rescue workers actually said this. Only such a belief could explain "The continual waste of devotion, energy, time and money on efforts to rescue endless processions of fallen women, while giving little or no attention to the public opinion which tacitly upholds the masculine demand" (*The Shield*, July 1916, p. 39). Defenders of the need for rescue work dwelt on the "belief that the girls to be rescued had lost something", perhaps "virginity". Tite suggested that to see the loss of virginity outside marriage as a "moral loss which is unique and irreparable" is unacceptable. She advocated that rescue work should be abandoned in favour of a general scheme to train and help all girls.

The dominant feminist approaches did not blame women or even particular kinds of women. The American feminist Maude E. Miner, in her 1916 book *Slavery of Prostitution*, said that the prostituted women who came through the Night Court and through the probation service for which she worked in New York were "much like other girls and women" (1916, p. x). She explained that these ordinary girls had techniques practised upon them by procurers which compelled them into prostitution. They were procured by promise of marriage, fake marriage, advertisements for workers, employment agencies, promises of fine clothes and high wages, and through force and violence. The "breaking-in system", as she called it, included threats and fear, promises of protection, and the provision of affection.

The League conducted a study on the rehabilitation of prostitutes, inspired by the apparent willingness of some regulationist countries to consider changing their policy if the League committee could come up with a solution to the problem of what to do with women discharged from the brothels as they were closed (League of Nations, 1939). The rehabilitation study looked at rescue work and decided that it was ineffective. Unless the women were very young when "rescued", they showed no lasting desire to be reformed. This led the committee to the conclusion that rehabilitation was likely to be less effective than prevention. The report of the study on prevention was published in 1943. The first part of the study, which focused on the history of prostitution, suggested that the causes of women entering prostitution which had previously been seen as most significant were becoming less relevant: "poverty and distress no longer played ... the important part they once had as principal causes of prostitution" (League of Nations, 1943, pp. 15–16). Women had also achieved some emancipation. The decisive cause of prostitution now was certainly men's demand. The report pointed out that "the causes of the demand have received less attention than those which result in the supply". It explained demand in terms of late marriage, men wanting variety, the advantage of no sentimental ties, but stated that the demand could only become "effective" if it "succeeds in calling a supply into existence— only where women are subordinate socially, intellectually, and, above all, economically, to men" (*ibid.*, pp. 25, 44).

When considering preventive measures, the report stated that these fell into two classes, those which attacked "the causes producing the demand" and those which attacked the "causes producing the supply". Since the demand determined the supply, "measures to reduce it are the more fundamental and offer the greatest hope of effecting a permanent reduction in prostitution" (*ibid.*, p. 33). Much of the time and energy expended in protecting young girls and rescuing prostitutes would be wasted "unless accompanied by efforts to combat the fundamental reason why prostitution continues to exist". Demand, it was suggested, could be reduced by increasing leisure facilities for young men as a diversion. But it was most important to change public opinion, since "in both regulationist and abolitionist countries, public opinion in general tolerates prostitution as long as it is practised freely and not under pressure" (*ibid.*, p. 34). For this there needed to be public instruction, particularly sex education.

Woman-blaming

But the League of Nations report on prevention contained a woman-blaming medical model too, from Dr Tage Kemp of Denmark, which threw the responsibility for prostitution back onto the women. He examined the "physical and psychological causes of prostitution". He did ask the question whether disabling disease was the result or the cause of prostitution, but clearly decided upon the latter. Illness, he said, made the prostitute unfit for any other work. The list of physical illnesses found in his study of prostitutes is very comprehensive:

impaired vision, severe strabism, reduced hearing, heart disease, results of traumata, congenital deformities, consequences of infantile paralysis, rickets, rheumatic fever, chorea minor and lupus ... chronic gastric or intestinal ulcer, nephritis, nephrolithiasis, severe hernia, abdominal tumours and results of abdominal operations (adhesions etc.), occasionally combined with oophorectomy, phlebitis, haemophilia, psoriasis, severe eczema and the after-effects of serious burns. [*ibid.*, p. 45]

Apparently the women he studied were often suffering from two or more of the above ailments. There was no control group, so Kemp had no way of knowing whether his study just showed the health problems of poor, working-class women.

Mentally, Kemp thought prostitutes were under par, and expressed sympathy for their boring mediocrity. Their "mental habitus" he described as "drab". They were "poorly equipped by nature, and the course of their lives is usually predestined to a mediocrity which is neither interesting, nor thrilling, nor romantic, but sad, colourless and deserving of pity" (*ibid.*, p. 47). Many studies, he asserted, have found "defective development of intellectual functions, rudimentary development of emotional life (emotional hypoplasia), constitutional inferiority (psychopathic) and insanity". He quoted recent studies "undertaken according to modern methods of psychiatric examination", such as that by Sichel of Frankfurt who found that of 152 prostitutes, 48 (31.6 per cent) were oligophrenics (retarded), 16 (10.5 per cent) feeble-minded and hysterical, 36 (23.7 per cent) psychopaths and 9 (5.9 per cent) abnormal in other ways.

Kemp's own study in Copenhagen had found only 29.45 per cent of prostituted women to be mentally normal. Apart from the feeble-minded and the psychopaths, he found 7 per cent had a range of other fascinating debilities such as "dementia paralitica, hysteria, cyclothymic temperament or schizoid tendencies, pronounced nervousness, neurasthenia, marked psycho-infantilism, climacteric insanity, dipsomania or psychogenic depression" (*ibid.*, p. 48). Others suffered from "alcoholism, criminality, workshyness, *Wanderlust*, mental instabililty, weakness of character or rudimentary sentiment development", and in a few cases, "hypersexuality and other sexual abnormalities". Despite Cyril Burt's determination, in the same volume, that "of all the factors making for sex delinquency in girls, an over-sexed constitution is at once the commonest and the most direct", Kemp did not find frequent cases of "hypersexualism or erotomania". Kemp believed that prostitution could be explained biologically in terms of "hereditary taint" (*ibid.*, p. 54).

Kemp's biological determinism was not the only variety of woman-blaming explanation available in this period. Psychoanalysis was becoming fashionable. In an International Bureau publication, Edward Glover explained that women who ended up in prostitution were suffering from arrested development, like that other variety of female sexual deviant, the lesbian. "In a word, prostitution exhibits regressive characteristics; it represents a primitive phase in sexual development. It is a kind of sexual backwardness" (Glover, 1943, p. 27). His investigation showed that 86 per cent of prostitutes exhibited "some degree of intellectual and emotional backwardness".

Understandably, a woman-blaming explanation of prostitution led to the suggestion of preventive measures which limited the freedoms of women. These included the care and supervision of the mentally abnormal; moral protection of young women workers and the prohibition of their working in restaurants and bars, in the entertainment industry, on highways and in public places; and restrictions by employers on the leisure of domestic servants. More alarmingly, it could lead to sterilisation. In late-nineteenth century Britain, there was considerable anxiety in the scientific and medical community about the eugenic effects of allowing the "feeble-minded" to breed. (For the importance of eugenics in this period, see Bland, 1995.) In the 1920s and 1930s, sterilisation of the unfit was much touted as a solution, and the practice was adopted in several countries including the United States and Germany. Mademoiselle Ulfbeck, at the 1937 congress of the

International Bureau for the Suppression of the Traffic in Women and Children, explained that a special law of 1934 in Denmark had introduced the possibility of sterilisation, and cases on the border between "backwardness and mental deficiency" were put into Protection Homes, often because of "sexual deviation" (International Bureau, 1937, p. 8). The report of the Italian Committee against Trafficking in Women to the 1937 League congress made it clear that relegation to an institution would not be voluntary. The prostituted women would be subjected to "a work of real moral reconstruction, which would provide training for a profession", but "this would not be possible if the women to be treated remain at large" (*ibid.*, Report from Italian Committee).

The position of *The Shield* was hostile to eugenics. In 1931 there was a very critical review of *Sterilisation for Human Betterment*. The reviewer commented that there was not yet a "sufficient body of sound experience and good and scientific judgement", and "Even among the diseased and defective of the population, good and successful parents are to be found, and people with a bad heredity often make good in life" (*The Shield*, December 1931, p. 223). Feminists generally contested all woman-blaming suggestions that prostituted women were somehow biologically unfit. At the 1937 congress, Madame Sundquist from Sweden objected, from a feminist perspective, to the practice in some countries of effectively imprisoning women even though they had committed no offence. She explained that women "may be treated as vagrants and sent by the police to a kind of reformatory which is not called a prison. It is an Institution whose aim is to give those girls reeducation". But men, she said, "were never sent to such reformatories for loose sexual relations" (International Bureau, 1937, p. 21).

Madame Wanda Grabinska from Poland, in response to Cyril Burt's paper on the medical causes of prostitution, emphasised the importance of economic causes, but said she wanted to "emphasise very strongly" that "The main cause of the prostitution of women is the demand created and supported by men" (International Bureau, 1943, p. 20). She pointed out that she had "never read, or even heard, a description of the moral and psychological features of the clients of prostitutes". This feminist alarm at what was identified as "neo-regulationism" grew in the period after World War II. Miss K. B. Hardwick expressed in *The Shield* her concern at a "disturbing feature" of the 1947 congress of the International Abolitionist Federation. This was the tendency of "non-abolitionists, and even of some abolitionists", to see prostitutes as "psychopathic anti-social persons". The effects were to restrict women's liberties yet again. It was becoming "a dangerously fashionable point of view" that these "psychopathic persons" had to be controlled by "neo-regulationary measures" (*The Shield*, February 1948, p. 7).

This argument over neo-regulation came to a head when the 1937 draft Convention was being reconsidered in the late 1940s. The AMSH and other feminist organisations sought to resubmit the 1937 draft without what they saw as woman-blaming amendments. They disputed the new Article 17, which committed signatories to "the establishment of a specialised social service for the prevention of prostitution and the rehabilitation of prostitutes" (*ibid.*, p. 88). The problem with this formulation was:

> taken with other articles, this focusses the eye on the prostitute as the very centre of the social problem. This was far from the aim of the 1937 Convention. The great steps forward that have been made in recognising man's responsibility for prostitution and the need for understanding and study of his promiscuity and other forms of sexual aberration are ignored and the prostitute is again assumed to be the core of the evil. This is retrogressive. [*ibid.*]

The feminist organisations feared that articles in the revised draft would be used to treat prostituted women unjustly in law, albeit in the guise of rescuing them. The idea of prevention and rehabilitation remained in the final Convention as

Article 16. The feminists remained opposed, but were unable to prevent its inclusion.

Pursuit of the equal moral standard: tactical limitations

Feminists expressed their opposition to prostitution in terms of the importance of the equal moral standard for women and men. In the feminist understanding, the idea of equality under law was integrally linked to the necessity of an equal moral standard in which men must emulate the chastity and morality they expected respectable women to display. The double moral standard led to prostitution by requiring the setting aside of a special class of women to be used by men. Alison Neilans, secretary of the AMSH, who espoused this position based upon a strongly christian morality, demonstrates its limitations. In a piece in *The Shield* in 1919 on "Principles of the International Abolitionist Federation", Neilans states: "Abolitionists hold that prostitution is a *vice* not a crime—a moral offence not a legal one" (*The Shield*, May–June 1919, p. 128). She believed that men and women needed to be convinced "*that the sex-impulse can be inhibited* when that is the only honourable course" to avoid "the gravest physical and spiritual deterioration of the race" (*ibid.*, p. 131). In 1920 she asserted that women who had little hope of marriage because of the effect of the war on the sex ratio, young unmarried women and war widows, must make a "voluntary renunciation of their individual emotional needs and physical impulses" to maintain a single standard of sexual morality and build up "a clean, wholesome, and happier world for those who will come after them" (*The Shield*, March–April 1920, p. 6). In 1926 she was still expressing her confusion over the difference between promiscuity and prostitution: "Prostitution is not a trade, it is an anti-social habit mutually indulged in by promiscuous men and women ... There is plenty of prostitution ... in which money does not figure at all" (*The Shield*, February–March 1926, p. 6).

But times were changing. In the decades after World War II

the idea of an equal moral standard became a millstone around the neck of the AMSH. Neilans and others in the AMSH continued their belief in the importance of a single moral standard of chastity for men and women right into the 1940s and in some cases the 1960s. Already after World War I there had been changes in sexual behaviour which caused anti-prostitution campaigners some confusion. Gladys Mary Hall in 1933 explained that the effects of the war and of new ideas of sex repression and sex psychology had led to a change in behaviour, so her study "Prostitution: A Survey and a Challenge" would include "'promiscuous sex relations paid or unpaid' as part of the prostitution problem of to-day" (1933, p. 21).

This position became even more anomalous after World War II and particularly in the period of "sexual revolution" of the 1960s. In the 1960s the AMSH metamorphosed into the Josephine Butler Society. Many of the old anti-prostitution campaigners were dying or already dead. Alison Neilans died in 1943. *The Shield* had become a once-yearly publication, and lamentations were frequent about lack of members for the society and lack of funds. This decline is likely to have been aided by the position of the Josephine Butler Society on the equal moral standard, which had remained unchanged since the Edwardian era. Dame Margery Corbett Ashby, an ex-suffragist and a longterm member of the society, expressed the difficulty of believing in the equal moral standard in changed times.

In one respect we have been disappointed. When we urged an equal moral standard we thought to raise men's standard of sex conduct and moral responsibility to that previously expected of women. Now it seems that an equal moral standard means promiscuity for both sexes, though soliciting for commercial prostitution is still punished in women and not in men. Perhaps this is a phase that will pass as we achieve a greater sense of mutual respect between the sexes. [Ashby, 1968, p. 16]

The call for women to be chaste was unlikely to be successful when women were claiming their right to experience sexual pleasures. It was because the equal moral standard approach confused the behaviour of men and women in prostitution with "promiscuity", that writers in *The Shield* in the 1960s mistakenly believed that "sexual freedom" would cause prostitution to die out (Catterall, 1968, p. 5). The sex experts of the sexual revolution also believed prostitution would die out, as we shall see in the next chapter. They considered that sexually liberated women would enthusiastically perform for men all the services they could possibly want from prostituted women. They too confused the sex of prostitution with what women might choose for themselves. The sexological literature of the sexual revolution combined with the efforts of pornographers and writers of "great" literature to create the ideology of sexual liberalism (Jeffreys, 1990). Feminist arguments about the equal moral standard would no longer suffice as a basis for challenging men's use of women in prostitution. The next stage of the feminist campaign would need a new language about sexual violence and human rights to deal with a different landscape of ideas about sex.

CHAPTER 2

the revolt of the johns:
prostitution and the
sexual revolution

Any woman who herself is ready to enjoy and
understand sex and meet her partner's needs
as fully as a professional but with love, can
outclass anyone hired ... She can learn from
periods and cultures in which the courtesan
was repository of the art of pleasing, but what
we call whores' tricks ought to be called
lovers' tricks. A woman who can make love
with love and variety needn't fear commercial
competition. [Comfort, 1979, p. 210]

The feminist campaign against men's use of
women in prostitution was achieving some success by the
1950s. The 1949 *Convention against the Traffic in Persons*
was now in existence, and both signatory and non-signatory
governments were seeking to put into effect the outlawing of
licensed brothels that the Convention required. Many countries—including in 1946 France—so long the target of feminist efforts were closing down licensed brothels, and this
meant that there was no longer such easy access to prostituted
women for their clients (Corbin, 1990). It is interesting that
this success in limiting men's prerogatives was closely followed by a considerable campaign of legitimising propaganda
from sexologists and historians. These male writers promoted
and celebrated prostitution. I call this chapter "The Revolt of
the Johns" because there are indications in this literature that

the authors had a more than academic familiarity with brothels and the practices of prostitution. This might explain the degree of anxiety that they express to the threat posed by feminists and progressive male politicians to men's access to women in prostitution.

I have analysed elsewhere the ideology of sexual liberalism which was created through the sexual revolution, and suggested that this was hostile to women's interests, setting in place a view of sex as the masculine need for sexual aggression which must be met by women's desire to submit and service men (Jeffreys, 1990). In this chapter I will go further and suggest that the theorists and publicists of the sexual revolution—sexologists such as Masters and Johnson and sex advice doctors such as Alex Comfort—constructed a theory and practice of sexuality based on prostitution (Masters and Johnson, 1970; Comfort, 1979, 1984). Prostitution formed the model for effective sexual functioning, men's sexual practice modelled on the johns and women's on the prostituted women.

The histories of prostitution produced in the sexual revolution played an important role in legitimising prostitution too. They presented a rosy view of prostitution in history and justified its continued existence in the present. In particular historians such as Henriques, Basserman and Bullough created a potent myth of origin which is being used to great effect by the prostitutes' rights movement today (Henriques, 1965, 1968; Basserman, 1967; Bullough and Bullough, 1987). Central to this myth are two "golden ages" of prostitution in which prostituted women were seen to occupy an elevated status: during sacred temple prostitution and in classical Greece. These histories have been used to argue that there is nothing wrong with prostitution, except the social prejudice of the present, and that prostitution can be returned to its past glories.

The sociology of the sexual revolution is important too in constructing the idea of prostitution. Deviancy sociologists named the prostituted woman as the paradigm case of the deviant (Goffman, 1974). Deviants, otherwise almost all men such as sex offenders and drug addicts, were romanticised as countercultural heroes. This view of the prostitute as deviant disappeared the "client" and the abuse. Johns, after all, were not deviant. The impact of these influences was to create a liberal context in which prostitution could be promoted as acceptable by the prostitutes' rights movement. This could not have happened before the 1970s.

Sexology

Feminist historians and sociologists of sex have written swingeing critiques of sexology from the founding fathers in the late nineteenth and early twentieth centuries to today, pointing out the way in which sexologists normalise a male sexuality based upon eroticising the subordination of women as simply what sex is (Jeffreys, 1985, 1990; Jackson, 1994). Male commentators as well as such feminist critics have thrown considerable doubt upon the "scientific" status of sexology. Thomas Szasz, best known for his influential *Myth of Mental Illness*, has written a damning critique of the credentials of sexology, arguing that it is simply a branch of the sex industry which gives the imprimatur of science to the practices of the industry (Szasz, 1980). Stephen Marcus, whose book *The Other Victorians* will be considered later in this chapter, offers a useful insight into the sexology of the nineteenth century. Marcus identifies this "science" of sex as incorporating the values and methods of pornography, a practice of prostitution. He describes the "scientific knowledge" of sexuality of the mid-nineteenth century as an "official fantasy" which shares many "qualities in common with pornography itself" (Marcus, 1970, p. 1). It should not cause too much surprise then, to discover that 1960s sexologists such as Harry Benjamin, Alex Comfort, and William H. Masters represented the practices of prostitution as simply "sex", and aimed to reconstruct female sexuality to more accurately replicate those aspects of using women in prostitution which most effectively served men's sexual interests.

The book by Harry Benjamin and R. E. L. Masters, *Prostitution and Sexual Morality* (1965), purports to tell the truth about prostitution. It is a work distinguished by its unselfconscious enthusiasm for prostitution and the shameless nonsense used in defence of maintaining the privilege of such access to women for men. The authors explain that they are outraged at the way in which, at the time of writing in 1964, an anti-prostitution stance was beginning to dominate international opinion: "A hysteria of puritanism has swept most of the world in recent years, doing a great deal of harm" (*ibid.*, p. 4). Hysteria, of course, is a "feminine" disease. Benjamin and Masters railed against the influence of feminists through the United Nations and the League of Nations.

> United Nations doctrine on the subject of prostitution, it should be added, derives mainly from feminists and the theoretical concepts of "liberal" do-gooders and bleeding-hearts of the varieties with which the world is now entirely familiar … The League of Nations played an important part in creating the popular bogey of a widespread "white slavery," something that did not exist in Europe and America to any significant extent. [*ibid.*, p. 267]

Their understanding of "white slavery" is that of a trafficking for prostitution effected by physical force and kidnap rather than the traffic in women who understood their destination. The latter was well documented by the League.

The influence of feminism threatened the maintenance of prostitution, but so did socialist politics. Benjamin and Masters were typical political conservatives of their time. They wanted the zeal being expressed against "madams", the women who ran brothels, to be "more often aimed at Communists, notorious gangsters and other real criminals" (*ibid.*, p. 258). They were disturbed by the tendency of progressive political regimes to take measures against prostitution. Many nations in both East and West had outlawed prostitution or taken other anti-prostitution measures "under the impact of the ever-growing influence of socialism and also as a consequence of various other factors". Gandhi was also called to task for having outlawed prostitution in India as a result of "erroneously" thinking that prostitution was made possible only by the unequal status of women (*ibid.*, pp. 419, 422). Benjamin and Masters were concerned that anti-prostitution legislation, under the influence of progressive politics and feminism and the "ever-growing influence of socialism", was being put in place worldwide as they were gripped by a Cold War hysteria against communism, particularly where it proved hostile to the use of women in prostitution.

There are indications in their book that the writers were personally familiar with brothels. Benjamin reminisces nostalgically about a madam he knows rather intimately. He talks of her "clients": "All of them were pretty steady customers in her New York apartment, where they were always sure to find a good time with excellent liquor, attractive girls, and a lot of conversation and fun, mainly supplied by Polly herself" (*ibid.*, p. 248). He considered that closing brothels would lead to serious social problems. There needed to be, he said, a massive government-funded research project to find the effects of closing brothels, to see whether this would increase "the incidence of homosexuality, delinquency, sex crimes, broken families, illegitimacy etc." Benjamin already knew the answer. There were, he said, "good reasons to believe that such may be the case" (*ibid.*, p. 255). The casual social intercourse of these sexologists with prostituted women and madams was extended to Alfred Kinsey, who was introduced by Benjamin to another madam who was a good friend. Kinsey then interviewed her "girls" (*ibid.*, p. 257). Masters was very familiar with brothels too. He visited them straight from school from the age of fifteen and informs us that one madam of his acquaintance only allowed schoolboys to engage in coitus in the house but, "Marie herself occasionally violated the prohibition against oral intercourse with 'pupils' of long-standing who initiated the activity" (*ibid.*, p. 259).

These writers provide reasons, supposedly based upon science, criminology and sexology, as to why the intercourse of men with prostitutes should not be constrained. They said the effect of anti-prostitution legislation would be the social evils of "masturbation, homosexuality, adultery, child-molesting, and carnal assault". Rape and attempted rape would increase because deviates used prostitutes and "Prostitution has been and can be a safety valve" (*ibid.*, p. 431). Use of prostitutes was crucial to prevent homosexuality, because "undifferentiated young males" would be made homosexual if they did not experience heterosexual relations to give them confidence. The answer was, "Accessible, healthy prostitutes, operating in a pleasant environment" (*ibid.*, p. 432). Masturbation was not a solution, because it was "neither physically nor psychologically" as satisfying as normal heterosexual intercourse. Psychological damage was done, and masturbation did not prevent homosexuality as efficaciously as using prostitutes did (*ibid.*, p. 434). The use of prostitutes provided a safety valve for men's aggression and violence, and upheld the heterosexual nuclear family. The most important task was to prevent men's "sexual frustration", or "the question of how sexual gratification may be made available to the greatest number of persons with the least harm to anyone" (*ibid.*, p. 118).

Benjamin and Masters were aware that feminists and other anti-prostitution campaigners were suggesting strategies which were threatening to men's "sexual gratification", such as penalising the client, and expressed considerable hostility to these "vice crusaders". "The more fanatical and therefore more dangerous type of the vice crusader is either impotent, a deviate, or both". They suffered from "psychosexual disturbances" (*ibid.*, pp. 361, 362). One of the most "senseless and harmful legislative measures of all ..." was the punishment of the "prostitutes' customer", and this "persistently recurring proposal" was "a product of an ill-considered feminism". It would be foolish to punish prostitutes, but "the social damage from so doing is slight as compared with what the effects of punishing the customer would be if such penalties were impartially enforced on a large scale". Whilst the prostitute can be jailed without "substantial loss to society", this was not true of the customer, "who is often an important source of support for family, business, church, state, and other institutions". Prostitution researchers such as Kingsley Davis (1937) and Abraham Flexner (1964) all said punishing customers would "disrupt and derange society". The customers, after all, had wives and children. The customer had "much more to lose than has the prostitute", so it was wrong to say the question was one of equal penalisation (*ibid.*, pp. 385–6). Men should not be treated in the same way as women because men were important.

Constructing the sexuality of prostitution

The sex that was being constructed through sexology and pornography in the sexual revolution can be seen to be the sexuality of prostitution. The sexologists and pornographers accepted the female servicing of men's ruling-class sexuality in prostitution as simply what good sex was, and sought to normalise this and promote it to non-prostituted women as their sexual liberation and sexual responsibility to their husbands. Alex Comfort, author of the quintessential sex education work of the sexual revolution, *The Joy of Sex*, was determined that heterosexual women should adopt the practices of prostitution to make sex full of "joy" for themselves and their male partners. Thus women are advised in his book to be prepared to dress like a "cross between a snake and a seal" by wearing leather and latex costumes. Throughout, Comfort stresses that male and female sexuality are different. Women would not expect men to perform as sexual objects covered in the costumes traditionally associated with prostitution; it was only men who would want this. If women were not prepared to comply, they were accused of being old-fashioned and prudish, and threatened with their husband's recourse to the divorce courts.

> Any woman who herself is ready to enjoy and understand sex and meet her partner's needs as fully as a professional but with love, can outclass anyone hired ... She can learn from periods and cultures in which the courtesan was repository of the art of pleasing, but what we call whores' tricks ought to be called lovers' tricks. A woman who can make love with

love and variety needn't fear commercial competition. [Comfort, 1979, p. 210]

The sex therapy techniques of Masters and Johnson, developed to cure what they considered to be sexual dysfunctions, mainly in men whose masculinity was injured by impotence or premature ejaculation, were based on the practices of prostitution. Masters began his research on human sexuality by interviewing "at length and in depth" 118 female and 27 male prostitutes. Edward Brecher, Masters's friend and populariser, tells us that he was "remarkably perceptive" or "exceedingly lucky" to study prostitutes as his pilot group, because they were the best-informed on human sexual response (quoted in Jeffreys, 1990, p. 136). They were experts because they had developed the skill of bringing a bored man who was not even sexually interested in them to orgasm, and this was to be the aim of sex therapy. So it is prostitution, a situation in which women service men's one-sided sexual interests for money, that was to form the template for the famous sex therapy which was to teach the Western world how to copulate from the 1960s onwards. Prostitution practices became the very model for successful sex.

It was not only sexologists who prescribed the practices of prostitution for wives and girlfriends. The 1960s historian of prostitution, Lujo Basserman, did the same in *The Oldest Profession* (1967), a book which rehabilitates prostitution through a sanitised view of its history. At the end of his "history", Basserman includes a large section in which he advocates that wives should be prepared to act as prostitutes to save their marriages and their husbands from the arms of other women (*ibid.*, p. 261). Wives should be prepared to behave in ways that seem to them "indecent" and that they might dismiss "under the vague description of 'perversity'", because this would create, "for the first time the climate required for true sexual intimacy and it is very often, too, the husband who needs it more than the wife" (*ibid.*, p. 262).

This requirement that wives should act like prostitutes to

excite their husbands he sums up in a phrase which he says has become a proverb in the United States: "High heels, happy homes" (*ibid.*). In other words the wife should dress in the uncomfortable and degrading fetish costume of prostitution for her husband's sake. There would still be work for prostituted women, though, even when wives had transformed their behaviour, because there would be some things that could not be done by wives. Only "harmless kinks" could be practised by wives, not "perversions of a more exacting nature". It would be little use for the husband to try to get a wife to wear the underwear of prostitution, for instance: "A wife's familiar figure is not rendered more attractive by the decorative underwear which the husband purchases with reluctance and tries out on her with a beating heart. She simply looks grotesque in it ..." (*ibid.*). The pathos of this description does seem to come from the author's heart. So, Basserman concludes, the husband will still have to go to a brothel to experience the real thrills of prostitution underwear.

Alex Comfort professes to be but the editor of *The Joy of Sex* volumes, though no other names are mentioned. The authors, whoever they are apart from Comfort himself, advise some fairly exact replications of the usual circumstances of prostitution as harbingers of the new sexual freedom. They are avid proponents of and participants in swinging, which, they recognise, provides all the excitements men might otherwise gain in brothels.

> The essential point is that, in spite of enthusiastic sex on all sides, it was wholly unlike a brothel, and wholly like a relaxed home, the keynote not being excitement or lasciviousness but innocence, once the freakout produced in strangers by its openness was over. [Comfort, 1984, p. 139]

Many of the practices advocated in his book, too, seem to derive from those traditionally enjoyed by men in prostitution. Comfort recommends three-way sex, for instance, as an accompaniment to massage sessions. One of the excitements of threesomes in or out of prostitution seems to be the opportunity for men to bond with each other through simultaneous use of a woman's body. In this recommendation from *More Joy of Sex*, for instance, it seems clear that the joy belongs to the male users.

> With two women and one man it much more commonly, and satisfactorily, ends in three-way oral sex; with two men and a woman it's more apt to end with her taking one of them orally and the other vaginally, if she was the one massaged. [*ibid., p.* 34]

When prostituted women describe their experience of this practice, it does not seem to be for the benefit of the woman. Linda Lovelace describes being used by five businessmen at one time in *Ordeal* (1981), and makes it clear that this is abusive.

> The man who had been called for the sandwich lay on his back and the others put me on top of him. Then I felt another man climbing on my backside. I understood then that they were talking about a human sandwich. I had never experienced anal sex before and it really ripped me up. I began to whimper. [*ibid.*, p. 35]

It does not seem likely that women would design such a practice for their own sexual satisfaction. Just in case the two men using a woman in Comfort's prescription become overenthusiastic, he reminds them, "Occasionally a threesome massage turns into what looks like rape but isn't ..." (*ibid.*, p. 34).

Another practice that men had traditionally been able to obtain only in brothels was that of watching other men using women sexually. Comfort recommends "watching" because it is "not only exciting but immensely instructive" (1984, p. 69). He is encouraging to reluctant, most likely female, readers, by explaining that the writers of *More Joy of Sex* have much experience of this sex industry practice. "Yes, we've watched dozens of couples, and a lot of the comment in this book is from direct observation ... Watching and being watched is exciting, friendly and encouraging—not intrusive and embarassing" (*ibid.*, p. 70).

The recommendations in *More Joy of Sex* refer in a cheerfully familiar fashion to the prostitution sex of massage parlours. The writer explains what the women readers need to know about the limitations, for men, of such commercial sex. Female partners engaged in massaging their men should not oil the penis. They are warned that they should not "automatically put [oil] on the penis even, as massage parlor girls do—it cuts sensation below trigger point in some males, though others enjoy it, especially if you're going to massage the glans itself" (*ibid.*, p. 31). Such advice, based upon a masculine familiarity with the practices of prostitution could be seen as an attempt to translate these practices into the home, but minus some small inconveniences. The sex of prostitution had other drawbacks which its replication in the home did not. Apparently it was much more exciting and instructional to watch other real live couples engaging in sexual activity than to watch pornography, because actors in pornography films were "not really enjoying themselves".

One practice recommended in *More Joy of Sex* replicates the use of women in prostitution particularly clearly. This is the use of sex "surrogates". "Surrogates" were female volunteers who were supplied by sexologists to men with sexual difficulties. The surrogates supplied sex therapy in the form of hands-on experience. The use of such female volunteers was described as more efficacious than the use of prostituted women because the latter were not sufficiently altruistic and enthusiastic.

The best way to learn to have sex if you're new to it or have problems is to have it with a clued, experienced, undemanding and turned-on partner. Unfortunately, most of our regular partners are also learning ... Hookers are clued, experienced and sometimes turned on, but the scene is wrong, and

a lot of them, by motivation and by experience, are basically
hostile to the opposite sex—also, unless you go to very expen-
sive call girls, their time is money and they time-stress you.
[*ibid.*, p. 185]

It is interesting to speculate on how the Comfort team know
about the problems of hostile "hookers" or time-stressing.
For those men familiar with such problems, surrogates—
women volunteers dedicated selflessly to men's sexual interests—would be seen as preferable. Surrogates were
recommended for men who are premature ejaculators and for
the male "with gay experience only" who "wants to acquire
heterosexual skills". The "sane" therapist was advised to send
such a man to a surrogate.

The surrogate would provide the selfless sexual use of her
body but without the disadvantages imposed by commercial-
ism. The surrogate would be a "woman with the necessary
skills, who enjoys sex and is supportive but doesn't make
demands" (*ibid.*, p. 186). She would represent, it seems, the
characteristics of the perfect feminine stereotype. She has
many of the qualities expected of the prostitute, such as not
getting "overinvolved with clients", but also those of the perfect wife: "The woman who is a surrogate has to enjoy sex, be
clued about handling male problems, and be warm and
caring." But she is to perform the task traditionally expected
of prostituted women in many cultures, sexual initiation.

He may never have had the chance to explore a woman's
body. Her job is to reinforce him without scaring him, to cul-
tivate his potency, to teach him social as well as sexual skills
in bed, and to concentrate on his presenting problem.

Comfort's team feels it necessary, though, to answer the criticism they suspect could be made of such arrangements, by
explaining, "far from being an exploitation of women, some
surrogates find their job an ideal expression of their own
needs, though it's hard work, like any other wet-shoulder

assignment" (*ibid.*). *The Joy of Sex* offers only a brief comment on the clear sexist bias of surrogacy arrangements.

> We say "he" and "woman" because that's the way around it is now: there are male surrogates, but from a cultural backlog women are very often less able to accept them than men are female surrogates, and there are psychodynamic differences. We don't know enough male surrogates to be able to judge how this will go. [Comfort, 1979, p. 185]

Masters and Johnson also provided surrogates for male "patients" and not for women and they explain that there is no "double standard" here. It would be inappropriate, they say, to supply male surrogates for women because it would conflict with their "existing value system" (Masters and Johnson, 1970, p. 147). Since women were not trained and culturally expected to use men in prostitution, the use of surrogates would not be suitable for their treatment.

The men's value system was not challenged. Indeed the male "patients" of Masters and Johnson were generally very familiar with the use of prostituted women and, according to the concerned sexologists, had learnt many of their problems, such as premature ejaculation, in prostitution. The "patients'" experiences with prostituted women seem to have been uniformly unsatisfactory. One man had been forced to doubt his "masculinity" because prostitutes laughed at him or caused him to ejaculate too soon (*ibid.*, pp. 170–1). One had suffered from the effects of participating in a gang-bang of a prostituted woman. Masters and Johnson politely call this, "a multiple coital episode in which the same woman was being shared". The problem for this unfortunate patient was that he was last, and "There were verbalised demands to hurry from his satiated peers and from the impatient prostitute." So, "Faced with a performance demand measured by a specific time span", he could not perform, and he experienced long-term adverse consequences. He found he could no longer function sexually either with prostituted women or those "within his social stratum", which presumably prostituted women were not (*ibid.*, pp. 135, 136). These unfortunate men who had suffered in the use of prostituted women needed the help of volunteers. The question of male bias was irrelevant because "incredibly vulnerable unmarried males" so desperately needed it. Masters and Johnson explain that curing sexual dysfunction is absolutely vital for men so that they can fulfil the political demands of male dominance. Without the use of surrogates, impotent men would be unable to assume "effective roles in society" (*ibid.*, pp. 140, 147).

Sometimes in the United States in the 1970s the sex industry was employed directly to educate medical students. Medical students were invited to bring their partners and lie in an auditorium where a great variety of pornographic films, depicting the full range of practices covered in pornography, was projected on the ceiling (Szasz, 1980). This was an SAR or Sexual Attitudes Reassignment, designed to remove any tendency to make judgements about sex so that doctors would be morally neutral about the disclosures of their patients. The use of these aspects of the sex industry in the 1960s and 1970s to teach sex shows how easily the sexual revolution had made prostitution simply the paradigm of what sex is.

The history of prostitution

It seems that the writing of a new authorised version of the history of prostitution was important to the new idea of sex that the sexual revolution was constructing (Basserman, 1967; Henriques, 1965, 1968). The stories these histories told were not dissimilar to those told in the works of the sexologists of an earlier period, such as Havelock Ellis, who also found it important to their work in creating a new sexual climate to interpret the history of prostitution. In the 1960s and 1970s, writing the history of prostitution became an important task once more for sexual liberals.

The attraction of writing about prostitution may have lain in sexual satisfaction. Lujo Basserman's *The Oldest Profession* was exciting to write, he says, because "The attractions of such a journey through the centuries are mainly due to the prizes which it offers. But I also found it pleasurable because it almost always led along the heights" (1967, p. x). His book is explicitly aimed at normalising prostitution. He declares that anyone who has objections to men's use of women in prostitution is mentally ill. "Anyone who ... finds the sight of an occasional prostitute or the mere existence of prostitution offensive should indubitably visit a psychiatrist." He considers prostitution, which he calls "the sale of sexual satisfactions", to be "an integral part of the urban life of mankind" (*ibid.*, p. xi).

Basserman's description of the "age of the *hetaerae*" has helped to construct the myth that this was a golden age for prostituted women.

> Those were centuries in which Greece flourished as it never did again. The nectar then harvested was quaffed by a few hundred beautiful women. No wonder they despised the men who made life so easy for them and who laid at their feet all the prizes they had collected for themselves ... During this era ... very few women exceeded the degree of emancipation achieved by the *hetaerae*. [*ibid.*, p. 26]

Fernando Henriques (1965) provides a similar account. The idea that the *hetaerae* of classical Greece experienced wealth, independence and high status has become part of the folklore of prostitution, even among feminists, as a result of uncritical acceptance of the "facts" in such histories.

British socialist feminist theorist Elizabeth Wilson repeats this idea uncritically in *What is to be Done About Violence Against Women?*

> The *Hetaerae* (the word may be translated as "partner" or "friend") were more like courtesans. They were the most, indeed the only educated women in ancient Greece, they attracted famous politicians and artists to their "salons", led lives of considerable freedom, and were both glamourized and respected. [Wilson, 1983, p. 90]

This myth of a golden age is extremely persistent, despite the fact that the evidence for it depends on the work of clearly biased male historians. It has been taken up by the contemporary prostitutes' rights movement with little concern for the accuracy of its origins. Nickie Roberts, from the contemporary prostitutes' rights movement, in her *Whores in History*, uses these male chroniclers to promote the same story. Her approach to this period adopts the celebratory tone of her sources. She reveals a class bias in her account by paying little attention to the masses of slave prostitutes in this period, the *dikteriades* or brothel prostitutes and *auletrides* or dancing girls, and concentrating on those she sees as having made serious money. Anyway, she remarks, slave status was not necessarily a problem, because "Theoretically, the *auletrides* were slaves, but such was their popularity and earning power that many were able to buy their freedom and go on to earn great fortunes for themselves" (Roberts, 1992, p. 29). She describes the activities of the moneyed prostitutes thus: "In the evenings, the garden would be crowded with beautiful women and their customers, flirting, joking, bargaining ... Their free and cultivated lifestyle could not", she says, "have provided a greater contrast to the seclusion and obscurity of married women" (*ibid.*, pp. 20, 21).

Like her male authorities, Roberts depicts the *hetaerae* as existing in a golden age when prostitutes could be the very model of the educated and cultivated woman whilst non-prostituted women were confined to the home. Aspasia, apparently, presided over a *gynaeceum*:

a school where aspiring *hetaerae* were educated and learned their trade ... [they] studied the arts and sciences of literature, philosophy and rhetoric. These students went on to become the wisest and most learned women in Greece ...

The gynaeceum links Aspasia and other *hetaerae* with the famous women-centred colleges that were known to have existed in Greece several centuries before the "golden" age of 5th-century Athens. [*ibid.*, p. 24]

Even male historians writing celebratory histories of prostitution have found little to praise about the Roman period. But Roberts still takes a positive tone. She explains that: "Generally speaking, prostitution in ancient Rome was a natural, accepted profession with no shame attached to the working women" (*ibid.*, p. 31).

Feminist historians tend to tell a rather different story. Eva Keuls in her book about sexual politics in Ancient Athens, *The Reign of the Phallus*, specifically repudiates the myth of the golden age of the *hetaerae*. She points out that "most of the prostitutes were slaves, completely deprived of will or choice" (Keuls, 1993, p. 154). She explains that we have no knowledge of the conditions prevailing in the brothels of Corinth and Athens, "but there is no reason to assume that they were any more commodious than the dark and stinking holes in which Roman whores practised their trade". In these holes the prostituted women of Rome lay on the bare ground to be used by men. Keuls states that between Athenians and "bought women of all classes the advantage was with the male all the way: his were the privileges of free status, citizenship, money, class, and gender" (*ibid.*, pp. 156, 174).

Her evidence centres upon vase paintings, and she points out that sexual encounters between men and *hetaerae* show abuse and battering. The *hetaerae* were brought to "symposia" in the homes of citizens which, far from being devoted to scholarly activity, seem to have constituted large-scale gang-bangs. Mostly intercourse was from behind, probably with anal penetration, and she sees this helping to achieve one of the purposes of the symposia, the development of "male supremacist behaviour in youths". Intercourse from the rear, and particularly anal intercourse, "was conceived as humiliating to the recipient, and hence a suitable culmination of initiatory sex" (*ibid.*, p. 176). The depiction of the money pouch in such paintings had the symbolic value of an "economic phallus".

A number of vase paintings show men beating *hetaerae* with various objects. At least two of these involve older *hetaerae* who are coerced to perform a sexual service which was apparently regarded as more repugnant than intercourse—namely, fellatio. [*ibid.*, p. 180]

Keuls quotes Demosthenes to show the attitude of Athenian men to the symposium, in which, she says, "sexual violence was an integral part" (*ibid.*, p. 182). "We've come together, a party of men with huge erections, and when we feel sexy, we strike and strangle whom we please" (quoted in *ibid.*, p. 153). She describes the idea that the city's *hetaerae* were "creatures of charm and culture, exercising control over their own lives" as "far off the mark" (*ibid.*, p. 153).

The myth of the *hetaerae* has been taken up by the post-modern theorist of prostitution, Shannon Bell (1994). Bell uses the classical Greek texts by men to prove that *hetaerae* such as Aspasia really did wield considerable power and influence. Having established the power of the *hetaerae* she seeks to prove that prostitute performance artists, such as Annie Sprinkle and Veronica Vera, are the direct descendants of these powerful forebears, part goddess and part whore. A myth has been used to support an equally dubious expression of prostitute power in the present. But the use of this myth by pro-prostitution writers like Roberts and Bell does suggest its durability and importance.

Another modern myth of prostitution which has wide circulation in the present prostitutes' rights movement, and again originates in the writings of male apologists for prostitution, is that of sacred prostitution. According to this myth, prostitution began with the phenomenon of sacred prostitution in prehistoric times when the priestess and prostitute were one and the same, holding sway through the sacred power of sex. In 1996 the magazine of the Prostitutes' Collective in Victoria had a double-page spread on the exalted status of the prostitute in history (*Working Girl*, Spring 1995, pp. 8–9). The evidence from *Whores in History* promotes Nickie Roberts' view of the noble past of prostitution in the service of the goddess. Roberts explains that the prostitutes' rights movement depends upon "whores ... rediscovering the glories and achievements of their ancient past". The result of this "reclamation of their old dignity" has been "the growth within the last two decades of a worldwide prostitutes' movement" (Roberts, 1992, p. 339).

Roberts places the origin of prostitution firmly in the temple. "It is here that the true story of prostitution begins; with the temple priestesses who were both sacred women and prostitutes, the first whores in history" (*ibid.*, p. 3). The priestesses were sex prophets and symbols of a golden age of sexual freedom.

> Within these prehistoric societies ... culture, religion and sexuality were intertwined, springing as they did from the same source in the goddess. Sex was sacred by definition, and the shamanic priestesses led group sex rituals in which the whole community participated, sharing in ecstatic union with the life force ... [*ibid.*, p. 3]

According to this myth of origin, when the patriarchs destroyed the matriarchy, they invented sexual morality and undermined the status of prostituted women. "If the male elites were decisively to overturn the whores' power, they had to invent a system of sex-repressive morality that would be sufficiently negative to make sacred women into social pariahs" (*ibid.*, p. 9). The sources that Roberts uses are almost entirely those of the male historians, such as Henriques and Bullough, who wrote rehabilitative histories of prostitution which relied on ancient male historical sources whose objectivity may be as suspect as that of their male interpreters. The feminist historian, Gerder Lerner, takes a rather different approach in *The Creation of Patriarchy* (1987). She separates the phenomenon, labelled by male historians as "sacred prostitution", from the origins of commerical prostitution. The latter she places in the invention of slavery and the acquisition of female slaves who were sold into prostitution. Roberts is aware that feminists have not been enthusiastic about the

interpretation given to "sacred" prostitution by male chroniclers. She explains that "middle-class feminist writers" sometimes mention "earlier forms of prostitution, the religious
practices of earlier civilizations" but reject the "similarity
between the high-status whore-priestesses of yore and the lat-
terday streetwalker" (Roberts, 1992, p. xi). Her book is dedicated to repudiating this distinction.

Rehabilitating Victorian prostitution

In the 1960s there was a wave of books by male sexual liberals
which sought to rehabilitate the prostitution and pornography
of Victorian England. Some simply described in positive terms
the use of prostitutes by Victorian men, in the causes of repudiating the myth that the Victorians were anti-sex, and showing up the hypocrisy of "Victorian" morality. Books of this
type were Pearsall's *The Worm in the Bud*, and Cyril Pearl's
The Girl with the Swansdown Seat. Others sought to rehabilitate the Victorian classics of pornography, such as the hus-
band-and-wife team Drs Phyllis and Eberhard Kronhausen,
who published an annotated edition of Walter's *My Secret
Life*. Still others, such as Wayland Young's *Eros Denied*,
sought to undermine the censorship of pornography, seen as
resulting from Victorian hypocrisy, by detailing what was
thought of as the sorry history of censorship of erotic works.
These books represented the Victorian underworld of prostitution and pornography as simply sex in its natural form.

Cyril Pearl's *The Girl With the Swansdown Seat* (1955)
predated the sexual revolution, but remained a classic which
influenced the later literature. His first chapter, "The Victorian
Myth", set the template for this kind of "rediscovery" writing.
He writes that there should be no generalisations about
Victorian morality, because "this pretty picture-postcard
oleograph of sex life in nineteenth-century England has no
more relation to reality than Edward Lear's description of the
domestic habits of the Jumblies" (Pearl, 1980, p. 1). But the
alternative view he gives is a celebration of prostitution, as can
be judged from his use of positive language to set his scenes:

"But it was also an age when prostitution was widespread and flagrant; when many London streets were like Oriental bazaars of flesh; when the luxurious West End nighthouses dispensed love and liquor till dawn ..." (*ibid.*, p. 5).

Ronald Pearsall's *The Worm in the Bud* (1969) took a similar approach. The enemy to be unmasked in the book was Victorian hypocrisy as espoused by the "repressed and inhibited classes" (Pearsall, 1971, p. 18). The heroes were johns.

In such a time, those who were not afflicted by the climate of repression stand out with uncommon clarity. Swinburne, working out his flagellation mania in an establishment in St John's Wood: Rossetti, commuting between the virginal Elizabeth Browning and his fat whores; Boulton and Park, gaily flaunting their transvestism in the theatres of the Strand— not only do these stand larger than life, they make their so-so-respectable contemporaries look like their photographs in old family albums—sepia-coloured and wooden. [*ibid.*, p. 19]

He represents the world of prostitution as glamorous and exciting: "in the streets the prostitutes perambulated like so many flagships on review at Spithead" (*ibid.*, p. 21).

"Gay" life, the life of prostitution, was contrasted with the "furtive gloom of the agonised and repressed" (*ibid.*, p. 22). It was an age in which prostituted women were simple and enthusiastic sexual innocents uncorrupted by Victorianism. Poor girls got clean living conditions, food and good clothing in brothels, he says, and he is blithely confident that "The fact that the girls had to open their legs to a succession of strange men was a matter of minor importance." His view of the working class was that they would undoubtedly enjoy it. They experienced, after all, the "doggy world of working-class sex" (*ibid.*, pp. 357, 391). The sexual revolution was expected, these sort of writings suggest, to blast Victorian hypocrisy out of the way and usher back in an age of innocent sexual enthusiasm, full of prostitution and pornography and poor girls grateful for a bed in a brothel.

My Secret Life, by "Walter" was analysed extensively and critically in that famous 1964 re-examination of Victorian sexual morality, Stephen Marcus's *The Other Victorians*. In contrast, the annotated 1967 edition of the book by Drs Phyllis and Eberhard Kronhausen is simply celebratory. The Kronhausens were American enthusiasts for pornography, particularly period pornography, and I have written elsewhere about their celebration of *Lady Chatterley's Lover* (Jeffreys, 1990). Their promotion of pornography in the sexual revolution is given a spurious authority from their medical qualifications. The Kronhausens use *My Secret Life* as a propaganda tool, to promote the sexual freedom that men might be expected to gain from the sexual revolution. The author, Walter, writes a chronicle of the use of hundreds of prostituted women of all ages. In his detailed descriptions, the women are always enthusiastic and nearly always orgasmic, as befits male pornographic fantasy. Walter's conduct is frequently brutal and often clearly rape, particularly when he is buying the virginity of 10-year-olds. The Kronhausens use his conduct to write a chapter on "The Psychology of the Sexually Active Male", of which Walter is supposed to be a prime example. He was a "sexually active male with more than average sex drive, or—as is more accurate—with fewer cultural inhibitions than is the case with most people" (Kronhausen and Kronhausen, 1967, p. 173). He was typical of male sex psychology because the "most outstanding feature of the sexually active individual, and certainly in the male, is the marked need for variety" (*ibid.*). An example from Walter of such typical behaviour goes as follows:

> Exceedingly nice women [prostitutes] were then to be met in the Quadrant from eleven to one in the morning, and three to five in the afternoon. I would have one before luncheon, get another after luncheon, dine, and have a third girl. [*ibid.*, p. 174]

Walter's behaviour may be more typical of the way that men should behave than readers might think, they consider, because "It could … be that the cultural norm may be artificially depressed, and that a sexuality such as Walter's may be more normal than the norm." Walter was a good example of the sort of rebelliousness required against "our sexual mores and institutions", because they "provide neither adequate sexual stimulation nor sufficient opportunity for sexual activity".There had, they said, always been people who rebelled against this "social castration", and "Walter is certainly a pertinent case in point" (*ibid.*, pp. 174, 180, 181).

But Walter was not just a good example of a sexual revolutionary: he was a sex expert too, an "amateur sexologist" who was really knowledgeable about how women felt sexually. In fact, the example the Kronhausens offer of his sensitive insight into women's feelings about sex may convince us of quite the opposite.

> What a joy a woman must have when, for the first time, she clasps in secrecy and security a good stiff stander, knowing that she may handle it and look at it at will, and that it will stretch her and give her the divine pleasure she has heard about! [*ibid.*, p. 217]

Stephen Marcus, the British literary critic, who is a more astute critic of this work, remarks that women tend to be less than enthusiastic about "stiff standers" in fact. But the Kronhausens hope their readers will be impressed with "the deep understanding of female sex psychology on the part of our amateur sexologist, based on his unusually wide experience with women". The Kronhausens tell us that "our amateur sexologist's erotic understanding of the female sex impulse" is "Astonishing", and so it is, but not so much for its accuracy as for its fantastic qualities (*ibid.*, pp. 230, 223). What is most interesting about the Kronhausens' approach is that they should confidently assert that a Victorian pornographer is an accurate sexologist or scientist of sex. This does support Thomas Szasz's notion that sexology is but a branch of the sex industry and draws its values from that source.

The Kronhausens' conclusion is that Walter is specially suited to embody the spirit of the sexual revolution. He may have a "message for us who live in an age of automation, egalitarianism, and paralysation of personal initiative" (*ibid.*, p. 326). They quote *Time* of 1965 to sum up what the sexual revolution can offer to men constrained by such circumstances as equality. It may well be "that sex itself is the real, perhaps the last great adventure, the 'last frontier' that permits modern man, hag-ridden by civilisation, to explore, to dare and to conquer" (*ibid.*). Considering, as Mary Daly explains, that the word *hag* is from an Old English word meaning "harpy, witch", it might not be unreasonable to see the threat to men's "last frontier" as coming from women and feminism (1979, p. 14).

The examples that Marcus gives of Walter's sexual behaviour are scarcely those of a representative sexual revolutionary, if we consider that a "sexual revolution" should be connected with socially radical tendencies. He procured girls of ten to deflower and, as Marcus informs us, "The scenes which describe the outcome of these desires are the most brutal and disgusting in the book" (1970, pp. 156–7). He quotes Walter unflatteringly as saying he has "probably fucked now ... something like twelve hundred women, and [I] have felt the cunts of certainly three hundred others of whom I have seen a hundred and fifty naked" (*ibid.*, p. 188). Marcus seems to suggest that, though the behaviour of sexual revolutionaries is brutal, it is necessarily so in pursuit of their political ideals. He says we should remind ourselves that "the struggle for sexual freedom, at least in the lives of individual persons, requires considerable stepping over the bodies of others and that it is not only in political revolutions that crimes are committed in the name of liberty" (*ibid.*, p. 159).

Nonetheless, despite an analysis of male sexuality and the motivation of the male client of prostituted women which differs scarcely at all from the radical feminism of a later period, Marcus wishes to hold onto the idea that there is something to be admired in Walter's behaviour.

If it were not for the fact that the activities we are discussing are of a compulsive nature, one would be tempted to regard them as in their way courageous—it takes some courage, after all, to live constantly on the brink of the meaningless ... Among the many extraordinary—and even admirable—qualities of the author of *My Secret Life* is the fact that he had the courage of his compulsions ...

What we have, therefore, in *My Secret Life* is the record of a real life in which the pornographic, sexual fantasy was acted out. [*ibid.*, p. 196]

So, despite Walter's brutal male sexual aggression against women and children, which Marcus characterises so well, he remains a suitable male hero of the sexual revolution. Perhaps this demonstrates the extent to which male sexual acting out of any fashion was seen to be inherently revolutionary in the 1960s. It was not possible, even for a male commentator with the insight of Marcus, to doubt the positive revolutionary value of men's sexual freedom.

The sociology of prostitution

In the period of the sexual revolution, male sociologists tended to take a deviancy approach to prostitution. Sociologists of sex, such as Henslin and Sagarin, argued that deviance must be a "major focus" of their work. The sociologists of sex needed to study "the activities of those persons who violate the normative expectations of society." Their job was to understand why anyone would want to violate these norms. The researcher, of course, was a man. "He will examine norm violations and norm violators in order to determine those aspects of society and culture that both push people toward and pull people away from deviance" (Henslin and Sagarin, 1971, pp. 16–17).

Erving Goffman, in *Stigma*, used the prostitute as his first example of the deviant who needed to be studied. In the field of enquiry called "deviance", he explains:

Prostitutes, drug addicts, delinquents, criminals, jazz musicians, bohemians, gypsies, carnival workers, hobos, winos, showpeople, full-time gamblers, beach dwellers, homosexuals, and the urban unrepentant poor—these would be included. These are the folk who are considered to be engaged in some kind of collective denial of the social order. [Goffman, 1974, p. 171]

Prostitutes have the place of honour as the supreme example of the deviant. So puzzled were these male sociologists as to why any woman would enter prostitution that they sought to examine the "career" of the prostitute. They were interested in how she managed what Goffman called a "spoiled identity". They developed the idea that the prostitute's career required an "apprenticeship" period, during which she would learn to handle experiences that might otherwise cause distress. Gagnon and Simon, for instance, explain how the prostituted woman learns to negotiate with clients.

One of the most complex of these tasks is learning the capacity to speak openly … about sexual acts and preferences … The structure of prostitute–client talk, once learned, becomes highly ritualised and predictable, though it varies from one social level of customer to another … [Gagnon and Simon, 1974, pp. 266–7]

The deviancy approach was criticised, even in its heyday, for its political biases.

Alexander Liazos wrote a persuasive critique of the sociology of deviance in 1972. He pointed out that there were three theoretical and ideological biases in the field of the sociology of deviance. One was that, despite attempts to show that the "deviant" is not different from the rest of us, the very emphasis on his/her identity and subculture may defeat that aim. Another was that certain forms of "deviance", especially by the economic and political elite, were neglected. The third and most damning bias, as far as the sociology of deviancy applied to prostitution was concerned, was that the analyses contained no exploration of the role of power in the designation of "deviance", despite many statements to the contrary. Liazos does not mention the male bias of deviancy sociology.

The masculine sociology of deviance romanticised what were seen to be deviant males as heroic rebels against social conformity. Sex offenders, for instance, became heroes in an extraordinary suppression of the points of view of women and children. The view of the perpetrators of sexual violence as heroes is well represented in a 1969 book, *The Twisting Lane*, which contains interviews with eight male sex offenders by Tony Parker, described as "a sociologist". The oral histories are described as "personal statements made at unknown cost and with inestimable bravery". Parker says he feels unable to thank them adequately but can only state his "respect and admiration for their courage and dignity". The interviewees include two serial child sex abusers, one serial rapist, one serial sexual harasser who grabbed women in the street and put his hands in their knickers, an indecent exposer, a man in prison for living off immoral earnings, and two men jailed for homosexual acts. The two homosexuals might well deserve his "respect", but scarcely the others who created such misery for women and children. In a section at the end entitled "some Brief Remarks", there are statements by women and men who have been sexually assaulted as children or adults declaring that these events had no bad effects on them and they feel really sorry for the men who assaulted them. The object of the book was to decriminalise or reduce the stigma attached to all these activities. This was an overt aim of the more "radical" deviancy sociologists. As Colin Sumner notes in his *The Sociology of Deviance: An Obituary* (1994), liberal male deviancy sociologists paid attention only to what they wanted to decriminalise.

Feminist sociologists began to point out by the late 1970s that deviancy sociology was relentlessly male supremacist in its values (Rodmell, 1981). It heroised male aggression and ignored the women and children who were its victims. The only women the male sociologists had noticed were prostitutes, but somehow they did not receive the same treatment of breathless respect that was accorded to male deviance. Sumner describes the absence of women from the field as "nothing short of spectacular" (1994, p. 287). He suggests that deviancy theorists would not have been able to continue with their ideological heroising of deviancy if they had been forced to notice male violence against women and children:

> it is hard to see how the violence of fathers against their children could generate much enthusiasm for a theory of crime as creative critique, a theory of crime as a function of urban ghettoes, a theory of crime as a subcultural solution to social contradictions or a theory of the dangers of social over-reaction to deviance. [*ibid.*, p. 294]

Deviancy theorists were excused, presumably, from studying the men who abused women in prostitution because they were not deviant and not interesting. The sociological fascination with deviance obscured the men and stigmatised prostituted women again as constituting the problem of prostitution.

Prostitution and sexual freedom

Sexologists and sociologists of the sexual revolution who saw the sex of prostitution as "just sex" often predicted that the positive effects of the sexual revolution would cause prostitution to die out or at least considerably reduce it. Liberated women would take up the sexual servicing of men that prostitution had provided. Alex Comfort (1977) predicted the demise of prostitution, but only when all women were doing the sex of prostitution, of course. Not surprisingly, the sexual liberation of women did not lead to the withering away of prostitution, because prostitution is not "just sex". Women in general were never going to become enthusiastic about giving unknown men blow jobs in alleys unless they were paid. After the sexual revolution, prostitution was alive and well, beginning to develop new forms and becoming globalised, but in no danger of dying out.

Some sexual liberals, on the other hand, expected that prostitution, instead of dying out, would become available on a more equitable basis to men who would not usually be able to afford it. According to the sociologist David Sternberg, in the 1960s:

> Swedish psychiatrists, psychologists and social activists debated with some seriousness the formation of a "Sex Corps", analogous to the American Peace Corps, which would be comprised of dedicated and idealistic young men and women who would provide sexual services to incapacitated, disabled, and emotionally disturbed persons, including prison, hospital, and mental health institution inmates, as well as troubled, aggressive male outpatients. [Sternberg, 1983, p. 86]

Lars Ullerstam, a Swedish doctor, whose book *The Erotic Minorities* was published in 1964, suggested mobile brothels. His book was dedicated to relieving the loneliness and sexual frustration of paedophiles and necrophiles and the erotically underprivileged. The mobile brothels would service "hospitals, mental hospitals, and institutions, paralyzed, housebound patients, and old people, as well as individuals who are too inhibited to visit such establishments themselves" (Ullerstam, 1964, p. 152). The employees would be called "erotic Samaritans" and be composed of "cheerful, generous, talented, and ethically advanced persons". A gender bias creeps in when he explains that the services of stationary brothels would be provided free to those who could not pay, such as "adolescent boys and people without an income" (*ibid.*, p. 151).

The sexual revolution provided a new language for talking about sex, one full of concepts such as repression and inhibition and the need for sexual liberation, whilst institutionalising men's sexual imperative and privilege as the driving force and determinant of sexuality. The sexual liberals in the fields of sexology, history and sociology who wrote about prostitution created a new climate for the discussion of this subject, which was sympathetic to the normalising impulses developed by some prostitutes' rights groups. The sexual liberals promoted the sex of prostitution as simply what sex was. They have been remarkably successful. As Kathleen Barry explains: "The legacy to women of the sexual liberation movement and the legitimization of pornography of the 1960s has not been women's liberation but rather the prostitution of sexuality (1995, p. 59). The "sex that is bought in the act of prostitution and promoted in pornography" she says, no longer, in the 1990s, looks "significantly different from the sex that is taken in rape, pressured in teenage dating, and apparently given in many private relationships" (*ibid.*). This change was necessary for the success of a pro-prostitution prostitutes' rights movement. A movement which spoke of prostitution as just a job like any other and even a form of sexual liberation could not have been conceived in the era of pre-World War II feminism, but after the "sexual revolution" there was more confusion than before about what constituted the liberation of women. Some proponents of the prostitutes' rights movement, as we shall see, saw women's sexual liberation in the sexual servicing of men, just as the 1960s sex professionals of sexology did.

CHAPTER 3

normalising prostitution:
the prostitutes' rights movement

> If we had legalised pornography and prostitution at the same time, we wouldn't be sitting on the powder keg of sex and violence we're sitting on in this country. [Margo St James of COYOTE, quoted in Jeness, 1993, p. 75]

In the 1970s a prostitutes' rights movement developed which transformed the way in which prostitution was thought about by policy-makers, non-government organisations, human rights activists and feminist theorists. Whilst the early groups argued, in ways which appealed strongly to feminists and socialists, that prostitutes were oppressed by unjust laws and persecuting and corrupt police forces, they did not celebrate prostitution but saw it as arising from women's dire economic necessity. Feminists found little to quarrel with in this politics and many offered support. But gradually the politics of some of these organisations changed. They began to argue that prostitution was a job like any other which women "chose", and even that it represented sexual liberation for women and was on the cutting edge of women's freedom instead of being in any way connected with women's oppression. Fierce controversy broke out over the issue within the feminist movement in the 1980s with the publication of three anthologies from feminist presses which promoted the new pro-prostitution politics (Bell, 1987a; Delacoste and Alexander, 1988; Pheterson, 1989a). The prostitutes' rights movement has been very successful in—as suggested by the title of Valerie Jeness's history of the American group COYOTE, *Making it Work* (1993)—changing the conception of prostitution in many circles to that of sex work. It has also, by the 1990s, made it very difficult for feminists to argue that the origins of prostitution lie in women's oppression.

Kate Millett predicted this furious controversy in *The Prostitution Papers*, which she wrote in the summer of 1970 soon after finishing her major work, the classic of radical feminist theory, *Sexual Politics*. Millett's analysis of prostitution was a clear and passionate example of the radical feminist approach. She saw prostitution as "paradigmatic, somehow the very core of the female's condition". It declared her "subjection right out in the open" more clearly than marriage, which hid the cash nexus behind a contract. It turned the woman into a thing to be bought, effecting her "reification". It showed that a woman is no more than "cunt".

> It is not sex the prostitute is really made to sell; it is degradation. And the buyer, the john, is not buying sexuality, but power, power over another human being, the dizzy ambition of being lord of another's will for a stated period of time. [Millett, 1975, p. 56]

By the 1980s feminists with this kind of analysis were being attacked by some prostitutes' rights activists, as hostile to prostitutes, endangering their lives by increasing "whore stigma" (Roberts, 1992). Millett describes the furore at a 1971 conference which gives a hint of the disagreements to come. Some prostituted women came to this women's liberation movement conference and became very angry with the feminists there. They became particularly enraged when a panel entitled "Towards the Elimination of Prostitution" was organised, including "everyone but prostitutes" (Millett, 1975, p. 15).

> Things rapidly degenerated into chaos. Prostitutes had gathered their still-nebulous rage against their own lives and

summarily redirected it towards movement women who appeared to be quite as summarily "eliminating" prostitution, the very means of their livelihood. [*ibid.*, p. 16]

A physical fight ensued. But Millett considered that authentic action around prostitution had to come from prostitutes themselves: "if anything, ultimately, is to be done or said or decided about prostitution, prostitutes are the only legitimate persons to do it" (*ibid.*, p. 15). This was to become a difficult position to hold in the 1980s when the views of prostituted and ex-prostituted women themselves became polarised into pro and anti-prostitution positions. Feminists without such experience were going to have to decide which "truth" of prostitution they were prepared to accept. The hostility of some prostituted women to the feminist analysis that prostitution must be eliminated was to provide a good reason for even serious feminist theorists to back away from their feminist understanding in later years, as we shall see.

Birth of the prostitutes' rights movement

The first prostitutes' rights groups in Britain and Australia had an economic analysis of prostitution. Prostitution was not celebrated, or characterised as work or choice, and certainly not as sexual liberation. The purpose of the groups was to fight the legal discrimination and police harassment faced by prostituted women. The prostitutes' rights movement in Europe was launched in Lyons in 1975, when French prostitutes occupied a church in protest at the ways in which they were treated by the police. The strike protested against the savage police repression and corruption in Lyons, which had been experiencing a wave of brutal murders of prostitutes. Women in Britain who were inspired by the example of the strike formed a prostitutes' rights group called the English Collective of Prostitutes (ECP). A prostitutes' collective on the ECP model was set up in New York, and others in Austalia.

Margaret Valentino and Mavis Johnson of the ECP provide an introduction to the volume of life stories of French women involved in the strike, and an analysis setting out the ECP position. They explained that "Prostitution was one way women had been fighting to get paid for housework—by getting paid for all the sexual services all women are always expected to give for free" (Valentino and Johnson, 1980, p. 25). The cause of prostitution was "poverty and women's refusal of poverty", and "the end of women's poverty is the end of prostitution" (ibid., pp. 26, 31). The ECP approach was abolitionist rather than celebratory.

> But we agree with those who say they want to abolish prostitution. That's not what we have in mind for ouselves and our daughters, that's not what our children and relatives have in mind for us. That's not what most women who have done it or who've never done it want to do, as the six women in this book make clear. [ibid., p. 30]

The six life stories make no attempt to glamourise prostitution. Indeed, Valentino and Johnson offer an explanation of why some prostituted women might want to do that. "If we sometimes glorify our job, it is to defend ourselves against the charge that we do it because we don't know the 'right' way to live" (ibid., p. 22).

Other British prostitutes' rights groups set up in the 1970s and 1980s also had a strong economic analysis and came from socialist roots. Eileen McLeod, of the Bimingham group PROS, explained that it was socialist feminists rather than radical feminists who found it easiest to throw their support behind prostitutes' rights campaigns:

> in the early days of PROS its support came more readily from feminists emphasising the economic and class origins of women's oppression, for example members of Women's Voice Groups, rather than those rooting the explanation of women's oppression in patriarchy as such ... to them women's comparative poverty and what was seen as the victimisation of working-class prostitutes were the major issues. [McLeod, 1982, p. 134]

In the United States the socialist roots of the prostitutes' rights movement seem to have been less strong. The original organisation of the prostitutes rights' movement was, according to its chronicler, Valerie Jeness, COYOTE, or Cast Off Your Old Tired Ethics, from San Francisco. It was founded on Mothers' Day in 1973 from WHO, Whores, Housewives and Others, "to bring attention to the abuses of local prostitutes and to provide numerous community services to women and prostitutes" (Jeness, 1993, p. 43). The leading personality, Margo St James, was an ex-prostitute and got money from the Point Foundation at Glide Memorial Church, and later $1000 dollars from the Playboy Foundation. The sex industrialists saw the potential of COYOTE to support their interests from the beginning. St James recruited 50 influential San Franciscans to form an informal advisory board, as well as local prostitutes to advocate reform. "Interested parties, including students, clients of prostitutes, politicians, media personnel, activists, and representatives from other advocacy organisations were invited and encouraged to become members of COYOTE" (ibid., p. 43).

Jeness attributes the founding impulses behind the prostitutes' rights movement to inspiration from the gay movement and feminism. She explains that "the gay and lesbian movement helped to create a socio-political climate more hospitable to prostitutes and their advocates ... the discursive themes of the gay and lesbian movement have been adopted by the prostitutes' rights movement." Also, themes from the women's movement "have proved instrumental in launching the prostitutes' rights movement, as well as defusing it" (ibid., p. 21). This connection needs some critical analysis. The oft-repeated assertion that lesbian and gay rights and prostitutes' rights are inevitably intertwined is based upon the erroneous view that the prostitutes' rights movement is one of sexual liberation. One of the ways in which the prostitutes' rights movement appealed to certain areas of the feminist movement was by promoting itself as a movement irrevocably tied to women's sexual liberation.

COYOTE seems to have been popular with liberal men, which is unusual for a feminist group. Jeness records that, in the first year of COYOTE's existence, the *Seattle Post-Intelligencer* reported that "Margo is 'in' socially this year. Well-to-do liberals invite her to things and seek her company" (*ibid.*, p. 44). The organisation was started in San Francisco because it was a tolerant environment, and many liberal men were on the original advisory board. Recruitment of prostituted women was difficult, ostensibly because prostitution was illegal. COYOTE staged media events to raise funds and publicity, which went down well with the male public. Each year they held the Annual Hookers' Convention and Annual Hookers' Ball. The slogan of the first ball was "Everybody Needs a Hooker Once in Awhile", and the *Chicago Tribune* reported, "for the press it was an orgy. They filmed, photographed, and interviewed anyone who was generous with her eyeshadow" (*ibid.*, p. 59).

According to Jeness, the prostitutes' rights movement was instrumental in changing ways of thinking about prostitution. Prostitution was transformed into "sex work".

> During the 1970s and throughout the 1980s a new image of prostitution emerged to challenge traditional views of prostitutes as social misfits, sexual slaves, victims of pimps and drug addiction, and tools of organised crime. It has become fashionable to refer to prostitution as "sex work". [*ibid.*, p. 1]

In a short time the movement had established a "vocabulary of sex as work, prostitutes as sex workers, and prostitutes' civil rights as workers" (*ibid.*, p. 1). Prostitution became firmly placed "in the rhetoric of work, choice, and civil rights".

Jeness argues that the movement "not only seeks to legitimate prostitution, but to celebrate it as well. It has developed a radical critique of popular views of prostitution by substituting a new ethic, one that affirms prostitutes' behaviour as sensible and moral" (*ibid.*, p. 4). This "new ethic" was not so obvious from the writings of the prostitutes' rights movement in Europe and the United States in the 1970s. The movement appealed to feminists for support to fight the discrimination, violence and harassment faced by prostituted women. Feminists recognised prostituted women as, in Kate Millett's words, our "political prisoners". But none of this meant the celebration of prostitution. It was quite possible to campaign against the oppression of prostituted women whilst still seeing prostituted women as victims of male abuse. I argued in a 1979 paper, written in response to the activities of the ECP and the French prostitutes' strike, that feminists who set up refuges to support battered women and campaigned to provide them with decent child-care and economic assistance did not feel the need to celebrate "marriage" (Jeffreys, 1985). It was possible to fight the wrongs women experienced in the institutions of male supremacy, marriage and prostitution, whilst still seeking to abolish those institutions.

COYOTE, along with prostitutes' rights groups in other countries, gained respectability, increased state funding and a higher public profile after the HIV/AIDS epidemic took hold. State concern to reduce infection led to reliance on organisations seen as having access to prostituted women and in a position to spread safe-sex messages. A similar phenomenon took place in relation to the lesbian and gay movement, leading to controversy over whether gay liberation became bureaucratised by a new respectable status (Altman, 1994). As Jeness puts it, "The prostitutes' rights movement moved from feminist discourse to public health discourse [and] inherited an opportunity to work within the system in a socially sanctioned way" (1993, p. 103). Symbolic alliances, she says, were forged with the gay and lesbian movement, as well as mainstream organisations such as the World Health Organisation, the American Civil Liberties Union, the UN Human Rights Commission, amd the US Institute of Public and Urban Affairs.

In the early 1980s, COYOTE met some serious competition. Prostitutes' organisations with a very different analysis of prostitution began to oppose pro-prostitution ideas. Women

Hurt In Systems of Prostitution Engaged in Revolt, WHISPER, was set up by Evelina Giobbe, an ex-prostituted woman who defines prostitution as commercial sexual violence. WHISPER works with prostituted and ex-prostituted women, offering support, organisation and training programmes. It does not celebrate prostitution. WHISPER was followed by the Council for Prostitution Alternatives and Standing Against Global Exploitation, SAGE, in San Francisco. Jeness, who clearly takes a COYOTE position, seeks to discredit WHISPER. She says it is an organisation "made up of volunteers, feminist scholars, and clergy who are concerned with saving prostitutes from the life of prostitution" (Jeness, 1993, p. 77). In fact the WHISPER newsletter and materials do not suggest a christian do-gooder approach at all. Nevertheless, the main implication of Jeness's description is that WHISPER is not composed of women with experience of prostitution.

This is an odd accusation, considering that Jeness thoroughly debunks the idea that COYOTE itself is composed of prostituted or ex-prostituted women. In a section of her book entitled "Institutionalising an Organizational Myth", Jeness explains that the myth is that COYOTE is an organisation of prostituted and ex-prostituted women. This myth gives it legitimacy, she says, particularly with the media. The media accepts and promotes the myth. In fact only a small percentage of members have worked as prostitutes. In 1981 COYOTE claimed to have a membership of 30,000 with 3 per cent of those being prostituted women. Media reports promoted the myth with references to COYOTE as a "'self-proclaimed prostitutes' union,' 'a national organization of hookers,' 'the biggest prostitutes' group in the U.S.,' 'the first prostitutes' guild,' 'the first prostitutes' union,' 'a hookers' union,' 'a hookers' organization,' and 'a prostitutes' trade union'" (Jeness, p. 114). Jeness quotes Margo St James debunking the myth herself: "That has always been the myth, the media's terminology for their idea of COYOTE. I'm not a working prostitute. I haven't worked for many, many years. Besides, a union for prostitutes is not possible now" (*ibid.*, p. 115).

Priscilla Alexander, at one time director and chief spokesperson for COYOTE, had never been in prostitution. COYOTE has actually lied about its composition to support the myth, Jeness explains. A 1988 copy of its newsletter, COYOTE Howls, declared on the first page that "most members of COYOTE are either prostitutes or ex-prostitutes, with a few non-prostitute allies" (ibid., p. 116). COYOTE does not, then, directly represent the views of women in prostitution any more than any other group organised around the issue, but it does represent a particular ideological viewpoint that is in favour of the sex industry and opposes feminist perspectives. As Jeness suggests, COYOTE seeks to normalise prostitution by presenting the media with an image of prostitutes as "ordinary, well-adjusted individuals trying to make a legitimate living" (ibid.). This is not a view from prostituted women and it is likely to be very partial.

International organising

The prostitutes' rights movement began to organise internationally in the mid-1980s. Gail Pheterson from the Netherlands worked in California with Margo St James of COYOTE in 1984. She developed her ideas on prostitution in the Netherlands in the 1980s, when public policy was being directed towards recognising the "choice" and "autonomy" of prostituted women. As we shall see in Chapter 11 on trafficking, the liberal sexual climate of the Netherlands has produced some of the most influential ideas and organisations involved in promoting a pro-prostitution position on the traffic in women. In 1985 the newly formed Netherlands prostitutes' rights group, the Red Thread, organised a congress which led to the forming of the International Committee for Prostitutes' Rights and the draft of a World Charter for Prostitutes' Rights was discussed and finalised at a second international congress in 1986. The politics of this international organisation are pro-prostitution. Its "Statement on Prostitution and Feminism" declares that prostitution is "legitimate work" (Pheterson, 1989a, p. 193). The World Charter includes a defence of johns, explaining that "The customer, like the prostitute, should not … be criminalised or condemned on a moral basis" (*ibid.*, p. 41). Whereas anti-prostitution and anti-pornography feminists see the interests of johns and prostituted women as being in opposition, the pro-prostitution position sees the johns as the basis of the prostituted woman's livelihood and is unable to portray them in a negative light.

It was the development of a strong feminist movement against pornography, St James (1989) explains, that made her realise the need for international organising against it. Pheterson and St James had already separated themselves completely from the sort of feminist anti-prostitution analysis expounded by Kathleen Barry (1979). Pheterson rejects the ideas that Barry expressed at a conference in 1982 in Rotterdam on female sexual slavery, inspired by her book of the same title. Barry, she says, "invalidates the words of prostitutes by pointing to their histories of abuse, their poverty and/or their inability to be objective about their situations" (Pheterson, 1989b, p. 20). Barry sought to end prostitution, and Pheterson and St James saw prostitution as acceptable work.

A queer perspective

A perspective on prostitution drawn from gay male theory began to have an influence in the 1990s. Andrew Hunter, of the Australian prostitutes' organisation Scarlet Alliance, is an exponent of this "queer" approach, which he sees as far more radical and progressive than earlier prostitutes' rights approaches. He explains that the Australian Prostitutes' Collectives in Melbourne, Sydney and on the Gold Coast in Queensland were originally affiliated with the English Collective of Prostitutes and accepted the ECP explanation of prostitution as "a reflection of economic circumstances". This was a useful position at first to get funding, he says, because it was "sometimes helpful to have an explanation that is full of holes as a starting point, in order to avoid the theory becoming dogma". Hunter characterised this "economic" approach as apologist. The ECP has an "acceptable" theory of prostititution, summarised by its slogan "for prostitutes, against prostitution". This acceptable position argued that "prostitution existed because of the economic inequality of the sexes" (Hunter, 1992, p. 110). This theory, he says:

> in retrospect, can be seen as the type of apologist position that many oppressed groups have taken in the first public airing of their cause. The gay movement started pre-Stonewall, in the same way, saying that it was not their fault they were different and that they just wanted to be accepted.

However, Hunter argues, the problem with this approach was that it was negative. It encouraged "people who had problems in the industry to come to the group", with the result that many of the positive aspects of sex work were not highlighted. One result of what he calls the "economic approach" is "the maintenance of a public perception that prostitution is a problem". And that would not do at all. The "negative approach" failed to emphasise "what people in the industry actually like about working" (*ibid.*, pp. 112, 113).

The more positive approach of seeing prostitution as "work" was taken up by Australian groups around 1987, he says. The new position was well encapsulated by Cheryl Overs from Scarlet Alliance.

> Consciously commercial sex which takes place in a workplace, regardless of how informal, is more accurately described as sex work (as distinct from prostitution). Those transactions can be recognised as a series of interrelated workplaces which form the commercial sex industry and which can be targeted for promotion and/or enforcement of sound work practices. [quoted in *ibid.*, p. 112]

One difficulty with this approach was that it excluded street prostituted women. They did not have a "workplace" in which conditions could be improved.

Hunter explains that this position has been followed by

one that is more positive still about prostitution. This new position on prostitution was derived from lesbian and gay and queer politics. This approach consists of:

> seeing sex work as an expression of sexuality—an expression which in itself is good. This position further posits that sex work, like other expressions of sexuality that deviate from the norm, will be oppressed, and sex workers will be discriminated against. [*ibid.*, p. 111]

This politics was developed through HIV/AIDS work and the fight against right-wing politics. This led to the recognition of prostitutes as a sexual minority. "Sex-worker" groups could now "look for allies amongst other groups of people who were stigmatised because of their sexuality and sexual expression". They came to be seen as "part of a broad 'pro-sex' movement, which includes the promotion of sexual minorities and action against censorship". The "concept of sex workers as a sexual minority, amongst other sexual minorities" provided a base from which to work "to destigmatise sex work, as part of a broader movement aimed at destigmatising sex and sexuality" (*ibid.*, pp. 111, 114).

Hunter's position is allied to the queer politics of the 1990s, which could be seen as "out and proudly out", and confrontationist rather than assimilationist. In Australia, in particular, gay male proponents of prostitution have been influential in constructing a pro-prostitution position, based on the experience of gay male prostitution which is significantly different from the situation of women in many ways (Perkins and Bennett, 1985). The influence of an inappropriate but powerful gay male theory and practice on the politics of the prostitutes' rights movement will be examined in detail in Chapter 4. From this "sexual minorities" position, in which everyone is fighting to celebrate and destigmatise their sexual practice, critical feminist politics of sexuality were roundly repudiated. They certainly do not fit the "queer" perspective (Jeffreys, 1994). The feminist argument that prostituted women do not enjoy their work showed, Hunter said, "an anti-sex/sexual difference position that has been taken by many 'progressive' groups towards sex work in particular and sex itself generally" (1992, p. 111). Acording to his position, prostitution represents sex, prostitutes are sexual revolutionaries working for everyone's sexual freedom, and critics are anti-sex. Certainly, the more the politics of the prostitutes' rights movement moved towards this position, the more difficult it became for feminists to support such groups.

The feminist controversy

Spokeswomen of the prostitutes' rights movement, such as Nickie Roberts (1992), castigate feminists for their refusal to listen to prostitutes. The problem, though, is in deciding which prostituted and ex-prostituted women to listen to. The positive and celebratory stance taken by a small number of prostitutes' rights activists seems to gain considerable publicity because it is popular with the media and with all the powerful economic and political forces which represent the interests of johns. The careful research on prostitution which involves qualitative interviewing does not support this relentlessly positive position (Hoigard and Finstad, 1992; McKeganey and Barnard, 1996). However, the work of anti-prostitution organisations such as WHISPER, which represent the interests of those prostituted and ex-prostituted women who find prostitution dangerous and damaging, is not so well known as that of COYOTE.

WHISPER, Women Hurt In Systems of Prostitution Engaged in Revolt, is an organisation of "women who have survived the sex industry" (Giobbe, 1990, p. 67). Its analysis of prostitution could not be more different from that of COYOTE. It explicitly opposes what it calls the "mythology" of prostitution constructed in part by some prostitutes' rights groups. The "mythology" claims that prostitution is a "career choice", that prostitution "epitomises women's sexual liberation" that prostitutes "set the sexual and economic conditions of their interactions with customers" (*ibid.*, p. 67). WHISPER declares that prostitution is a "crime committed against women by men in its most traditional form. It is nothing less than the commercialisation of the sexual abuse and inequality that women suffer in the traditional family and can be nothing more" (*ibid.*, p. 80). But even the writings contained in the three anthologies from feminist presses mentioned earlier, which take a pro-prostitution editorial position and are dominated by the perspective of the prostitutes' rights movement, contain much that would support an opposite view.

One of the editors of *Sex Work: Writings by Women in the Sex Industry* (1988) is Priscilla Alexander, co-director of COYOTE, who might be expected to take a COYOTE position. *A Vindication of the Rights of Whores* (1989) is edited by Gail Pheterson, who is co-founder of the International Committee for Prostitutes' Rights. The Canadian volume, *Good Girls, Bad Girls: Sex Trade Workers and Feminists Face to Face* (1987) originated in a conference stimulated by the hostility of the Canadian Organisation for the Rights of Prostitutes (CORP) to feminist organisers of the International Women's Day march, who had distributed a leaflet attacking pornography as harmful to women. This volume does include material written by self-identified feminists as well as material which is hostile to feminism. The contributions to these collections are mostly in the form of oral history or statements from individuals. They are not based upon research into the experience of prostitutes. However, because they have the authority of coming from feminist presses and are widely circulated within the feminist community, they have been important in shaping the views of feminists about prostitution.

In the anthology *Sex Work*, many contributions by prostituted and ex-prostituted women speak of prostitution as abusive (Delacoste and Alexander, 1988). At the Canadian conference covered in *Good Girls, Bad Girls*, ex-prostituted women directly contradicted the statements of pro-prostitution activists in very heated exchanges. Peggy Miller, a member of Toronto's CORP, was positive about the sex in prostitution. "What is so terrible about fucking for a living? I like it, I can live out my fantasies" (Bell, 1987a, p. 48). Another participant challenged her, saying that she had been a prostitute for eight years since the age of fifteen:

> I don't know how you can possibly say, as busy as you are as a lady of the evening, that you like every sexual act, that you work out your fantasies! Come on, get serious. How can you work out your fantasies with a trick that you're putting on an act for? ... Can you count how many tricks you have had? You mean you have that many fantasies? Isn't it about having money to survive? ... If I had had to fuck one more of them—boy, I would have killed him! [*ibid.*, p. 50]

One woman at the conference pointed out that, whilst some women purported to enjoy their work when they were speaking publicly, more negative stories were being told in private.

Despite the efforts of some prostitutes' rights organisations to put a positive face on prostitution, as soon as women speak out about their experience it becomes clear that many women want to condemn the oppression of prostitution rather than celebrate it. Feminists who wish to discover the truth of prostitution by listening to women with experience find that there are diametrically opposed points of view. It becomes necessary to decide which view to accept. The making of this decision is not assisted by the fact that some prostitutes' rights activists have retreated into personal abuse towards any feminists who challenge prostitution.

Hostility to feminism

As the ideology of most organisations within the prostitutes' rights movement has moved more and more in the direction of the celebration of prostitution, the vituperation against feminists who oppose men's use of women in prostitution has, perhaps not surprisingly, become more extreme. Andrea Dworkin (1997) has written powerful fiction and analysis informed by her own experience of prostitution. She is commonly seen as representing the unpopular anti-prostitution position. Susie Bright, first editor of the American lesbian pornography magazine *On Our Backs*, objects to Dworkin's portayal of prostitution in her novels, *Ice and Fire* and *Mercy*. She proclaims, "If you understand that Andrea Dworkin is the reincarnation of the Marquis de Sade, her whole thing makes sense! She's a severely repressed sadist" (Juno, 1991, p. 201). Dworkin is not alone in receiving this hostility. Nickie Roberts, the ex-prostitute author of *Whores in History*, describes a paper I gave at a 1980 Women Against Violence Against Women conference in Leeds as "paradigmatic" of the radical feminist view of the "sex industry" (Roberts, 1992, p. 341). I am accused of having "silenced prostitutes and reduced them to objects" by

> making the same careless mistake as most other outside observers of the sex industry: she equates prostitutes with prostitution, asserting that "Payment reduces the woman to a bought object". In fact, what is being bought is not the woman, but the sexual services she offers. [*ibid*., p. 342]

It is significant that this kind of reversal is so common. Feminists who challenge the objectification of women are seen as the ones who make women objects, not men. Feminists who fight the victimisation of women are seen as making women victims (Roiphe, 1993; Wolf, 1993). I, and feminists with a similar position, are seen as helping the "moral reactionaries who are always waiting in the wings, ready and eager to jump out at any time and blame prostitutes for all of society's ills" (Roberts, 1992, p. 342).

The most damning accusation against those of us who criticise men's abuse of women in prostitution is that we are endangering women's lives by increasing the negative public image of prostitutes: "the concrete effects of this kind of theorizing are wearily predictable, costing many whores their livelihoods and, all too often, their lives, as the whore-stigma is translated into violence on the streets" (*ibid*., p. 343).

A study of the "sex industry" in the state of Victoria in

Australia by Donna Macik (n.d.) is available from the Prostitutes' Collective of Victoria. Macik also accuses me and Andrea Dworkin of creating dangerously negative and patriarchal stereotypes of prostitutes.

> Dworkin and Jeffreys, by focussing negatively on prostitution, intensify the stigma attached to sex industry workers, perpetuating a "power over" position, denying prostitutes workplace industrial rights and reinforcing a "victim"/inferior status that reinforces attitudes feminists define as patriarchal. [Macik, n.d., p. 12]

The possibility of being accused of endangering other women is a potent weapon against those who might wish to be critical of the institution of prostitution. It silences opposition to this form of male abuse. The Australian political scientist Barbara Sullivan (1994) explains that she changed her mind about the origins of prostitution lying in male supremacy because she was criticised by sex workers for being anti-prostitute. Consequently, she now takes the public position that prostitution is just about teaching sexual skills and in the future men and women will all be doing it. Faced with anger from those holding a pro-prostitution position she chose to recant and decide that she no longer wanted to criticise prostitution: "Feminist approaches which attempt to support sex workers but not the sex industry do not make logical or practical sense" (ibid., p. 268). Sullivan's volte-face does suggest the power of the pro-prostitution rhetoric that has emerged from the prostitutes' rights movement, from post-modern and queer theory and sexual libertarianism. The pro-prostitution position is influential because it comes from some women involved in the industry, as well as from the johns, and a failure to accept it could look like a denial of women's experience.

Anger at feminists in the arguments of prostitutes' rights activists can become quite caustic. Valerie Scott, Peggy Miller and Ryan Hotchkiss of CORP express considerable hostility in the Good Girls, Bad Girls collection (Bell, 1987). They are very sympathetic towards men, and castigate feminists for not having this sympathy. Of the johns, they say: "You want ... to be sensitive to his needs as a person. He's a person. He's not a fucking animal—he's a person! He may just need to be held, he may just need you to act out some fantasy ...". The strength of their sympathy with the plight of men makes them angry with feminists who tend to be critical of male behaviour. The johns, they say, are "people, and we're tired of the feminists treating them like they're not" (ibid., pp. 209, 210). The interview is called "Realistic Feminists" because the CORP members say they are the real feminists, not those who purport to be. They are the "only feminists around", in fact, because they are the only ones listening to men.

> We think whores are more conscious of feminism from a healthy perspective than most other feminists. The reason is that we're constantly interacting with men and conscious of where they're coming from, so in that sense we're really hearing them. [ibid., p. 210]

This is an unusual definition of feminism, of course. Liberation ideologies do not usually arise from listening intently to the oppressor and serving his wants and needs with utmost care. The English Collective of Prostitutes takes a rather different position on johns. It has a socialist perspective which stresses that the interests of the workers are in conflict with their employers: "We see prostitute women's interests in connection not with the police, the media, politicians, academics and clients, but with all others who share poverty and repression with us" (Delacoste and Alexander, 1988, p. 275).

According to CORP, prostituted women are more "realistic" feminists than others because those who usually call themselves feminists are hung up sexually.

> We're more realistic feminists. A prostitute is a realistic feminist as opposed to an idealistic, hypocritical, shadowy feminist who doesn't want to confront the facts of life, the facts of her

own negotiating and trade-off in the marriage situation, the fact that the male is her brother and not the enemy and the fact that she's afraid of sex. [Bell, 1987b, p. 211]

They accuse feminists of "pimping our ass" (*ibid.*, p. 212). Feminists should stop doing this and "start listening to us" and "stop looking at us as victims", and feminists should "address sexuality as it really is" i.e. presumably, the sex of prostitution.

The problem, they say, is that feminists are prudes and puritans and "can't even hear their own bodies". Feminists are unable to understand and accept what the CORP spokeswomen say because of sexual inhibitions: "Feminists are so blocked sexually around what's politically correct, what's madonna-like" (*ibid.*, pp. 213, 214). As women lose these inhibitions, and realise what sexuality is really about, and get "more financial power", then they will, and already are, using men in "escort services" just as men have used women. But first of all they need to understand what they need sexually and realise that they need to buy commercial sex just as men do. "The first step is getting a woman to understand that her sexual needs are what they are and they're valid. She's entitled to that" (*ibid.*, p. 217). If prostitution is sexual liberation, then women must be included in this vision, whether this is realistic or not.

Proponents of prostitution seek to discredit contemporary anti-prostitution feminists by associating them with a hostile stereotype of the nineteenth-century feminists involved in a similar struggle (Jeness, 1993, p. 35). They characterise the anti-prostitution feminists of the period, who campaigned against the *Contagious Diseases Acts* in Britain and the double standard of morality, as prudes and puritans who were against women and against sexual liberation. The usual approach is to associate contemporary feminists with the hostile caricature they have constructed of nineteenth-century feminists in order to delegitimise contemporary campaigners. (McLeod, 1982; Roberts, 1992). Nickie Roberts makes the connection thus:

It is no coincidence that many feminists remain ambivalent towards the whores' movement, and that the anti-pornography/prostitution faction of contemporary Western feminism has tended to reproduce the attitudes of the predecessors, the "First Wave" feminists of the nineteenth century. [Roberts, 1992, p. 340]

Eileen Mcleod is another of the many who make similar arguments. She says that, among feminists who were resistant to supporting prostitutes' rights groups like PROS in Birmingham, "there were some echoes of the fact that feminist action against the *Contagious Diseases Acts* became transmuted into the social purity movement early in this century" (McLeod, 1982, p. 134). Closer attention to the arguments and actions of nineteenth-century feminist campaigners does not support the caricature, as I have argued elsewhere. (Jeffreys, 1985).

Prostitution performance art: public relations for the sex industrialists

In the late 1980s a new phenomenon developed out of the pro-prostitution movement. This consisted of prostituted and ex-prostituted women, like Carol Leigh, Annie Sprinkle, Veronica Vera, who turned their life's experience of being abused by men in prostitution into careers as "performance artists" and "sex educators". They took the sex of prostitution in which they were well versed, and marketed it to women and men as sexual liberation, as a new sexual "feminism". These women wrote for the feminist anthologies on "sex work", and fronted for prostitutes' rights organisations. They were not protesting the conditions of prostitution: mostly they said it was just lovely in the sex industry. Rather, they were promoting prostitution as the very model, not just for sex and self-determination, but for art, commerce, feminism, even a new religion. They have achieved some success, if success is measured by the regard in which they are apparently held by the world's patriarchal media, which loves to market prostitution as women's liberation.

The ideas and practices promoted in this new phenomenon of prostitute performance art are well represented in the work of Annie Sprinkle. Sprinkle was an activist in the prostitutes' rights group PONY (Prostitutes of New York). She reported in 1991 that she had worked for sixteen years as a 42nd Street dancer, as a pornography film star with one hundred and fifty feature films, twenty videos and fifty 8-mm loops behind her in 1991, and as a prostitute in massage parlours (Juno, 1991). She came to New York to be the mistress of Gerard Damiano, who made the pornography movie *Deep Throat*, in which Linda Lovelace performed at the behest of a violent pimp who threatened her with a gun (Lovelace, 1981). Sprinkle became an apprentice pornography film-maker. In 1985 she became a "performance artist" and began a successful career performing in many countries as what she calls a "Post-Porn Modernist". One show is called *A Public Cervix*, in which Sprinkle invites audience members to inspect her cervix with a speculum and flashlight. She masturbates and uses a vibrator to orgasm on stage and pees into a toilet, including wiping with toilet paper. This is treated as art by the cognoscenti. It is interesting that Sprinkle has managed to pornographise a practice begun by feminists for self-empowerment. Feminists in the early 1970s used specula to examine each other's cervixes in consciousness-raising and women's health groups, to get to know and demystify their bodies, and take power back from the medical establishment. Sprinkle displays herself for an audience and still claims that this is something to do with women's sexual empowerment.

In Australia, Sprinkle was a star at the prestigious Adelaide Fringe Festival in 1996 and also performed in theatres in Sydney and Melbourne. It is perhaps not surprising that some women performance artists learnt their skills in prostitution. They are, after all, simply providing similar performances, though to larger audiences who see themselves as intellectuals and art lovers rather than johns, and in theatres rather than peep shows. Somebody is being had. Sprinkle comments, "Almost all the top women performance artists have told me (because

I've met all my favorites) that they were in the sex industry as streetwalkers, go-go dancers" (Juno, 1991, p. 39).

Sprinkle has had a spiritual transformation since the old days when she just did striptease and regular pornography. She has developed a new persona called Anya, and promotes a New Age sexuality with tantric healing rituals. She styles herself a "sex educator" who is bringing sexual liberation to women. "Annie Sprinkle likes sex with transsexuals, midgets and amputees: Anya makes love to the sky, mud and trees" (*ibid.*, p. 33).

> Post-Porn Modernists celebrate sex as the nourishing, lifegiving force. We embrace our genitals as part, not separate, from our spirits. We utilise sexually explicit words, pictures and performances to communicate our ideas and emotions. We denounce sexual censorship as anti-art and inhuman. We empower ourselves by this attitude of sex-positivism. And with this love for our sexual selves we have fun, heal the world and endure. [*ibid.*, p. 23]

A celebratory article in the colour magazine of the *Australian* newspaper details the degree of esteem in which Sprinkle is now held by the establishment.

> Revered in some circles as a woman who can provide genuine insights into the lives of sex workers and the role of sex in women's lives, she has lectured at Brown and Columbia universities and the Museum of Modern Art; her *Sluts and Goddesses* video was screened at the Whitney Museum and she is in great demand as a teacher of workshops for women, including The Secrets of Sacred Slutism, and Sex for Healing, Meditation and as a Path to Enlightenment. [Krum, 1996, pp. 31–2]

Sprinkle's "genuine insights" are aimed at making prostitution seem like a fine career for a woman. She does not dwell on the negatives that so irritate proponents of prostitution.

Sprinkle had no sexual abuse in her past, she says, but

went into prostitution six months after losing her virginity, because she needed the money. She loved her first job working in a massage parlor; "For 3 months I worked and didn't even know I was a hooker—I was having such a good time!" She particularly liked sex with men she found physically repulsive: "I wanted to see what sex was like with somebody you couldn't even 'stand', so for awhile I had my 'Beauty and the Beast' fantasy: being with the 'creepiest' kind of guys ..." (Juno, 1991, pp. 24, 26). Her understanding of love is that it can exist in the experience of a few minutes of sexual use by a paying customer.

> When I was in that massage room having sex, I *loved* that person! I was truly having a *deeper relationship*. And *they* loved me! I think as a child I didn't get enough attention ... So in a way prostitution was perfect: I needed to feel sexy; I needed people to tell me I was sexy—because I thought I was ugly. [*ibid.*, p. 26]

Sprinkle's message for those women in prostitution who have a rather harder time is that it must be their fault.

Anything negative that happened to her, Sprinkle explains, was her own responsibility.

> And I think that if I was a victim, in a sense I was just as responsible as the victimiser—that sounds harsh, but whenever that happened I'm sure I created a lot of it. I did have a low self-image and self-worth, which affected how other people treated me. So I take responsibility for any exploitation that occurred. [*ibid.*, p. 28]

She does comment, though, that many men were "far less than 'respectful'" and "abusive in some ways" but "mostly ... I came out a winner!" (*ibid.*) Even women who get arrested for prostitution bring it on themselves, she considers. She was never arrested for prostitution because she exercised the power of positive thinking. Nothing happened to her because she was "never afraid". But she knew "women working in the same places I did who have been arrested 5 or 6 times—they were so afraid of being arrested, that they *were* arrested!" (*ibid.*, p. 38).

Despite this very positive account, there clearly were negatives to Annie Sprinkle's work experience. One of her performances was called "'A Hundred Blow Jobs', because out of the two or three thousand blow jobs I'd given, a hundred had been really lousy—really horrible experiences where I'd cry afterwards" (*ibid.*, p. 32). In the performance she "gagged on this huge dildo", and "got in touch" with her pain. Apparently "All the sexual abuse I'd ever suffered came out of my throat", which is a surprise considering the positive portrait she has been painting. In the same interview she declared, "I've never been raped—nothing horrible has ever happened to me. I've never been really scared; I've had this really lucky life" (*ibid.*, p. 32). The "Blow Jobs" performance allowed her to "feel *free*—free from all that abuse I suffered ...". It seems that the public relations role for the sex industry that has been taken on so profitably by "sex educators" like Sprinkle is sometimes difficult to maintain.

Some of the forms of erotic entertainment that Sprinkle engaged in at the New York sadomasochist club, Hellfire, in the late 1970s certainly have the appearance of being abusive, except that, according to John Heidenry in his history of the sexual revolution, she apparently chose and relished these experiences. He describes Sprinkle as thinking up "little sex games".

Once she invented something called oatmeal wrestling, then enlisted two dozen men to wash the oatmeal off her body with urine. Another time she orchestrated a circle jerk of twenty men around her ... She had sex with a forty-two-inch-tall dwarf, a black man with a penis three times normal length, a man named Erhardt who liked to have sex in a Nazi uniform ... She also accommodated ... piercing scenes, a Great Dane that enjoyed fellatio, an eight-foot boa constrictor ... [Heidenry, 1997, p. 161]

The accounts of prostituted women that we shall consider in subsequent chapters suggest that Sprinkle's apparent enthusiasm for experiencing extreme degradation is most unusual. Most prostituted women, after all, say they take no pleasure in even the most ordinary practices of prostitution (see Hoigard and Finstad, 1992). Her particular enthusiasms and experience do not equip her well to be a prostitutes' rights spokesperson representing the interests of such women. As a sex educator for those interested in a sexuality of equality, she may be equally poorly qualified.

The practice of sexual performance art is not limited to the United States. Linda Sproule, an Australian performance artist, echoes Sprinkle's idea that women can make positive political statements by opening up their bodies to the male gaze in a way that has traditionally only taken place in the sex industry. In the Australian journal *Artlink*, Sproule is seen as comparable to "New York artists Annie Sprinkle and Karen Finley who believe that in terms of drawing attention to the second-rate treatment of women in our society, active protest may succeed where feminist theory has not" (King, 1994, p. 60). Sproule's "active protest" requires that she injure her body before the performance so that she can show the audience real wounds. She throws off a negligee on stage, dons high heels, and the viewer is "confronted with Sproule's naked body, bruised and newly lacerated, and as she minces through the audience on the high heels she becomes a ghastly parody of woman as object of desire" (*ibid.*, p. 61). She gives viewers a torch and bends over so that they can examine the wounds. In the photographs accompanying this piece, men and women are shown shining a torch onto her buttocks and one man fingers the lacerations upon them. We are told that "feminists and misogynists alike" have misread the piece as "confirming women's second-rate status". As disproof of this hypothesis the writer, Amanda King, says that "self-mutilation has precedents" in the art of women who self-inflict razor cuts and invite the audience to cut off their hair (*ibid.*, p. 61). The bodies of these women are called here "artists' materials" and the "artists" re-enact upon them the abuse of women that is inflicted upon women by men in the world outside the gallery. It is hard to see how the appropriation of this abuse for art challenges the abuse of women that is not identified as artistic.

Sexual performance art is now highly regarded by some in the academic feminist community. Post-modern theory is invoked in Shannon Bell's book *Reading, Writing and Rewriting the Prostitute Body* (1994), to support the notion that prostituted women are more than simply women doing a job like any other, or even just doing a job which happens to bring them the ultimate in sexual excitement and fulfilment. For Shannon Bell, prostituted women are sacred healers and goddesses. Invoking the golden age myths about periods in history when prostituted women were held in high regard, she chooses to trace the prostitute's "lineage to the ancient sexual, sacred, healing female body" (Bell, 1994, p. 1). Bell is impressed at the way in which prominent prostitute activists, such as Annie Sprinke, Veronica Vera, Candida Royalle, are taking their politics and their sex industry, expertise into the making of video and performance "art". This "art", whilst apparently making ironical comments upon the sex industry, also employs—and celebrates—its practices. In this prostitute performance art, Bell believes, prostituted women manage to reconcile the great dualism of goddess and whore which has been used historically to divide women.

The ideas and the practices of the prostitutes' rights movement developed in the 1980s and 1990s in ways which made it very difficult for feminists to support them without giving up a feminist analysis of prostitution. Feminists were required to abandon all the insights that feminist theorists and activists had been offering for a century about the connections between prostitution and the oppression of women, in order to accept that prostitution was a job like any other, or possibly rather better, and even a form of sexual service or sexual liberation. However, there was a problem. Many prostituted and ex-prostituted women told a very different story and failed to see any positive aspects to prostitution. Groups like

WHISPER developed, which contained prostituted women and declared that prostitution was a form of violence against women which must be eliminated. How were feminists to decide which analysis they found most convincing? The pro-prostitution position gained most publicity and funding because its message was more in sympathy with prevailing male opinion. It was—and is—an easier cause to support, even if it means abandoning those women who remain worryingly negative, and it avoids the invective of pro-prostitution activists who are very angry at the feminist critique of prostitution. In succeeding chapters I will examine the arguments of pro-prostitution activists that prostitution is about choice, that it is a job like any other, that it is sexual liberation—and suggest that prostitution is none of these things for the women involved, but rather a form of sexual violence.

CHAPTER 4

homosexuality and prostitution

When I first started doing punters, I had a lot
of trouble. God, I'd feel like heaving with
most of them, they were so nasty. [Paul in
Gibson, 1996, p. 85]

A gay male or "queer" perspective has been
important in constructing the idea of prostitution in the
1980s and 1990s. The prostitutes' rights movement has been
influenced towards seeing prostituted women as a variety of
sexual minority like lesbians and gay men. A complacency
towards prostitution in the feminist and lesbian communities
can be seen to have been encouraged by a gay male acceptance of the practice. Critical analysis of the relationship
between male homosexuality, lesbianism and prostitution is
necessary to an understanding of how prostitution has been
normalised at the end of the twentieth century.

The use of prostituted men and boys has played a significant part in gay male sexual behaviour historically. This has
not been the case for lesbians, who are much more likely to
have been prostituted for men than to have played the part of
johns. However, the experience of prostituted men has not
been subjected to feminist analysis. There are clearly some crucial differences from the experience of prostituted women,
such as the fact that some young gay men seem to see it as raising rather than lowering their status to be offered money for
sex. But in other ways the experience of boys in prostitution,

particularly those who are homeless, shares considerable similarities with that of women and girls.

The theory of prostitution arising from gay male culture and contemporary "queer" theory does not take account of differences between prostituted women and men. It does not look at the way in which the power relationship between the sexes constructs the phenomenon of prostitution. Yet the idea that prostituted women and men constitute a sexual minority, a category of sexual deviant worthy of inclusion in the ranks of queer, a notion dependent on traditional masculine definitions of sex, has gained some considerable influence within lesbian, gay and general academic theorising of sexuality. This is deeply problematic for feminist theorising of prostitution, since pro-prostitution gay and queer theorists are strongly opposing the idea that prostitution constitutes a violation of human rights or a form of sexual violence, preferring to see it as a liberatory practice. This chapter will analyse the theory and the practice of gay male and lesbian prostitution to understand what is going wrong with queer approaches to prostitution.

Sexual minorities

The queer theory of the present tends to lump together what are described as sexual minorities. It regards them as representing equally "transgressive" "sexualities". The roots of this kind of approach lie in the work of Michel Foucault and his popularisers, such as the British gay historian Jeffrey Weeks. According to Foucault, the sexological categorisation of sexuality that took place in the late nineteenth century, when non-reproductive sexual practices were labelled as perversions, was converted by homosexuals to a more positive purpose when the sexual deviants used sexology to argue for tolerance. This development has been called a "reverse discourse". Those who were the objects of the sexological categorising were able to use those very categories which gave them a sense of identity to form political movements and fight back: "homosexuality began to speak in its own behalf, to demand that its legitimacy or 'naturality' be acknowledged, often in the same vocabulary, using the same categories by which it was medically disqualified" (Foucault, 1978, p. 101). Social and economic changes enabled the geographical concentration of homosexuals in large numbers in particular cities and areas so "politicised sexual identities" could develop (Weeks, 1985, p. 193). The effect is that "Many openly homosexual men today see themselves as belonging to a 'sexual minority', a term that has been taken up and used more recently by other sexual groupings, such as paedophiles and sado-masochists." The idea of sexual minorities has been a powerful one because: "'Minorities' can lay claim to 'rights'. There is a hallowed tradition in liberal democracies of recognising ... the claims of minorities" (*ibid.*, p. 195).

The "sexual minorities" that Weeks cites are a strange collection. They include practitioners of paedophilia, which feminists have analysed as sexual abuse of children, and sadomasochism, which anti-pornography feminists identify as the promotion of a sexuality of cruelty with dire consequences for women and prostitutes. All are perceived through a queer lens as somehow equivalent to lesbians and gays (Jeffreys, 1990, 1993).

> Erotic groupings which can never expect to achieve obvious social weight or whose tastes apply only to a minority of a minority—sado-masochists, paedophiles, transvestites, prostitutes come to mind—have to rely in large part on association with related sexual groupings. Only in a city like San Francisco has it been possible for a sizeable subculture of sado-masochists to emerge. [Weeks, 1985, pp. 192–3]

Less popular sexual minorities would require the support of lesbians and gay men, and this, of course, is achieved through queer politics which incorporates these practitioners into a broad platform of the sexually transgressive (Jeffreys, 1994).

These minorities, who would adhere into "movements of affirmation" and take to the streets in the assertion of a "radical sexual politics", seem always to include prostitutes in Weeks's formulation. Prostituted women and men are defined as a group of people striving for the freedom to practise their sexual tastes. For women prostitutes this inclusion is inappropriate.

> Transvestites, transsexuals, pedophiles, sado-masochists, fetishists, bisexuals, prostitutes and others—each group marked by specific sexual tastes, or aptitudes, subdivided and demarcated into specific styles, morals and communities, each with specific histories of self-expression—have all appeared on the world's stage to claim their space and "rights". [Weeks, 1985, p. 186]

Prostitution does not fit here. It is not a sexual practice for the women involved, and it was not "discovered" and categorised as a perversion by sexologists in the same way. Prostitution, unlike the other practices, is performed for money and has nothing to do with the "sexual tastes" of the practitioners. It is unlikely to have a great deal to do with "aptitudes" either in most manifestations. A woman who has to let a man put his hand into her vagina in a massage parlour is not necessarily showing a special aptitude.

It might be argued that it is the very different experience that gay men have of prostitution that causes this inappropriate inclusion of prostitution in a list of sexual minorities. Nevertheless there are influential lesbian theorists thinking along the same lines. These ideas have been taken up by the American lesbian theorists of sadomasochism, Gayle Rubin (1982) and Pat Califia (1981, 1982, 1994). They too seek to give a revolutionary status to prostitution. Rubin and Califia were founding members of the San Francisco lesbian sado-masochist group Samois in 1980. Rubin (1993) has gone on to devote her intellectual energies to documenting the gay male leather community in the United States, as well as developing a theory of sexuality which justifies sadomasochism as revolutionary. Califia has produced a volume of sex education and several volumes of sadomasochist pornography (1988, 1989).

The connections between the emerging cult of sado-masochism and prostitution were strong from the beginning. Dominatrixes from the malestream sex industry have been important members of SM groups. Others, like Califia (1994), made a point of entering prostitution as part of their SM practice as a top or sadist, most often practising on straight or gay men. Sadomasochism is interesting for other reasons in relation to prostitution. It is a sexual practice which has strong links to the sex industry, as shown when the prosti-tutes' rights activist Annie Sprinkle made her debut in the Hellfire club in New York. Clubs like the Hellfire, of which there are now versions in Australia too, can be seen as one aspect of the sex industry in which an audience pays to watch sadomasochistic acts carried out on both paid and voluntary participants. Rubin and Califia make prostitution central to their ideas about sexuality, and they have been very influential in the creation of a libertarian politics of sex which sees pros-tituted women as an erotic minority seeking liberation.

Gayle Rubin's article "Thinking Sex" has had great influ-ence on both feminist and gay theorising of sexuality (1984). Its popularity is reflected in its republication as the keynote chapter in the first reader in lesbian and gay studies in 1993 (Rubin, 1993). Rubin sets out to create an "accurate, humane, and genuinely liberatory body of thought about sex-uality", a "radical" theory of sex which "must identify, describe, explain, and denounce erotic injustice and sexual oppression" (ibid., p. 9). She calls for the liberation of non-reproductive practices. She explains that the sexual value system separates sexual practices into what is "good", "normal", "natural" and "blessed", and what is "bad", "abnormal", "unnatural", and "damned". Prostitution—or, as she defines it, "commercial sex"—is included in "bad" sex along with homosexual, unmarried, promiscuous or non-procreative sex. Unlike Weeks, Rubin does comment that prostitution differs from other "sexual minorities" in being

"an occupation" while "sexual deviation is an erotic preference" (*ibid.*, p. 18). But, she says, "they share some common
features of social organization".

Her political aim is a "democratic" morality which would
"judge sexual acts by the way partners treat one another, the
level of mutual consideration, the presence or absence of coercion, and the quantity and quality of the pleasures they provide" (*ibid.*, p. 15). She considers that "whether sex acts are
gay or straight, coupled or in groups, naked or in underwear,
commercial or free, with or without video" should not be
"ethical concerns". Her idea of a "democracy" which can be
created out of sexual exploitation is in direct opposition to
the feminist position that prostitution arises precisely from a
lack of "democracy" between women and men.

Rubin identifies radical feminist politics opposed to
pornography and sexual violence politics as "less a sexology
than a demonology". This is a perspective, she says, that
"implies that sexism originates within the commercial sex
industry and subsequently infects the rest of society" (*ibid.*,
p. 28). This is not an accurate description of these politics,
since feminist theorists do not maintain that the oppression of
women originates in commercial sex, but rather the opposite.
For Rubin, this feminist position is "nonsensical". She says
that the sex industry is affected by sexism but plays no part in
causing or maintaining it. In her view, "We need to analyze
and oppose the manifestations of gender inequality specific to
the sex industry", but this does not mean "attempting to wipe
out commercial sex" (*ibid.*, p. 28). Commercial sex is innocent then, simply tainted by sexism.

Rubin states that "sexual liberation has been and continues
to be a feminist goal" (*ibid.*, p. 29). She considers it to be hostile to the "sexual minorities" to ask such questions as whose
liberation the practitioners, such as paedophiles, represent or
where the sexual practices of these minorities came from. It
was a hostile question to ask where homosexuality came
from, she says, as this implied less legitimacy for homosexuality than for heterosexuality for which the same question was

never asked. Since prostitution is included in all her lists of sexual deviants, erotic minorities, sexual subjects etc., it must be assumed that asking questions about the etiology of prostitution which might illuminate why it is so gender-specific would be seen as equally hostile. Though Rubin is committed to social constructionism, as she explains in this piece, her commitment is strangely limited. She, like Foucault, is interested in how certain practices become stigmatised at particular times in history and how sexual actors then create "movements of affirmation", but the practices themselves—whether sadomasochism or prostitution—are treated as transhistorical and beyond question. They simply *are* what sex is.

Rubin argues that gender and sexuality must be separated analytically. She suggests that there are two systems of oppression: that of gender, which oppresses women, and that of sexuality, which oppresses "sexual minorities". Feminists are characterised as exceeding their brief in seeking to analyse sexuality; they should deal only with gender. It is precisely this separation which allows prostitution as well as paedophilia and sadomasochism to be excised from feminist considerations of material power differences, for instance, and considered as liberatory sexual practices. The separation works well for those gay theorists who are uncomfortable with feminist analyses of sexuality. It allows their sexual practice to escape critical scrutiny. Certainly male gay theorists have been enthusiastic about the Rubin formula. Andrew Ross, for instance, makes a similar argument.

> Gender-based reforms, such as those proposed by anti-porn groups, are likely to be antagonistic to the interests of sexual minorities, and have, in fact, already added to the suppression of minority rights only tentatively extended under the protection of the privacy of sexual conduct. A politics of sexuality that is relatively autonomous from categories of gender may be needed to achieve and guarantee the full sexual rights of sexual minorities. [quoted in Stychin, 1995, p. 73]

The implications of this separation, which forbids feminists to theorise sexuality and effectively gives it into the hands of male gay theorists, are troubling (Jeffreys, 1994).

Rubin admits that gender might be relevant to an analysis of the sexual system, but only so far as recognising that women have been discriminated against in this system, particularly by being denied participation as clients and proprietors in the sex industry.

> Part of the modern ideology of sex is that lust is the province of men, purity that of women. It is no accident that pornography and the perversions have been considered part of the male domain. In the sex industry, women have been excluded from most production and consumption, and allowed to participate primarily as workers. [Rubin, 1993, p. 33]

The solution, then, is to facilitate women's participation in what Rubin seems to assume to be natural and essential sexuality. Women too must become users of prostitutes of both sexes in equal numbers to men. In this classic form of sexual liberalism, women must have access to male sexual privileges.

Pat Califia's approach to sexuality is similar, but less carefully worded and less intellectual. Prostitutes were enlisted by Califia to support her own sexual preference for sadomasochism in her first public position paper on the issue in 1979. Prostitution, here, is just another "sexual preference". "Drag queens, leathermen, rubber freaks, boy-lovers, girl-lovers, dyke sadomasochists, prostitutes, transsexuals ... our difference is not created solely by oppression or biology. It is a preference, a sexual preference" (Califia, 1994, p. 157). Her attitude to prostitution is one which prostituted women might find hard to understand. Califia has eroticised the idea and the practice of prostitution. For her, prostitution must continue because of the role it plays in the pleasures of sexual outlawry, regardless of what it means for women who have no choice but to be in the institution, and what it means for women in general. This is expressed in her feelings when her partner is fucking her with a dildo: "I become pornographic, a slut, a whore—an identity that has been denied me with as much ferocity as the pleasures of masculinity" (*ibid.*, p. 177). Most women in prostitution, of course, have not been "denied" the identity of prostitute, but found it imposed upon them and seek to escape its grip. Historically, prostitution has not been a denied identity for poor women, but rather the opposite. But for sadomasochists who do "choose" the excitements of dominance and submission, prostitution is simply assumed to be exciting for those who are used because it is so clearly about inequality of power. The arrogance of the libertarians seems to make it difficult for them to grasp the fact that prostituted women do not "choose" and are not excited.

Califia does choose to work as an SM prostitute by placing De Sade advertisments in a local paper. She believes that prostitution will always exist. "I doubt very much that a just society would (or could) eliminate paying for pleasure" (*ibid.*, pp. 222, 242). Such an approach naturalises male sexuality and sees the present masculine practice of objectification as essential for all human beings instead of historically contingent. Women would use prostitutes if "women had the same buying power that men do". But presently they do not, and she provides a list of motives for men's use of women in prostitution which give some insight into male privilege. "Some of my slaves", she says, "have had wives who were ill" (*ibid.*, pp. 243, 222). The implication is that men have a right to sexual servicing and can go elsewhere if this part of the housework is not being done properly.

Califia obviously thinks that the sex in prostitution is what sex is because she thinks that prostituted women can teach all there is to know about "sex".

A talented sex worker could introduce brand new players to all of their sexual options, show them appropriate ways to protect themselves from conception or disease, and teach them the skills they need to please more experienced partners. [*ibid.*, p. 245]

In fact it is the sexuality of male dominance and female subordination that is taught in prostitution. It is interesting that Califia is so keen to tout prostitution's educative role. In relation to pornography as well as other areas of the sex industry, libertarian theorists have determinedly repudiated any suggestion that negative education could result, but prostitution is seen as having a positive teaching role (Jeffreys, 1990).

Interestingly, Califia identifies the effects of feminism as a reason for men's greater need of prostitution. Feminism, she considers, has created problems for men. Men have been forced to "pay child support and alimony" while being deprived "of their homes and the custody of their children" (Califia, 1993, p. 244).

> In a world of prenuptial agreements and lawsuits for breach of promise and sexual harassment, the "good" woman who was once valorised by men ... is increasingly perceived as a leech and a liability. More men may come to believe that "nice girls" are revolted by sex and will take all their money, while "fallen women" like cock, like sex, and want only a hundred dollars or so. [*ibid.*]

It is easy to see from such views whose side Califia is on. She has sympathy with heterosexual men who are being deprived of their privileges and comforts as women demand the financial recognition of their labour and their right to sexual self-determination. Like Rubin, Califia's political identification seems to rest with men rather than women. Where women's interests threaten the privileges men have derived from their position of power, men's interests are given priority.

Califia considers that sex work could even find its "sprituality" restored (*ibid.*, p. 246). Once the stigma attached to prostitution was removed, then:

> Everybody might expect to spend a portion of her or his life as a sex worker before getting married ... Perhaps there would be collective brothels where people could perform

community service to work off parking tickets or student loans. [*ibid.*, p. 247]

Califia's notion that prostitution will always exist is matched by her notion that "gender" is necessary to sexual excitement and will survive women's freedom. She does not accept that "gender", like prostitution, is constructed specifically from women's subordination. "In a world where men and women were equal, people might choose to exaggerate (rather than abandon) their differences, if only to preserve erotic tension between the sexes" (*ibid.*, p. 152). For Califia the "difference" between the sexes provides simply a benign form of sex toy rather than a form of social organisation of inequality that keeps male supremacy in operation.

Differences between male and female prostitution

Those like Weeks, Rubin and Califia who see prostituted women and men as a sexual minority make no distinction between the experience of women and men in prostitution. If the "sexual minority" is taken apart, widely different experiences can be discovered between men, women and male-to-constructed-female transsexuals. Thus lumping them all into one category can be seen as a profoundly problematic homogenising of women's experience into that of men. Interestingly, some male theorists of prostitution are saying that feminist analysis is faulty for failing to consider the differences between male and female prostitution. Garrett Prestage (Gary Bennett) in a 1994 Australian collection says that feminist debate has always ignored male prostitution and "how it might impact on a feminist analysis of prostitution" (1994, p. 174). He implies that the feminist attitude to prostitution is too negative and could be improved by a consideration of how pleasurable and positive prostitution is for gay men.

Gay male theorising and practice has been so influential in constructing contemporary theorising of prostitution that a consideration of the differences and the connections that are being made is necessary. Lesbian and gay sexual libertarian theorising of prostitution has excluded the majority of those involved in the industry, women who do not see themselves as a sexual minority, as "queer", or even as involved in anything to do with sex. As Prestage and Perkins point out when considering the problem of terminology in addressing prostitution:

> The difficulty in trying to include prostitutes within a broader category called "queer" is precisely that the term simply has no resonance with them. The issues of concern to gay men, lesbians, bisexuals and transsexuals do not necessarily relate to those of prostitutes; nor do prostitutes, especially heterosexually identified female prostitutes, necessarily see themselves as having similar interests to these other groups. [Prestage and Perkins, 1994, p. 17]

The latter "generally view themselves as very ordinary and normal people" for whom their apparently deviant behaviour is "not viewed as relevant to their sense of who they are". "A term such as 'queer' is actually offensive to such people". Prestage and Perkins sensibly go on to point out that "To attempt to create an 'umbrella identity' for all these groups", especially when many lesbians, gays and transsexuals do not accept the term, is "simply not possible" (*ibid.*).

Male and female prostitution have one thing clearly in common: the customers are overwhelmingly male. Prostitution exists to serve the sexual interests of men almost exclusively (Perkins and Bennett, 1985; Gagnon and Simon, 1974). The numbers of women using men in prostitution seem too tiny to be of note, and women using women are mostly doing so as part of a couple where the man wants a threesome, and is still serving his own sexual interests. It is this very commonality which suggests the differences that will follow. If it is the power differences between men and women that have created men's prostitution of women, then we might expect those power differences to be reflected in both men's and women's experience of being used by men in prostitution.

One signal difference relates to the sexual pleasure that prostituted women and men gain from their work. Prostituted women overwhelmingly report that their work does not provide sexual pleasure (McLeod, 1982; Millett, 1975; Hoigard and Finstad, 1992). For male prostitutes, it appears to be different (Gagnon and Simon, 1974). For female prostitutes, orgasm is rare and usually regarded as distressing, since it threatens the careful dissociation the prostituted woman has created to protect her sense of self; but for prostituted men and boys, it is usual. In fact, it is the client of the male prostitute who is likely to forgo orgasm rather than the other way around. Men are more likely to mention sexual pleasure as their motivation.

Garrett Prestage explains, as a result of his work in Sydney, that the motives for entering prostitution and the meaning of the experience are quite different for men than they are for women. Women enter for economic reasons and see it as a "job". Most men engage in prostitution only casually and gain a very small part of their income from it. He puts the proportion of women entering prostitution at 0.03–0.16 per cent, whereas 20–25 per cent of gay men have been used in prostitution and a similar proportion of gay men have used the services of prostitutes (Prestage, 1994). In another survey of young gay males in Sydney, one-third were found to have worked in prostitution at some time or another (Perkins and Bennett, 1985, p. 22). Perkins and Bennett suggest that an element of prostitution is a normal part of a beat or cruising ground; "any reasonably attractive gay man can expect to be offered money ... for sex at any time at any beat" (*ibid.*, p. 36). The lesser role played by economic necessity is also illustrated by the class backgrounds of male prostitutes. Perkins and Bennett point out, "A very noticeable feature of the professional gay male hustlers interviewed were [sic] their relatively non-working-class backgrounds." They were predominantly from lower-middle-class backgrounds. The full-time street hustlers were a "mixed grouping of relatively middle-class young men ... and young working-class men" (*ibid.*, p. 27).

There is a difference too, in the risk attached to prostitution for men and women. The women are often abused by johns, whereas male prostitutes report few assaults by johns and the johns themselves are wary and have much to lose. Male prostitutes and their johns have something in common. Both johns and the men they use face the stigma of homosexuality. Women have little in common with their johns, and the johns do not face stigma. Perkins and Bennett suggest that in homosexual prostitution, "client and prostitute suffer together and have an affinity for each other's position"; whereas in heterosexual prostitution, "the contact only intensifies the hostility and distance between women and men" (*ibid.*, p. 14). In male prostitution, Prestage suggests, the "issue of exploitation" tends to be much less relevant.

Jeffrey Weeks, in his interesting work on homosexual prostitution in England in the ninteenth and early twentieth centuries, demonstrates that these differences have existed historically in Western culture. He explains that there was no "legitimizing ideology for homosexual prostitution similar to that which condones heterosexual prostitution". Though the female prostitute was condemned, her john was not. Male prostitution carried a double stigma. Weeks suggests that one difference between male and female prostitution in this earlier period was the significant lack of a developing culture and community between the men in homosexual prostitution. Women prostitutes did create such a community to help each other to survive. No separate community developed amongst prostituted men, but there was a "close, indeed symbiotic, relationship between forms of prostitution and the homosexual subcultures" (Weeks, 1991, p. 197). Homosexual prostitution was less public, since all male homosexual activities were at this time illegal and there was an increased risk of violence and blackmail.

Interestingly, Weeks explains the existence of male homosexual prostitution as resulting from the oppression of male homosexuals, and the restricted opportunities for homosexual expression. Such an explanation suggests that prostitution is not inevitable, but indeed historically contingent, and will cease to exist when homosexuality ceases to be oppressed. This explanation might help us to understand why prostitution has been so significant in gay male culture and remains so today, with a resulting lack of outcry amongst political gay men about the prominent role of the sex industry in gay culture. But it cannot be a sufficient explanation, since heterosexuality is not suppressed and does not have to be hidden but heterosexual prostitution thrives. Also lesbians have had to be hidden too, but prostitution was never historically an important part of lesbian culture in the same way. Where it was part of lesbian culture, this was because prostituted women who were used by men were often lesbians or in lesbian company because of a shared outlawry. This is a rather different connection.

By the 1870s, Weeks says, any sort of homosexual transaction was described as "trade", a word whose continuing currency suggests the central role of the sex industry in gay male culture. The furtiveness and the disparities in wealth and position created by the determination of upper-class men to have sex only with their social inferiors meant that the cash nexus dominated gay sexual culture. "Middle class men generally had nonsexual relations with friends, sex with casual pickups" (ibid., p. 203). Perkins and Bennett explain that, because "there is no sharp distinction between sex within and outside prostitution", the most important question to ask of a male prostitute is how he became part of the deviant subculture of homosexuality rather than prostitution; "since they are already stigmatised as homosexuals, a further stigma as prostitute has little meaning" (1985, p. 219).

The difference between male and female prostitution is exemplified in the description offered by Perkins and Bennett of "street hustlers" in Sydney.

These are mostly gay men who stand along the kerb and solicit passing pedestrians and motorists in much the same way as women streetwalkers. This parallel with female street soliciting ends when it is realised that hustlers are sometimes working alongside "charities", that is, young men looking for sexual contact without payment. [*ibid.*, p. 9]

The difference is thrown here into stark relief. Women prostitutes do not solicit on streets filled with women who are just looking for a bit of action with men. The role of cruising is insignificant in women's sexual practice, whether heterosexual or lesbian (Bell and Weinberg, 1978). Moreover, men who are cruising may on occasion accept money to perform the very same acts that they are seeking to perform on a "charitable" basis; this is also rather different from the situation of women. Male gay sexual practice, which values quick, impersonal contacts in public places, does not differ greatly in procedure from what will take place for money. The act of being prostituted does not demean the man taking part. He may even, it seems, gain in status. The offer of money may confirm his masculinity and sexual desirability even more than free sex could. A male sex worker explains his motivation:

there was a certain "glamour" in being a male prostitute. It seemed to me that I could not express my sexuality in a better way: the thought of having men gloat over my body and then pay to be next to it was definitely appealing. [Goodley, 1994, p. 126]

This man reports feeling entirely integrated, as a prostitute, into the local gay scene. "I have never really felt stigmatised by other gay people as a result of my working ... it's no big deal to be known as a male prostitute ... This makes being a sex worker a viable career in the gay scene" (*ibid.*, p. 131). This supports Weeks's contention that in the late nineteenth century male prostitutes were part of the homosexual subculture. But other male prostitutes in the study by Perkins and Bennett suggested that the sexual part of full-time prostitution was a lot less glamorous. One speaks of the damaging effects of prostitution.

In a way it can make you really insensitive. It can make sex a mechanical business. I mean, I had a lover at one stage and there were times when I'd be having sex with him and I'd flash on to an old man that I'd had the night before and then I'd just have to stop, you know. It can destroy your sex life. [Perkins and Bennett, 1985, p. 152]

Another said that the work caused a loss of interest in sex and a greater need for affection: "you have so much sex and so you're not really interested. What you need is affection" (*ibid.*, p. 166).

Though writers like Perkins and Prestage emphasise the difference between male and female prostitution and assert a more positive experience for gay men, there seems to be a variety of male prostitution which clearly shares characteristics with the experience of women. This is the prostitution of young men who have experienced sexual abuse and/or are homeless and living on the streets. Their situation seems to share much of the powerlessness and vulnerability to abuse of women involved in street prostitution. A London study of male street prostitution found that the young homeless men who are prostituted not only come from harsh social and economic circumstance and backgrounds of physical, sometimes sexual, abuse and institutions, but also are likely to lead a life after prostitution, of drifting, of homelessess or institutions, and harsh economic need (West, 1992). As Cudmore Snell notes in his study of *Young Men in the Street* in the United States, there is little research on young male prostitutes (1995, p. 4). Snell found that the young men had experienced sexual victimisation, including sex for money at very young ages.

The mean age of the first sexual encounter for money or favors was 15 years, with 5 years as the youngest age and 32 years as the oldest age of the first encounter. One respondent reported that at age 5 he received a special favor for sex and regarded this as his first prostitution experience. Sixty-one per cent of the respondents were between the ages of 5 and 15 at the time of their first prostitution experience ... [*ibid.*, p. 41]

Interestingly, Snell noted that there was a difference in the rate at which black and white young men swallowed the semen of their sexual partners: 69 per cent of white males would never do so, compared with 30 per cent of black; and 31 per cent would do so occasionally compared with 70 per cent of black males (*ibid.*, p. 65). Black males were also less likely to change their sexual practices in response to AIDS. This suggests that racially oppressed young men are more likely to be severely victimised in prostitution because of their greater vulnerability.

A book of oral histories of six prostituted young men from London presents a picture of men who are badly damaged by their prostitution experiences. Barbara Gibson worked with Streetwise Youth, which supported homeless prostituted men in London. This collection is rare in the detail it provides about the lives and experiences of such young men. In selecting the interviewees, she says she chose those who showed a wide range of "typical experiences" of the "streetwise client" (Gibson, 1996, p. ix). The young men report considerable abuse before entry to prostitution. They became vulnerable to sexual exploitation through having to leave home and through their desperate search for affection. Madser (now dead of HIV/AIDS) and Jason/Zoe had been first sexually abused at ten years old. Madser had also been physically abused in his family. Paul was first used for sex at thirteen and paid by a man he met in the public toilets. He says: "When I met this man, I was looking at him as a father, which I wanted more than anything. I thought that sex was love and that he was showing me love (*ibid.*, p. 68). Simon/Simone was sexually abused in the form of anal penetration from the age of five by his babysitter's son, who was twenty. The abuser's friend raped him too. Simon's attitude to the abuser is ambivalent, because the abuser was the only one who gave him affection. "He was a comfort throughout them years, from the torment of my foster parents. That sexual abuse was quite a comfort because he was also my friend" (*ibid.*, p. 96). Simon and his brother, also abused, tried to commit suicide.

Simon is a self-mutilator, and was abused at school for being "girly". Adam was sexually abused by a member of his stepfather's family in childhood, and was used in prostitution from seventeen (*ibid.*, p. 139). Only one respondent did not report sexual abuse.

The techniques the young male prostitutes reported using to survive are similar to those used by women in prostitution. Madser used alcohol and dissociation. He said, "I didn't mind having to do the sex, I just blanked it out in me head. That's what I've been doing all me life anyway" (*ibid.*, p. 20). These young men did not report sexual pleasure in prostitution. Several said they were "frigid" both in prostitution and out of it. Jason/Zoe explains:

> I didn't like going with punters [johns] ... I was very frigid. I still am. I clam up. I can't relax. I hated anyone going down on me. When it was with punters I could switch off: but when it wasn't, I was really frigid. [*ibid.*, p. 38]

Another pre-operative transsexual respondent, Simon/Simone, had a similar lack of sexual response.

> I'm not able to come. I get the feeling of it, but nothing will come out. It's not frustration, it doesn't matter, the hormones switch off whatever it is in there anyway ... It's not important as I don't like sex anyhow, and I'm not really interested in downstairs. [*ibid.*, p. 90]

Adam says he was "always sexually frigid" (*ibid.*, p. 152). He drank to survive the abuse, and when he was drunk lost his inhibitions: "It was the only way I could have sex."

Simon's johns were interested in a "chick with a dick" (*ibid.*, p. 88). It would have been a financial disaster to have surgery performed on "downstairs". He is ambivalent about the experience of prostitution, seeing it as the only way in which he can exercise any "power" but still finding it disgusting.

You get these dirty bastards who want to come around and see a girl with a willy and shove it in their mouth and give you ninety quid. I cope with it, because I'm getting paid, the power is one of the biggest thrills. It's powerful: they come here into my room to pay me. I have the power in that room. I have what I want, I make them do what I want. ... Oh yeah, you feel dirty, you don't want them touching you. But you just think money. It's an easy way to make money. It's the buzz. That's the only reason I'm here. I wouldn't be here otherwise. I can earn more money in a day than most do in a week. [*ibid.*]

The johns were "nasty-looking". Afterwards he would want to scrub himself out and he didn't like the after-effects that reminded him of childhood abuse: "... it's all the wet on my bum, I don't like that feeling. I'm left to feel whatever ... I don't like the feeling, just like the feelings I got as a kid from my abuse" (*ibid.*, p. 89).

Jason/Zoe suffered considerable emotional damage from the abuse of prostitution.

After I'd worked the Dilly [Picadilly] for about six months, I started getting really fucked up in the head. I never went out with anyone, apart from for money. I started feeling dirty and used. I kept thinking, why is it that people are doing this to me? [*ibid.*, p. 42]

He decided to transsex and started taking hormones by private prescription at seventeen and had surgery at eighteen. Another of the respondents who decided to transsex linked the decision to his childhood experiences of sexual abuse and not wanting to stay in the body of a man. The connections between prostitution and the self-mutilation of transsexualism need to be studied. The two young men who transsex here learnt about transsexualism through friends, social workers, the media. Their transsexualism is socially constructed out of abuse and poor self-image resulting from the stigma attached to their homosexuality. It is possible that the abuse of prostitution is an additional contributory factor. Such abuse may damage the victim's perception of himself as properly a "man", since a "man" has power and status.

Paul was in prostitution at the age of fourteen. At fifteen he was beaten by a former MP and his boyfriend, all for 40 pounds. Of the MP, he says: "He got me pretty stoned before he caned me. He was disgusting, it was painful. He'd got loads of toys for hitting people with ..." (*ibid.*, p. 72). Paul worked at the age of fifteen and sixteen in a brothel in Amsterdam. At that stage, he had "warts on my penis, up my bum, gonorrhoea and crabs". In the brothels some of the boys were effectively slaves, kept without their passports and trafficked from one brothel to another. The johns were abusive. In a German brothel, "Most punters would treat us badly; fucking would be like bang, bang, bang ... I had my seventeenth birthday there. I was so depressed" (*ibid.*, pp. 76, 80). The johns, he said, treated young boys like "pieces of meat, just to get their rocks off".

> They don't think we are worth anything. I've met quite a few who just get off on going with prostitutes, just the fact that they are paying for it. That fucked me up. Yet in the end money was more important to me than my body. [*ibid.*, p. 86]

He coped by using drugs. "When I first started doing punters, I had a lot of trouble. God, I'd feel like heaving with most of them, they were so nasty. I then started doing E's [ecstasy], and the sex with anyone was fab ..." (*ibid.*, p. 85). Drugs helped him: "Drugs helped me cope with hating myself and missing home" (*ibid.*, p. 86). Of prostitution he concludes:

> I'm dead against prostitution. I got into it because I thought sex was about love, and underneath it all I was looking for a dad ... It's done me no good mentally ... I've lost all respect for myself for doing it. I wouldn't recommend it to anyone. [*ibid.*, p. 86]

Whilst in prostitution, he was beaten up "lots of times", "forced to have sex" and "ripped off": "People had sex with me while I was asleep, I was abused loads of times", and several times he felt suicidal (*ibid.*, p. 86). He is now HIV positive and his friend is dead.

One of the black prostituted youths in Gibson's book reported the racism of the sexual abuse he suffered. Ryan got into prostitution when unemployed and homeless, having suffered bad beatings from his mother and harassment at school for his club feet. He hated it from the beginning.

> It was a nightmare for me every time someone picked me up ... I just felt so dirty the whole time.
>
> Punters want black boys to be slaves. They want to whip and beat them up, and make them wear slave collars. They want to totally degrade the boys. They think all black guys have got big cocks. [*ibid.*, p. 129]

Ryan ended up in prostitution because he had to leave the hamburger place he was working at because of the pain in his feet. He had to wait six months for the dole since he was seen as voluntarily leaving work, and had no alternative but prostitution.

Despite suffering experiences that most observers would consider to be clearly and relentlessly abusive, it is possible for prostituted women and men to romanticise their abuse. I have discussed elsewhere how the sort of raunchy sexuality expected in gay male culture makes it difficult for gay men in particular to give serious attention to the issues of sexual abuse and rape (Jeffreys, 1990).

Transsexual prostitution

Male-to-constructed-female transsexuals are heavily over-represented in prostitution, compared with their total numbers in any population. Perkins and Bennett estimate that "as many as half of all transsexuals may have moved in and out of prostitution at some stage of their lives" (1985, p. 12). This high incidence is, they suggest, the result both of prejudice that makes them "virtually unemployable" and the high cost of medical expenses for the transsexual process. Two sexologists offer a different explanation for the involvement of transsexuals in prostitution. Transsexuals see prostitution as attractive because it affirms their "femininity" if johns are prepared to see them as women. "Prostitution sometimes becomes a tempting substitute for marriage. There is no greater confirmation of femininity than that of having normal heterosexual men again and again accept her as a woman and even pay for her sex services" (Block and Tessler 1971, quoted in Raymond, 1994b, p. 92).

This notion is undermined by the fact that most of the transsexuals in prostitution, in the Sydney study by Perkins and Bennett, were pre-operative. Mostly the johns were aware of their transsexual status and deliberately chose them. Post-operative transsexuals were apparently able to charge the same prices as those whom Perkins and Bennett refer to as "natural-born women", whilst male prostitutes earned less than women. One transsexual "parlour" prostitute explained the motivations of johns.

> Transsexual prostitution, like all other forms, is necessary … but more than the others it is growing in demand. It's a variation of the male/female role because clients don't feel homosexual as they do with the boys, and they don't feel unfaithful to their wives as they do with the natural girls. [Perkins and Bennett, 1985, p. 35]

Garrett Prestage suggests several reasons for the demand from johns for transsexuals in prostitution:

> some simply like the sensibility and particular appeal of the "trannies"; some are attracted by the "kinkiness" of sex with a transsexual; some are attracted by the idea of (experimenting with) sex with another man but are reluctant to choose a partner who actually is a man; and some enjoy particular

sexual activities which require that their partner has a penis even though they prefer female partners. [Prestage, 1994, p. 177]

Prestage remarks that this demand is increasing in respect of pre-operative transsexuals who retain their penises. It would be interesting to speculate on what this means in the context of supposed greater "gay liberation" in the last decade. The use of transsexed men in prostitution is common to many societies, in which it seems to imply lack of acceptance of homosexuality and a high degree of male dominance. In societies such as those of India, Brazil and Thailand, young men are required to cross-dress or transsex to provide a class of prostitutes that men can use without endangering their masculinity or male privilege (Calkin, 1994). This phenomenon has destructive results for the young men involved. The fact that transsexuals are increasingly in demand in Australia, as in other Western countries, suggests the strength of male dominance and the necessity to shore up its foundation in masculinity, even in countries where gay culture and the gay political lobby have had some success.

Transsexuals seem likely to be more subject to abuse and violence in prostitution than men and, Prestage implies, perhaps more than "natural-born" women too. In an Australian study, 45 per cent report being assaulted and 34 per cent raped. They suffer a double stigma and in general have little in common with the johns. "In a sense these men often seem to view their transsexual partners merely as a sexual tool, a means to explore their sexuality" (Prestage, 1994, p. 179). Transsexuals in prostitution receive the violence that is visited upon women in prostitution, plus the violence directed at those suspected of being homosexual.

Gay male defence of pornography

To understand the lack of condemnation of using young men and boys in prostitution amongst gay theorists, we only need to look at the reverence displayed towards gay pornography.

The vital role attributed to pornography in constructing gay identity, politics and culture provides a stumbling block to recognition of the abuse involved in all areas of prostitution. Male theorists of pornography explain that it is crucial to the formation of gay male identity, and post-modern theorists pronounce that gay male pornography is revolutionary and will speed feminist aims as well as gay liberation. Certainly, pornography seems to be accorded a puzzlingly high status. In a non-fiction collection entitled *Taking Liberties* (1996), containing essays written by poets, novelists and short story writers on "Politics, Culture and Sex", Christopher Hogan treats pornography with great respect. He writes reviews of gay pornography videos with the kind of seriousness which others might accord to arthouse movies. Not only does pornography help "establish what gay male culture defines as erotic", but it also has become "the safest forum in which gay men can examine their culture ... Within the gay community, men who avoid overt political or cultural discussions are engaged in these issues through pornography (Hogan, 1996, pp. 239, 244).

Charles Isherwood, in his biography of a dead gay male pornography star, Joey Stefano, concurs on the importance of pornography. He says that gay men lack role models. Thus porn stars are "the only gay movie stars" and get attention and respect in gay culture (Isherwood, 1996, p. 84). In a world where gay men have no positive images, they have to find them in pornography, which is the only place where gay male sexuality is represented. He says that whereas heterosexuals have "a large store of romantic and/or sexual imagery to draw upon in forging relationships", gay men and women have not:

So gay men have to find visual representations of men relating sexually to each other the only place it is to be found: in porn. For many a gay man, stumbling upon a gay porn magazine may be the first concrete indication that there are others like him out there. [*ibid.*, p. 85]

Having mentioned "gay women", he quickly drops them from his argument. Lesbians do not fit well into this idea because pornography is relatively recent and still insignificant in lesbian culture. The question of how lesbians are gaining their identities if pornography is so crucial is not addressed. If it is true that gay male identity resides in pornography, in the depiction of objectifying and often sadomasochistic anonymous sexual acts, then this is a tragedy worthy of serious concern. This is an impoverished vision of identity indeed, and one unlikely to facilitate a strong and positive gay community and politics.

Isherwood quotes two other male theorists who proclaim an extraordinary status for pornography. John Burger writes that "Pornography makes gay men visible", and Richard Dyer says that it constitutes "an attempt by gay men to rewrite themselves into American history". Dyer argues that pornography "has made life bearable for millions of gay men" (*ibid.*, p. 86). In the view of gay legal theorist Carl Stychin, gay pornography is even more important. It is the vehicle of gay and women's liberation.

Stychin proposes that the law should specially protect gay pornography from censorship because of the important political role it performs for the sexual minority of male homosexuality. "In legal terms, gay pornography becomes protected speech, but based upon its role in securing the political rights of a subject forged from a marginalised political experience." Gay pornography is a "point of resistance in an oppositional discourse to male dominance" because it "makes visible what has been made invisible by male heterosexual culture" (Stychin, 1995, pp. 62, 63). Presumably, then, women should be grateful for the way in which gay male pornography will make them free. Yes, Stychin says, gay pornography contains the themes of dominance and submission of heterosexual pornography, but it does not really mean the same because "the marginalisation of gay men may mean that the reception of the pornography signifier by the viewer can change the very meaning of the sign *because* of its relocation". He uses post-modern theory to prove that pornography will have different meanings to the viewers depending on the context, so just because it looks male supremacist doesn't mean that the viewers will see it that way (*ibid.*, pp. 63, 65).

Quoting the lesbian queer theorist Judith Butler, Stychin asserts the revolutionary potential of pornography. The use of heterosexual male values in a gay setting will show that these values are not natural but socially constructed, and thus "undermine heterosexual hierarchical gender construction ... Consequently, not only can gay representation resignify the meaning of the symbols of dominant culture, it also reveals, through a parody of gender, the contingency of the relationship between signifiers and signified" (*ibid.*, p. 67).

The gay psychoanalytic theorist Leo Bersani argues that gay pornography is revolutionary because it empowers the bottoms. Gay pornography usually features men who are seen as straight taking the active role, penetrating men who are gay and do not become famous. The latter are called bottoms. Whereas heterosexual pornography may empower men by always having men in a top position, gay pornography, says Bersani, has powerful bottoms and so subverts hierarchy. A "revaluation of the powerlessness essentially involved in sexuality" takes place.

> This redemption of the value of the loss of the coherent self in sex thus becomes a profoundly anti-phallocratic manoeuvre. Gay male porn and sexuality are subversive to the dominant order because they represent a decision to shatter the boundaries of the self in an act of eroticism. The alleged focus of gay male sex on sadomasochism underscores that a male sexual identity can centre upon the demeaning and debasing of the self, which may in turn undermine the existing definitions of maleness ... [*ibid.*, p. 70]

Reading such post-modern exuberance, it is easy to see why the civil rights perspective has a problem with the feminist analysis of pornography. The latter is seen as depending on outdated notions of the importance of respect for the "boundaries of individual sexual subjecthood", instead of "how those boundaries might be transcended to give meaning and to give pleasure" (*ibid.*, p. 71).

Apparently it will help women and men if gay men transcend subjecthood and transgress boundaries through practices like sadomasochism. Losing respect for subjecthood might be a tall order for women who are still pursuing the right to have any subjecthood at all in a world in which women are reduced to objects. But gay men like Bersani can show women how to transgress the boundaries of this illusory goal of subjecthood.

Fortunately, the marketplace will help liberate gays. Capitalism supports sexual liberation.

> The amorality of the marketplace has proven a useful tool for the liberatory imagination of gays. In the face of widespread regulation and oppression in the name of morality, capitalism has provided the most consistent doctrine in support of sexual liberation. [Andrew Ross, quoted in *ibid.*, p. 73]

Stychin thinks the marketplace of pornography should not be totally deregulated, but the regulation should be "sensitive to sexual difference" (*ibid.*, p. 74). This means "a focus on employment standards" and "greater participation of sexual minorities in the production and control of the porn industry". Then the market can be "strategically useful, creating greater possibilities for the subversion of dominant culture".

Stychin wishes to pursue special legal protection for gay pornography because it is threatened by the ideas and practice of feminists who do not realise that "sexuality at the margins of the dominant discourse is qualitatively different", so that gay pornography cannot be criticised in the same way as heterosexual pornography. Anti-pornography feminists, he says, have failed to recognise "the usefulness of the subversive acts of gay men operating at the fringes of the dominant sexual discourse". Gay pornography must be insulated from feminist threat, because "Pornography may be a means of achieving both resistance to the dominant culture and, potentially, gay liberation" (*ibid.*, p. 75).

There is an obvious omission in Stychin's argument, and in that of other pro-prostitution gay intellectuals. They do not consider the effect of being used in the production of the "revolutionary" materials of pornography, on prostituted young men who may be having a far from revolutionary experience. The bottoms are not really powerful. There is little research on the experience of young men used in the making of pornography, but there is an interesting biography of one porn star, Joey Stefano, which suggests some difficulties with Stychin's free-market liberalism. Stefano is the pornography name of a young man who was sexually abused and left home and school at fifteen. The home was middle class, but otherwise his career follows much the same trajectory as those of other abused and homeless boys. He went into prostitution to support himself. When he went into pornography, he was unusual in becoming a star as a bottom. According to his biographer, Stefano was "very proud of being a bottom" (Isherwood, 1996, p. 62).

As a bottom he experienced considerable abuse in the pornography which caused damage to his self-esteem, and he also became HIV positive. He ended up taking a drug overdose at twenty-six after a previous suicide attempt. He was held in contempt "by the very people who were paying for his services" in prostitution and despite his pornography stardom (*ibid.*, p. 97). He was unable to leave the industry because he was uneducated and untrained. He was constantly pressured to have things done to him on film which were dangerous to his health and sense of personhood. One of these things was unprotected sex, but other kinds of physical abuse were inflicted. "I try so hard, and I do too much sometimes! I've done things onstage that I never do myself. I've been fisted, taken two dildos up my ass, and I would never do that in my personal life" (*ibid.*, p. 103). His appeal declined and he found it hard to make money. Tops are apparently more marketable, since they can sell rubber "approximations of their anatomical assets". As Isherwood puts it: "Stefano, pegged as a bottom, couldn't supplement his income with such sidelines and had to make more movies" (ibid., p. 106). The porn industry was viciously exploitative and did not pay well, giving only one-time fees of $500 to $1500. Thus Stefano was forced to continue in prostitution and stripping, as were most porn stars. Having been fisted on film, he lost status: "Afterward all I heard from every queen around was how I got fisted in New York and how I was this big slut" (ibid., p. 116). He was not a proud and confident gay, man despite the supposed "empowerment" the pornography he created inspired in the consumers. He was devastated to discover that a lover with whom he was happy was actually bisexual, i.e. not completely heterosexual. A homosexual lover was less valuable. Such internalised gay-hating is reminiscent of the decades before gay liberation, when effeminate gay men were routinely attracted to the masculinity of supposedly straight partners (see Jeffreys, 1990).

The details of Stefano's life, and probably of other bottoms, do not suggest that the values of male supremacy are inverted and subverted in pornography, at least not for the men and boys who are used, and this should surely be of some concern. Despite the determination of gay post-modern theorists, free-marketeers and sexual liberals who see their consumption of pornography as central to their lives, to defend its revolutionary nature it may be necessary to challenge the consumption of the prostituted men who are abused in making the supposedly liberating materials.

Prostitution in lesbian politics

Prostitution has played a very different role in lesbian history and culture. Women have been the objects rather than the subjects of the sex industry, and that is no less true for lesbians than for heterosexual women. Lesbians have worked as prostituted women, and prostituted women and lesbians have socialised and drunk together in bars, but lesbians have not, historically, been johns. In contemporary lesbian culture, though, two developments have influenced the ways that prostitution is being theorised by feminists. One is the romanticisation of the lesbian connection with prostitution, which is clearest in the writings of Joan Nestle. The other is the role of lesbians who work as prostituted women in the malestream sex industry in "sex education" within the lesbian community.

Joan Nestle is a lesbian theorist of role-playing. Her politics owe much to the libertarian approach of Califia and Rubin. Pat Califia, for instance, is a contributor to Nestle's 1992 anthology on role-playing, *The Persistent Desire: A Fem/Butch Reader*. Role-playing is frequently included in lists of "queer" lesbian varieties, along with sadomasochism. Like Rubin and Califia, Nestle romanticises prostitution as a form of "outlaw" sexuality which is in natural alliance with the struggle of lesbians. Her contribution to pro-prostitution ideology, "Lesbians and Prostitutes: A Historical Sisterhood", has been seen as so important to the prostitutes' rights movement that it is included in two of the three anthologies published in the 1980s on this subject, *Sex Work* and *Good Girls, Bad Girls* (Delacoste and Alexander, 1988; Bell, 1987a), Nestle says that looking at the historical connections between lesbianism and prostitution might undermine the feminist anti-prostitution position. "I hoped that by putting out the bits and pieces of this shared territory I would have some impact on the contemporary feminist position on prostitution as expressed by the feminist anti-pornography movement" (Nestle, 1988, p. 232). The association of lesbians with prostitutes is intended to support the redefinition of prostitution as a positive avocation for women.

The first connection that Nestle draws is the fact that, when she came out as a lesbian in the 1950s and 1960s, lesbians and prostitutes shared the same social spaces and had relationships with one another.

In the bars of the late fifties and early sixties where I learned my lesbian ways, whores were part of our world. We sat on barstools next to each other, we partied together and we made love together. The vice squad ... controlled our world, and we knew there was little difference between whore and queer when a raid was on. [*ibid.*, p. 232]

The connection arose out of shared oppression. Lesbians and prostitutes shared public censure and punishment. This comradeship in adversity was broken, Nestle says, when she discovered lesbian feminism, because then "whores" were seen as the enemy. For Nestle, there were other personal connections to prostitution. Her mother "turned tricks to pay her rent", and she had herself "entered the realm of public sex". In this realm she not only writes "sex stories for lesbian magazines", poses for "explicit photographs for lesbian photographers" and does "readings of sexually graphic materials dressed in sexually revealing clothes", but she has also "taken money from women for sexual acts" (*ibid.*, pp. 232–3).

Nestle uses material from men's histories of prostitution which suggests that lesbianism was rife amongst prostitutes such as the *auletrides*, or flute girls of Athens. She suggests that lesbian history might be found in the records of prostituted women, if only middle-class feminist historians were prepared to accept it. As an example she cites the descriptions of lesbian activity in Cora Pearl's *Grand Horizontal: The Erotic Memoirs of a Passionate Lady* written in 1873. Feminist historians might be chary of using such sources in lesbian history, because the facts are likely to have been packaged for men's titillation rather than constituting an independent and accurate memoir.

Nestle sees both prostituted women and lesbians as women who daringly expressed their independence. Both "were and are concerned with creating power and autonomy for themselves in seemingly powerless social interactions". She quotes a lesbian prostitute saying that it is the prostituted woman who is in control when with a john: "we set the terms of the relationship" (*ibid.*, p. 245). But the sexual autonomy of lesbians and prostitutes is not analogous. The narrow possibility that a woman working as a prostitute has to keep herself safe in a

situation of risk is rather different from the rebellion involved
in refusing to service men sexually at all and instead enjoying
making love with a woman.

Another influential development of the last fifteen years has
been the way in which workers in the malestream sex industry
who are also lesbians have diversified their practice to include
the lesbian community. Strippers and prostituted women have
moved into the creation of lesbian commercial sex activities,
pornography, prostitution and the provision of "sex education".
The most influential vehicle for this legitimation of prostitution
has been *On Our Backs*, the American lesbian pornography
magazine. Its sex industry links are very clear. The founder,
Debbie Sundahl, started out as a stripper in the malestream
sex industry and financed the first issue of *On Our Backs* by
putting on strip shows for lesbians. Strippers and prostitutes
such as Sundahl and Annie Sprinkle filled what they perceived
to be a void in lesbian culture, the "explicit" discussion of sexuality. Prior to the establishment of a lesbian sex industry, lesbianism had been a staple ingredient of the malestream sex
industry. Men's pornography had featured fantasies of lesbian
sex for centuries (Faderman, 1985). Simulated lesbian sex was
important in prostitution too. Prostituted women were
required to perform sexual activities with other women in
brothels or in threesomes at men's pleasure. In the early days
of the lesbian feminist movement, these representations of lesbianism were rejected as hostile stereotypes. Feminists were
calling for a "self-defined" sexuality for women which was
defined as the very opposite of the masculine version designed
for men's consumption in the sex industry. It was therefore a
considerable and disturbing surprise to lesbian feminists that a
lesbian sex industry should be set up for lesbians, staffed and
inspired by precisely those who had learnt their sexuality in
men's service, and which would recycle all the limited reper-
toire of lesbianism in men's pornography, mostly around
sadomasochism and role-playing.

Debbie Sundahl purports to "love being a stripper". She
says she majored in women's studies and history and worked

with Women Against Violence Against Women. Half of the sixty "performers" in the place where she was working were lesbians, and they began to feel that the stripping business was sexist because "very few women would come to the theater to watch us perform" (Sundahl, 1988, p. 177). The sex industry was a "boys' club" and this had to be changed. The lesbian strippers decided to demand "equal access to sexual entertainment". So Sundahl started the "first women-only strip show" at a lesbian bar in San Francisco in 1984. The strippers loved it because they had more "freedom of expression" and were "treated with awe in their communities" (ibid., p. 178). Then she set up *On Our Backs* and an X-rated video company. These lesbian prostitutes and pornographers support and participate in the malestream sex industry. They sell lesbianism as the same sort of sexual commodity it has always been in men's pornography. Susie Bright, editor of *On Our Backs*, was published in *Penthouse*'s Forum, and *Hustler*. Her 1986 piece in *Hustler* was entitled "Confessions of a Teenage Lesbian" by Susie Bright, "a real live dyke" (Summer, 1993, p. 238). There is profit to be made by women from turning lesbians into more marketable commodities in men's sex industry.

The phenomenon of women advertising their sexual services to other women in gay newspapers has become sufficiently common that Jackie James felt she needed to write about it for a British anthology on "Lesbian Transgressors", which threw into unlikely conjunction lesbian separatists and sadomasochists (1996). It is not possible to know whether the advertisements receive a response, or to what extent. James interviewed a client, Ruth, about her experience of using a woman in prostitution. She seems to have the same difficulties as other women who try out using women in this way, the inability to feel comfortable treating another as an object and being treated just as a john. "What I found most strange was not talking and being close after the sex was over ... But when you pay a woman to do something for you, whether it's cleaning your house ... it makes you unequal" (ibid., p. 152).

James seems convinced that women using women in prostitution will become as institutionalised as men using women, so that "In another ten years it may be widely accepted that women pay for sex, and many of those women are likely to be lesbians" (*ibid.*, p. 154).

Toby Summer wrote "Women, Lesbians and Prostitution: A Working-class Dyke Speaks Out Against Buying Women for Sex" in opposition to the development of a lesbian sex industry. As an ex-prostitute who considered prostitution to be "the abuse of women" and "sexual slavery", she could not "stand it that lesbians are buying women for sex and calling it progress, freedom, our sexuality, lesbian politics" (Summer, 1993, p. 234). Summer agrees with Nestle that "Lesbian pimps have always been around. Lesbian prostitutes have always been around." Summer adds, "Lesbian johns have always been around", though studies of prostitution such as that of Perkins and Bennett in Sydney in the mid-1980s found only negligible numbers of women customers of any sort. But simply stating that lesbians were there too does not, Summer asserts, challenge the "harm done to those women who are positioned to be bought and sold" (*ibid.*, p. 237). She attacks the attempt by some lesbians to join the existing power structure of male supremacy by asserting their own right to use women in prostitution or make a profit out of them. "It is the failure of 'feminism' to leave the structure of male supremacy intact while women pry their way into it" (*ibid.*).

Some of those lesbians who are currently romanticising prostitution seem to be moved by a desire for outlawry. Some identify closely with the interests of gay men, as Rubin and Califia do. Some are women who have been damaged by sexual abuse in childhood and in prostitution. They seek to gain acceptance and income from recycling that abuse as sex within the lesbian community. Others are indeed likely, as Summer suggests, to want entry to what have been seen as male privileges, such as access to women's bodies.

The experience of men in prostitution, which differs according to whether they are playing a "masculine" or "feminine" role, and the experience of transsexuals who are representing the despised classes of women and homosexuals, should alert us to the political dynamics of prostitution. Prostitutes do not simply represent a "sexual minority" struggling to be free. The existence and experience of prostituted women demonstrates the way that the subordination of women is practised and constructed through male sexual dominance. The greater tolerance for the use of women and boys in prostitution that exists amongst some lesbians and many gay men seems to arise from the association of both homosexuality and prostitution with sexual outlawry. Without questioning the political construction of prostitution, many are able simply to identify with a group who are, like them, subject to stigma and repression on the grounds of sexual activity. But other interests operate here too. Male and female sexual liberals who consider that freedom means having equal object choices, and who believe in the ability of the free market to deliver such goods, are fighting to retain these excitements in direct opposition to the feminist challenge.

The legitimisation of prostitution through queer and postmodern theory presents a serious obstacle to the acceptance of a feminist analysis and needs to be vigorously contested. Critical research into the experience of prostituted men and boys from a feminist anti-violence perspective will provide the basis of a radical challenge to gay male sexual exploitation in theory and in practice. Such research will explore the experience of the young, the poor, the racially oppressed, the sexually abused, who are used and damaged through the exercise of the privileges of bourgeois gay male consumers, and provide the fuel for a politics of resistance.

CHAPTER 5

prostitution as "choice"

Women who are compromised, cajoled, pressured, tricked, blackmailed, or outright forced into sex ... often respond to the unspeakable humiliation ... by claiming that sexuality as their own. Faced with no alternative, the strategy to acquire self-respect and pride is: I chose it. [MacKinnon, 1989, p. 149]

As we have seen in Chapter 3, the development of the prostitutes' rights movement introduced the language of "choice" to the discussion of prostitution. Since some women were saying they "chose" to be in prostitution and were happy with that "choice", feminist theorists have been faced with the problem of disbelieving women. Feminist method has been based upon women's truth-telling about their experience and, as MacKinnon (1989) argues, this is what distinguishes feminist methodology. But problems arise when some women make truth claims that feminist theorists find problematic. This leads to questions such as whether it is reasonable for feminists to attribute false consciousness to other women, and whether someone who has no experience of a situation has the right to interpret it on behalf of others. Another complication for feminist theory is the advent of post-modernism, which has introduced a concern to discover women's agency even in the most apparently unlikely situations. This chapter will consider the significance of these ideas for theorising prostitution, choice, women's agency, false consciousness, representing the prostitute.

The contemporary defenders of prostitution use the rhetoric of "choice" to make prostitution seem acceptable. The language of choice is deeply problematic from a feminist perspective. It is the language of sexual liberalism. The idea of choice is used by the prostitutes' rights movement and by male defenders of men's sexual rights. In relation to prostitution, men's rights are concealed beneath the idea of women's choice. An example of this tactic is the magazine *Gauntlet* in the United States. Edited by Barry Hoffman, it is a civil libertarian magazine, which concentrates on promoting the rights of pornographers and paedophiles, with occasional references to other issues, such as "media pandering to Black cultists, gays ..." (Hoffman, 1994, p. 1). The issue is called "In Defense of Prostitution" and subheaded "Prostitutes debate their 'choice' of profession". In his editorial, Hoffman explains that the coverage of the topic will be balanced: "Rape, police harassment, deplorable working conditions are discussed, as well as the choice many prostitutes have consciously made to enter and stay in the field" (*ibid.*, p. 5).

It is surprising to discover that those supporting the rights of women employ exactly the same language and concepts as those supporting the rights of men to use, and profit from the use of, women. But prostitutes' rights activists who purport to be pursuing women's rights do use the same language of "choice" as the johns do. Nickie Roberts, as we saw in Chapter 2, is a British ex-prostitute woman who espouses choice arguments in her celebration of the history of prostitution, *Whores in History*. She characterises the feminist and gay movements, as well as that for prostitutes' rights, as campaigning for freedom of choice.

The feminist and gay movements especially have made important steps towards opening up freedom of sexual choice for everyone, whatever their orientation. Uncomfortable as it may be for some feminists, though, it is implicit in the demand that women have control over their own bodies that they also have the right to sell their own sexual services, if they wish to. [Roberts, 1992, p. 355]

Prostitution, of course, is not an "orientation". The right to choose to love someone of the same sex is not an appropriate comparison to the right to choose to be used as the raw material in a massive capitalist sex industry.

The idea of choice in liberal theory

The language of choice in relation to prostitution relies upon the popularity in the 1970s and 1980s of a particular variety of liberal thought which emphasises the importance of choice. In *The Sexual Contract*, Carole Pateman details the dangers of adopting this kind of liberal theory for such issues as marriage and prostitution. She focuses her critique on contract theory, which she sees as part of a landscape of liberal ideology centred upon the importance of choice. Contract theory's "new lease of life" is

> bound up with wider political developments centred on an interpretation of democracy as individualistic initiative (or choice), which can be summed up succinctly in the slogans of private enterprise and privatization. The whole political package is marketed under the name of freedom. [Pateman, 1988, p. ix]

When feminists promote "choice" in relation to reproductive surrogacy, breast implants and prostitution, they do not usually reference the male theorists of liberalism from whom this approach derives. But a consideration of this literature is instructive in showing the sort of political agenda that "choice" proponents tend to uphold overall.

Within Kantian liberalism, expressed in recent times by liberal theorists such as John Rawls and Robert Nozick, the human being's ability to reason is seen to raise "him" above the animal. As *Gender Justice*, a book committed to applying these ideas to "gender", puts it:

We begin with the philosophical underpinnings of this liberal position, the understanding of human beings as distinguishable from other species by their capacity for autonomous action and the commitment to liberty as a way of honoring this core human trait. [Kirp, et al., 1986, p. 13]

Eighteenth-century male theorists wanted to believe that they were superior to animals. They based their political philosophy on maximising the opportunity for "man" to demonstrate and freely practise this skill which differentiates "him" from animals. Women, of course, were considered to be deficient in reason, so this philosophy was not meant to cover them. Man's capacity to reason, however, would be evidenced in his exercise of "rational choice" only if the state's interference was minimised.

Gender Justice provides a useful example of the problems that arise from applying these ideas to feminism. The authors—two American male law professors, David Kirp and Mark Yudof, and a female PhD student, Marlene Strong Franks—consider that the way to achieve gender justice is through the maximisation of choice and small government. "We pose, as our central question, whether government should aspire to alter societal outcomes, as these vary by sex, or—very differently—to free up the processes by which individuals make life choices for themselves" (*ibid.*, p. 4). The "law" of the market, as understood by libertarian economists, is applied to all areas of social decision-making here. It is wrong for governments to seek to shape society through policy, since a better result will always be achieved by the rational exercise of the unfettered free choice of citizens who pursue what they perceive to be their best interests. "In setting the engine of process in motion, as in the paradigm case of the marketplace, we imagine rational individuals who pursue their self-interest and posit that such personal calculations benefit society generally." In this approach, "choice itself, not some specified social arrangement, becomes the yardstick of goodness" (*ibid.*, pp. 11, 12). The development of "this capacity for individual choice is central to becoming a person", they quote David Richards as saying. They proclaim that "Respect for individual choice, however mysterious its origins, is a necessary condition of social justice" (ibid., p. 15). Denigrating free choice, they assert, is the same as denigrating human worth. They quote the influential liberal philosopher Robert Nozick to express this: "Without free will we seem diminished, merely the playthings of external causes" (ibid., p. 64).

The authors of Gender Justice, motivated by what they call "classical liberalism", indignantly reject large parts of a mainstream feminist agenda. They note that delegates to a 1978 National Women's Conference in the United States declared that government should

> eliminate violence in the home and develop shelters for battered women, support women's businesses, eradicate child abuse, provide federal funding of nonsexist day care, assure full employment in order that all women who wish to work may do so, protect homemakers who would make their marriages into partnerships, end the sexist portrayal of women in the media, establish reproductive freedom and end involuntary sterilization, revise the criminal codes dealing with rape, eliminate discrimination on the basis of sexual preference, establish nonsexist education, review all welfare proposals for their specific impact on women, and so forth. [ibid., p. 125]

To feminist eyes this might seem a reasonable list and one that would certainly require state intervention for fulfilment, since the laws of the market do not protect women's interests as women. Kirp et al. are appalled. They call this a "litany" and "naive" and a desire for "thought control" by "big sister". The "basic principles of sound gender policy", they aver, "if liberty is to have meaning", are to remove barriers to choice so that individuals "have the opportunity to choose, the capacity to make choices, information on which to base preferences, and a climate of tolerance in which to explore alternatives" (ibid., p. 133).

In recent decades a whole school of ideas based on such notions has developed within political science and economics, called "public choice". Through these ideas theorists seek to promote the advantage of small government and to prove that the exercise of "rational choice" will lead to public welfare (Hauptmann, 1996; Stretton and Orchard, 1994). As critics of these ideas have pointed out, the idea of the primacy of some constant human motivation, of mysterious but inconsequential origin, does not match feminist experience, let alone theory. Feminists have sought to change the motivations of women and men with a considerable amount of success and with the help of some government intervention and economic changes (*ibid*., p. 236). As Hugh Stretton and Lionel Orchard point out in their critique of public choice theory, motivation is not stable but "a main subject of debate, choice and action" (*ibid*.).

Liberal theorists who privilege the idea of choice often relate their pedigree back to John Rawls, *A Theory of Justice* (1972). Rawls was not an extreme libertarian, but nonetheless exemplifies some of the great difficulties those who ascribe to liberation philosophies have with choice theories.

> The main idea is that a person's good is determined by what is for him the most rational long-term plan of life given reasonably favorable circumstances. A man is happy when he is more or less successfully in the way of carrying out this plan. We are to suppose, then, that each individual has a rational plan of life drawn up subject to the conditions that confront him. This plan is designed to permit the harmonious satisfaction of his interests. It schedules activities so that various desires can be fulfilled without interference ... The expectations of representative men are, then, to be defined by the index of primary social goods available to them. [Rawls, 1972, p. 92]

Such an approach shows no interest in where the choices originate. It makes no allowance for the circumstances of oppression. Rawls does point out that what is rational for a man who is in a particular situation might not be rational for another. But this seems inadequate to address the difference in "choice" available to an unemployed Aboriginal youth in Sydney's Redfern and that available to a youth who has attended the best school and university in the land, between a woman who sees no alternative to prostitution if she is to eat and one who can "choose" between medicine and the law. Taken to extremes, the pursuit of choice in American liberalism can lead to some odd political platforms. Some liberal theorists, such as Milton and Rose Friedman in *Free to Choose* (1980), use the sacred ideal of choice to oppose not just communism and command economies, but also seat-belt legislation.

The idea that democracy should be founded upon and dedicated to the protection of "choice" was adopted by Margaret Thatcher's conservative government in Britain. David Evans, in his *Sexual Citizenship*, explains that in the 1970s and 1980s "the balance of citizenship rights shifted away from social rights of welfare towards civil rights of an economic kind (i.e. market access related) such as the right to buy council houses and to purchase shares in privatised industries" (1993, p. 3). The Tory citizen turned into a consumer with choices. This was formalised in the White Paper in July 1991, the *Citizen's Charter*, in which a new model of citizen and taxpayer was legitimised with the language of "choice".

> The *Citizen's Charter* is about giving more power to the citizen. But citizenship is about our responsibilities—as parents for example, or as neighbours, as well as our entitlements. The *Citizen's Charter* is not a recipe for more state action: it is a testament for our belief in people's rights to be informed and choose for themselves. [quoted in *ibid.*, p. 5]

The "power" of the citizen was to be exercised through choice, which was a problem for those not economically or socially in a position to make "choices". The citizen's rights were reduced to "the freedom to make a well-informed choice of high quality commodities and services in public and private sectors, and to be treated with due regard for their 'privacy, dignity, religious and cultural beliefs.'" (*ibid.*, p. 10).

Choice as consent in prostitution

In the 1980s the language of choice was adopted unquestioningly by many prostitutes' rights advocates, such as COYOTE. Its conservative origins were carefully overlooked, and the right of prostituted women to "choose" to be prostitutes was represented as progressive and feminist politics. Feminist anti-prostitution theorists have been incisively critical of this liberal ideology as it has been applied to prostitution. Kathleen Barry (1995) demonstrates the uselessness of "choice" in explaining prostitution by pointing out that prostitution is not about or for women, but for men. It does not, therefore, matter whether women claim the right or choice to be prostituted or whether they see themselves as victims of men's abuse. How or why female bodies get into the male consumer market is irrelevant to the market. In theory, the main way in which prostitution is typically differentiated from rape is on the issue of "choice" or, as it is usually posed in this context, "consent". Rape is defined as sexual intercourse without consent, and prostitution as sexual intercourse with consent. Consent is not a very effective way to distinguish between abusive and non-abusive sex, as feminist analysts of marital rape and sadomasochism have pointed out (Russell, 1990; Hawthorne, 1991; Jeffreys, 1993). Barry explains that "consent" is not a good divining-rod as to the existence of oppression, and consent to violation is a fact of oppression (1995, p. 65). Oppression cannot effectively be gauged according to the degree of "consent", since even in slavery there was some consent if consent is defined as inability to see, or feel entitled to, any alternative.

> If, for example, consent was the criterion for determining whether or not slavery is a violation of human dignity and rights, slavery would not have been recognized as a violation

because an important element of slavery is the acceptance of their condition by many slaves. [*ibid.*, p. 66]

She explains that pro-prostitution activists "collapse the experience of harm into the act of consent". They make harm invisible. In particular, ideas of choice or consent transform the sex of prostitution from being a class condition of women to one of the personal choice of the individual.

Barry revised her important early feminist analysis of prostitution *Female Sexual Slavery* (1978), and published it as *The Prostitution of Sexuality* (1995). In the later book, she explained that she had been trapped, in her first book, into using a forced/free dichotomy, which implied that prostituted women could be divided into those who "chose" or consented and those who had no "choice" and did not consent. In her 1995 book she pays considerable attention to demolishing the distinction.

According to the feminist human-rights concepts I am developing in this work, "consent" is not the indicator of freedom, nor is absence of consent the primary indicator of exploitation. The liberal construction of consent narrows the feminist analysis of oppression to individual wrongs and drowns feminism in the ethics of individualism. It confines sex to a matter of consent and will and does not consider how sex is used, how it is experienced, and how it is constructed into power. [Barry 1995, p. 89]

She explains that the idea of "consent" has been instrumental in making feminists reluctant to see prostitution as sexual violence. Feminists have "falsely separated prostitution from rape, legally and socially", whereas the movement against sexual violence should include prostitution "just as it includes the sexual subordination of women in marriage and of teenagers in dating" (*ibid.*, p. 90).

Barry explains that feminist anti-rape politics have often been based on an uncritical liberal individualism, as evidenced in the acceptance of "consent" as the crucial demarcation of that which is rape and that which is not. She is critical of the way in which the ideology of consent has been used to obscure the real effects of women's multi-layered oppression on their ability to exercise individual free will. She shows how the early anti-rape slogan used on Take Back the Night marches, "No Means No", supports the idea that unless a woman recognises herself as having not consented, no violation has taken place. This use of the consent idea "shifts oppression from a class condition of sexual exploitation to individual experiences of it" (*ibid.*, p. 84).

> That is how women in prostitution are excluded from being recognised as sexually victimised. Prostitute women are made to be the "other"—the women for whom the act of abusive, violating, dehumanizing sex is meant—because their consent is established in the market exchange, where they take money for sex. [*ibid.*, p. 84]

The idea of consent or choice in prostitution effectively separates prostituted women from other women. Non-prostituted women, including feminists who take this approach, can then exclude themselves from the discussion of prostitution. Since these women would not "choose" to be prostituted, prostituted women must be a different kind of woman for whom experiences that other women see as violating can be quite acceptable, or even desired.

When prostituted women themselves use the language of "choice", they can be seen to be engaging in what deviancy sociologists call "neutralising techniques". Sociologists use this term to describe the way in which socially despised and marginalised groups create rationalisations which enable them to survive their marginal condition (Sykes and Matza, 1957). Such techniques may be employed because the only alternative available may be the painful one of self-contempt. The idea that prostitution is freely chosen is such a technique. When pro-prostitution activists and theorists employ the idea of choice, they incorporate the dehumanisation of prostitution into the identity of the prostituted women. As Barry explains it, the prostituted woman is to live the fragmentation of her self as actively chosen. The result of the adoption of the ideology of personal choice, which Barry describes as "apolitical", to explain how women come to be violated is, she says, that "the critiques of power relations that characterised the feminist movement in the late 1960s and early 1970s" have been submerged (Barry, 1995, p. 82).

As the free-market ideology of personal choice has been combined with the sexual liberalism of those who see themselves as progressive and left-wing, the language of choice has gained the ascendence. "Hyper-individualism and elevation of personal choice as the only and therefore ultimate condition of freedom, if it prevails over the feminist movement, will be its final deconstruction." Personal choice is thus elevated "above any concept of a common good or collective well-being". Personal choice politics are a manifestation of "capitalist market liberal ideology that emphasises individualism to serve market competition and promote consumerism" (ibid., p. 83). The question of how people in general, or women in particular, come to "choose" and what they have to "choose" from is carefully avoided.

Ann Jones, in Next Time She'll Be Dead: Battering and How to Stop It, sees the rhetoric of choice, however inappropriate, as serving the function of protecting those who adopt it from having to face their own vulnerability. Women who would not like to think that they could be battered, or who cannot see any commonality between themselves and prostituted women, can use the idea of "choice" as a distancing mechanism. They would not "choose to stay" or "choose" to enter prostitution, so battered and prostituted women come to be seen, as Jones puts it, as pariah groups "who apparently choose to live 'abnormal' and dangerous lives because of some peculiar kinks of background and personality" (Jones, 1994, p. 14).

Blaming the victim

The language of choice puts the responsibility for prostitution upon women. Men's abuse of women in prostitution is explained in terms of the actions of the women they abuse, i.e. a woman's choice to be there. In relation to other areas of violence against women, asking the question why women stay—or in other ways putting the responsibility upon the victim—is recognised by feminists as victim-blaming. Only in relation to prostitution is this still seen as a legitimate tactic.

Feminist theorists and activists of the anti-rape movement have exposed the "rape myth" that women cause rape by their own behaviour (Russell, 1975; Brownmiller, 1975). Since the courts in most countries still employ these myths when dealing with rape, it is clear that the ideology of victim-blaming is still very effective. Women are blamed for wearing the wrong clothing, being in the wrong place at the wrong time, leading men on, accepting a lift, being prostitutes. This practice has academic back-up in the work of the victimologists who, since World War II, have sought to blame women for men's violence against them. The work of Menachim Amir, for instance, has been well critiqued by feminist anti-rape theorists since the early 1970s (Brownmiller, 1975). Victim-blaming has been a dominant form of explanation for other forms of male violence too, such as child sexual abuse where sexologists have blamed female children for being too affectionate, for accepting sweets, and other forms of precipitating behaviour (Jeffreys, 1982).

Victim-blaming in relation to men's battery has taken the form, as in other areas of violence, of asking what personality characteristics cause a woman to get herself battered. But the most common form of victim-blaming has been to ask why women stay. A questionnaire answered by 216 randomly selected community members in the United States found that more than 60 per cent agreed that if a battered woman was really afraid she would leave (Barnett and La Violette, 1993, p. 76). Anti-violence theorists have sought to answer this question by showing how violence develops in relationships in such a way as to preclude easy decisions about leaving; how women are affected by the prolonged torture of battering so that making assertive decisions becomes difficult; how women receive little help from friends, police or other agencies; how women are dependent economically on the batterers, particularly when they have children; and how women, encouraged by a whole culture of victim-blaming, blame themselves. Battered women are also sensibly aware that attempting to leave may occasion their deaths, since often enough this is precisely what happens. This issue has come to prominence in the United States over the O. J. Simpson case (Schneider, 1996). Staying and accepting the violence can seem better than death, or a life of hiding and being stalked.

Despite this sensitive and very extensive work on the reasons why women are not able to leave, even feminists sought to attribute blame to Hedda Nussbaum. This was a case which caused considerable dissension amongst feminists. Nussbaum was tortured by the man she lived with, Joel Steinberg, in ways that are extreme even by the often horrifying standards set by battered women's accounts.

> Steinberg had kicked her in the eye, strangled her, beaten her sexual organs, urinated on her, hung her in handcuffs from a chinning bar, lacerated a tear duct by poking his finger in the corner of her eye, broken her nose several times and pulled out clumps of hair while throwing her about their apartment. [Caputi, 1993, p. 10]

Steinberg used a blowtorch on her and caused burns all over her body. But the problem for some feminist commentators was that Steinberg was also torturing Lisa, a child he illegally adopted. Nussbaum did not seek to protect the child, and in fact watched over her for three hours whilst she was dying, without calling for help. Susan Brownmiller, author of the early and influential feminist critique of rape, *Against Our Will*, denounced Nussbaum's collusion in the violence to Lisa and criticised the view of Nussbaum as victim. She argued that feminists should not support

> unquestioningly the behaviours and actions of all battered women ... The point of feminism is to give women the courage to exercise free will, not to use the "brainwashed victim's" excuse to explain away the behaviour of a woman who surrenders her free will. Victimhood must no longer be an acceptable or excusable model of female behaviour. [*ibid.*, p. 11]

Note that Brownmiller in speaking of "free will" has adopted the language of American liberalism. As Jane Caputi argues, this approach takes the focus off Steinberg; it concentrates not on how the man could have done this, but how the woman could have let him. "It seeks the reason for the battery in the personality of the woman ... and not in male dominance" (*ibid.*, p. 11). Caputi argues that Nussbaum's failure to summon emergency help for the abused Lisa as she lay dying, must be sought in the "nuclear family and in her status as a torture victim" (*ibid.*, p. 12).

It is interesting that the very naming of men's battery has enabled the practice of obscuring male culpability. Terms such as *domestic violence* and *spouse abuse* conceal men's agency and make it look as if battery in relationships is gender-neutral. In prostitution, this problem of naming is extreme. The word *prostitution* does not include the agents of the abuse, men, in the picture at all, and enables prostitution to be seen as something for which women are responsible and which women perhaps practise all on their own. The term *prostituted women* is useful in at least indicating that there is an agent involved. But a term which really demonstrates male responsibility does not yet exist. Naming is important and such a term would be useful in rebalancing the debate towards the role of men.

Victim-blaming in prostitution is demonstrated by the male sexologists, sociologists and psychologists who seek explanations in the personalities and lifestyles of the victims for why women become involved. Harold Greenwald gave the psycho-analytic perspective in *The Call Girl* in 1958. From his case studies, he decided the call girl had an "extreme type of behavior disorder" (Greenwald, 1964, pp. 12–13). Stella, for instance, had "difficulty in establishing close relationships" and in "trusting", and rejected female identification. She wanted to revenge herself on a cold and indifferent mother and "seemed to feel the need to debase herself" (*ibid.*, pp. 84, 92). Other psychoanalysts identify prostituted women as frigid and markedly hostile towards men, but these characteristics are seen as explaining their prostitution rather than resulting from it. Glover, in *The Psychopathology of Prostitution*, suggested that the prostituted woman "unconsciously seeks at the same time to block and to punish herself for her original incestuous (infantile) strivings by denying herself normal adult love and marriage" (1969, p. 12). Such approaches are no longer so popular, at least amongst feminists, but, I suggest, the concentration on women's "choice" in entering prostitution is just an updated version of victim-blaming. It is a clever one, because it masquerades as an explanation for prostitution which attributes agency to women and fulfils feminist aims of seeing women as strong, powerful and capable. But it obscures entirely the role of men. Indeed in the literature which concentrates on showing how women "choose", the johns are rarely mentioned at all. Prostitution appears to exist as a benign industry created to answer women's need for a remunerative occupation, which continues because women continue to "choose" it.

Sexual and reproductive liberalism and choice

In an illuminating contribution to the critique of "choice" entitled "Sexual and Reproductive Liberalism", Janice Raymond examines why many feminist theorists and activists have started to use the language of choice as if this provided a radical way forward for women. As she notes, previously most feminists recognised the problems associated with the liberal idea of choice: "there was a feminist consensus that women's choices were constructed, burdened, framed, impaired, constrained, limited, coerced, shaped by patriarchy" (Raymond, 1990, p. 103). This did not mean, as some proponents of "choice" aver, that feminists saw women as incapable of making decisions and taking action in their own interests.

> No one proposed that this meant women's choices were determined, or that women were passive or helpless victims of the patriarchy. That was because many women believed in the power of feminism to change women's lives, and obviously, women could not change if they were socially determined in their roles or pliant putty in the hands of the patriarchs. [*ibid.*]

Then, Raymond explains, some feminists began to talk about the importance of not seeing women as victims. She sees this as the result of some women starting to gain benefits out of male supremacist society and being unable to understand why other women did not.

> More women went to graduate and professional schools, grew "smarter", were admitted to the bar, went into the academy, and became experts in all sorts of fields. They partook of the power that the male gods had created and "saw that it was good." [*ibid.*]

There was a shift from feminist radicalism to feminist liberalism. This was evident in sexual liberalism, i.e. the pro-pornography position, and also in reproductive liberalism, which promoted the new reproductive technologies as having positive advantages for women. Both these groups use the rhetoric of a woman's "right to choose" and "have invested an old, liberal discourse about choice with a new and supposedly feminist content" (*ibid.*, p. 105). These feminists want to see women as agents of their status in pornography or their role as surrogates in reproduction, and see women as needing the choice to take part in these practices to be free.

They wanted, for instance, to see Mary Beth Whitehead as having chosen to sign her contract (Raymond, 1994). Whitehead contracted with William Stern to be inseminated by him and bear a child for him. She was a working-class mother, he was an upper-class man. She changed her mind after bearing the child and discovering that it looked like her other daughter and, having breastfed the child for four months, decided that she wanted to keep her. Stern went to court and gained custody, hunted Whitehead down with police and private detectives, and removed the child. As Phyllis Chesler (1990) points out, the surrogacy contract is not about equality. The surrogate mother faced all the risks of pregnancy for nine months, carried the baby and felt it moving inside her, went through labour, delivered, began to lactate and breastfed the baby, and "throughout her life she was being socialised into motherhood". But "pro-choice" feminists were able to see Stern as within his rights because Whitehead chose to sign a contract. They said, "We must have a right to make contracts. It's very important. If a woman can change her mind about this contract—if it isn't enforced—we'll lose that right!" (*ibid.*, p. 101). They did not consider that the contract was unethical and should not be seen as legitimate, or that Whitehead's decision to embark on this contract for $10,000 meant a payment rate of only 50 cents per hour.

Janice Raymond points out that it is deeply problematic to identify as agency the situations in which women opt into oppressive institutions which originate precisely in the subordination of women. Radical feminists, she explains, have seen women's agency as most clearly expressed in their "resistance to those oppressive institutions, not in women's assimilation to them" (Raymond, 1990, p. 109). Those who choose to see women as agents when they opt into oppressive institutions do not mention the agency of those women who resist oppression, those who testify to their abuse in pornography, or ex-surrogates who fight in court for themselves and their children. As Raymond comments, "If we want to stress women's agency, let's look in the right places." Prostitution survivors say that leaving prostitution is a great deal more worthy of the term "choice" than their entry. A woman who was in prostitution for three and a half years from the age of fifteen was interviewed for Maggie O'Neill's study of prostitution in Birmingham, England. As O'Neill explains, "For her, 'choice' and 'control' were exercised by leaving prostitution" (1996, p. 139). The liberals, Raymond says, have not defended women's agency "in the creation of a culture that defies patriarchy", but only in supporting male supremacist culture.

There are good examples of this approach amongst many of those researching prostitution for whom it is currently fashionable to attribute agency to prostituted women. When prostituted women are credited with agency, this is presented as respectful of the women. Graham and Annette Scambler take this approach in the 1997 British collection *Rethinking Prostitution*. They explain in the introduction that the first of the themes they "wish to identify" in the book is "agency".

> Opposing the tendency, implicit in many social theories of prostitution, to regard women sex workers as more or less passive victims of their backgrounds or circumstances, we would advocate a presumption of wilful rationality ... insist that the "starting point" for any analysis be the respectful attribution of agency. [*ibid.*, p. xv]

The solution for the problems faced by prostituted women favoured by those concerned to attribute "agency" is generally "empowerment". This is proposed by the Scamblers in their conclusion. They do not want the end of men's abuse of women in prostitution but, "the reconstruction or 'displacement' of the flawed British sex industry of the 1990s via the empowerment through full citizenship of all its current sex workers" (*ibid.*, p. 188). Since the woman is exercising "agency" to get into prostitution then getting her out could not be a solution. This would disrespect her agency. She must be "empowered" to stay in.

Choice and women's agency: a post-modern approach

The language of "choice" has received particular emphasis in the currently fashionable development of post-modern feminism. In their anxiety to see women as rational, free-willed individuals whose ability to exercise choice must be protected above all, some feminist post-modern theories resemble the conservative rhetoric of American liberalism (Halberstam, 1994). Kathy Davis's book *Reshaping the Female Body* (1995) on cosmetic surgery is a good example of this approach. Davis seeks to emphasise women's agency and is most concerned not to see women as "victims". Her book is based upon interviews with women who have had breast augmentation and reduction surgery. As a result of the damaged health suffered by thousands of women who have had silicone breast implants, organisations of "survivors" have been set up in the United States and in Australia to support injured women. Throughout the world women are seeking compensation payments from the makers of the implants. In 1994 there was a $4.2 billion award against the implant manufacturing companies of Dow Corning, Bristol–Myers Squibb, and Baxter International in the United States. In the same year there was a moratorium in the United States on the use of silicone in reconstructive surgery. Activists in this struggle estimate that 20 per cent of women implant patients suffer symptoms of toxicity, and 4000 women in Australia alone have registered their silicone-related illnesses with consumer organisations (Dumble, 1995).

Davis is aware of the dangers implants pose for women's health. She states that the chance of what she calls "side effects" from breast augmentation is 30–50 per cent. The least dramatic and most common, she explains, are decreased sensitivity of the nipples, painful swelling and congestion of the breasts, hardening of the breasts which makes it difficult to lie down comfortably or to raise the arms without the implants shifting position, or asymmetrical breasts. More serious is encapsulation, which occurs in nearly 35 per cent of cases overall, and affected 50 per cent of her interviewees. In such cases, the patient or doctor has to "massage" the implant to break it up, causing enormous pain and much greater risk of leakage of the silicone. If the massage does not work, the implants have to be removed, which can, as Davis describes it, mean chiselling them from the patient's chest. Rupturing or leakage can lead to damage to the woman's immune system, resulting in arthritis, lupus, connective tissue disease, respiratory problems, or brain damage. The implants need replacing after fifteen years. Unsuccessful operations are disfiguring, and result in unsightly scars that may leave the woman with a much worse problem than she had before (Davis, 1995, p. 27).

Considering the degree of damage and the worldwide campaign to gain compensation, it is perhaps surprising that Davis selects this particular practice for her exercise in demonstrating women's agency. Davis explains that she is most determined not to represent her interviewees as "cultural dopes" who have simply imbibed the negative messages of the beauty culture about the inferiority of women's bodies. She wants to see the women's decisions in a more positive light. She says that such cosmetic surgery is an "intervention in identity", which can allow a woman to "open up the possibility to renegotiate her relation to her body and construct a different sense of self". Though many feminists might see cosmetic breast surgery as the result of women objectifying themselves in line with their representation in Western male supremacist culture, Davis chooses to see it as "disempowering" the "entrapment of objectification".

> Cosmetic surgery can provide the impetus for an individual woman to move from a passive acceptance of herself as nothing but a body to the position of a subject who acts upon the world in and through her body. It is in this sense that cosmetic surgery can, paradoxically, provide an avenue toward becoming an embodied subject rather than an objectified body. [ibid., p. 113]

Though Davis disapproves of breast implants and other cosmetic surgery practices and professes to be aware that circumstances constrain agency, she manages to remain determined to protect the right to "choice" which gives women agency. She discusses positively, for instance, the argument of Lisa Parker, who attacks the decision of the American Food and Drug Administration in 1992 to restrict availability of silicone implants due to health risks. Parker argues that this decision is paternalistic and tramples on "women's right to informed consent". Davis likes this approach, she says, because:

> taking the decision out of the recipient's hands is not only paternalistic, but misrepresents women's competence to make a choice on the basis of the information available. More seriously, by denying women the power to decide to have cosmetic surgery, it also forecloses the opportunity for them to decide not to have it. Rather than encroaching upon women's rights to making decisions about their bodies, it is my contention that we need to think about ways to effectuate their decision making: by providing information, support, and opportunities for reflection and deliberation. [*ibid.*, p. 155]

Davis becomes quite lyrical about the "choice" for cosmetic surgery. For her, it represents, by the end of the book, something beyond even a simple necessity to relieve suffering and provide empowerment. It is a means of achieving moral and just outcomes: "Cosmetic surgery is about morality. For a woman whose suffering has gone beyond a certain point, cosmetic surgery can become a matter of justice—the only fair thing to do" (*ibid.*, p. 163).

Victimism

The determined quest to find agency for women and deny victimhood, even in unlikely cases, has been gaining momentum in feminist theory in the last few years through the books of popular liberal feminism produced by authors such as Katie Roiphe (1993), Naomi Wolf (1993) and Rene Denfeld (1995), who are far from post-modern. These women have attacked anti-violence feminists for making women into victims rather than agents (Deutchman, forthcoming). Feminists who emphasise the significance of men's violence in maintaining the oppression of women are now characterised by some liberal feminists as "victim feminists". They, rather than men, are seen as responsible for women's victimisation (Faust, 1994). This is an example of what the feminist theorist Mary Daly has called patriarchal reversal (1984, p. 86). The role of men in violence against women is obscured by an attack on the women who call that violence into question. The whistle-blowers are accused of being the ones who actually oppress women.

In the case of liberal feminists like Beatrice Faust in Australia and Katie Roiphe in the United States, this attack seems designed to protect such women from the feelings of powerlessness and humiliation that might be seen to follow a recognition of their actual vulnerabillity. Roiphe, in her book *The Morning After*, seems determined to believe in her exemption from the realities of the sex industry. In her comments on the lecturing style of Catharine MacKinnon on college campuses, she comments indignantly, "but the pornography industry that MacKinnon describes—with all of its diabolical machinations, the nude dancer under bright lights—takes place far from our world" (Roiphe, 1993, p. 152). Radical feminist theorists have indeed started from the understanding that all women are linked in a common oppression and that what happens to any woman affects and should be of concern to all; their approach is "Ask not for whom the bell tolls". In contrast, liberal feminists rejoice in what they see as their own immunity.

Roiphe attacks feminist campaigns against sexual harassment and date rape for making women passive victims. Feminists have created a "stock plot" for the woman of the 1990s which is the equivalent of the "love and marriage" of the 1950s: "the sensitive female, pinched, leered at, assaulted daily by sexual advances, encroached upon, kept down, bruised by harsh reality ... a new identity spinning ... around ... passivity and victimhood" (*ibid.*, p. 172).

The sexual libertarians defend pornography and sado-masochism and are another group which attacks anti-violence feminists as victim feminists (Vance, 1984; Califia, 1994). At first sight, these two groups might not seem to have a great deal in common. The conservatism of Roiphe (1993), Wolf (1993) and Denfeld (1995) looks an odd bedfellow for the robust piercing enthusiasm of proponents of lesbian sado-masochism such as Pat Califia, but they have in common a determination to protect the "privacy" of sex. In the case of the libertarians, their object is the defence of their own sexual pleasures which they believe are under threat from the feminist analysis of sexual violence and sexuality. For Roiphe and others like her, the emphasis is on the protection of their view of themselves as powerful, free-willed agents of their own destinies who are not limited by the victimhood of women.

The difficulty of accepting the humiliation of actual rather than potential victimhood affects those who have been prostituted. Toby Summer, in her refutation of the arguments of the *Sex Work* anthology, says that she found it extremely difficult to write her rebuttal of pro-prostitution arguments, because "Confronting how I've been hurt is the hardest thing that I've had to do in my life." It is hard to admit hurt, because "It is humiliating to acknowledge victimization. It is really quite simple: if you lose, you don't win. One cannot be hurt and not be a victim to the perpretrator ..." (Summer, 1993, p. 234). Catharine MacKinnon offers a similar explanation of the difficulty of admitting victimisation.

Women who are compromised, cajoled, pressured, tricked, blackmailed, or outright forced into sex ... often respond to the unspeakable humiliation ... by claiming that sexuality as their own. Faced with no alternative, the strategy to acquire self-respect and pride is: I chose it. [MacKinnon, 1989, p. 149]

In fact, anti-violence feminists have striven to avoid what has been seen as the stigma of victimhood for women who have been abused. After the early years of the campaigns against rape and sexual abuse of children, the term *victim* was abandoned in favour of *survivor*. This was intended to prevent what Kathleen Barry, in her 1979 analysis of prostitution, calls "victimism". Barry describes the advantages of the term "survivor" for women who experience prostitution: "More than victims, women who have been raped or sexually enslaved are survivors. Surviving is the other side of being a victim. It involves will, action, initiative on the victim's part" (1979, pp. 46–7).

Barry stresses that survivorhood is active, a state in which women are choosing strategies for survival. Passivity might be chosen as a strategy, and perhaps a misguided one, but it is likely to be the result of a determination to survive.

Louise Armstrong, whose book *Kiss Daddy Goodnight* (1978) is a foundational text in the feminist campaign against father rape, explains that feminists chose to use the word *survivor* because *victim* had connotations of permanent injury. The word *survivor* "allowed for the notion of serious injury without classifying the injury as necessarily permanently deforming" (Armstrong, 1994, p. 30). But, she explains in *Rocking the Cradle of Sexual Politics*, though feminist activists certainly never victimised women, an "incest industry" has been set up by therapists since the 1970s which has revictimised women by concentrating all attention on them as if they are permanently damaged goods, whilst avoiding any need to stop or penalise the abusers.

Considering the savage attacks that have been launched against anti-violence feminists on the grounds of their victimising women, there may be a case for readopting the word *victim*. The avoidance of the word *victim* and the terminology of survivorhood may have left the way open for these attacks. As lesbian feminists adopted the term *lesbian* with pride to divert the ways it could be used to attack women, so perhaps the term *victim* could be rehabilitated (Radicalesbians, 1988).

Victim would have a literal meaning in describing the recipient of violence and abuse, but need not signify a permanent state of "victimism".

The limitations on choice

It is important to examine the conditions of prostituted women's lives to understand why the rhetoric of "choice" is inappropriate. Such feminist analysis of the limitations of women's choices has been criticised by liberal feminists for being condescending to women. Janice Raymond points out that Marx is respected for his insight into the fact that people do not make choices under conditions they have created, but feminists who apply a similar understanding to the condition of women are criticised for turning women into victims. Nonetheless researchers and survivors of prostitution provide a great deal of evidence to undermine the idea that prostitution is a "choice".

JoAnn Miller, in a collection entitled *Sexual Coercion* (1991), places prostitution within the framework of coercion. She argues that, rather than representing "choice", prostitution is a situation in which "members of less powerful groups are compelled or forced, physically or psychologically, to engage in a sexual act, [so] prostitution is fundamentally coercive and exploitative". The entry of women to prostitution, she says, is "about as voluntaristic as a young man's decision to join boot camp after he was drafted during wartime" (*ibid.*, pp. 47, 54).

Jane Anthony, who has worked in prostitution, wrote a piece in *MS* magazine specifically entitled "Prostitution as 'Choice'", opposing the liberal ideology which privileges "choice" arguments (1986, p. 86). She points out that of the few women putting forward the "choice" argument for prostitution, most do not "choose prostitution for themselves". These spokespersons who are picked up enthusiastically by the male-dominated media have either "abandoned it; some never worked as prostitutes; some work as 'madams' selling other women's bodies ... a few actually work as prostitutes'. She sees the "choice" argument as completely decontextualising commercial sex from "the cultural constraints burdening women's 'choices'—job discrimination, gender inequality in the courts, and in general, sexism so pervasive it is often invisible" (ibid.).

The study by Hoigard and Finstad (1992) of prostitution in Oslo shows how little choice, in the sense of real alternatives, the women they interviewed had. The average age at which women turned their first trick was fifteen and a half, an age which is below the legal age of consent in most countries. They entered prostitution before any other possible method of earning money was open to them. Their social background was often the bottom end of the working class, and fitted the same pattern as indicated by other prostitution research. What was particularly startling was the extensive experience of institutionalisation. Only three of the twenty-six interviewees had never been institutionalised at all. Some had been in many kinds of institution. Fifteen were institutionalised before their first trick, and thus rejected by society. The institutions often trained the young women for prostitution. Prostitution did not seem more distressing for many than other life experiences which had already conditioned them. Anita, for example had a seventy-year-old man as her first trick, and commented: "It was totally disgusting. But I didn't think about it too much. I'd done so many weird things, I'd been doing group sex since I was a little kid. My sex life was already screwed up" (ibid., p. 17). When girls have been sexually abused in childhood, as prostituted women often have, it is hard to see them as having a really free choice.

Most of the young women who entered prostitution in Oslo had associated with other street kids for quite a while before they turned their first trick. They were in gangs and turned tricks to get money or paint thinner. At first they would be able to share the paint thinner of girls who were already being prostituted, and then would have to join in themselves so as not to be seen as leeching. There was a subculture of sharing in which prostitution was an act of solidarity and abstention was sponging. As Hoigard and

Finstad explain, "all women in our society have at some time, most likely many times, come up against the notion that our greatest asset is our body". But the women did not see themselves as having made a "choice" from a well-informed position. One commented, "If I'd known what I know today, I'd never have started" (*ibid.*, pp. 18, 22).

Prostitution was not a typical solution for young women faced with unemployment or unattractive jobs. For those who did get prostituted, this was because

> through their own experiences and the cultural milieu [they] acquired a view of their personal value and their bodies that makes prostitution an alternative to other forms of support. It is this combination of self-image and an oppressed position in class society that can be fateful. [*ibid.*, p. 76]

The sort of jobs available to them, and which they had tried, were untrained ones such as cleaning, sales, caring for children or the elderly, and waitress jobs. They feared exposure of their prostitution experience, which generally predated any other paid work, and this often led to their leaving jobs.

Hoigard and Finstad identify other factors influencing the decision, such as being addicted to drugs, which offers only the choice between prostitution and crime because of the need for large amounts of money. A perceived lack of alternatives resulted from the fact that all the young women's friends from the children's home were prostituted. They could gain from entering prostitution a sense of "mutual friendship" and togetherness against society. Some gained a sense of power through using men's sexual need and, as Hoigard and Livstad comment, "When sexuality is the woman's only means to power, she would have to be extremely strong, not to use her sexuality as a means of power" (*ibid.*, p. 83). This had the effect, though, of creating an instrumental relationship to sexuality. These women were not turned out by violent pimps and would probably be seen in much literature as having "chosen" prostitution, but when their circumstances are looked at closely, it is clear that their "choice" bears no relation to that which would face the middle-class commentators who make these judgements. Women's economic status in the United States, for instance, suggests that the "choice" of prostitution is not often made from amongst many viable alternatives. Women are two-thirds of all economically poor adults, according to the US Bureau of Census; full-time female workers earn 60 per cent of the male wage, and the average female college graduate earns less than a man with a mere high-school diploma (Barnett and LaViolette, 1993, p. 24).

The crisis in providing good support for girls in care seems to be providing recruits to prostitution in many Western countries. Maggie O'Neill, who works with prostituted women in Birmingham writes:

> Some are young women who drift into prostitution on leaving care because of financial problems and their association with the street culture; others are clearly pimped and coerced into prostitution whilst in care through their developing "romantic" relationships with local pimps. All of these young women have profoundly sad backgrounds: child sexual abuse; physical or emotional abuse; family breakdowns; multiple placements in care. [O'Neill, 1996, p. 135]

Older women, she explains, entered prostitution as a way to resist poverty for themselves and their children.

It might be better to use a different word to describe what women do in situations which are constrained. I prefer *decision* to *choice*. The word *decision* has the advantage of being able to convey the hard task women have when in a situation of few alternatives, where perhaps all of them are undesirable to a greater or lesser extent. The word "choice" implies that there are viable alternatives to select from. The private school and Harvard-educated man who might make rational choices in a Rawlsian view of the world, might indeed have medicine, law or the officer class of the army as alternatives. The word *choice* is not appropriate for a woman whose "choice" is between low-paid service work which does not fit in with child-care, and the chance of a better income with more flexible hours through the violation of her body. Women can indeed express agency by making decisions, but it is likely to be an anguished agency much constrained by circumstance and devoid of the exultation of "choosing" between glorious possibilities for the exercise of their talents.

Believing women

The ideology of choice can be criticised for its theoretical underpinnings in extreme libertarian individualism, and for its practical weaknesses for understanding the situation of women, but it is a stumbling block for many feminists that some prostituted women do speak of choice. Scepticism about their choices might seem to be disbelieving women, and much of feminist theory and practice has been based upon the idea that women should be believed. Feminist ideas on methodology, ways of establishing the truth of women's experience, tend to rely on what women recount without any very effective way of dealing with the conflicting truths that can result. Socialist feminist theorists, such as Alison Jaggar, Dorothy Smith, Sandra Harding and Nancy Hartsock, have developed what has been called feminist standpoint theory as the basis for a feminist analysis. Radical feminist theorists, most notably Catharine MacKinnon (1989), have developed a methodology based on consciousness-raising. Both approaches rely on women's accounts of their experience, but do not require an acceptance of totally conflicting accounts as equally accurate.

The socialist feminist theorists use Marxist ideas about class consciousness to support the notion of a "feminist standpoint". Nancy Hartsock argues that, if human activity is structured in fundamentally opposing ways for two different groups, such as men and women, "one can expect that the vision of each will represent an inversion of the other, and in systems of domination the vision available to the rulers will be both partial and perverse" (quoted in Harding, 1991, p. 121). Alison Jaggar explains:

Like both traditional Marxists and radical feminists, socialist feminists view knowledge as a social and practical construct and they believe that conceptual frameworks are shaped and limited by their social origins. They believe that in any historical period, the prevailing world view will reflect the interests and values of the dominant class. [Jaggar 1988, p. 369]

Jaggar's understanding of how class position affects consciousness applies neatly both to the attitude of influential ruling-class men to prostitution, and to the views expressed by prostituted women who have adopted a libertarian rather than a feminist perspective. The men who use prostituted women are unlikely to recognise that they are being abusive.

Because their class position insulates them from the suffering of the oppressed, many members of the ruling-class are likely to be convinced by their own ideology; either they fail to perceive the suffering of the oppressed or they believe that it is freely chosen, deserved or inevitable. They experience the current organization of society as basically satisfactory and so they accept the interpretation of reality that justifies that system of organization ... [ibid., p. 370]

Prostituted women, from this perspective, could be expected either to seek to adapt to the view that their johns hold, because ruling-class ideology is powerful, or to come to the realisation that they are being abused.

Oppressed groups, by contrast, suffer directly from the system that oppresses them. Sometimes the ruling ideology succeeds in duping them into partial denial of their pain or into accepting it temporarily but the pervasiveness, intensity and relentlessness of their suffering constantly push oppressed groups toward a realization that something is wrong with the prevailing social order. [ibid.]

This idea, however, does not provide a ground for distinguishing between the sometimes opposing interpretations of their "lives" that women recount. Sandra Harding explains that not all the things women say about their experience provide "reliable grounds for knowledge claims", because

> women (feminists included) say all kinds of things—misogynist remarks and illogical arguments; misleading statements about an only partially understood situation; racist, class-biased, and heterosexist claims—that are scientifically inadequate. [Harding, 1991, p. 123]

The problem of simply believing what women say lies in the fact that women's interpretations of their experience, before they become feminists, have been so shaped by social relations that:

> women have had to learn to define as rape those sexual assaults that occur within marriage. Women had experienced these assaults not as something that could be called rape but only as part of the range of heterosexual sex that wives should expect. [ibid., p. 123]

What is true of rape in marriage is likely to be true also for prostitution. Women are likely to minimise or deny the abuse they have suffered, as I discuss in Chapter 9 on the sexual violence of prostitution. Standpoint theorists agree that the feminist standpoint is not just any account by women, but one created out of political struggle. As Nancy Hartsock points out: "the standpoint of the oppressed represents an achievement both of science (analysis) and of political struggle on the basis of which this analysis can be conducted" (1983, p. 288).

I have argued elsewhere that when feminists are confronted with differing accounts of the truth of prostitution, we should not simply retire from the field but exercise a critical political intelligence (Jeffreys, 1996). We need to measure what we are being told against what we already know about sexuality and sexual violence from our extensive feminist knowledge and our own experience.

Beyond choice: understanding oppression

The privileging of the notion of "choice" for women who embark upon breast augmentation, reproductive surrogacy, or prostitution depends upon ignorance of the complexity of women's oppression. William Ryan's study of the paucity of notions of equal opportunity in relation to race in the United States, *Blaming the Victim* (1971), shows that simply removing the most obvious obstacles to "equality" and expecting the oppressed to then hoist themselves by their own bootstraps is merely reinforcing their victimhood. Once "equality of opportunity" has been provided, the failure of black Americans to enter the upper echelons of business in large numbers can be seen to prove their innate inferiority. Any more sophisticated understanding of oppression might suggest that the dismantling of the legacy of racism—the reconstruction of a racist state, economy and education system, into one that is less hostile to the interests of black Americans—is a radical and long-term task. The ideology of "equal opportunity" protects the privileged from thinking their situation unfair whilst soldering inequality into place.

Catharine MacKinnon criticised the idea of the level playing-field that underpins the liberal view of the state in similarly scathing terms, but from a feminist perspective, in *Towards a Feminist Theory of the State* (1989). She explained how a masculine frame of mind has constructed work and sport and all the other institutions of the masculine state so that women, disabled by not matching the male model, can never perform "equally". Similarly, Carole Pateman (1988) has shown that the model of the individual and the worker are quintessentially masculine.

Feminist theories on how heterosexuality becomes compulsory show that the oppression of women is subtle as well as coercive. Adrienne Rich (1984) argues that heterosexuality is forced on women through everything from simple economic means, through the erasure of lesbian existence, to the use of the chastity belt. Feminist theorists of education, literature, history, as well as theorists of sexuality, have demonstrated the multiple mechanisms through which women learn to be women, learn to service men, and learn to tailor their sexuality, gestures and use of space, as well as their emotions, to men's needs (Henley, 1977; Graham, 1994). As MacKinnon points out, consciousness-raising has demonstrated how it is that women come to be "thingified in the head" (1989, p. 99).

Women are clearly not just victims without agency. The very existence of feminism as a mass movement proves the ability of women to resist oppression and seek to alter their own circumstances and those of all women. But the practice and theory of feminism has also shown the array of forces which exact the conformity of women to their oppressed situation in the form of marriage or prostitution. A full understanding is needed of all the social forces which deliver up to men a woman to be used simply as a hole, and create in men the desire or "need" so to use women. Liberal feminism, which privileges the notion of choice, has an impoverished idea of what is wrong with the condition of women. It recognises the overt discrimination of laws and practices which clearly and deliberately disadvantage women, but, for example, on the forces which might cause a woman to submit to unwanted sexual intercourse in marriage, despite her severe distress, it is mute. Liberal feminism really believes that women have nothing to lose but their chains, unless they have learnt to enjoy wearing them, and when women are not obviously wearing chains they are assumed to be replete with free will and exciting opportunities.

CHAPTER 6

just a job like any other?
prostitution as "work"

> Even those who find it regrettable, or less
> than perfect, might come to see it as one of
> the helping professions, a service like medi-
> cine, social work or the law which helps
> people cope with their problems. [Perkins and
> Bennett, 1985, p. 222]

Pro-prostitution prostitutes' rights organisations have, since the 1970s, promoted the idea that prostitution is simply a form of work and should be seen as such.
The objective was to change the way in which prostitution
has historically been regarded: as deviant sexual behaviour on
the part of the prostituted women. Promoting prostitution as
"work" was supposed to counter what pro-prostitution
activists have called the "whore stigma", which blamed prostituted women as dirty and bad for the ways in which they
were used by men (Pheterson, 1996). Clearly, being used in
prostitution is not "sexual behaviour" by the women
involved. It is onerous and is undergone for the sake of remuneration, not out of perverse desire. Stressing that prostitution
is work recognises these elements and can be seen to challenge
the misconceptions based upon traditonal morality. However,
pro-prostitution activists do not usually stop at simply asserting that prostitution is work, but demand acceptance of men's
use of women in prostitution as legitimate work, no different
from any other. Some pro-prostitution theorists even argue

that prostitution is a superior form of work, a skilled profession.

The consequences of the argument that prostitution is legitimate work like any other, or even superior, are of considerable concern. This argument is being used to institutionalise prostitution as an industry. I will not argue that prostitution is not "work", but instead that it should not be regarded as *legimitate* work by the International Labour Organisation, by governments or trade unions. This is a difficult line to follow, since failure to accept that prostitution is legitimate work is represented by some pro-prostitution activists as being hostile to prostitutes, failing to recognise their skills, talents and rights. It is even depicted as exposing prostituted women to harm, since an acceptance of legitimacy is a necessary precursor to improving the conditions in which men use women in prostitution and to protecting their physical safety. I shall seek to explain in this chapter why it is necessary to challenge the notion that prostitution is legitimate work, despite the danger of being thus misrepresented.

What kind of work is prostitution?

Traditionally, male sexologists have regarded prostitution as anything but work on the part of prostituted women. In the 1960s Harry Benjamin and R. E. L. Masters were arguing that women entered prostitution precisely because they did not want to work—they were lazy and anti-social: "The hostile prostitute is likely to think of herself as having 'outsmarted' the society by evading one of its most forceful and universal edicts—that to reap its benefits, one must work" (1965, p. 107). But they contradict themselves later in the same book, when they argue firmly for accepting prostitution as legitimate work. They say that prostitution should be "quietly placed on the same level as any other occupation, and its workers accorded the respect that ought to be their due" (*ibid.*, p. 440). Benjamin and Masters make it fairly clear in their writing, as we have seen, that they are familiar with brothels, and it is interesting to note that acceptance of prostitution as legitimate work was a demand of the "clients" before it was taken up by the prostitutes' rights movement. Many of the arguments in Benjamin and Masters are precisely those that prostitutes' rights organisations were later to develop. For instance, Benjamin and Masters argue, as pro-prostitution lobbyists began to argue in the 1970s, that a prostituted woman sells not her body but "sex as service" (*ibid.*, pp. 277–8). This should be of concern to pro-prostitution feminists since it is not usually the case that traditional male supremacist interests match precisely with the demands that feminists make in the interests of women's liberation.

It is useful to examine the arguments of pro-prostitution lobbyists and theorists in order to establish precisely what kind of work they consider prostitution to constitute. The American prostitutes' rights organisation COYOTE, credited by its historian Valerie Jeness as the main force in changing the idea of prostitution to that of sex work, sees it as service work. Jeness argues that the most important proposition of COYOTE is that prostitution "is service work that should be respected and protected like work in other legitimate service occupations" (Jeness, 1993, p. 67). The co-directors of COYOTE, Margo St James and Pricilla Alexander, stated in 1977:

> A rather profound misconception that people have about prostitution is that it is "sex for sale", or that a prostitute is selling her body. In reality, a prostitute is being paid for her time and skill, the price being dependent on both variables. To make a great distinction between being paid for an hour's sexual services, or an hour's typing, or an hour's acting on stage is to make a distinction that is not there. [quoted in *ibid.*, p. 68]

At this early stage, they seem not to have been quite so sure what sort of work prostitution was. After all, typing and acting are not service work. Later the language became that of selling sexual services. Dolores French, prostitute and president of the Florida branch of COYOTE, president of HIRE

(Hooking Is Real Employment), and an appointee to Atlanta Mayor Andrew Young's Task Force on Prostitution argued:

> A woman has the right to sell sexual services just as much as she has the right to sell her brains to a law firm where she works as a lawyer, or to sell her creative work to a museum when she works as an artist, or to sell her image to a photographer when she works as a model or to sell her body when she works as a ballerina. Since most people can have sex without going to jail, there is no reason except old-fashioned prudery to make sex for money illegal. [*ibid.*]

Those involved in the prostitutes' rights movement describe what constitutes the "work" of prostitution in different ways. Eva Rosta, an English prostitute and "sex counsellor" argues, "all work involves selling some part of your body ... I choose to sell my vagina" (Pheterson, 1989, p. 146). Presumably this is analogous to the idea that academics sell their minds and production-line workers sell their hands. Roberta Perkins is a male-to-constructed-female transsexual who was involved in setting up the Australian Prostitutes Collective. With Gary Bennett (Garrett Prestage) he researched and wrote *Being a Prostitute* in 1985. These two male authors do see prostitution as a job like any other, despite the fact that they include in their book a considerable amount of evidence of how abusive the "job" is for women. They say it has the advantage of offering women the chance to run their own small business. Some prostitutes, like those who work on the street, Perkins and Bennett tell us, "are working for themselves rather than for the boss ... They are similar to the owner of the corner shop, the small business proprietor or the street pedlar" (1985, p. 214). But their survey results show that 83 per cent did not like working in prostitution, and they might well have been much more enthusiastic about running the corner shop if they had had the resources to do so.

Perkins and Bennett seem to believe in the biological, hydraulic model of sexuality whereby men must have outlets

for their sexual needs or become a menace to the community
(Gagnon and Simon, 1974).⎬The prostitute provides a service
in helping men find the outlets necessary for their mental
health, they say. Thus prostitution might even be of a higher
status than shopkeeper. It might be more like the job of a
lawyer:

> a social service providing a sexual outlet or the possibility of
> sexual fulfilment that may help to prevent the traumatisation
> of many men, and in some cases psychological disturbance.
> Even those who find it regrettable, or less than perfect, might
> come to see it as one of the helping professions, a service like
> medicine, social work or the law which helps people cope
> with their problems. [Perkins and Bennett, 1985, p. 222]⎬

It is hard to believe that, given the opportunity, many women
would choose prostitution over law or medicine.

There seems to be some consensus, though, that being used
in prostitution is equal to providing a service. If this is so,
then increased employment opportunities in prostitution
might form part of the tendency in the late twentieth century
towards more employment in service rather than in primary
industries. In this approach, the service provider that the
prostituted woman most resembles is the therapist. ⎬The
Canadian pro-prostitution organisation, CORP, sees prostitution as "a legitimate service, and we'd like to be able to provide it to all people" (Bell, 1987b, p. 207). The unfortunate
gender bias in the industry is to be overcome by offering the
"service" to women as well as to men.⎬

> As far as we're concerned, there are a lot of women who
> could use this kind of service. They've never had a good fuck
> in their life. They need the service, and it would be well worth
> the money to pay and have a good service and awaken their
> sexuality. We think that it's a legitimate service that anyone
> should be entitled to ... [ibid.]

Prostitution is a profession which should be able to set "professional standards", and this is inhibited by criminalisation. CORP suggests that prostitution is analogous to psychotherapy: "Imagine therapists trying to give good service to someone if they're seeing them on the side because they could be put in jail" (ibid.).

| Pro-prostitution theorists and activists who seek to raise the status of prostitution to that of a profession speak of the advanced "skills" which the prostituted woman possesses. Prostitution is rather unsuited to the usual definition of a profession. Professions such as the law, medicine or teaching require the aspirant to attain a body of skills and reach an examinable standard assessed by their peers. Professional bodies play gatekeeping roles to ensure that the lucrative opportunites open to the professionals are not undermined by cheaper, unqualified labour. Though prostitution does not obviously fit such a definition, this does not deter the American feminist philosopher, Laurie Shrage, from attempting to make it do so. She suggests that individual prostitutes should be licensed, and that to get the licences they would have to undertake courses at university to equip them for their profession. Licensing boards would impose standards which |

> reflect the kinds of knowledge and skill required for the sex provider's work, and required to protect the society from any harm ensuing from her work. For example, candidates for this license could be expected to complete some number of college-level courses on human sexuality from the perspectives of biology, psychology, history, medicine, and so on. [Shrage, 1994, p. 159] |

Certainly there are forms of prostitution in which social skills are important. The degree of social skills required seems to differ according to the niche the prostituted woman occupies in the market. Escort agency workers might be required to conduct conversations in restaurants with the men who will later sexually use them. Women working on the streets are unlikely to have lengthy conversations expected of them. But the skill of maintaining a conversation does not seem sufficient to qualify prostitution as a profession, and such social skills are not a necessary part of the "work" of prostitution. Women in street prostitution who lift their skirts in dark alleyways do not need such skills (McKeganey and Barnard, 1996).

Other pro-prostitution commentators suggest that prostituted women possess particular sexual skills (Sullivan, 1994, 1995). Street prostituted women speak of the skills of getting men to ejaculate quickly so that they do not have to undergo the discomfort of being used for too long. But this skill, consisting of moving around and making noises, does not seem to be more specialised than the practices routinely learnt by heterosexual women who are not getting paid, and want the men they live with to end unwanted sexual intercourse quickly so that they can go to sleep. Masters and Johnson, who used the practices of prostituted women as the template for their model of sex therapy, were impressed by the ways in which prostituted women were able to encourage erections in elderly or intoxicated clients (Brecher, 1972). These "skills" are likely also to be shared by those unpaid heterosexual women who have accepted that they should thus service their partners. A multitude of sex therapy and sex education books explain these techniques, some of which are no more sophisticated than wearing fetishistic and objectifying underwear.

The problem with the idea that prostitution involves special skills which require it to be recognised as a profession, particularly as a therapeutic profession, is that the basic act which the average john wants to perform in the body of a prostituted woman can be performed without the exercise of any special skills on her part. Opportunistic rapists who use the body of their sleeping partner or that of a drunken woman at a party do not require that women exercise skills. Unlike those manual trades which do require skill, such as bricklaying, just having an orifice does not. The argument as to special skills could be seen as window-dressing, designed to make out that prostitution is something that it is not. The use of a woman as orifice in an alley or car, the most basic form of prostitution, does not greatly resemble psychotherapy. The skills that all prostituted women must develop are those which allow them to *survive*, such as dissociation, being alert to danger, and limiting the activities that the customers request to those the prostituted woman is prepared to accept without too much damage to her health and sense of self. These are rather different from the skills that college courses or apprenticeships develop in other professionals and in skilled workers.

The dignity of work?

At a time when forms of work are changing rapidly at the end of the twentieth century towards large-scale permanent unemployment, the decline of traditional male jobs in favour of service industries, and the casualisation of the workforce, it might be expected that exciting discussion would be taking place amongst socialists about what constitutes worthwhile and dignified work. If such a discussion were taking place, then a discussion of prostitution surely ought to be a part of this. But there does not appear to be such a discussion. As the socialist ethicist Bernard Cullen remarks in a piece on whether there is really a "Right to Work", it is "scandalous that the concept of work itself has received so little discussion among socialists in recent years—and almost no discussion at all on a philosophical or theoretical level" (1987, p. 166). He admits to being puzzled that "a highly romanticized and sentimental view of work has tended to predominate" in much of the recent discussion about unemployment, among "academics, journalists, and politicians". He suggests that it may be precisely because of mass unemployment, which has made paid work so unobtainable for many in the rich countries of the West, that work can now be romanticised. Cullen remarks that work seems an unlikely cause to be celebrated, since so many people say their work is "boring, demeaning, and so on" but also points out that being stuck at home is even more "boring, demeaning and depressing". But work, he recognises, does have positive values, such as giving people a "sense that they are making a useful contribution to the social fabric", and work "seems to be bound up with the need to be secure in one's standing as a responsible adult member of the community" (*ibid.*, pp. 172, 173, 174–5). It is unlikely that prostitution will secure such "standing" for women. Cullen does have a sense that socialists should not just accept any remunerative activity as work, since he specifically speaks of the right to "socially worthwhile, healthy and satisfying work for everyone who requires it". He speaks only of men, does not mention women, and seems to himself romanticise the new service industry jobs which will provide "satisfying, socially useful, and healthy work". What he would think of the old-fashioned "service" job of prostitution we cannot know.

It is, of course, feminists who have provided much of the most interesting thinking about work in the 1980s and 1990s. The perspective of women, who have been outside the scope of traditional men's jobs, casts some light on the notion of "work". Marilyn Waring has argued in her most illuminating book, *Counting for Nothing*, (1988), that women's massive contribution in unpaid work is left out of economic statistics, that masculine economics has never been able to recognise the patterns of women's economic activity. Male economists have defined work as that which is paid: "when work becomes a concept in institutionalised economics, payment enters the picture" (*ibid.*, p. 21). According to the traditonal masculine account, for instance, no housewives are workers.

Feminist scholars have shown how certain forms of work come to be seen as "women's work" and attract lower status and remuneration. These include those which require the same qualities and labour as women traditionally perform unpaid in the home and as part of the sexual contract of marriage, such as kitchen work, cleaning, child-care, nursing. These feminist insights can help us to understand the particular indignities of service work. Arlie Hochschild has contributed greatly to our understanding of "women's work" through her study of flight attendants. She finds the most damaging element of this form of "service" work to consist in the necessity to commercialise emotion. Her book, *The Managed Heart* (1983), is exceptional in being a detailed and sensitive study of the damaging effects of service work. The arguments that prostitution is service work do not seem to consider that the joys of service work may not be unalloyed.

Hochschild points out that Marx considered not only the injustice in economic terms of becoming an "instrument of labour", but also the human cost involved. C. Wright Mills argued that workers sold their personalities in the course of selling goods or services, and that this was a "seriously self-estranging process, one that is increasingly common among workers in advanced capitalist systems" (*ibid.*, p. ix). But, Hochschild says, Mills failed to recognise the "active emotional labor involved in the selling". She investigates the experience and harms of this active emotional labour by female flight attendants, which

> requires one to induce or suppress feeling in order to sustain the outward countenance that produces the proper state of mind in others—in this case, the sense of being cared for in a convivial and safe place. This kind of labor calls for a coordination of mind and feeling, and it sometimes draws on a source of self that we honor as deep and integral to our individuality. [*ibid.*, p. 6]

The difference between physical and emotional labour lies, she considers, "in the possible cost of doing the work: the worker can become estranged or alienated from an aspect of self—either the body or the margins of the soul—that is used to do the work" (*ibid.*, p. 7). The emotional labour of flight attendants resembles that engaged in by women in other traditional female jobs. Hochschild explains that women are better at engaging in these forms of labour, which include prostitution, than men because they have learnt the skills of how to behave as a subordinate in relation to men, and the skills of emotional labour are those of deference.

The deferential behavior of servants and women—the encouraging smiles, the attentive listening, the appreciative laughter, the comments of affirmation, admiration, or concern—comes to seem normal, even built into personality rather than inherent in the kinds of exchange that low-status people commonly enter into. Yet the absence of smiling, of appreciative laughter, of statements of admiration or concern are thought attractive when understood as an expression of machismo. Complementarity is a common mask for inequality in what is presumed to be owing between people, both in display and in the deep acts that sustain it. [*ibid.*, p. 84]

One of the "skills" of prostituted women, then, can be seen as emerging from women's subordinate position. The emotional work of women creates status enhancement for men.

The effects of doing this emotional work, for female flight attendants, resembles to some extent the effects described by prostituted women. Hochschild defines as "emotive dissonance" the "separation of display and feeling [which] is hard to keep up over long periods" (*ibid.*, p. 90). This has some similarities with the phenomenon that researchers of prostitution and the slave labour of child sexual abuse call "dissociation". Another consequence of emotional labour, she points out, is sexual harassment. The airline advertisements often used words combined with the ubiquitous emblem of emotional labour, the smile, that led to male passengers having sexual expectations of staff. One of Hochschild's interviewees did make the connection between her experience and what is euphemistically called in the 1990s "sexual entertainment", albeit a high-class form of the latter: "you have married men with three kids getting on the plane and suddenly they feel anything goes. It's like they leave that reality on the ground, and you fit into their fantasy as some geisha girl. It happens over and over again" (*ibid.*, p. 93).

The job of prostitution is not equally open to men and women, since the predominantly male customers of women prostitutes would not be equally happy to use men. But the job of flight attendant is open to men, and Hochschild points out that their experience is very different. For women, the principal task was to deal with the "displaced anger and frustration of passengers" expressed towards women because they do not have the "status shield" provided by a higher position in the social hierarchy. The principal task for a man was to "maintain his identity as a man in a 'woman's occupation' and occasionally to cope with tough passengers 'for' female flight attendants" (ibid., p. 171). Hochschild shows that men and women receive different emotional treatment on account of their different social positions. High-status people tended to "enjoy the privilege of having their feelings noticed and considered important". Low-status categories, on the other hand—"women, people of color, children—lack a status shield against poorer treatment of their feelings" (ibid., pp. 172, 174). Women flight attendants also had to deal with resistance to their authority, whereas the men were usually seen as authority figures even if gay. All of these insights raise interesting points of similarity to and difference from the job of prostitution, particularly the different experience that the women and men in prostitution might have when both are used by male clients.

The most interesting similarity of all is Hochschild's understanding that the female flight attendant's workplace difficulties, in terms of being treated with decent respect, stemmed from the fact that she was seen to "symbolise Woman".

> they are not simply women in the biological sense. They are also a highly visible distillation of middle-class American notions of femininity. They symbolise Woman. Insofar as the category "female" is mentally associated with having less status and authority, female flight attendants are more readily classified as "really" female than other females are. And as a result their emotional lives are even less protected by the status shield. [ibid., p. 175]

Flight attendants were expected to enact "two leading roles of Womanhood, wife and mother and glamorous career woman". If this was true of the job of flight attendant, one which was open to men as well as women, then it is much more likely to be true of prostitution in which men specifically seek women in yet another important female role: as sex objects. The problem of symbolising womanhood is taken to its extreme in prostitution, where a woman is seen, as Kate Millett puts it, simply as "cunt" (1975, p. 56). If symbolising womanhood means being treated as subordinate, this might explain why prostitution is such a particularly dangerous job for a woman, since it is the one in which the subordination of women is most clearly represented. One problematic result of having to symbolise woman was that it led some female flight attendants to "feel estranged from the role of woman they play for the company" (Hochschild, pp. 182–3). In fact some women experienced a "loss of sexual interest" and "preorgasmic problems", and also lost their liking for men. This is even more likely to be true for prostitution in which being used physically as a sex object is the job.

Prostitution as an equal contractual arrangement

The feminist political scientist Carole Pateman has challenged the rhetoric of prostitution as just a job like any other. She has concentrated her critique on the arguments of the contractarians. These male liberal theorists argue that prostitution can take the form of an equal contract between the parties. Pateman rejects the notion of the possibility of an equal contract for any kind of employment, let alone prostitution. Contractarians see contracts as compatible with equality, because they are entered into voluntarily between two free and equal parties. The basis of the contractarian argument, she explains, is that the employment contract is different from slavery because there is a sharp distinction between the sale of a slave (as a commodity or piece of property) and sale of a worker's labour power (a commodity external to himself, the owner). In this view, individuals own their labour power and stand in relation to their property in their body and capacities in the same relation as to their property as property owners.

Thus "abilities can 'acquire' an external relation to an individual, and can be treated as if they are property", so that in the employment contract the worker's whole person is not sold but only her labour power, an argument we saw being made by prostitutes' rights activists above (Pateman, 1988, pp. 146–7). The individual was seen as able to "contract out any of his pieces of property, including those from which he is constituted, without detriment to his self" (*ibid.*, p. 149). Pateman considers that socialists should understand very well that it is a fallacy that labour power can be separated from the person of the worker. It is an interesting anomaly that socialist feminists, who might be expected to be suspicious of the idea of an equal employment contract, sometimes seem to overlook the inequality involved in the prostitution "contract" (McLeod, 1982; Sullivan, 1994, 1995).

Some even argue that women in prostitution have power over their johns, as if prostitution were a quite distinct and free category of employment. Priscilla Alexander of COYOTE expresses this argument about the equality of the contract with useful clarity.

Prostitution ... involves an equation of sex with power: for the man/customer, the power consists of his ability to 'buy' access to any number of women; for the woman/prostitute, the power consists of her ability to set the terms of her sexuality, and to demand substantial payment for her time and skills. Thus, prostitution is one area in which women have traditionally and openly viewed sex as power. [Alexander, 1988a, p. 188]

It is surprising that prostituted women are seen to have such power. In other situations in which women find themselves alone with unknown men who expect to use them sexually, they are more likely to feel vulnerable. Payment does not make a difference since, as Pateman explains, employment, marriage and prostitution contracts create social relations of subordination, not equality. Workers, she says, are "paid to obey" (Pateman, 1988, p. 148).

Both socialists and feminists have been seduced into the acceptance of contract as a way forward, Pateman considers. Socialists are attracted to the idea of contract because it "suggests that contract capitalism can be replaced by contract socialism". Socialists mistakenly believe that the problem in employment lies in "exploitation" resulting from an unequal exchange, whereas in fact it lies in contract itself which creates subordination and allows exploitation to take place. Feminists are seduced by seeing an "anti-patriarchal argument in contract if women were recognised as owners of their bodies" (*ibid.*, pp. 152, 153).

When prostitution is defended by contractarians, Pateman points out, the prostitute is represented as an owner of property in her person who contracts out part of that property in the market. She is said to be able to "contract out use of her services without detriment to herself", and prostitution is said to be a trade that anyone could enter (*ibid.*, p. 191). But prostitution is not "mutual, pleasurable exchange of the use of bodies, but the unilateral use of a woman's body by a man in exchange for money", Pateman asserts. The sex industry is based upon, and reminds men and women of, the law of male sex-right (*ibid.*, p. 199). Men's demand is part of the contemporary expression of masculine sexuality.

The prostitution contract, though, is different because it is with a woman. The woman enters the contract often with another worker, not a capitalist. The prostitution contract is with the customer and not with an employer. The customer, Pateman considers, gains control of the prostitute in the same way that an employer does with a worker, but with one important difference. Whereas employers are generally happy to replace workers with machines because they are cheaper, the customer wants the body of a real live woman. In prostitution it is the body of the woman which is the subject of the contract.

Pateman goes on to consider what such use of the body might mean. In this respect she is clearly using the insights of radical feminism, since socialists, including socialist feminists, have not been eager to embrace an understanding of the significance of bodily experience. Pateman explains, "There is an integral relationship between the body and the self." As an example, she gives the use of sexually significant body parts as terms of abuse for women and for men. Identity is inseparable from the sexual construction of the self, she says (*ibid.*, pp. 206, 207). Thus:

> sale of women's bodies in the capitalist market involves sale of a self in a different manner, and in a more profound sense, than sale of the body of a male baseball player or sale of command over the use of the labour (body) of a wage slave. [*ibid.*, p. 207]

This is demonstrated in the defensive strategies used by prostituted women. Prostituted women have to distance themselves from what is happening to them because of the intimate connection between sexuality and sense of self. As Pateman points out, this is a problem for johns who do not want the prostitutes they use to distance themselves. The distancing undertaken by prostituted women impairs the satisfaction that johns expect to gain, their sense of mastery. Her conclusion is that "men gain public acknowledgement as women's sexual masters—that is what is wrong with prostitution" (*ibid.*, pp. 207, 208).

What characteristics does prostitution share with slavery?

The sense of mastery is a fundamental satisfaction of the slavemaster too, Orlando Patterson argues, and in this way prostitution has something very much in common with slavery. Patterson's *Slavery and Social Death* (1982) has provided inspiration for feminist thinking on prostitution. Though most feminist theorists would agree that prostitution in most of its contemporary forms does not constitute slavery, there are nonetheless significant ways in which it can be seen to resemble some of the elements of slavery. Patterson's work is useful because he provides a philosophy of slavery, explaining what the slavemaster sees in the slave and what the effects are for the enslaved. Prostitution does not usually conform to Patterson's definition of the extreme power and powerlessness of the master–slave relationship: "Slavery is one of the most extreme forms of the relation of domination, approaching the limits of total power from the viewpoint of the master, and of total powerlessness from the viewpoint of the slave" (ibid., p.1). However, there are ways in which the experience of prostituted women, even of so-called "free" prostituted women in Western countries, does seem to replicate the conditions of slave life. Patterson talks of slavery meaning "social death", in which the slave, "Alienated from all 'rights' or claims of birth ... ceased to belong in his own right to any legitimate social order. All slaves experienced, at the very least, a secular excommunication" (*ibid.*, p. 7). Prostituted women suffer a social excommunication arising from their work, which is surely unprecedented in other forms of work, at least in Western culture. As Kathleen Barry (1979) points out, one of the acknowledged practices of pimping and trafficking involves separating women from their connections, family and known locations so that they are entirely within the control of the pimp.

Patterson also talks of the way in which the bodies of slaves are marked to denote their status: "Masters all over the world used special rituals of enslavement upon first acquiring slaves: the symbolism of naming, of clothing, of hairstyle, of language and of body marks" (1982, p. 8). In the Americas branding was used for this purpose. Head shaving was used on slaves in Africa, China, highland Burma, amongst primitive Germanic peoples, the nineteenth-century Russians and many other peoples. The shorn head had a highly symbolic function representing "castration—loss of manliness, power and 'freedom'" (*ibid.*, pp. 59, 60). Moreover, slaves are given new names. "The Nootka of the northwest coast of America, the Icelanders, and the Kachin of highland Burma are all typical of peoples who took special delight in giving to female slaves names that demeaned both their status and their sex" (*ibid.*, pp. 54–5). Similarly, pimps rename women when they "turn them out" into prostitution. Historically, prostituted women have had clothing regulations enforced upon them, yellow hair or a particular colour of clothing, or clothing representing sexual availability.

Most significantly, in terms of analysing the similarities with prostitution, Patterson explains how the master–slave relationship served the purpose of enhancing the power and social status of the owner, rather than being about work that the slave could do and other obvious material benefits. He speaks of the master acquiring honour only insofar as the slave lost it.

> What was universal in the master–slave relationship was the strong sense of honor the experience of mastership generated, and conversely, the dishonoring of the slave condition. Many masters, especially among primitives, acquired slaves solely for this purpose. But even if the motivation was chiefly materialistic, the sense of honor was still enhanced. [*ibid.*, p. 11]

When he explains how the slave experienced this enhancement of the master, there are similarities with the way prostituted women speak of their experience of loss (*ibid.*, pp. 11–12). The counterpart of the master's sense of honour is the slave's experience of loss. The so-called servile personality is merely the outward expression of this loss of honour.

> What the captive or condemned person lost was the master's gain. The real sweetness of mastery for the slaveholder lay not immediately in profit, but in the lightening of the soul that comes with the realization that at one's feet is another human creature who lives and breathes only for one's self, as a surrogate for one's power, as a living embodiment of one's manhood and honor. [*ibid.*, p. 78]

Prostitution shares this characteristic with slavery.

Indeed, the function of prostitution in establishing the power of the john is an important element in distinguishing it from other forms of work. Pateman argues that this is the very essence of the job of prostitution. In using prostituted women, men establish their difference from and superiority to women. This constitutes the excitement of prostitution for males in contemplation. Hoigard and Finstad (1992) describe how johns in Oslo would drive for hours past street prostituted women, experiencing the excitement of imagining their use. They also explain that one of the pleasures of prostitution is the anticipation, often over a whole day, with which the men contemplate buying a woman. For some, just contemplating and looking at women available for their delight is sufficient satisfaction. They do not need to part with money to experience enhancement of their status. The power of men—or, as those theorists embarassed at attributing power to men directly would put it, masculinity—is created by establishing difference from its opposite. Manhood cannot exist without womanhood, freedom not without slavery. In such an equation, where one gains power by establishing the lack of power of the other, it is hard to see this as an equal exchange. What one gains, the other loses.

Patterson explains that cases of what he calls "transparent personalistic power", which share some characteristics with slavery do exist in some forms in advanced capitalist societies, such as the relations between many husbands (potentially all) and wives. Patterson compares, as Pateman does, the employment contract with the property component of slavery.

When one buys or hires a person's labor, by implication one purchases the person's body for the negotiated period. There is no such thing as a disembodied service, only the discreet willingness to suspend all disbelief in such disembodiment. [Patterson, 1982, p. 24]

The difference he identifies between slavery and employment is that "Non-slaves always possess some claims and powers themselves *vis-à-vis* their proprietor" (*ibid.*, p. 26).

Interestingly, Patterson suggests that slaveholding societies possess certain characteristics created by that practice. Household slaves in Ancient Greece, for instance, who performed child-care, helped create the arrogance, authoritarianism and timocratic nature of that culture. He says that some of the research on slavery, such as that on the Celebes Islands, suggests that tribes without slaves are more democratic and less authoritarian than slave-owning ones (*ibid.*, pp. 88, 85). Prostitution is so prevalent in contemporary societies that it is not commonly asked what characteristics the display of women to be bought is likely to encourage in a society. But it might be expected that prostitution would encourage the development of the characteristics of male dominance. The British ethicist Bob Brecher (1987) argues, from the perspective of moral philosophy, that the acceptance of reproductive surrogacy will create precisely a society in which people may own other people's bodies. He makes similar arguments for the damaging repercussions of pornography.

Patterson's comments on the way that slaves have to behave in the presence of the master, and the effect this has on their sense of self, also provide some clear analogies with the behaviour extracted by the prostitution "contract" and with the commercialisation of emotion, so typical of women's work, that Hochschild describes. He quotes the poet son of two runaway slaves, Paul Lawrence Dunbar.

> We wear the mask that grins and lies,
> It hides our cheeks and shades our eyes,
> This debt we pay to human guile:
> With torn and bleeding hearts we smile.
> [Patterson, 1982, p. 208]

Another way in which prostitution and slavery are related is in their history. The feminist historian Gerder Lerner, in *The Creation of Patriarchy* (1987), argues that prostitution has not always existed but is the result of the development of slave-holding. She does not share the fashionable view of pro-prostitution advocates that commercial prostitution derives from the practice of sacral or temple sexual practices in which women would engage in sex with men, but sees it as quite a separate phenomenon.

> It is likely that commerical prostitution derived directly from the enslavement of women and the consolidation and formation of classes. Military conquest led, in the third millennium BC, to the enslavement and sexual abuse of captive women. As slavery became an established institution, slave-owners rented out their female slaves as prostitutes, and some masters set up commercial brothels staffed by slaves. The ready availability of captive women for private sexual use and the need of kings and chiefs, frequently themselves usurpers of authority, to establish legitimacy by displaying their wealth in the form of servants and concubines led to the establishment of harems ... [Lerner, 1987, p. 133]

If prostitution did in fact originate in slavery, then it is not at all surprising that there are so many past and present parallels between them.

Julia O'Connell Davidson is a British feminist sociologist who has entered the debate on the similarities between prostitution and slavery. She argues that problems around issues of power, control and consent suggest that "prostitution fits neither slavery or wage labour and is a challenge for contemporary social theory" (Davidson, 1996, p. 182). It is, however, a challenge which contemporary social theory seems remarkably reluctant to take up. Davidson carried out an ethnographic study of a successful and independent white British prostitute, identified as a member of an elite group, her receptionists and "clients". The prostituted woman she studied is not a slave, in Davidson's opinion, because "she exercises more control over her working life than do a majority of workers" (ibid., p. 183). She is not powerless in relation to a john, having more experience than him whilst he is uncertain. Davidson argues that her tape-recordings of interactions, which document the nervous laughter of the john, suggest that Desiree is in control.

> This kind of client relies on Desiree to script the encounter and she can get such men in and out of the house in fifteen minutes ... but even when dealing with punters who regularly visit prostitutes, who are confident and who know exactly what they want, D's far greater sexual skill and knowledge allows her to exert some control over how much of her sexual labour she provides for a set fee. She is highly skilled at getting clients to come (and therefore to go) very quickly. [*ibid.*, p. 185]

Desiree, she says, "dictates the limits and terms of their interaction". Desiree is "far from simply the 'passive, inert, and open' object conjured up by, for example, Dworkin's ... feverish rhetoric". She is, in contrast, "As both dominatrix and 'straight' prostitute [performing] intensive and highly skilled emotional labour in exchange for the client's money" (*ibid.*, p. 187).

However, Davidson is firm about the negative side of prostitution. "Whether he is submissive, flattering or abusive, the client's treatment of the prostitute represents a denial of her subjectivity and humanity, and this process of denial both draws upon and reinforces profoundly misogynistic images of women" (*ibid.*, p. 189). She argues that, as well as paying for the sexual pleasure, physical labour and/or the making available of body parts, the john is effectively paying the prostituted woman to be a person who is not a person: "the essence of the transaction is that she is an object, not a subject, within it". Even the very privileged prostituted woman, Desiree, fulfils much of the definition that Patterson offers of slavery. She "becomes what Patterson ... might term 'socially dead' for the duration of each transaction, that is, a person without power, natality or honour". The prostituted woman, like the slave, cannot, "exercise claims, rights and powers over things or other persons", because she cannot make claims or demands of the john. She is without natality because her identity is concealed from the john, and without honour because her degraded status dissolves her entitlement to the protection and respect accorded to non-prostituted women. Prostitution is unique as a form of work, in Davidson's view, because the prostituted woman becomes "a person who is not a person, a slave who is not a slave, and a wage worker who is not a wage worker" (*ibid.*, pp. 191, 188).

Prostitution is a construction of male supremacy

Another aspect of prostitution which can be seen to mark it off from other areas of work is that it is a construction of male supremacy. Whereas other forms of work might be expected to survive the ending of male supremacy, prostitution would not. Christine Overall takes this position in her continuation of Pateman's question in *The Sexual Contract*, "What's Wrong with Prostitution?" She starts from the position that she cannot "respect" sex work. She seeks to discover why this is so and what makes prostitution worse than "cooking, secretarial service, or professional work?" (Overall, 1992, p. 709).

> Assuming that all labor now occurs within the constraints of capitalist exchange, I am asking the deliberately essentialist question of whether there is anything inherent in sex work as practiced today that renders it inevitably morally problematic in a way that other forms of work are not, and whether it is possible to change sex work in such a way as to overcome those moral objections. [*ibid.*, p. 710]

She explores the arguments most frequently made by feminists about why prostitution is different from other kinds of work, and finds most of them less than persuasive. She decides that prostitution is not distinguished by the bad working conditions attached to it, because these could be improved. She rejects the idea that women cannot "choose" prostitution and considers that women do, even from limited options, exercise choice. She considers the idea that women inevitably surrender power in prostitution, and suggests that unionisation might improve the power of the prostituted woman. Prostitution is not distinguished by the retailing of intimacy, she thinks, because other forms of work in contemporary American society, such as that of the psychotherapist, also contain this element, and the idea of sex without love does not have to be a problem. Unlike Pateman, she does not apply radical feminist insights which would allow her to consider the profound experience of the body involved in the retailing of intimacy involved in prostitution. She does not take account of the ways in which the self and sexuality are linked.

Overall asserts that the main distinction between prostitution and other forms of work lies in the fact that prostitution is the only form of labour constructed solely from the oppression of women. It is not equally open to men, and could not be; the very idea of prostitution, of men's imperative sexual urges and that women should be used in this way, is a political construction arising from male supremacy. This distinguishes prostitution from other forms of women's work such as child-care or housework or cooking, all of which can be performed by anyone and do not depend for their very existence upon a political system of oppression.

> In a culture where women's sexuality is used to sell, and women learn that sex is our primary asset, sex work is not and cannot be just a private business transaction, an exchange of benefits between equals, or an egalitarian trade. Like rape, sexual assault, sexual harassment, and incest, prostitution is inherently gendered, a component and manifestation of the patriarchal institution of heterosexuality. [*ibid.*, p. 721]

Women's "choice" to enter prostitution, then, is severely constrained: although women might have the freedom to choose their form of bondage, "we do not have the freedom to choose the institutions that shape our decisions and severely limit the options we have." Prostitution represents, says Overall, the archetypal sexual interaction of male supremacist North

American culture, "the willing, economically dependent, always available, sexually seductive and irresistible woman serves the needs of the virile, strong, aggressive male with an irrepressible sex drive who can buy the means for satisfying his desires" (*ibid.*, p. 722). This leads to her conclusion:

> Sex work is an inherently unequal practice defined by the intersection of capitalism and patriarchy. Prostitution epitomises men's dominance: it is a practice that is constructed by and reinforces male supremacy, which both creates and legitimises the 'needs' that prostitution appears to satisfy as well as it perpetuates the systems and practices that permit sex work to flourish under capitalism. What is bad about prostitution ... [resides] in capitalist patriarchy itself. [*ibid.*, p. 724]

This conclusion is proven, she considers, by the irreversibility of prostitution. Capitalist and patriarchal conditions create the sexual needs of men and the ways in which women fulfil them. Sexual equality in prostitution is therefore not attainable.

Laurie Shrage, in *Moral Dilemmas of Feminism* (1993), is critical of Overall's conclusion. Shrage takes a cultural relativist position; she argues that the idea that capitalist and patriarchal conditions are the cause of prostitution is disproved by the existence of the prostitution of women for men in situations where no such conditions exist. It is true that Overall's thesis applies only to situations where capitalism exists, whereas prostitution certainly exists in pre- and non-capitalist societies. This is the difficulty of seeking to fit prostitution into a predominantly socialist analysis. But Shrage does not convince at all in her examples of supposedly non-patriarchal conditions. One example is colonial Kenyan prostitution, in which working-class males working away from home use prostituted women who are classifed by Shrage and her source, historian Luise White, as "petty bourgeois".

In other words, commoditised sexual labour here is not the expression of class or social privilege, but the expression of

the context-specific needs of men transformed in the colonial
context from peasant sons to wage laborers, and the context-
specific needs of women transformed in the colonial context
from peasant daughters to petty-bourgeois entrepreneurs.
[*ibid.*, p. 108]

What Shrage fails to understand, and interestingly this is a
common mistake of socialist commentators, is that the
absence of class superiority on the part of the men using the
women in prostitution does not negate the hierarchy of gender.
The reduction of the relations of male supremacy to those of
class is mistaken and allows, in this case, a cultural relativist
account of prostitution which disappears the subordination of
women. Men's use of women in prostitution affirms their sex
class status as male and superior, whatever the social origins of
the women they use. The hierarchy of men over women is created and confirmed through prostitution.

Overall omits consideration of the profound experience of
the body that is involved in prostitution. Perhaps because she
starts from a socialist feminist perspective, she is unable to
countenance the way in which the sexual nature of prostitution distinguishes it from other work. This is a common limi-
tation of socialist feminist theorists who are chary of speaking
of matters of the body lest they stray into the forbidden
realms of essentialism. Carole Pateman, who combines a
socialist feminist tradition with a radical feminist understanding enriched by the knowledge engendered by working
against male sexual violence, is not so limited, and is able to
envisage the particular violation that prostitution constitutes
for the self of the prostituted woman.

A profound experience of the body

There is one significant way in which prostitution differs from
the vast majority of that which is usually accepted as work,
and this is in the profound involvement of the woman's body
and therefore her self. Bob Brecher asks us to consider
whether any remunerative activity should be considered as

work in a provocative article on the trade in kidneys for transplant. Brecher recognises that there are interesting comparisons between the kidney trade and prostitution, because the kidney trade concerns the body, as prostitution does, and raises questions about its inalienability. His perspective on the kidney trade is conveyed in the subtitle of his article, "the customer is always wrong". The customer is wrong because he/she is making a commodity out of other human beings. Brecher suggests that "Our moral concern ... needs to focus on the customer's actions rather than the seller's; and on the implications for larger questions of the considerations to which this gives rise" (1990, p. 120).

When a lively trade in kidneys through a private hospital in London was discovered in 1989, the British Prime Minister protested about the unacceptable nature of such an enterprise. Brecher points out the contradiction involved in such a protest, by a government so in favour of the free market and the creation of an "enterprise culture", at "people making use of their assets in such an enterprising way". Clearly, even for free-marketeers, there is an understanding that the market should have limits. Brecher asks, "What is it about selling a part of one's body that people consider so reprehensible?" Brecher suggests that some make a greater objection to the selling of kidneys than to the sale of blood or to prostitution, all forms of hiring out the body or parts of the body, because they see the sale of irreplaceable organs such as kidneys as leading to serious consequences. But, he responds, "it is entirely unclear that I am suffering more harm by selling a kidney than, for example, by renting out my body, especially with all the attendant risks of the latter" (ibid., pp. 120, 121). Brecher indicts the customer of these practices, arguing that he/she is responsible for the consequences such as premature ageing or death from cancer resulting from the unsafe employment practices that create consumer goods or profits.

What is required, however, is that we focus attention not on the seller—the victim—but on the customer. It is the customer, the generator of demand, who is always wrong in the sorts of transaction I have been discussing. The point about buying a pint of blood, or a kidney; renting someone's body for an hour or two; or living off other people's ill-health is that all these are forms of exploitation based on making a commodity of human beings. [*ibid.*, p. 122]

Brecher argues that those who object to kidney trafficking are "logically committed" to opposing "the sale of blood, renting of bodies, and physical exploitation of labour". The problem in all such cases is the "commoditisation of human beings". In this it resembles prostitution, certain forms of surrogacy, and page three of the British newspaper *The Sun*, which is devoted to women's naked breasts, in symbolising, partly constituting, and encouraging "a moral climate within which the commoditisation of human beings proceeds apace" (*ibid.*). He condemns the supporting cast behind the kidney trade, such as the doctors, owners of the private hospital, proponents of a market view of medicine, and the "ideologues of wealth", as well as the recipients. Similarly, of course, prostitution is supported by a cast who must share in blame and responsibility: politicians, credit-card agencies, corporations, property owners. Brecher concludes that outrage from free-marketeers at the kidney trade is the result of their recognition that such a trade shows up the defects of their ideology in an embarassingly obvious way. In fact, the sale of kidneys is not different from the sale of blood or prostitution, but serves to symbolise the "nature of all these transactions".

In prostitution, certain profound experiences of the body are implicated which make prostitution not just a job like any other. In *Sex Work on the Streets*, women interviewed by the authors spoke of the extreme precautions they take to ensure they are not impregnated by their abusers (McKeganey and Barnard, 1996). Some used two forms of contraception with clients. They spoke of the agonies of doubt if they became pregnant, and of the effect of this on their relationships with men they loved. The possibility of pregnancy should surely be seen as an unreasonable risk of paid work and throw the acceptability of that work into question. Outside prostitution, the possibility of pregnancy is treated with seriousness and some awe, yet prostituted women are expected to treat this as just part of the job. This is similar to the way in which prostituted women are expected, by the defenders of prostitution, to be able to deal with being used by prostitution abusers in ways which non-prostituted women find it difficult to imagine surviving. Profound experiences of the body, fraught with significant meanings in the cultures in which prostituted women live, are expected to be dealt with as simply part of the routine. Thus prostituted women are expected to be different from other women, perhaps born to it, or as a degraded class of persons suited to such work, less sensitive or deserving.

Socialist feminist theorists have generally taken the approach that concentrating too much on what is significant about women's experience of the body is essentialist and counterproductive. In this respect socialist feminists have taken a stance similar to that of liberal feminists, who have agued that women's sameness and not "difference" should be emphasised to make women worthy of "equal opportunities" with men who do not possess women's biology (MacKinnon, 1989). Socialist feminist campaigning has not tended to concentrate on bodily matters, save in the area of demanding a woman's right to "choose" abortion. But some radical feminists too have been most concerned to avoid the suspicion of essentialism, the attribution of characteristics of women's behaviour or status to their biology.

Christine Delphy and Diana Leonard, for instance, argue in *Familiar Exploitation* (1992) that feminists have erred in giving too much attention to sexuality and reproduction in the oppression of women.

Some continue the error by arguing that women's oppression is specific and special in that it concerns "the body"; which is often accompanied by the assertion that men's power is especially, overwhelmingly, concerned with the sexual and

reproductive use and abuse of women ... But the fact that
women's oppression concerns their bodies, or that women's
whole identity becomes tied up in being a mother, is not specific to women's oppression only. The oppression of wage
workers also concerns their bodies and their whole personalities. Men and women employees' bodies are used and exhaust-
ed and maimed and objectified ... [Delphy and Leonard,
1992, p. 22]

Of course men's and women's bodies are affected by the work
they do, but it is important to notice the specificity of the particular use of the body involved in prostitution. Sexuality,
identity, sense of self, are all damaged in being used sexually.
Bricklaying does not have the same consequences. There is a
determination here not to notice the specific bodily experience
of women. Delphy and Leonard are unusual radical feminists
in downplaying the significance of such experience.

With the development of a fashion for post-modernism
amongst many erstwhile socialist feminist thinkers in the
1980s, there has been a renewed attack on the possibility of
taking the body seriously. In theory, post-modern and queer
theorists have professed a real interest in and intellectual
excitement about the body. There has been a proliferation of
books and university courses and research centres focused,
apparently, on the body. Renate Klein, in a useful critique of
this trend entitled "(Dead) Bodies Floating in Cyberspace:
Post-modernism and the Dismemberment of Women",
explains that she wondered whether to be delighted at this
new concentration on the body until she read the new body
writings. She discovered that these writers wrote of the body
in ways which should be of concern to feminists who wanted
to stress the importance of women's lived experience in the
body and the inseparability of the body and the self.

The bodies I have been reading about in post-modern feminist
writings do not breathe, do not laugh, and have no heart.
They are "constructed" and "refigured". They are written

about in the third person: " ... human bodies have the wonderful ability to ... produce fragmentation, fracturings, dislo-
cations ..." ... Women are absent and although speaking of
"embodiment" and "corporeality", much of the post-modern
feminist discussion perceives a body as a "thing" that can be
used by its "owner" and others ... As texts, bodies are
objects, (thinking) fragments, or surfaces, to be inscribed,
marked, written on, written. [Klein, 1996, p. 349]

Klein points out that this post-modern approach has been
used in relation to prostitution too, as in Shannon Bell's
Reading, Writing and Rewriting the Prostitute's Body (1994).
The title should inform us before we read this book that it is
not concerned with the actual meaning of prostitution for real
live women's bodies, but only for the "body" in and as a text.
Klein characterises Bell as conceptualising the "flesh-and-blood
female body" as an object, with the result that her project
"rewriting the prostitute body" consists of putting a positive
construction on prostitution by discussing prostituted women
"... inscrib[ing] their own bodies in divers and contradictory
ways ...'". Klein sees this approach as posing serious dangers
for women. She concludes: "Maintaining that women *are* Our
bodies—Ourselves, that being human equals integrity of
mind/body/spirit, that we have a humanity that must not be
violated, is feminism's heresy of the 90s. But it is crucial for
survival" (*ibid.*, pp. 355, 357).

The implications of accepting prostitution as work
There has been considerable movement towards the acceptance of prostitution as just work like any other in some areas
of Australia, particularly Victoria and the Australian Capital
Territory. In these two areas, for instance, in which brothel
prostitution has been legalised and regulated, the Australian
Liquor, Hospitality and Miscellaneous Workers' Union has
been signing up brothel prostituted women. When this was
announced with loud fanfares in the media in early 1996, it
was represented as a world first for a traditional malestream

union to target prostituted women. The union argues that "sex work" is just a job like any other. Ruth Frenzell from the union declared that the only difference between "sex workers" and their other members, such as zookeepers and child-care workers, was negative community attitudes (ABC, Radio National, 1996).

The union is seeking an "award" for sex workers. This means that workers would have their minimum wages and conditions laid down by a tribunal, including job security and training. There is no doubt that the current situation of brothel prostituted women is one of unprotected exploitation. Brothel owners say they are not employers, they just rent rooms to private contractors. Thus they pay no retainers. The prostituted women get paid only per john, and could spend ten hours waiting in the brothel and earn nothing. They get no sick pay, maternity pay, lunch hours. An award would gain the recognition that the brothel owners are employers, the women would get benefits and conditions available to other workers, and they would get a minimum rate per hour to recognise the work they put in by being on the premises, submitting to sexual objectification by potential johns even if they do not get used for sex.

One irony of the situation is demonstrated by the title of a radio programme in which these issues were discussed in Australia. It was called "You Can Touch Me. I'm Part of the Union" (*ibid.*). This shows how the recognition of prostitution as just a job like any other undermines the demands of other women union members, who are precisely arguing "You Can't Touch Me. I'm Part of the Union" in respect to sexual harassment. Prostituted women are being paid to receive exactly the treatment as sexual objects that other women workers are seeking to abolish. Indeed, the difficulties likely to be experienced by brothel prostituted women in establishing their right not to be touched in sexual harassment extraneous to their "contract" are considerable. It would be interesting to know whether the union will sue the employer on behalf of prostituted women who experience unwanted touch—johns who grab their breasts—and whether the employers will put in place policies against harassment. To provide a safe working environment, the union would need to insist on AIDS and STD testing all johns. Such measures to protect the prostituted women from terrible forms of abuse would be likely to make the men's use of women feel less exciting and spontaneous.

The acceptance of tabletop dancing as "just work" is already placing an obstacle in the path of women's equal opportunities in Melbourne. Tabletop clubs, unlike brothels, are licensed for the sale of alcohol, and offer better possibilities for men to socialise with each other. Two clubs in Melbourne are now competing with each other to attract businessmen to have lunch and hold meetings on their premises. Presently a network of professional men, "including judges, radio executives and managers in the finance sector do this" (Blake, 1996, p. B3).

> Both clubs have Board Rooms for corporate functions. The room at the Men's Gallery has a long board table, a white board and a lectern. They can even provide pens and notepaper. Dancing girls are supplied on request.
>
> The corporate board room at Goldfingers caters for meetings of about twenty men in a more informal setting. Peanuts, girls, cocktails. After-work gatherings are also encouraged in the Cigar Bar, an enormously popular concept in the United States ... [*ibid.*]

One customer explains, "A lot of business gets done in here. It's very good for business and it just happens to be a place where women take their clothes off" (*ibid.*). Women can be paid to strip naked "at point blank range" and present their genitals and anuses for men to gaze into. Suburban pubs are introducing "lap-dancing nights and topless lunch hours".

The efforts of feminists and individual women to break open the executive culture, so that women may reap the benefits currently available only to men, are likely to be entirely superseded by the culture of sexualised male dominance for middle-class males being developed by the sex industry. According to a survey of 124 of Australia's largest companies, the proportion of women senior managers has declined from 2.5 per cent in 1984 to 1.3 per cent in 1992 (Sinclair, 1994). Amanda Sinclair has studied the reasons why the Australian executive culture is so hostile to women. She suggests that the systematic exclusion of women may be related to the fact that executive culture is "the stage on which constructs of identity, masculinity and leadership are being established and asserted through traditional managerial scripts and masculine discourses" (*ibid.*, p. 6). The sex club is a very masculine "discourse" indeed, and women managers are unlikely to take part in the business decisions and camaraderie that their male counterparts are shaping out of the sexual exploitation of a group of poorer and more vulnerable women.

Prostitution is not just a job like any other

Prostitution is distinguished from other kinds of "work" in many crucial respects. It is a form of work which arises from a particular system of political oppression—male supremacy—and is unthinkable outside the political construction of what it is to be a man or a woman, and what sex is understood to be, in that system. Prostitution performs the function within that political system of creating "manhood", raising men's status by enabling them to use the subordinate class of women specifically for what they are seen to represent and be "for" in that system. Woman is used as "cunt" in a system in which it is precisely the possession of a "cunt" that places her in a subordinate class. Andrea Dworkin explains that in the sex class system women are subordinated as a class, based upon their biological sex and through their sexuality. As members of the same sex class, women experience a common condition. They are: "Subordinate to men, sexually colonised in a sexual system of dominance and submission, denied rights on the basis of sex, historically chattel, generally considered biologically inferior, confined to sex and reproduction ..." (Dworkin,

1983, p. 221). The result of categorisation as a member of this class is that "Women are defined, valued, judged, in one way only: as women—that is, with sex organs that must be used ... Women are born into the labor pool specific to women: the labor is sex" (*ibid.*, p. 64).

Prostitution uses that part of a woman's body which signifies her second-class status, and it is this that is likely to provide its excitement to the men whose superior status is created by such use. It is hard to imagine another form of work that is similar, in which the sign of a social group's inferior status is the centre and meaning of the "work". There are other kinds of service work in which the status of individual customers can be enhanced by being serviced by subordinates. It is, however, peculiar to prostitution that the servicing and status enhancement are organised according to a strict structural hierarchy, that between the ruling class of men and the subordinate class of women. It is this political significance of prostitution that causes it to be a job which endangers women's lives, and causes the physical and emotional damage that women suffer from abusive johns, pimps, male passers-by. It is hard to think of another job in which workers are required to receive the contempt appropriate to an inferior position in the political hierarchy to the extent of possible brutal death. It is in the area of the experience of the body, however, that prostitution is most sharply distinguished. What is done to women's bodies in the ordinary acts of prostitution, abuse so threatening that prostituted women must dissociate to survive, forms the subject of the next two chapters on the sex of prostitution and sexual violence.

CHAPTER 7

'why cars? who's driving?'
prostitution and the
theorising of sexuality

Post-Lacan, actually post-Foucault, it has
become customary to affirm that sexuality is
socially constructed. Seldom specified is what,
socially, it is constructed of, far less who does
the constructing or how, when, or where ...

"Constructed" seems to mean influenced
by, directed, channeled, as a highway constructs traffic patterns. Not: Why cars? Who's
driving? [MacKinnon, 1989, p. 131]

The key to understanding prostitution lies
in the theorising of sexuality. Prostitutes' rights organisations
and feminist academics who have adopted their arguments
call the activity that men perform on and in the bodies of
prostituted women "just sex". In this they agree with the
wisdom of christian divines, pornographers, philosophers,
and more recently, sexologists, the scientists of sex. But in
order to represent prostitution as "just sex", they have to
regard the "sex" of prostitution as a natural essence of sexuality and deliberately avoid noticing the body of feminist
theory that has developed over the last quarter-century which
casts grave doubt upon the naturalness of the sex of male
supremacy. In this chapter I shall consider the sort of theorising of sexuality which has allowed the cheerful acceptance of
the sex of prostitution as "just sex" by sexual liberals. I shall
contrast this with the critical perspective of radical feminist

theorists, who place the "sex" of prostitution within a broader analysis of the role of sexuality in constructing men's power in the political system of male supremacy.

In the nineteenth and early twentieth centuries sexologists had an essentialist approach to sexuality, believing that men's imperative sexual urges were biologically inevitable, and that women were possessed of little sexual enthusiasm by nature (Acton, 1987a, b). Though they may have lamented men's use of women in prostitution, they saw it as a natural result of men's lack of alternative outlets caused by late marriage and the expectation of premarital chastity for women. Later, in the "sexual revolutions" of the 1920s and 1960s, "progressive" sexologists expressed their belief that prostitution would die out as the result of women's greater enthusiasm to service men's sexual interests (Russell, 1972; Comfort, 1979). Men's sexual urges and practices were seen as natural, and the success of the "sexual revolutions" was to be judged by the zeal with which women satisfied these natural desires. In the 1950s and 1960s, however, radical sociologists questioned the whole idea that sexual practices, or even the experience of sexual pleasure, were based upon biology. They developed social constructionist explanations of these "natural" facts. Symbolic interactionists were ruthlessly social constructionist long before post-structuralism became fashionable in the late 1970s. Then Lacanians and Foucauldians came to be seen as the ultimate social constructionists. It was no longer possible to talk about "sexuality"; only "sexualities". These approaches, though differing greatly over the importance they attribute to biology in explaining sexuality, have something very much in common. They explain sexual practice and sexual feelings with no reference to the power relationship between the sexes.

Feminist theorists pointed out that radical social constructionism created a great mystery. Catharine MacKinnon asks, "Why cars? Who's driving?": what forces were at work shaping the social construction of sexuality? (1989, p. 131). Feminist theorists sought to understand who and what was constructing sexuality, and in whose interests. Maybe it was not such a great mystery after all.

Essentialism

Sexology, the "science of sex", developed in the late nine-teenth century. It was built upon a belief in the naturalness of a sexual drive or instinct. August Forel, one of the founding fathers of sexology, describes the "sexual appetite" in non-human animals:

> The desire to procreate dominates everything. A single plea-sure, a single desire, a single passion lays hold of the organism and urges it toward the individual of the opposite sex, and to become united with it in intimate contact and penetration. It is as if the nervous system or the whole organism felt as if it had for the moment become a germinal cell, so powerful is the desire to unite with the other sex. [Forel, n.d., p. 73]

In human animals too "the sexual passion intoxicates for the moment all the senses. In his sexual rut even man is domi-nated as by a magic influence, and for the time he sees the world only under the aspect inspired by this influence" (*ibid.*, p. 75). Forel's picture of the natural form of what he calls "sexual desire" in man is very well suited to the use of women in prostitution.

> Man represents the active element in sexual union, and in him the sexual appetite, or desire for coitus, is at first the stronger. This desire develops spontaneously, and the role of fecunda-tor represents the principal male activity. This appetite pow-erfully affects the male mind, although sexual life plays a less important part in him than in the female. [*ibid.*, p. 77]

Moreover, in Forel's world, men were naturally possessed of a "desire for change" which led to polygamy and prostitution (*ibid.*, p. 83).

The sexual appetite in woman was rather different. Forel,

like many sexologists, was convinced that women were devoid of such appetite. In a "considerable number" he observed, the sexual appetite was "completely absent". Where it did appear, it was likely to take the form of emotional submission.

> Her smaller stature and strength, together with her passive role in coitus, explain why she aspires to a strong male support. This is simply a question of natural phylogenetic adaptation. This is why a young girl sighs for a courageous, strong and enterprising man, who is superior to her, whom she is obliged to respect, and in whose arms she feels secure. [*ibid.*, p. 93]

Freud is another sexologist of the period who embraced the idea of the imperative nature of male sexual urges. His concept has been called by critics the "hydraulic" or "drive-reduction" model of sexuality. This assumed a powerful natural sexual instinct which pressed against the bonds of social control. Radical social constructionist of sex in the 1960s rejected this notion. Sociologists John Gagnon and William Simon identify the legacy of Freud as the view that sex is a dark, anarchic, "innate and dangerous instinct" (1974, p. 10). They argue that this idea was adopted uncritically by the early sociologists of sex, such as Kinsey. They describe how sex came to acquire a revolutionary lustre in the post-Freudian period. The seventeenth-century image of the indvidual against the state was translated by Romantic tradition into a contest between the individual and his culture. The Hobbesian view of man as possessed of natural instincts struggling against imposed constraint was moved by Freud to the arena of the mind, sexuality, and the parent–child contract. Thus in Freud's politics, "sexual instinct presses against cultural controls ... as sociocultural forces in the form of parents (leviathan writ large) block, shape, and organise the sexual drive and convert it ..." (*ibid.*, p. 11).

Social construction

Gagnon and Simon are radically social constructionist in their approach. They are radical in their questioning of the natural-ness of the sexual urge. They suggest that sexual feelings themselves are not natural but constructed: "The very experi-ence of sexual excitement that seems to originate from hidden internal sources is in fact a learned process and it is only our insistence on the myth of naturalness that hides these social components from us" (*ibid.*, p. 9). They argue that a "sexual script" has to be learnt before the potential for sexual activity could ever be realised. They assert that coitus itself, the sup-posedly most natural of sexual acts, usually unquestioned as what "sex" is, in fact requires complex learning to be per-formed at all. It "involves a vast array of human learning and the coordination of physiological, psychological, and social elements", and is the "outcome of a complex psychosocial process of development" (*ibid.*). Such an approach would cer-tainly suggest that men's use of women in prostitution is not "natural" or just sex. Coitus may take place, itself the result of complex sexual scripting, but much more needs to be explained: how men gain the idea that they may buy and use a strange woman's body in this way, and how they have learnt that such use is erotically exciting. These male sociologists, however, do not ask the questions that are interesting to fem-inists, such as why the sexual script should take the form of imperative male urges and male-dominant coitus. They have no interest in the "political" construction of sexuality, the system of power relationships that mould a potential for sexual activity into the form considered "normal" under male supremacy.

This mystery as to the origins of the social construction of sexuality deepened in the 1970s as the result of the work of a generation of gay male sociologists of sex. Following the ideas of Michel Foucault, gay sociologists such as Jeffrey Weeks and Ken Plummer are convinced that sexuality is socially con-structed, but their approaches to sexuality contain precisely the elements of essentialism that Gagnon and Simon identify in the work of the followers of Freud. Though they are apparently great believers in social constructionism, they seem to rely on the idea of sex as dangerous instinct. Weeks states, for instance, that "social categories of sex are imposed upon a sexual flux, a ceaseless turmoil of sexual possibilities of the body", and speaks of "the dangers of desire, many-sided, polymorphous, malleable but disruptive" (1985, pp. 176, 179). Freud's legacy is obviously flourishing in gay male theory in the 1980s and 1990s. This is clear in the title of Weeks's book *Sexuality and its Discontents*, which refers to Freud's *Civilisation and its Discontents*. The chapter from which the above insights come is entitled "Dangerous Desires." It is quite true that the exercise of contemporary male sexuality holds many dangers for women, of rape and sexual abuse, even sexual murder. The romanticising of the dangerousness of "sexuality" by such theorists, however, seems to reify a historically specific and politically constructed form of sexual practice as simply what sex is.

The sexual politics of meaninglessness: symbolic interactionism and post-structuralism

Jeffrey Weeks is a British historical sociologist. In *Sexuality and its Discontents* (1985) he does not ask about the origins of the social construction of sexuality, because the work of Foucault renders such considerations invalid. No source could be sought because it was much too complicated.

> The organisation of sex does not operate through a single strategy of control. On the contrary, power relations addressing sexuality operate through a multitude of practices and of apparatuses (medicine, psychology, education, the law), each of which has its specific structures of regulation. [*ibid.*, p. 181]

Weeks is determinedly vague about what "sources shape sexual patterns". He suggests, "kinship and family systems", "economic and social changes", "changing forms of social regulation", "political context", "cultures of resistance". As a gay theorist, he is most impressed with the last category, which includes the male gay liberation movement and constitutes the "rock on which many forms of sexual regulation have crashed" (*ibid.*, p. 179). He does not include male power as one of the shaping sources.

Weeks states unequivocally that there is no point in searching for a unifying way of understanding sexuality. The new "politics of desire ... undermines any idea that accepted social definitions of sexuality reflect a deeper reality or truth" (*ibid.*, p. 176). This insight, he explains, comes from the work of Foucault.

> "Sexuality" plays upon, ideologically constructs and unifies, as Foucault has suggested, "bodies, organs, somatic localisations, functions, anatomo-physiological systems, sensations and pleasures ..." which have no intrinsic unity or "laws" of their own. The body is a site for the deployment of power relations ... [*ibid.*, p. 177]

But the question of "whose power" is deemed inappropriate here. This vagueness has not been without its critics: thus Anthony Giddens comments, "What Foucault terms power—that 'power' which mysteriously does things of its own volition—was in some fundamental respects gender power" (1992, p. 171). Since, for Weeks, there are so many different sources, "The corollary is that many forms of sexuality result, differentiated along lines of class, generations, geography, religion, nationality, ethnic and racial groupings. There are sexualities, not a single sexuality" (Weeks, 1985, p. 179). Weeks is an exponent of radical sexual pluralism.

Weeks writes in a time when feminist analyses of sexuality have been influential. The adoption of the radical pluralist approach with its determined focus on "sexualities" and rejection of unifying explanations, is a challenge to this influence. British feminist sociologists Sheila Allen and Diana Leonard muse on the retreat from recognising the importance of feminist approaches in their account of the 1994 conference of the

British Sociological Association. The theme of "sexuality" was transformed into "sexualities". This may, they consider,

> indicate an approach to sociology more broadly in which the very fact of difference justifies the impossibility of any gener-alisable theoretical statements or political practice ... Thus it appears that in much of the recent research on sexuality, sexual practice has somehow become detached from gender— or to have superseded it. [Allen and Leonard, 1996, p. 26]

This trend could be explained by "exploring the impact of financial support for AIDS research, influences of gay and men's studies and growth of queer theory" (*ibid.*, p. 31; see also Jeffreys, 1994). The "sexualities" approach conveniently disallows any question of whose power is being "deployed" in a Foucauldian anaysis. "Sexuality" becomes naturalised and individualised into the feelings and practices of black or white, working-class or middle-class, male or female, hetero-sexual or homosexual or bisexual, paedophile or sado-masochist, transsexual or transvestite, "sexualities". The "powers" of repressive state apparatuses and economic sys-tems, or any of the other numerous factors occasionally men-tioned, "play" upon and regulate the way these "sexualities" are expressed; but the similarities between them and how they come to exist, let alone the question of how they might relate to male supremacy, is not seen as relevant.

Another British gay male sociologist who takes a symbolic interactionist approach to sexuality also embaces the politics of meaninglessness. Ken Plummer writes of the "Culture of Sexual Storytelling". He says there can be no "Grand Conclusion" because "in the late modern period such Grand Stories are no longer possible". There are only "fragments of stories" left, and the "all too tempting desire to place them into a coherent and totalising narrative structure", i.e. to seek meaning, must be resisted (Plummer, 1996, p. 50). Plummer is a symbolic interactionist who has adopted post-structuralist language and ideas. British feminist sociologists Allen and

Leonard criticise symbolic interactionism for being counter-theoretical and allowing no relation of individual events or "stories" to their social context. In the late 1960s and 1970s, they say, it became fashionable "to counter abstracted theory by concentrating on the situation, without placing the directly observed or experienced relations of individuals into a framework capable of explaining or understanding them" (Allen and Leonard, 1996, p. 28). The problem of social theory with no concept of society, as represented in symbolic interactionism, has been continued, they suggest, with work that takes a post-structuralist or post-modernist perspective.

Where definite forces of construction are recognised in recent gay theory of sexuality, these may determinedly ignore the power relations between men and women. David Evans, in theorising the *Sexual Citizenship* of homosexual men and other sexual minorities, is critical of the vagueness of symbolic interactionism, for instance. He takes a materialist Marxist approach, and asks of the sexual script theory of Gagnon and Simon:

> Why are some scripts available and not others? In whose interests are particular scripts? How do they represent and reproduce existing power relations? Are their effects universal ... Are scripts available and negotiated solutions dependent upon the relativities of material power and citizenship status? These are some of the questions left unanswered by symbolic interactionism. [Evans, 1993, p. 31]

These are all very good questions. But Evans is a rather pure Marxist whose understanding, even of sexuality, turns out to be uncontaminated by feminist insights. He explains that there is a need to "establish the material contexts within which sexual discourses and scripts occur; those of capital, class and the state" (*ibid.*, p. 32). It is remarkable that a theorist who references much feminist theory in his work can manage to avoid noticing that sexuality might be constructed out of the power relationship between men and women, but he does. Considering the lengths to which some male theorists will go to ignore the role of male dominance in constructing sexuality, it is, perhaps, not surprising that radical feminist analyses of prostitution which start from here have fallen on stony ground. It is hard to understand prostitution when relying on theory that is impossibly vague, or ignores the significance of there being "men" and "women" involved in sex.

Radical feminism

The radical feminist theorist of sexuality Catharine Mac-Kinnon explains that those who see themselves as progressive and on the left are likely to subscribe to the notion that sexuality is socially constructed, particularly those who follow the masters of post-modernism, but they fail to ask the crucial question of what does the constructing and for what purpose.

Feminist theory of sexuality is social constructionist too. In the work of those theorists who have adopted male gay analyses, post-modernism and Foucault, such as the American proponent of sadomasochism, Gayle Rubin (1993), this social constructionism can share in the mysteriousness that we have highlighted above. Radical feminism, though, does offer explanations of what forces are constructing sexuality and for what purposes. Stevi Jackson is a British feminist sociologist of sex who has been influential in the feminist assault upon essentialist sociological and sexological understandings of sexuality. She developed the social constructionist framework in a feminist direction by showing that it is the organisation of male power which dictates the direction of this social learning. She explains the difference between "sex" identified as sexual activity, and "sexuality", a term used by sociologists and feminist theorists to describe that system of social meanings within which sexual behaviour is learnt, understood and practised. She defines sexuality as "not just ... genital activity, but ... all the attitudes, values, beliefs and behaviours which might be seen to have some sexual significance in our society" (Jackson, 1978, p. 3). Her critique of those theorists who have treated sex as natural provides a good rationale for criticising those theorists who represent the sex of prostitution as natural in the present.

> Sexual behaviour is social behaviour; it is not just the consummation of some biological drive. Heterosexual sexuality involves at the very least a social relationship between two people, and the pattern of that relationship arises out of the larger socio-cultural context. [*ibid.*, p. 2]

As Jackson explains, feminist theorists started their enquiry into the social construction of sexuality from their concern about the power relations that are so clear in heterosexual sex; they "began by questioning the relations of dominance and submission inscribed in conventional heterosexual practice". People learn to be sexual within "a society in which 'real sex' is defined as a quintessentially heterosexual act, vaginal intercourse, and in which sexual activity is thought of in terms of an active subject and passive object" (Jackson, 1996a, pp. 25, 23).

Fundamental to radical feminist approaches is the understanding that members of two unequal political categories, "men" and "women", are involved in dominant heterosexuality. According to radical feminist theory such as that of Monique Wittig (1992), "men" and "women" are political categories similar to those of class. The category "men" is the ruling class and can exist only in relation to its opposite, "women". The idea of "men" does not make sense without "women". The Australian sociologist Robert Connell expresses this idea: "The categories 'male' and 'female' are not categories of social life and sexual politics; the categories 'men' and 'women' are" (1995, p. 137). In heterosex these two political categories meet in a potentially intimate activity which involves the very organs which represent the status category of the participants. As many feminist and profeminist theorists point out, this "sex" is likely to be the activity most constructive of the category "men". This makes sexuality fundamentally constructive of sexual politics, as it is fundamentally constructed by sexual politics.

Catharine MacKinnon actually defines a feminist theory of
sexuality specifically as one which recognises that sexuality is
"a social construct of male power defined by men, forced on
women, and constitutive of the meaning of gender" (1989,
p. 128). She criticises socialist, including socialist feminist,
thought for failing to have a theory that will explain the
oppression of women, and suggests an alternative perspective
which posits sexuality as the organising principle of male
supremacy. "Sexuality is to feminism", she argues, "what
work is to Marxism: that which is most one's own, yet most
taken away" (ibid., p. 3). Sexuality produces gender, creating
the political categories "women" and "men".

> The molding, direction, and expression of sexuality organises
> society into two sexes: women and men. This divison underlies
> the totality of social relations. Sexuality is the social process
> through which social relations of gender are created, organised,
> expressed, and directed, creating the social beings we know as
> women and men, as their relations create society" [ibid.].

She identifies sex, "that is, the sexuality of dominance and
submission", as "crucial, as fundamental, as on some level
definitive" in the process of subordinating women to men.
Male supremacy is distinguished from other forms of oppression by being sexualised, i.e. experienced as erotically exciting, as well as utilising sexuality to organise relations of
inequality between men and women in many other ways. As
MacKinnon explains: "Male dominance is sexual. Meaning:
men in particular, if not men alone, sexualise hierarchy;
gender is one." As a result, "The male sexual role ... centers
on aggressive intrusion on those with less power" (ibid., pp.
128, 127). According to MacKinnon, the genders of masculinity, male dominance, and femininity, female subordination, are constructed through the workings of the desire of
male supremacy, a desire which eroticises hierarchy.
   Sexuality is a force through which gender is moulded. The
desire of male supremacy, which eroticises objectification,

constantly recreates the inequality necessary to its satisfaction. MacKinnon's approach "reveals" this sexuality, "reduction of a person to a thing, to less than a human being", as "the dynamic of the inequality of the sexes" that is generally referred to politely as "sexual difference". What is called sexuality, she says, "is the dynamic of control by which male dominance ... eroticises and thus defines man and woman, gender identity and sexual pleasure. It is also that which maintains and defines male supremacy as a political system" (*ibid.*, pp. 127, 137). This kind of radical feminist analysis, which recognises sexuality as not only socially constructed but constructive of the political system of male supremacy, cannot regard the sex of prostitution as in any way natural or inevitable.

Equal opportunities feminism
Feminist accounts diverged radically in the 1980s. Whilst radical feminist theorists such as MacKinnon defined what was understood to be "sexuality" as male sexuality and attributed to it a fundamental role in maintaining male supremacy, sexual libertarian feminists took a very different approach. They decided that the problem with "sexuality" was one of equal opportunities (McLintock, 1992; Califia, 1994). Radical feminist theorists defined the supposed imperative nature of sexual urges and the shape that sexuality was supposed to take—objectifying, sadomasochistic, compulsive—as the results of male supremacist construction; but "sexual libertarian" feminists accepted this "sexuality" as natural and simply what sex is. The problem for women was getting access to it. Women had been repressed and unfairly excluded from the excitements that men were allowed. Women needed equal access to sexual goods. Unfortunately those sexual goods generally required the exploitation of *women's bodies*. Women's sexual freedom, like that of men, was based upon the right to use women in pornography and prostitution. Sexual libertarians demand access to the sexual privileges of men without recognising that those very privileges are constructed out of

men's ruling-class status and would not exist without a subordinate class of women.

It is this equal opportunities approach which is employed today by defenders of prostitution to argue that there is nothing wrong with prostitution except the unfortunate gender bias in the industry (Sullivan, 1994, 1995). It has been developed in reaction to the feminist challenge to pornography. Some pro-pornography feminists pursue the ascension of women to the status of sexual "subjects" as a crucial aspect of women's "sexual freedom". The identity and experience of the objects is carefully skirted over. Carole Vance, a prominent campaigner in Feminist Anti-Censorship Task Force, which was set up to oppose the anti-pornography ordinance proposed by Andrea Dworkin and Catharine MacKinnon, explains, "Feminism must insist that women are sexual subjects, sexual actors, sexual agents" (1984, p. 24).

Another pro-pornography feminist, Linda Williams (1989), also uses the language of subjecthood. She argues that hardcore pornography can be revolutionary. It can empower women as sexual subjects. "Feminists are beginning to recognise that the perverse sexuality of the 'other' can be crucial to the empowerment of women as sexual agents" (Williams, 1992, p. 234). Hard-core pornography allows the "sexual perversions" to come out into the open. The "sexual fantasies of 'perverse others'" can take their place "as *authoritative subjectivities*" and "sexual agents" (*ibid.*; my italics). If women are to inhabit "authoritative subjectivities", then authorityless objects must exist to enable the occupation of this superior position. These objects are unlikely to be heterosexual men. The objects in pornography are women, and it is the objectification of some women that will allow others to achieve subjecthood. Kathleen Lahey criticises the development of this "feminist" sexual liberalism incisively:

if the ability to engage in economic and sexual exploitation is the essence of the liberal bourgeois revolution, then women can only now be said to be emerging from feudalism ...

Women now can—and do—play the Marquis to our sisters ...
[Lahey, 1990, p. 200]

Female sexual liberals maintain that they are daring rebels
bravely challenging sexual conservatism for their right to
more "object-choices". The popular term for their rebelliousness presently is "trangression". This philosophy of sexuality
is ideally suited to the defence and maintenance of prostitution. Men's abuse of women in an institution set up to service
their interests is much harder to oppose when some feminists
are demanding the right to lord it as sexual subjects over
sexual objects too.

The radical feminist theorist Susanne Kappeler explains
that "feminist" sexual liberalism is simply an attempt by
women to join in the tradition of men's sexual liberalism. The
story of sexual liberalism, she says, tells of men's aspiration
towards a masculine freedom presaged upon women's subordination. She explains that the origin of the word *liberal* lies
in the concept of that which is "fit for a gentleman", as in a
"liberal education". Men's sexual liberalism demands a
sexual freedom from the paternal state, which "is in fact the
license to continue to regard the other *as* sexual object, vehicle for the individual's sexual pleasure, and not to have to
recognise that other as also an individual subject" (Kappeler,
1990, p. 178). The sexuality of men's quest for sexual freedom is the sexuality of a subject realising his subjecthood by
turning another into an object. Kappeler demonstrates, by reference to the works of the great masters, how male philosophers and psychologists have always understood desire to
mean the desire for subjecthood over the object status of the
other. The "other" was always identified as "the feminine".
"What is required for an erotic relationship is thus not simply
a "neutral" subject and an attribute of difference in the Other,
but a virile subject and another who by her very nature *is*
Otherness" (Kappeler, 1995, p. 146).

Kappeler argues that, though those usually attributed the
status of sexual objects, i.e. socially subjugated groups, are

gradually loosening the chains of subordination and fretting at their status, nonetheless the subject/object theme remains whole and entire in masculine systems of thought on sexuality.

> Although questions of sexual consent—i.e., the consent of the other—are increasingly having to be muted due to the technical, legal emancipation of black people from slavery, of women from male custody, of peoples from colonial subjugation, conceptually the emancipation of the other has not yet impinged on the ideological structures of western thought, structures shaped by slavemasters, custodians of women, and colonial imperialists. [Kappeler, 1990, p. 178]

In sexual liberal thought, Kappeler explains, sexuality is "constructed as pertaining to the individual"; it is not understood as "sexual relations or sexual politics" (*ibid.*, p. 179). The result is that the theories of contemporary sexual libertarians are founded on the importance of the individual having access to as wide a range of "object-choices" as possible. Gay "gentlemen", then, in their sexual liberalism, are not concerned with, do not even notice, the oppressions of class or gender.

> What masquerades as a (male) challenge to compulsory heterosexuality is in fact a demand for increased choice on the part of the sexual subject, the individual, the gentleman, choice from a wider range of desirable objects: not just women-objects, but also men-objects, and children-objects. [*ibid.*]

The result is an enthusiastic embrace of sexual consumerism by these "gentlemen", and women and children are invited to join in. One male proponent of this sexual liberalism who emphasises the importance of such choices is Jeffrey Weeks: "There exists a plurality of sexual desires, of potential ways of life, and of relationships. A radical sexual politics affirms a freedom to be able to choose between them" (1985, p. 210).

Old-fashioned gentlemanly sexual consumerism is here transformed into a "radical" politics of sexuality.

But, as Kappeler points out, this sexuality depends on the existence or creation of objects to be consumed if these consumers are to be satisfied:

> this pleasure so rigorously structured around object-choice, where the chosen object is a demoted subject, could not exist in a democracy of equals where everyone was fit to be a subject and consumer: there would be no one left to be chosen and consumed as object. [Kappeler, 1990, p. 180]

It is the sexual liberals, she says, who are in the forefront of the attempt to bury feminist insights to protect the gentlemen from this threat to their privileges (*ibid.*, p. 182).

So feminist perspectives on prostitution came to be divided. Where once, in the nineteenth century, feminists had been united in blaming men for the abuse of women in prostitution, at the end of the twentieth century there seems to be a feminist position that justifies prostitution and encourages its continued existence, as well as one that sees it as violence against women. In the theorising of sexuality that pertains to sexual liberalism there is considerable reluctance to analyse the plight of the objects, to observe critically the nitty-gritty of what happens in prostitution, the sex. In the next chapter I shall examine the sex of prostitution in some detail.

CHAPTER 8
prostitution as "sex"

... a person turning off her emotions, being
psychically somewhere else while someone
who despises her is making love to her.
[Summers, 1988, p. 118]

It is important to examine the sex of prosti-
tution critically. The idea proposed by some prostitutes' rights
campaigners and pro-prostitution theorists that the sex of
prostitution is simply "sex" has worrying implications for
women. Prostituted women themselves speak of dissociating
to survive, of the horror of experiencing the physical sensation of orgasm in prostitution when they are seeking to separate their selves from what is being done to their bodies. An
acceptance of what is being done to them as simply "sex"
normalises precisely the sex of male supremacy: the objectifying, dominating male sexual practice in which a woman's
body is used simply as an object irrespective of her wishes and
personhood. This is the form of sexual practice that has been
systematically criticised by feminist activists and theorists for
150 years. In *The Prostitution of Sexuality*, Kathleen Barry
describes the sex of prostitution thus: "When sex is objectified
and human beings are reduced to vehicles for acquiring it,
sexual domination enters into and is anchored in the body.
This is the foundation of prostitution and its normalization in
the prostitution of sexuality" (Barry, 1995, p. 26). This construction of sex in which oppression is carried into women's

bodies is not consonant with women's freedom. In this chapter I shall investigate exactly what happens in the "sex" of prostitution, what it means for the women who have this "sex" acted out upon them, what it means for the johns, and what it means for the struggle of feminists and women in general to create a sexuality of equality and respect.

Prostitution and male sexuality

One basic assumption of pro-prostitution ideology is that johns are just doing what comes naturally, acting out biologically created, imperative urges in the bodies of prostituted women. Sexologists who have sought an explanation for prostitution have concentrated on the women, since it was the women who were seen as acting abnormally. The sociologists of prostitution analysed the women's behaviour as deviant, but not the men's. Even feminist research into prostitution has neglected the johns, partly because access to the johns is difficult. This is particularly surprising since the sex of prostitution is so clearly male sexuality. The prostituted woman is not required to be anything but a receptacle in prostitution, though johns often like the women they use to simulate a sexual response. Prostitution can only be explained through an understanding of male sexuality. A feminist understanding of sexuality, as constructed by and constructing of male dominance, should make it difficult to see the men who use women in prostitution as simply acting out "natural" sexual urges. Indeed, as I shall argue, men's use of women in prostitution represents the model form of the sex of male supremacy.

Male sociologists of sex such as John Gagnon and William Simon (1974) argue that even the act of coitus requires social learning. It is reasonable, then, to expect the behaviour of the john to require complex learning processes. The john needs to experience himself as having sexual urges that require outlet. He needs to learn that he can use women in prostitution as an "outlet", and that such use is acceptable. He needs to learn to use another human being as an object on whom and in whom he can act out his urges in a way that makes her "desires" and pleasure, even her personhood, irrelevant. He needs to find such use of women exciting. Then he needs to find out how to access prostituted women's bodies and the customs involved in this practice. His "desire" to use women in prostitution, then, rather than being natural, is a political construction. Sexological and sociological literature does not usually take this approach, but seems to assume a biological need and an innate know-how on the part of men to use women in prostitution.

Little literature exists on the motivations of johns compared with that on prostituted women, because the men's motivation is considered to be self-evident; only the women are seen as acting unnaturally. In the literature that does exist, the commonest form of explanation clearly assumes the imperative nature of the male sexual urge and the naturalness of seeking outlets for it in the bodies of women who are paid for such use. Havelock Ellis devotes a whole chapter of *Sex in Relation to Society* (1946) to prostitution. But, following sexological tradition, most of his attention is directed to why women are prostitutes; very little is directed to the johns. Ellis explains the necessity of prostitution as arising from the contemporary requirement of chastity for women outside marriage and the phenomenon of late marriage which left single men with a lack of outlets. This suggests that he saw men's urges towards using women in prostitution as simply natural and imperative. Men needed sex, and without available women as outlets they would use prostituted women. Married johns required a particular explanation, since in theory they already had an outlet to hand. Their outlet was unavailable because their wives refused them; or they wanted variety; or they were "sexually perverted" and wanted to engage in acts that their wives would refuse, or they felt they could not inflict upon them (Ellis, 1946, pp. 184–6).

The sexologists Harry Benjamin and R. E. L. Masters suggest a range of explanations which relate to sexual frustration. This shows that they too believe in a sexual imperative that requires outlets. The johns need variety, they may be shy or insecure, handicapped or too old, they may have deviate urges which it would be dangerous to society to frustrate, they may be impotent, they may want to avoid impregnation or emotional involvement, they have no time or money for courtship, or find prostitutes simpler, safer and cheaper, they may be disabled or soldiers (Benjamin and Masters, 1965, p. 194). Benjamin and Masters reject the theories of psychoanalysts, such as Wilhelm Reich, which suggest that johns are psychosexually unhealthy. Since they suggest that 80 per cent of all men use prostituted women, and seem from their writings to have considerable familiarity with brothels themselves, the idea that johns are less than normal would not appeal.

Even some more recent researchers who identify themselves as feminists retain an approach which assumes the reasonableness and naturalness of men's sexual needs. Eileen McLeod's work on prostitution in Birmingham shows some sympathy with the idea that men have a right to satisfy their "needs", with no idea that these "needs" might be constructed or why women do not seem to have been endowed with them. She writes:

> prostitution does not provide an example of men enjoying an undifferentiated experience of dominance. This would be a crude denial of the ways in which men's emotional and sexual experience can be stultified. Male clients emerge largely as a result of the failure of marriage, cohabitation and conventional sex roles to cater for men's emotional and sexual needs. Encounters with prostitutes act to some degree as a palliative or source of refreshment ... [McLeod, 1982, p. 2]

All of these approaches assume that men's use of women in prostitution is simply "sex" and are to be explained by the various reasons for which these men find their usual sexual "outlets" unsuitable. They do not ask how the idea is constructed in the john's mind that finding and paying to use a woman he does not know as an object to masturbate in is a reasonable idea. They do not ask what is exciting about it.

The existence of a politically constructed male desire which is excited by objectification is necessary for prostitution to work.

But as Catharine MacKinnon explains, to question the idea of desire, to suggest that it is politically constructed, is not usually popular even with theorists of sexuality. She analyses male supremacist desire as the excitement of eroticised hierarchy.

> To list and analyze what seem to be the essential elements for male sexual arousal, what has to be there for the penis to work, seems faintly blasphemous, like a pornographer doing market research ... To suggest that the sexual might be continuous with something other than sex itself—something like politics—is seldom done, is treated as detumescent, even by feminists. It is as if sexuality comes from the stork. [MacKinnon, 1989, p. 130]

That which is understood to be sexual in male supremacist society is whatever "gives a man an erection". This turns out to be "Hierarchy, a constant creation of person/thing, top/bottom, dominance/subordination relations does" (*ibid.*, p. 137). Prostitution, from this perspective, rather than representing "natural" sex, provides an efficient way for men to achieve the excitement of eroticised hierarchy and objectification.

The feminist psychoanalyst Ethel Spector Person uses a similar idea to explain the phenomenon referred to as the high male sex drive, uncontrollable urges. She asks, "What so stokes male sexuality that clinicians are impressed by the force of sexuality?" and explains that it is not the result of biological instinct but of "the curious phenomenon by which sexuality consolidates and confirms gender". She, like many men's studies theorists influenced by psychoanalysis, considers that masculinity is "fragile" and needs therefore to be constantly reinforced by sexual acting out because this is the easiest way for men to reassure themselves of their masculine dominance.

"First, sexuality represents domination; witness the widespread rape, control, and transgressive fantasies among men. Consequently, anxiety about any threat to masculine power can be assuaged by sexual encounter." Another reason men feel the need to act out sexually is that they can only experience "dependency" through sex. For men, she says, "dependency needs can be disguised as sexual" (Person, 1980, p. 57).

John Stoltenberg is one of the founders of Men Against Pornography in New York and a theorist of male sexuality who has developed this idea of objectification to explain how it works to shore up masculinity. It is objectification, he argues, that is fundamental to the construction of what he calls "the male sex".

> The male sex is socially constructed. It is a political entity that flourishes only through acts of force and sexual terrorism. Apart from the global inferiorization and subordination of those who are defined as "nonmale", the idea of personal membership in the male sex class would have no recognizable meaning. [Stoltenberg, 1990, p. 38]

According to this analysis, sexual acting out is a prime way in which men can assure themselves of their membership in this male sex class. Like Catharine MacKinnon, Stoltenberg considers that sexuality creates gender rather than the other way around. "My point is that sexuality does not *have* a gender; it creates a gender" (*ibid.*, p. 40). The need to feel like a man can be realised through coitus.

> For many people, for instance, the act of fucking makes their sexual identity feel more real than it does at other times, and they can predict from experience that this feeling of greater certainty will last for at least a while after each time they fuck. [*ibid.*, p. 39]

A man's feeling that he wants to "fuck", the fabled male sex urge, can be explained through the need to reassert masculine dominance, rather than through biology: "the very idea of a male sexual identity produces sensation, produces the meaning of sensation, becomes the meaning of how one's body feels. ... The drive does not originate in the anatomy. The sensations derive from the idea." This reassertion of dominance comes from the process of objectification which is fundamental to the "fuck": "all male sexual objectifying originates in the common predicament of how to identify and feel real as a male in a male-supremacist culture" (*ibid*., pp. 38, 58).

Through this process of realising masculine dominance, the person who is "fucked" is made not a real person.

> Sexually objectifying a person makes them seem absent, not really "there" as an equally real self, whether or not the person is physically present. In this way, the one who is sexually objectifying interposes a distance between himself and the person he sexually objectifies; it is a gulf between someone who experiences himself as real and someone whom he experiences as not-real. [*ibid*., p. 54]

The act of using a woman in prostitution could be seen as the purest form of objectification. An unknown body which is paid for is likely to offer more effective gratification in this regard than a woman who is known and may intrude demands and make comments which might remind her user that she is a real person. The danger for women of this male practice is sexual violence, since "every act of sexual objectifying occurs on a continuum of dehumanization that promises male sexual violence at its far end" (*ibid*., p. 59).

Prostitution as "sex" for women

If prostitution can be seen as "just sex" for men, it is rather harder to understand how it could be seen as "just sex" for women. The johns, after all, have orgasms and experience "sexual pleasure", even if that is a particular political construction of what is pleasurable. Research on prostitution contains much straightforward repudiation from prostituted women themselves that they do their work for the sex or that they enjoy the sex (McLeod, 1982; Hoigard and Finstad, 1992). This lack of sexual pleasure is supported by the ubiquitous reports of the techniques used by prostituted women to numb themselves or dissociate so that, as Hoigard and Finstad put it, they can protect their sense of self. Yet one notable feature of the prostitutes' rights movement has been the argument by some proponents that the sex of prostitution is enjoyable for the women involved, that it can be a perk of the job, or even that the sex of prostitution enables prostituted women to provide a model of that objective for which feminists hanker, sexual autonomy.

Some pro-prostitution lobbyists argue that the sex of prostitution is sexual liberation for women. Priscilla Alexander, who is the co-author of the anthology *Sex Work*, was the secretary of Margo St James who founded the original US prostitutes' rights group COYOTE. She explains that she does not have experience of work in prostitution, but she sees prostitutes as simply doing "sex" and the right of women to be prostitutes as central to the sexual rights of all. She argues that one motivation of women in becoming prostitutes is that they "enjoy sex and have no qualms about enjoying sex as work" (Alexander, 1988a, p. 15). In another pro-prostitution anthology, Terry van der Zijden from the Netherlands says prostitution allows women to enjoy sex without complications. She says that working in prostitution is "one way to become sexually autonomous" (Phetersen, 1989, p. 161). She suggests: "if we experiment with sexuality within the framework of prostitution, we have the possibility of arriving not just at sexual self-determination, but also at self-determination in all other areas of our existence as women" (*ibid.*). It is quite difficult to imagine how a woman working in prostitution could "experiment" with what she might like sexually, as if prostitution were a kind of Garden of Eden, when her subsistence depends on doing what a man wants. But van der Zijden has persuaded herself that this situation, of serving a man's sexual desires for money, is the very model for the liberation of women. It is a rather circumscribed view of women's liberation.

Accounts by other women with experience of prostitution, in the anthologies from which these overblown sentiments come, do not support this view. As one erotic dancer declared, "nobody—not myself, not the other women—enjoys being pawed, poked, prodded and fucked by men we wouldn't give the time of day if we met them elsewhere" (Morgan, 1988, p. 25). A French prostituted woman rejects utterly the argument that prostitution has anything to do with sexual liberation:

> And don't think, either, that prostitutes—because they're prostitutes—are "liberated". Just the opposite. Prostitution and sexual liberation have got nothing to do with each other, they're exactly the opposite. Accusations of debauchery, pre-conceived notions that there'd be girls who'd do this for plea-sure, are quite absurd. [Jaget, 1980, p. 112]

She explains that she does not feel "free" with her body. In fact she feels "bad about it" and "self-conscious", and com-ments: "I don't really feel like my body's alive, I think of it more as bruised, as a weight" (ibid.).

Sexual response during prostitution does sometimes happen, but is not usually interpreted by prostituted women as "pleasure". Judy Edelstein wrote about her distress at having an orgasm with a john during oral sex in a massage parlour.

> Afterwards I'm sitting in one of the empty massage rooms with the muzak turned off, feeling kind of shaky. I just can't believe that I had an orgasm with that jerk. I try to forget him, to think about making love with Laura, the woman I'm with right now. But all I can see is the customer's all-American face. [Edelstein, 1988, p. 63]

Orgasm is a physiological response which can result from stimulation in situations which cause severe emotional pain and could not in any way be seen as positive or desired. I have discussed elsewhere the problem that results in Western culture from the absence of words to describe or even conceive of negative sexual response (Jeffreys, 1990). This is a problem in other forms of sexual abuse in which women are not paid. Survivors of child sexual abuse and of rape sometimes experience orgasm and feel a particular distress at the experience of their bodies betraying them and seeming to make them complicit in the abuse. The experience of orgasm makes it more difficult for the prostituted woman to separate herself from her work. Some prostituted women find that, far from setting in train their sexual liberation, their experience of being used in prostitution causes them to lose sexual feeling altogether. One of the women speaking in *The Prostitution Papers* describes feeling "sort of neuter" (Millett, 1975, p. 27).

Other ex-prostituted women explain that their experience of sex outside their work is adversely affected and that the damage can last for years after leaving prostitution. Toby Summer speaks of the damage she sustained through being sexually abused in prostitution.

> Consider the fact that I learned what sexuality meant from johns and pimps before I could find out what it might mean with the girl I loved. This lesson is not erasable. My body remembers all of it. It seems that bodies learn—in the body, physically—how sex is to be felt, not just done or gone through. [Summer, 1993, p. 232]

Rather than expressing her sexuality through prostitution, this lesbian speaks of expressing the sexuality she learnt in prostitution even years after the event. Once out of prostitution and in subsequent relationships she found that her sexual responses were affected very seriously by her experience, though that would not necessarily be clear to an observer.

> I'm talking about how orgasm felt. How the sexuality itself felt. Fucking my way to heaven with thousands of orgasms

and many truly loved partners did not "heal" the abuse. It may actually have deepened the learned sexual dynamic; it certainly caused confusion between this dynamic and any regard and respect we enjoyed with each other. [*ibid.*, p. 234]

She explains that the practice of numbing, or dissociation, which prostituted women regularly use for emotional survival, can create problems in having sexual responses in any but abusive situations (see Chapter 9). She explains that the numbing cannot easily be overcome and "sets women up for tolerating abuse, especially prostitution and sado-masochism" (*ibid.*, p. 233).

The practice of numbing which so many prostituted women describe as crucial to their survival is in sharp constrast to the claim by some of the new-style prostitutes' rights activists, that prostitution is a form of sexual self-determination and liberation. Numbing and sexual self-determination don't go well together. The johns, and the apologist literature by men which represents the johns' interests, have always maintained that women gain sexual pleasure by servicing men for money. Havelock Ellis maintains, for instance, that many prostituted women are of "coarse sexual fibre" and "show a marked degree of sensuality" (1946, p. 173). It is interesting that this argument is now being made by some women in prostitution, despite the wealth of evidence from the writings of prostitutes that this masculine argument is spurious.

Stigma

Proponents of prostitution, whether prostitutes' rights lobbyists or academics, state that prostitution can be reformed. They say that prostitution is such a hazardous and despised activity in contemporary society because of the stigma attached to it. This stigma is explained as the result of unreasonable and antiquated prejudices left over from the nineteenth century. Removal of the stigma would cause the conditions and status of prostituted women immediately to improve. The way to combat the stigma is to propagate the view that prostitution is choice and work, so that the old cultural myths, that prostitution is immoral or oppressive to women, will shrivel and wither away.

Prostitutes' rights activists make liberal use of this argument. Priscilla Alexander argues, "most of the problems associated with prostitution are directly related to the prohibition and the related stigma associated with sex and especially with sex work" (1988b, p. 17). Prostitution would never disappear, she thought, whatever social reforms are implemented, but the stigma could be eliminated. Veronica Vera, a prostitute performance artist and rights activist from New York, makes a clear distinction between the positive "service" that she believes prostitution potentially to be, and the effects of social prejudice.

> Sex work ... is a great service that is couched in all sorts of negative stuff. The "bad" part is the negative stuff that we put on it: from the client's feeling of sexual guilt to bad laws and cops harassing women on the street. [Bell, 1994, p. 110]

Other prostitutes' rights spokeswomen call this prejudice the "whore stigma" (Pheterson, 1996).

Such a perspective can create a problem for feminists who continue to see men's use of women in prostitution as abuse in and of itself. Feminists who propound this perspective can be seen as contributing to the creation of stigma, and therefore responsible for preventing an amelioration of the abuse prostituted women face. The Australian political scientist Barbara Sullivan, for instance, sees the violence attached to work in prostitution as simply the result of prejudice. Feminist efforts, she says, should be directed towards "shifting cultural meanings and on bringing marginalised discourses about prostitutes as rebels and empowered women into the mainstream". Feminists, in her argument, have become part of the forces making life dangerous for prostituted women. If prostitution is "problematic because of contingent, culturally based assumptions about the bodily submission involved in sex work", then feminist condemnations of sex work could simply reinforce prejudices (Sullivan, 1992, p. 264).

From a feminist perspective, it is not just unreasonable social prejudice which prevents the sex of prostitution from being seen as healthy and reasonable, as simply what sex is. Suzanne Hatty, who has researched prostitutes' experience of violence in Australia, rejects the argument that the violence and death associated with prostitution are the result of illegal status and stigma (Hatty, 1992, p. 73). She sees "Harassment, abuse and violence" as "integral" to prostitution, rather than simply a result of a temporary stigma. Toby Summer has replied angrily to the idea that it is only the "stigma" that is wrong with prostitution. She considers that the "stigma" argument hides the harm that women suffer in prostitution:

> Identifying "stigma" as what is wrong is a re-naming of reality that unfocuses perception of real harm to women in prostitution ... The shift from seeing harm to criticizing emotional responses emanating from the perception of harm targets a non-primary issue. [Summer, 1993, p. 238]

The argument that stigma is the problem is idealist. It represents a political problem of power relations, of the oppression of women, as one of problematic old-fashioned cultural attitudes. A feminist approach sees the sex of prostitution as representing the most oppressive aspects of the sex of male supremacy, a problem that goes rather deeper than stigma.

One ex-prostituted woman from New York, whilst envisioning a future in which all "sex" will be different, characterises the sex of prostitution very well as "a person turning off her emotions, being psychically somewhere else while someone who despises her is making love to her" (Summers, 1988, p. 118). This is the form, she points out, that "sex in this culture" often takes. She does not see the sex of prostitution as "natural", and it is hard to see how stigma could reasonably be removed from this "sex". The stigma attached to the way in which a john uses a prostituted woman may be well deserved. The problem with the "whore stigma" is that prostituted women receive the contempt that should more reasonably be directed at the perpetrators. The tradition of denigrating prostituted women misdirects the blame.

Sexual intercourse

The idea that, once the stigma is removed from prostitution, the activity involved will miraculously become "just sex" is unrealistic. There is no such thing as "just sex" in a male supremacist culture where sexual acts confirm and create political status. The act which men most commonly perform on prostituted women is penis-in-vagina sexual intercourse. There is nothing "natural" about that act. Kate Millett's *Sexual Politics*, which is a foundational text of radical feminism, started from the understanding that the power relationship between men and women could be read from the way in which men thought about, wrote and practised sexual intercourse. As she explains:

> Coitus can scarcely be said to take place in a vacuum; although of itself it appears a biological and physical activity, it is set so deeply within the larger context of human affairs that it serves as a charged microcosm of the variety of attitudes and values to which culture subscribes. Among other things, it may serve as a model of sexual politics on an individual or personal plane. [Millett., 1972, p. 23]

Millett effects a brilliant analysis of the political meaning of the sex portrayed in the work of acclaimed male novelists, Lawrence, Miller, Mailer and Genet. There is nothing marginal or insignificant about the meanings these men apply to sex; their work is central to male Western twentieth-century culture.

Henry Miller's heroes are johns. They use prostitutes in his novels as a matter of course: "At the hotel … I rang for women like you would ring for whiskey and soda." The language in which he describes sexual acts shows "the disgust, the contempt, the hostility, the violence, and the sense of filth with which our culture, or more specifically, its masculine sensibility, surrounds sexuality". He dumps these feelings on women, "for somehow it is women upon whom this onerous burden of sexuality falls". Miller describes female genitals as a "'crack'; a 'gash'; a 'wound'; a 'slimy hole' ... [a] 'festering, obscene horror'" (ibid., pp. 298, 295, 307–8). He is revolted by the smell of women. His hero delights in punishing them for being so disgusting. Millett provides a compilation of his descriptors for his female sexual partners to demonstrate his puritanical horror of women and sex.

> "The dirty bitches—they like it," he apprises us; clinical, fastidious, horrified and amused to record how one responded "squealing like a pig"; another "like a crazed animal"; one "gibbered"; another "crouched on all fours like a she-animal, quivering and whinnying"; while still another specimen was "so deep in heat" she was like "a bright voracious animal ... an elephant walking the ball". [ibid., p. 306]

Andrea Dworkin's *Intercourse* takes up the task which Millett began of examining the politics of the act of sexual intercourse. She explains that sexual intercourse cannot reasonably be seen as a private activity when, in fact it is so important as to be hedged around by law, laid down in statute. The very idea of privacy is simply, she states, "a means of protecting the active sexual dominance of men over others" when, in fact, "intercourse is, in essence and in reality, social, not private" (Dworkin, 1987, p. 148). Intercourse is, she explains, a social act deemed of great importance to the state.

> Intercourse both presumes and requires a society of at least two persons before it can occur at all; and the state is concerned about the nature of that society—how it is constructed, that it be hierarchical, that it be male-dominant. In each act of intercourse, a society is formed; and the distribution of power in that society is the state interest at stake ... Gender is what

the state seeks to control: who is the man here? which is the woman? how to keep the man on top, how to keep the man the man; how to render the woman inferior in fucking so that she cannot recover herself from the carnal experience of her own subjugation. [*ibid.*]

It is in the act of intercourse that woman's subjection to man must be clearly established. Women's failure to make obeisance to male power in the act is interpreted as resistance. "Rebellion here, in intercourse, is the death of a system of gender hierarchy premissed on a sexual victory over the vagina. The triumphant fuck is virtually synonymous with masculinity" (*ibid.*, p. 149). In my books *The Spinster and Her Enemies* and *Anticlimax*, I showed the great political significance accorded the act of sexual intercourse in the works of sexologists throughout the twentieth century. Sexologists from Havelock Ellis to Alex Comfort have been concerned that sexual intercourse should take place in the correct male-dominant form, and with sufficient frequency to ensure the efficient reproduction of male dominance in the marital relationship. But they were concerned with the construction of sexual pleasure too. The woman, in sexual intercourse, must not just be penetrated, but be swept away in a delicious submission to the will of her master and mate. The experience of female orgasm was supposed to signify and effect the woman's subjection. For this reason sexologists remained in a high state of anxiety for decades about women's resistance in celibacy, lesbianism, frigidity, lack of enthusiasm, for such women remained unconquered.

The language the sexologists used was unequivocal. It is the language of warfare and conquest and belied any notion that, for the sex experts, sexual intercourse was a matter of private pleasure. The political purpose in regulating male dominance and female submission is clear in this 1940s statement from the popular British sexologist Eustace Chesser. He is explaining to wives that they must "surrender" in sexual intercourse. He writes that a woman may find it impossible to surrender herself completely in the sex act. And complete surrender is the only way in which she can bring the highest pleasure to both herself and her husband. Submission is not the same thing as surrender. Many a wife submits, but retains, deep within herself, an area which is not yet conquered, and which, indeed, in fierce opposition to submission. [quoted in Jeffreys, 1990, p. 30]

Sexual intercourse, as Dworkin explains, "is what the society—when pushed to admit it—recognises as dominance" (1987, pp. 125–6).

Dworkin, like Millett, demonstrates from the work of famous male intellectuals that sexual intercourse, and by extension women, are seen as dirty and disgusting. Words applied by male-supremacist cultures to female genitals demonstrate this, as in *pudendum* from *pudere*, "to be ashamed". *Uterus* in Jewish and Islamic tradition means grave. Dworkin shows the great difficulty Freud had with finding women horrifying. He decided that "just seeing those genitals turns a man gay or makes him rub up against rubber for a lifetime". He wrote to Jung, "Oh yes, I forgot to say that menstrual blood must be counted as excrement" (*ibid.*, pp. 182, 183). Dworkin disdains the idea that sex can suddenly be made healthy without changing the subordination of women which constructs the idea that sex is disgusting in the first place.

> Current dogma is to teach by rote that sex is "healthy" as if it existed outside social relations, as if it had no ties to anything mean or lowdown, to history, to power, to the dispossession of women from freedom. But for sex not to mean dirt—for sex not to be dirty—the status of women would have to change radically ... [*ibid.*, p. 173]

This is precisely the problem with the notion that what is wrong with prostitution is stigma and that once prejudice is removed, then prostitution will be revealed as perfectly fine. If in fact the status of women were to change, then the sex of prostitution would likely become unthinkable rather than suddenly healthy. But meantime, the idea that stigma is the problem is used to suggest that the violence that prostituted women suffer is a temporary inconvenience which can be removed with a change of image. In fact, the sex of prostitution is a distillation of the sex of male supremacy, a sex in which men find women disgusting objects requiring and loving their subjugation. The johns are unlikely to be possessed of attitudes to sex quite different from those of the novelists, sexologists, pornographers which construct and suffuse the culture in which they learn to be sexual. If they had positive attitudes, they might not be able to conceive of using women in prostitution at all. If johns are simply men, imbued with the ordinary values attributed to women and sex in male supremacist culture, then prostitution is a very dangerous job, physically and mentally, for women to be doing.

The stigma attached to the sex of prostitution has its provenance in the way that sex, women and women's bodies have been constructed in a society of male dominance. The words which have been used in popular culture for the act of sexual intercourse and for the parts of women's bodies used in that practice suggest a contempt for women and the "sex" which is embodied in the sex of prostitution. Feminist cultural critics have demonstrated that woman-hating values permeate the literature of high art as well as popular culture and pornography, and that these values are concentrated in representations of women as the proper objects of appalling contempt and naked violence. bell hooks, in *Outlaw Culture*, analyses "gangsta rap", to show that the values of woman-hating it represents are simply those of patriarchal America and not the specific product of black culture. She gives as an example the image on the cover of a record called *Doggystyle* by Snoop Doggy Dogg. This showed a "doghouse, 'Beware the Dog' sign, a naked black female head in the doghouse, her naked butt sticking out", and interprets this as showing the woman to be "waiting to be fucked from behind" (hooks, 1994, p. 119).

Gangsta rap is part of the antifeminist backlash that is the rage right now. When young black males labor in the plantations of misogyny and sexism to produce gangsta rap, white supremacist capitalist patriarchy approves the violence and materially rewards them. [*ibid.*, p. 122]

It is hard to believe, as the contemporary defences of prostitution seem to suggest, that the sexual intercourse that takes place in prostitution is somehow free of this political significance. The sex of prostitution, if it is just sex, as its defenders assert, must somehow be "natural" and free, marvellously innocent of the politics attached to just such acts in science, great art, pornography and the whole of popular culture. The men who carry out acts of prostitution on women must be paragons of educated anti-sexism who have reconstructed the primary political act of male supremacy. But is that likely? Some evidence suggests that clients are ordinary sexists, precisely those men whose opinion of women is low (Davidson, 1994). And this would make sense. Those who use women in prostitution are sexist men, not sexual free spirits engaging in acts of liberation.

Pornography and prostitution

The values of what is considered to be "sex", or at least male sexuality, can be gleaned from pornography. Catharine MacKinnon suggests that pornography clearly represents dominant male-supremacist sexual values, or it would not be so massively profitable.

If pornography has not become sex to and from the male point of view, it is hard to explain why the pornography industry makes a known ten billion dollars a year selling it as sex mostly to men; why it is used to teach sex to child prostitutes, to recalcitrant wives and girlfriends and daughters, to medical students, and to sex offenders ... [MacKinnon, 1989, p. 139]

But the values of pornography are the values of prostitution.

Pornography and prostitution are indivisible. The testimony of prostituted women about the use of pornography to season them, its use in brothels, the filming of them for pornography suggests that pornography and prostitution are integrally connected (Everywoman, 1988). Mimi Silbert and Ayala Pines (1984) report from their research that 38 per cent of the prostitutes they interviewed had been used in pornography when under sixteen years old. They did not ask direct questions about pornography, and consider that if they had, the correlation would have been much higher.

Pornography and prostitution are indivisible too, because pornography is the representation of prostitution. Pornography records the commercial sexual use of women. Diana Russell, long involved as an academic and activist in anti-pornography work, suggests that it would be more honest and realistic to refer to the women in pornography as prostitutes rather than using terms such as *model, porn actress,* or *star* to differentiate these "photographed or filmed women from other prostitutes despite the fact that they, like all prostitutes, are paid for the exploitation of their bodies" (1993, p. 18). Russell comments on the "extraordinary inconsistency" that prostitution is illegal in all states in the United States except Nevada, yet pornography is defended as free speech.

> Does it really make sense that an act of prostitution in front of a camera is more acceptable than the same act performed in private ... These women are not simulating sex. They are literally being fucked, tied up, spread-eagled, having ejaculate sprayed over their faces and bodies, having anal, oral, and vaginal sex with three different men at the same time, being urinated on, and so on. [*ibid.*, p. 18]

The sex of pornography is no more "just sex" than the sex of prostitution. MacKinnon explains that pornography shows what men want sexually and permits them to have whatever they want sexually. It is their "truth about sex". "It shows what men want and gives it to them."

From the testimony of the pornography, what men want is: women bound, women battered, women tortured, women humiliated, women degraded and defiled, women killed. Or to be fair to the soft core, women sexually accessible, have-able, there for them, wanting to be taken and used, with perhaps a little light bondage. Each violation of women—rape, battery, prostitution, child sexual abuse, sexual harassment—is made sexuality, made sexy, fun, and liberating of women's true nature in the pornography. [MacKinnon, 1989, p. 138]

Pornography, says MacKinnon, "constructs women as things for sexual use and constructs its consumers to desperately want women, to desperately want possession and cruelty and dehumanization" (*ibid.*, p. 139). MacKinnon suggests that pornography does clearly represent dominant male supremacist sexual values.

The titles of pornographic materials give a good sense of the woman-hating nature of their content. Racist and sexual hatred are often combined to provide a particularly heady brew of vicious excitement. The following titles were obtained by a researcher from six stores and comprise those featuring "people of colour" on their covers (Maynall and Russell, 1993, p. 170). Titles featuring Asian women were:

Bawdy Tales of Wu Wu Wang
Bloody Encounters
Geisha's Girls
Geisha's Torment
Japanese Sadist's Dungeon
May Ling's Master
Oriental Sadist's Pet
Samurai Slave Girl
Teen Slaves of Saigon
Vietcong Rape Compound
Whips of Chinatown.

In the six shops there were eleven Nazi titles about sexual

violence to Jewish women and four which featured Arab women and which were explicitly sadistic:

Bound Harem Girl
Harem Hell
Raped by Arab Terrorists
Sheik's Hand Maiden.

The majority of pornography, though, is not explictly violent in this way. So-called soft-core pornography is the variety which is most likely to be seen as "just sex" by pro-prostitution lobbyists. *Playboy* and *Penthouse* are the most available and legitimate soft-core pornography, mainly because they do not show erect penises or nude men. But there are several ways in which they can be shown to represent and promote woman-hating attitudes. Andrea Dworkin and Catharine MacKinnon cite *Playboy*'s ideology of women as "bunnies" to demonstrate the sexism of the magazine: women are turned into less-than-human animals. Also the women in *Playboy* are "presented in postures of submission and sexual servility. Constant access to the throat, the anus, and the vagina is the purpose of the ways in which the women are posed" (Dworkin and MacKinnon, 1993, p. 79). Careful consideration of the cartoons in *Playboy* demonstrates the background attitude towards women in which the soft-core pictures are embedded. Diana Russell's book *Against Pornography* (1993) reproduces cartoons from mainstream pornography that show children enjoying rape and office-workers loving sexual harrassment, and text which teaches boys how to rape disabled girls.

Dworkin and MacKinnon illustrate the sexism of soft-core with the behaviour of its founder Hugh Hefner. Hefner has traditionally used the women who work for *Playboy* for his own sexual satisfaction. Linda Marchiano, whose prostitution name was Linda Lovelace, was, as they put it, "pimped" to Hefner, who "sodomised her and tried to have her have intercourse with a dog" (Dworkin and MacKinnon, 1993, p. 80). Marchiano has written about the situation of sexual slavery she lived in with this pimp who controlled her with guns to her head (Lovelace, 1981). A *Playboy* centrefold named Dorothy Stratten was tortured, raped and later murdered by her husband, who sold photos of her and access to her to Hefner. Hefner was made aware after her death that Stratten had hated being used for pornography made of her. He responded by issuing more videotapes of Stratten posing, and her estate has been unable to prevent the trafficking of Stratten in these videos. Dworkin and MacKinnon point out that the women used by Hefner personally, and in the magazine, are rarely over eighteen, and that Stratten was under-age when pimped to Hefner.

The sex of pornography, then, is not "just sex" but a particular kind of sex premised upon and constructed out of women's subordination and men's domination, just like the sex of other forms of prostitution. It is hard to believe that johns are egalitarians who love women, that they have managed to escape any influence from pornography and retained a pure ideal of sex quite unrelated to women's oppression. That would indeed be surprising.

The controversy within feminist theory over prostitution replicates that over pornography. It is to be expected that this should be the case, since the acts which take place in the making of pornography are precisely the acts of prostitution, i.e. sexual acts for money. There are, though, certain important differences between the ways in which feminist discussion of pornography and of prostitution have taken place. One obvious difference is the very strength and directness of the feminist campaigns against pornography. These campaigns have not been equally strong in every country, but the examples I shall give here refer to the United States and Britain, in which such campaigns have had considerable influence. Feminist campaigns in the United State—such as Women against Violence in Pornography and the Media, and Women against Pornography—and in Britain—Women against Violence against Women—have generated, since the late 1970s, considerable feminist activism and theory. These campaigns have not, until recently, directly challenged prostitution. This is not because the most significant theorists of pornography have avoided the issue. Andrea Dworkin is the best known anti-pornography feminist theorist, and she has made the connections between pornography and prostitution very clear in her works such as *Pornography: Men Possessing Women* (1981) and *Right Wing Women* (1983). Dworkin explains in *Pornography* that the word actually means writing about whores, *porneia*. It would be hard, then, to ignore the link. If, as seems reasonable to conclude, pornography is an expression of prostitution rather than the other way round, it is puzzling that anti-pornography activists do not target prostitution.

It may be that it is easier for women to see that they are personally affected by pornography than by prostitution. Perhaps choosing to ignore the reality of the women used allows women to fight pornography without having to confront the arguments of some women in prostitution and pornography that they "choose" their avocations and feminists have no right to criticise them. For whatever reason, the significant campaigns against pornography have not targeted prostitution and there has been little attempt to make the connections.

Prostitution and the construction of sexuality

Feminist research has shown that women over the last century have sought to transform the dynamics of sexual practice away from the male-dominant/female-submissive model of the sex of prostitution towards a sexuality more suited to women's pleasure and women's freedom (Bland, 1995). At the height of the powerful feminist movement of the late nineteenth and early twentieth centuries, feminist theorists and campaigners against men's sexual abuse questioned the importance of sexual intercourse. Some argued that sexual intercourse should be embarked upon only for the purposes of reproduction (Jeffreys, 1985). The massive sexologically inspired movement for sex reform in the same period enforced male-dominant/female-submissive sexual intercourse as what constituted sex (Jackson, 1984; 1994, Jeffreys, 1997). But feminists before World War I in Britain were still seeking to express their profound discontent with their experience of sexual intercourse as sex. One woman in a feminist magazine which provided a platform for the debate on sex reform wrote of the "absolute indifference or dislike of the sexual act in many women", and suggested this might have something to do with their feeling instinctively that "the man does despise them and hold them in contempt and they despise themselves" (quoted in Jeffreys, 1997, p. 52).

The fact that sexologists and other sex advice experts felt that a massive campaign was necessary throughout the twentieth century, a campaign which continues today, to attack women's "frigidity", their "dyspareunia" or "sexual anaesthesia" and train them to respond appropriately to the dominant form of male sexuality, suggests that there has been tremendous resistance by women. I detailed in *Anticlimax* the fury of sexologists at the forms of resistance that husbands reported to them. Women in the 1950s would, apparently, continue to read their novel or apply nail polish to their toes whilst their husbands sought to carry out the act that proclaimed their manhood (Jeffreys, 1990).

Shere Hite's famous report on female sexuality in 1977 suggested quite massive discontent amongst her large sample with the pattern of sexual intercourse that her respondents had experienced. When women were asked how they would like the "bedroom scene" changed, they came up "over and over" with demands that men not fixate on "cocks and cunts". They wanted more whole-body sensuality. Men's idea of what constituted sex left them profoundly dissatisfied even when they did have orgasms. "I've always felt that my sexual enounters have been only beginnings; they've never been even nearly carried as far as I would like them to be". Another said: "I always felt rather badly for my lover because it seemed that for him it was like scratching an itch—relieving himself of something negative—where for me it was absolute bliss" (Hite, 1977, pp. 530, 532). Women in Hite's study generally wanted much more touching, hugging, physical affection which did not necessarily lead to sex, and many felt desperate—some spoke of feeling like crying—because they could not get this from men, only brief encounters of sexual intercourse. Hite's study found that orgasm was rare for women from sexual intercourse alone. Only 30 per cent of her sample orgasmed regularly from sexual intercourse without direct manual clitoral stimulation at the same time.

The sex of prostitution constitutes a serious barrier to the desire of women, whether self-consciously feminist or not, to transform sexuality. Eileen McLeod in her 1982 study of prostitution offers the reluctance of wives to cater to the men's sexual "needs" as a motive for men visiting prostitutes. One john explained that he visited prostituted women because his wife would not provide for him the sex of prostitution.

I did suggest we could be a bit more adventurous. To her it was as though she was embarrassed. Some of the things I mentioned to her she thought was disgusting. I took some books home ... I even borrowed a blue movie off a friend of mine and a projector and showed it her. And after that her [sic] was as randy as hell. [ibid., p. 77]

Oral sex was a practice that wives seemed unwilling to provide for their husbands, so they used prostituted women for access to their mouths and for the performance of other practices that they wanted and their wives did not. Thus the existence of prostitution enforced in these men the idea that the sex of prostitution was what sex was, and what they had the right to demand, either from wives or prostitutes. The ability to use prostituted women enabled men to avoid having to have an egalitarian sexual relationship in which sexual practices needed to be negotiated and pleasing to both parties. As one john put it, prostitution gave him "the freedom of not having to do things the way your wife wants you to do them" (*ibid.*, p. 70). McLeod seems willing to accept that the sex of prostitution is indeed what sex is. In regard to men's demand for oral sex, she suggests that wives will eventually be persuaded to provide it. Wives will eventually provide all the services that men presently visit prostitutes for, and men will change their demands of prostitutes over time.

> Perhaps what is going on represents the time lag between what is discussed as sexually permissible and what couples commonly engage in. Prostitutes are then turned to to make good the difference. Presumably as decades pass so what men most want from prostitutes will change. [*ibid.*, p. 80]

This perspective suggests that men's use of prostituted women will act to enforce the sex of prostitution on all women and constantly maintain men's "needs" as what sex is. There is no conception here of what "wives" might want from sex or what a feminist vision of "sex" might be.

A contemporary example from a women's magazine serves to illustrate this problem. In an article entitled "When wife meets prostitute", Ginny, whose marriage broke up after the revelation that her husband had been visiting a prostitute for years, meets Sue, the prostituted woman, and discusses her husband's behaviour with her. Ginny was devastated by the discovery because she saw it as a betrayal of the trust she expected to be able to have in a husband. "I thought we had mutual love and respect and all that crap. What's the point of trusting anyone if one partner is just going to ruin it all with their own agenda?" (Bailey, 1995, p. 32). Ginny was particularly distressed in this discussion to discover what the "sex" her husband engaged in with Sue consisted of.

> Robert was quite adventurous after a while. He liked me to dress up. I think he enjoyed feeling like he had done something naughty more than the actual doing it. ... We only had penetrative sex every now and then. The rest of the time it was dressing up, talking dirty. He much preferred to have oral

sex with me as well ... He liked dirty sex, stilettos, fishnets, crotchless knickers, lots of make-up—that kind of thing. [*ibid.*, p. 30]

Ginny, who is described as having a successful career in publicity, is angry because the "sex" Robert went to Sue for is precisely that which she sees as demeaning.

My god, that's really disgusting. Well, he certainly never got that from me. I'm not wearing bloody suspenders for anyone ... It's degrading. It's such a degrading attitude towards women. Can you imagine me in crotchless knickers—yuck ... I'm not going to be thought of like that. Men can take me how I am or forget it. [*ibid.*]

It is clear from this example that Robert's ability to get the sort of sex which represented women as dirty and as subordinate sex objects from a prostituted woman affected Ginny's ability to create an equal relationship. As she struggled to create a sexual practice and sexual feelings which represented dignity, respect and trust, her husband could simply undermine her efforts through prostitution.

The "sex" of prostitution, it seems, can provide a reservoir of access to sexist behaviour towards women as this becomes less acceptable in the workplace, in the home and in marriages. For women as a class, the ability to transform sexual practice, to achieve respect from men as equal human beings and thus break out of their subordinate status, is undermined by the ability of men to escape from the responsibility of acknowledging women's equality. Men's use of women in prostitution stands directly in the way of women's efforts to improve their status. As the sex industry expands in its forms, in its worldwide organisation and in its acceptability, its effectiveness in preventing such an improvement is likely to intensify considerably.

The sex of prostitution is not "just sex", but male sexuality. It represents contemptuous attitudes to sex and those who are identified as representing it, women. The cacophony of rage that greets feminist attempts to challenge prostitution, the response that feminists must be "anti-sex" for wanting to challenge it, shows that the sex of prostitution is the model for what is understood to be "sex" under male supremacy, and the difficulty, even for some libertarian feminists, of imagining any alternative. Prostitution cannot be saved, then, by removing the stigma, when it is precisely the attitudes identified as "stigma" that create the phenomenon of prostitution in the first place. The johns must hold certain ideas about sex and women to enable them to use prostituted women. If those attitudes were to change, then prostitution could not survive. But attitudes towards sex and women are likely to be slow to change whilst the massively powerful force of the sex industry, through its considerable financial clout, is able to promote ideas directly in opposition to changing sexuality and the status of women.

CHAPTER 9

prostitution as male sexual violence

> Prostitution is sexual abuse because prostitutes are subjected to any number of sexual acts that in any other context, acted against any other woman, would be labelled assaultive or, at the very least, unwanted and coerced. [Giobbe, 1991, p. 159]

Prostitution in the public mind and that of sociologists and sexologists has tended to be seen as deviant *female* sexuality or, more recently, as *female* choice and work. Men, the johns who use prostituted women, have scarcely entered the picture. The analysis I shall give here is very different. I suggest that prostitution constitutes a variety of *male* sexual violence towards women. There are many ways in which the prostitution of women has been understood both to result *from* and to result *in* violence. Many studies, for instance, suggest that the percentage of prostituted women who have been sexually abused in childhood is very high (James and Meyerding, 1977; Farley and Hotaleng, 1995). The high rates of violence that prostituted women suffer in connection with their work—from rape to murder—have also been documented. But the feminist understanding that the acts carried out on and in the bodies of prostituted women are in themselves sexual violence is only just beginning to develop.

In the last twenty-five years, feminists theorists and activists have gradually uncovered different varieties of men's

violence towards women. They have done so usually in ignorance of the massive campaigns carried out by their foresisters
of the late nineteenth and early twentieth centuries on many
of the same issues (Jeffreys, 1985; Jackson, 1994). The first
objects of feminist action were rape and "domestic" violence.
In the late 1970s sexual abuse of children and sexual harassment at work were subjected to analysis. Sexual abuse of children was brought out into the open by the courage of
individual women victims inspired, by feminist analysis of
violence, to tell their stories (Armstrong, 1978). The first feminist theoretical approach to incestuous abuse was published
at this time (Rush, 1980). Catharine MacKinnon's pioneering
work *The Sexual Harassment of Working Women* (1979)
gained recognition for the damage of workplace harassment
as sex discrimination in this period. In the early 1980s it was
marital rape which was exposed to scrutiny, with Diana
Russell's groundbreaking survey, *Rape in Marriage* (1990,
first published 1982). Though these forms of abuse were
uncovered at different stages, research on them all has continued and the connections have been established, as in the work
by Liz Kelly (1989) on the continuum of violence. It is time
that prostitution was placed on this continuum. In this chapter I shall show how unreasonable it is to omit prostitution
from the feminist understanding of violence against women,
and consider the body of feminist theory and research which
now exists to support its inclusion.

Definitions

The question of how to define the violence and the sex of
men's abuse of women has been an issue of intense debate
between feminist theorists of male violence. This debate began
over rape. Many feminist theorists of rape seek to define it as
a crime of violence rather than a crime of sex. An example of
this approach is the Australian criminologist Patricia Easteal's
Voices of the Survivors (1994). She opens her book by refuting
myths of rape, and includes as one of the "myths" the idea
that "Rape is a sexual act". She states unequivocally:

> Rape is not a sexual act. Rape is an act of violence which uses sex as a weapon. Rape is motivated by aggression and by the desire to exert power and humiliate. Just as wife battering had to be taken out of the privacy of the home and made a crime in order to effect any change, rape must be taken out of the sexual realm and placed where it rightly belongs: in the domain of violence against women. [Easteal, 1994, p. 4]

She goes on to assert that the view of rape as a "sexual act ... is perhaps one of the most pervasive, enduring, and damaging myths". The purpose of this redefinition by feminists was to challenge the masculine notion, still influential in the justice system, that rape is just ordinary sex in which a man goes a bit too far or where a woman changes her mind after the event. The idea that rape is a crime of violence has also been employed to support the notion that sexually violent crimes would have an easier passage through the justice system, and women would be happier to report, if they were defined as, and taken as seriously as, other forms of physical assault (Fudge, 1989).

Catharine MacKinnon has been most influential in contesting this definition of rape as violence and not sex.

> What I see to be the danger of the analysis, what makes it potentially cooptive, is formulating it—and it *is* formulated this way—these are issues of violence, not sex: rape is a crime of violence, not sexuality; sexual harassment is an abuse of power, not sexuality; pornography is violence against women, it is not erotic. [MacKinnon, 1987, p. 85]

She sees the feminist adoption of this distinction as resulting from a fear of being seen as anti-sex—a reasonable fear considering that such an accusation has been a potent slur against feminists (see Chapter 3). She considers that rape is experienced as sexual by raped women because: "A common experience of rape victims is to be unable to feel good about anything heterosexual thereafter—or anything sexual, or men at all" (*ibid.*, p. 87). Since a woman is affected sexually, then certainly the abuse was sexual for her. The abuse is certainly sexual for the rapist, particularly since he often is unable to distinguish between what he has done and perfectly normal sex. She explains:

> What is sex except that which is felt as sexual? When acts of dominance and submission, up to and including acts of violence, are experienced as sexually arousing, as sex itself, that is what they are ... Violence is sex when it is practiced as sex. [*ibid.*, p. 6]

The distinction between violence and sex, MacKinnon argues, is employed to maintain the illusion that there is a whole realm of good and normal sex which has no connection with violence. In fact, she considers, no such clear distinction is possible because sexuality is politically constructed "gendered to the ground", and no pure sex, unadulterated by male supremacist values, exists (MacKinnon, 1989, p. 198). The violence/sex distinction is employed as a loyalty oath to true sex, to keep it sacred. MacKinnon's explanation of the reasons for the violence/sex distinction is helpful to our understanding of why the abuse of prostitution is so regularly invisible or denied. The "sex" of prostitution is so close to what is viewed, promoted and clung onto as normal sex under male supremacy, i.e. a woman's body used by a man for his pleasure irrespective of her personhood or will, that its classification as violent would be fundamentally destabilising to the sexual foundations of male power. Thus prostitution must be seen as just about "sex".

MacKinnon includes woman-battering within her understanding of sexual violence, because all violence against women tends to be eroticised. Therefore it is mistaken to say that when a man batters a woman he is not involved in a sexual act:

> it is very difficult to say that there is a major distinction in the level of sex involved between being assaulted by a penis and

being assaulted by a fist, especially when the perpetrator is a man. If women as gender female are defined as sexual beings, and violence is eroticised, then men violating women has a sexual component. [MacKinnon, 1987, p. 92]

There may, however, be a problem in the routine inclusion of all forms of violence and abuse towards women by men within the definition of sexual violence. I share Catharine MacKinnon's determination to illuminate the importance of sexuality in organising the oppression of women. To this end, however, I would like to distinguish, where that is possible, between violence that is effected towards women in the way in which it might be towards another hated group, and violence which is specifically sexual in nature and has a quality particular to the oppression of women. A man might, for instance, routinely denigrate women by saying that they are hopeless at driving, or maths. This is not a sexual insult so much as the kind of insult which might be directed at any despised group. Similarly it is possible that violence against women on some occasions might indeed be because women are women but not specifically sexual. I consider that there is some good purpose in keeping sensitively aware of the specificity of sexual violence. I suggest a definition of sexual violence which incorporates some sense that the violence in question refers to, is experienced as, or affects the sexuality of, either the man who is abusing or the woman who is abused.

In the anthology *Femicide: The Politics of Woman Killing* (1992), Jill Radford considers that the term *sexual violence* is useful because it "moves beyond the debate over whether rape is sexual assault or violence" by combining the two ideas. She states that "Femicide, the misogynous killing of women by men", is a form of sexual violence. This debate is limited, she considers, by "a narrow definition of the term sexual, one that rests on whether the man is seeking sexual pleasure" (Radford and Russell, 1992, p. 3). She prefers the term *sexual violence* because it "focuses on the man's desire for power, dominance, and control". But this interpretation loses any sense of that which is specifically sexual. Femicide includes articles on practices of woman-killing that do not seem to have a sexual element, such as infanticide. There can be murders of women because they are women, or female, which do not necessarily speak of sex to the perpetrator or the one who is killed.

MacKinnon is unusual in unequicovally including prostitution in her definition of the "vast amount of sexual abuse" uncovered by feminists since 1970. "Rape, battery, sexual harassment, sexual abuse of children, prostitution, and pornography, seen for the first time in their true scope and interconnectedness, form a distinctive pattern: the power of men over women in society" (MacKinnon, 1987, p. 5). Most of even the most sensitive and profound feminist analysis of male violence avoids prostitution entirely. As Jill Radford points out, "the concept of a continuum allows us to identify and address a range of forced or coercive heterosexual experience" (Radford and Russell, 1992, p. 4). Liz Kelly, for instance, in her deservedly influential *Surviving Sexual Violence*, includes a particularly wide range of abusive male practices within her *continuum* of sexual violence but does not mention the violence of prostitution. There is nothing, though, about Kelly's definition that would exclude the abuse of prostitution, and much that would seem to relate to it. Her definition is:

> any physical, visual, verbal or sexual act that is experienced by the woman or girl, at the time or later, as a threat, invasion or assault, that has the effect of hurting or degrading her and/or takes away her ability to control intimate contact. [Kelly, 1989, p. 41]

Unlike the conventional wisdom, this definition does not mention notions of choice or consent. It allows understanding of the harm to be recognised later rather than at the time. These two elements of the definition, which are significant additions to our understanding of sexual violence, readily include the violence of prostitution. The practices of prostitution, as many feminist theorists are now arguing, involve men engaging in acts towards women that can be seen as "threat, invasion or assault". The point over which I take issue with this definition is in its inclusion of "physical, visual or verbal" acts which can hurt or degrade women. I consider it important to retain a definition of "sexual violence" which gives significance to the specifically sexual nature of much of the violence directed towards women.

Surprisingly, Kelly's book, though entitled *Surviving Sexual Violence*, nowhere mentions the violence of prostitution and pornography upon the women abused, as forms of violence that women might need to survive. The sex industry is cited as a form of work in which sexual harassment is particularly severe, and the use of pornography, when shown to women and used as educational material, is seen as a form of sexual violence, but not the abuse of women that is constituted by the normal practices of prostitution. But within the British feminist anti-violence tradition, prostitution was included within the spectrum of men's violence by the early 1980s. Two papers on prostitution, one by myself and one by Maureen O'Hara, were included in the national Sexual Violence Against Women Conference in Leeds in November 1980. This conference sought to direct feminist attention, which had been focused on rape through the rape crisis movement, towards less-recognised examples of sexual violence, and to include within the analysis practices such as sexual initiation, gynecology, indecent exposure, as well as prostituton (McNeil and Rhodes, 1985).

Jill Radford seems specifically to exclude the violence of routine everyday prostitution from her list of what she calls the "continuum of antifemale terror". She includes only forced prostitution in a wide variety of practices which are abusive to women, such as:

rape, torture, sexual slavery (particularly in prostitution), incestuous and extrafamilial child sexual abuse, physical and emotional battery, sexual harassment (on the phone, in the streets, at the office, and in the classroom), genital mutilation (clitoridectomies, excision, infibulations), unnecessary gynecological operations (gratuitous hysterectomies), forced heterosexuality, forced sterilization, forced motherhood (by criminalizing contraception and abortion), psychosurgery, denial of food to women in some cultures, cosmetic surgery, and other mutilations in the name of beautification. [Radford and Russell, 1992, p. 15]

The absence of ordinary, everyday prostitution from this list stands out as a glaring omission.

One element of the feminist definition of sexual violence which is not well suited to the inclusion of prostitution is the idea that it is always enacted as part of a system of social control. Feminist theorists tend to quote Kate Millett's understanding in *Sexual Politics* (1975) that the oppression of women, like other political systems, is held in place by force, and expand this notion of force to include the wide variety of sexual violence that men enact against women. The act and the fear of rape, sexual abuse, sexual murder, sexual harassment, are seen to control women's movements and behaviour, even their clothing and ways of sitting and walking. The work of Betsy Stanko (1993) demonstrates how the fear of men's violence, even without direct experience, organises women's lives. But this understanding does not, to my mind, allow sufficient scope for the idea of recreational violence by men, which is not meant to curtail a woman's movement and may not have the effect of doing so. The violence of prostitution, because it is organised within a cash nexus, may not lead to the social control of making a woman fearful lest she will be assaulted. The assault is controlled by being paid for. Traditional defences of prostitution by male apologists like St Augustine and Thomas Aquinas, as well as some prostituted women themselves, actually argue that non-prostituted women should feel safer from sexual violence because men are venting their uncontrollable urges upon the sacrificial class of prostitutes. Use of prostituted women is seen as a form of catharsis. But such ideas simply abandon the class of prostitutes as appropriate targets of acts that these analysts themselves seem to recognise as intimately linked to non-commercial violence against women.

The power of naming

Liz Kelly introduces *Surviving Sexual Violence* by commenting on how difficult it was and still is to get public recognition of the significance of men's violence against women.

> When radical feminists point to the appalling incidence of sexual violence we are seen by many as hysterical and, even by other feminists, as placing too much emphasis on women's victimization. Most men and many women do not want to acknowledge the extent of sexual violence in, and its impact on, women's lives. It is still illegitimate for us to refer to it as being of "epidemic" proportions, threatening women's "basic human rights". [Kelly, 1989, p. ix]

When the extent of sexual violence in the forms currently recognised—rape, child sexual abuse—is denied by some feminists, it is not surprising that prostitution abuse cannot be taken seriously. Most feminists have probably not yet contemplated seeing what is done to women in prostitution as violence at all. Liberal feminists resist most strongly all suggestions that sexual violence is pervasive as a force in women's lives (Roiphe, 1993; Wolf, 1993). Yet, as Kelly points out, the fundamental assumption of liberal democracy, protection of life and liberty, is tenuous for women and girls. That this is not yet a "major source of concern", she states, "suggests that there are vested interests at stake here—men's interests" (Kelly, 1989, p. x). The aim of her work is to enable the "prevalence and impact of sexual violence in women's lives" to be more readily publicly acknowledged. She considers it vital that the "extent and range of sexual violence continues to be documented" (*ibid.*). Documentation of the sexual violence of prostitution, as this chapter will show, is proceeding apace. It is to be hoped that its inclusion in what feminist researchers routinely understood to constitute sexual violence will follow.

Liz Kelly interviewed sixty women in depth for *Surviving Sexual Violence*, to identify the continuum of violence in their lives. Like many other feminist anti-violence researchers, she found that the power to name their experience as sexual violence was something that the interviewees came to only through struggle, often through being alerted by media articles or conversations with other women. When they are unable to name their experience as violence, women may feel unease or distress but are unable to place what has happened to them in a context in which it could be understood as abuse. As Kelly points out, it is feminists who invented terms such as *battered woman, domestic violence, sexual harassment, sexual violence* and *incest survivor*, and created the possibility for women to understand their experience in new ways. Naming, she says, "involves making visible what was invisible, defining as unacceptable what was acceptable and insisting that what was naturalised is problematic" (*ibid.*, p. 139). Of the forty-five women she interviewed who had experienced rape, incest and/or domestic violence, 60 per cent "did not define them as such at the time although half of those experiencing domestic violence did so as the abuse continued". Women's definitions of sexual violence, she points out, can and do change over time (*ibid.*, pp. 139, 140).

The anthology *Femicide: The Politics of Woman Killing* seeks to gain recognition of the political significance of the murder of women as a form of sexual violence. Jill Radford and Diana Russell point out that the absence of a term to describe the phenomenon, which has generally been hidden within the particularly inappropriate term *homicide*, has made it difficult for feminists to organise against it. They define *femicide* as "the killing of women by men *because* they are women" and comment:

> We have long needed such a term as an alternative to the gender-neutral *homicide*. Establishing a word that signifies

the killing of females is an important step toward making known this ultimate form of violence against women. Naming an injustice, and thereby providing a means of thinking about it, usually precedes the creation of a movement against it. [Radford and Russell, 1992, p. xiv]

One of the difficulties particular to naming prostitution as abuse of women is that it has not just been ignored or considered natural like other aspects of male violence, but has actually been renamed to be specifically neutral or positive. Naming the abuse in prostitution as work or entertainment makes it particularly hard for women to identify what is happening to them as abuse. The cheerful accounts of stripping or tabletop dancing that are obtained by journalists or researchers who do not start from a sensitive understanding of male violence are possible only because the prostituted women have not developed ways of talking about sexual harassment (see Anon., 1995).

One common finding in Kelly's interviews was that women "minimised" the abuse that they had suffered. She suggests that this was one way of coping with it. "Minimising" which meant "not defining what had happened to them as sexual violence", was the result of either "the influence of dominant meanings" or of the "desire to not see themselves, or be seen by others, as someone who had been assaulted" (Kelly, 1989, p. 145). Judith Herman in *Trauma and Recovery* points out that, "Conventional social attitudes not only fail to recognise most rapes as violations but also construe them as consensual sexual relations for which the victim is responsible" (1994, p. 67). The result is that, under these circumstances, "many women may have difficulty even naming their experience. The first task of consciousness-raising is simply calling rape by its true name." Hoigard and Finstad (1992), in their study of street prostituted women in Oslo, explain that their respondents engaged in minimising at first. They did not start mentioning the violence they suffered with any seriousness until they had known and trusted the interviewers for some considerable time.

One of Kelly's interviewees spoke of seeing sexual harassment as a joke: "I suppose it's my way of coping, my way of interpreting the situation so they don't get through to me" (1989, p. 146). This technique was useful to women because it removed the need to act, and taking action could result in punishment. It was also useful in a situation where the woman was unable to take any action. This latter use of "minimising" would be particularly useful in prostitution, where accepting the sexual harassment is in fact the job for which the woman is paid, and she certainly cannot end it and continue to make a living. Battered women, Kelly explains, adapt techniques of neutralisation to minimise their experiences. They cannot afford to acknowledge the psychological impact of the abuse until after some time, or after they leave the batterers. For prostituted women, this is likely to be after they leave prostitution.

One of Kelly's interviewees explained how minimisation worked in relation to the sexual harassment she endured at work: "They'd chat you up. They'd put their arms around you and press up against you. I always passed it off as being part of the job and never considered it sexual harassment till I left" (ibid., p. 151). Kelly concludes that, in order to make it easier for women to define their experiences of abuse as problematic, feminists need to make a priority of "campaigning around the construction of male-defined stereotypes, particularly in the mass media", and continuing to work to "present feminist alternatives to a wider public" (ibid., p. 157). This is particularly hard in the case of prostitution, in which there is virtually no voice in the public domain which will allow prostituted women to see what happens to them as abuse. On the contrary, there is a cacophony of voices in women's magazines, newspapers, pornography and other media, telling them they "choose" or "enjoy" or should be ashamed of what is being done to them. The difficulties of enabling women to identify the abuse of being prostituted is on a scale considerably harder than naming even such abuses as marital rape and sexual harassment. Kelly points out that many women were able to redefine their experience as a result of finding alternative ways of understanding through articles, programmes or conversations informed by a feminist perspective. But women reading about prostitution from what purports to be a feminist or prostitutes' rights perspective have a good chance of finding a celebration of prostitution. The feminism of sexual liberalism will make it harder rather than easier for prostituted women to identify abuse.

Toby Summer is the pseudonym of an ex-prostituted woman who has written very persuasively of the pressures that caused her to resist naming her experience as abusive. She seeks to explain how prostitution can be said to have "something to do with women owning our own bodies", while at the same time these bodies are being sold "to men who hate women, whores and lesbians" (Summer, 1993, p. 233). She says that, though not always a feminist, she had always wanted to be "free". She felt "closer to freedom" when espousing what she calls the "Man's lie" about her independence in prostitution:

> when I told myself that I chose what happened (even the rapes), that I felt OK about what was done to my body (even against my will) ... that the nausea-alienation-bruises-humiliation-STDs ... poverty-abortion all were somehow fixable with what amounts to an EST positive attitude. [*ibid.*, p. 233]

She lied to herself, she says, because this made her feel better. The lie "attempted to turn my degradation into something else, something more human". She explains that this was a renaming of reality, not a changing of it; and that she maintained this lie after leaving prostitution, even though it allowed no explanation of why she chose to work in a "hot commercial laundry for $1.00 per hour [rather] than fuck another man" (*ibid.*, p. 233).

Unpaid violence in prostitution
Much research over the past twenty years has found that prostituted women suffer high rates of rape and battery from

johns, and battery from pimps and partners. They are all too frequently murdered as a result of their work, or of being seen as prostitutes. One contributor to the *Sex Work* anthology places the number of prostitutes and suspected prostitutes murdered in the Seattle area from 1983 to 1986 as eighty-one (Summers, 1988, p. 117). This is violence which is related to their work in prostitution, but not the violence which constitutes their work. To make this distinction I shall call it "unpaid violence". Advocates on behalf of the prostitution industry tend to see such violence as a workplace hazard that can be eliminated by improving the working conditions and social status of prostituted women and eliminating the social stigma which presently attaches to them.

Nineteen of the twenty-six women interviewed by Hoigard and Finstad had experienced violence as a result of being used in prostitution. But the commonality of the experience meant that they "banalized" violence and could relate "kidnappings, confinement, rapes, and death threats as if these were almost normal occurrences" (Hoigard and Finstad, 1992, p. 62). Partly this was because their childhoods were most often full of violent experiences too, and it fitted their expectations. They were "socialised to accept violence as a part of life".

> When life is otherwise characterized by degradation, humiliation, and insult, then perhaps violence doesn't appear as intolerable and extraordinary. Violence is uncomfortable, but not dramatic or unexpected. Life is not a bed of roses, after all. [*ibid.*, p. 63]

Farley and Hotaling (1995) discovered in their study that 55 per cent of their respondents had been assaulted by johns, 19 per cent of them in the past week. Most of them, 88 per cent, had experienced physical threat in prostitution, 33 per cent in the week before they answered the questionnaire. Rape is common: 68 per cent of their respondents had been raped since entering prostitution, 46 per cent by johns; and 48 per cent had been raped more than five times since being prostituted. Farley and Hotaling found that 49 per cent of their respondents had been badly beaten in childhood by a caregiver. Susan Kay Hunter (1994) from the Council for Prostitution Alternatives reports from her work that prostituted women are raped approximately once a week.

The prostituted women interviewed by Eileen McLeod in Birmingham also reported much unpaid violence. She comments: "Almost without exception, prostitutes I have had contact with have experienced some form of serious physical violence from their clients" (McLeod, 1982, p. 53). The violence was not used to get sex, necessarily, but:

> a prostitute may be punched if a man can't "come" or may be driven off somewhere or threatened if a man wants his money back and she is not prepared to give it to him, or he does not want to pay in the first place. [*ibid.*, p. 54]

The prostituted women adopted a fatalistic attitude, she found, and saw such unpaid violence as "one of the hazards of the job". An Australian study found that one-third of the women had experienced some kind of non-sexual violence, 11 per cent experiencing it on more than seven occasions. One-fifth of these women had been raped at work (Perkins, 1994, p. 172). A contemporary female brothel owner in Sydney with lengthy experience does not see the situation in respect of violence against prostitutes as improving: "The modern client is more demanding, wanting to pay less, looking for kinkier sex and, I believe, more likely to turn to violence" (*ibid.*, p. 139).

Connection between childhood sexual abuse and prostitution

Another way in which many researchers have understood prostitution to be linked to male violence is in the high percentage of prostituted women who report having been sexually abused in childhood. Evelina Giobbe of WHISPER, Women Hurt in Systems of Prostitution Engaged in Revolt, found in the Oral History Project that 90 per cent of the women who participated had been subjected to an "inordinate amount of physical and sexual abuse during childhood: 90 per cent had been battered in their families; 74 per cent had been sexually abused between the ages of 3 and 14". Of the sexually abused women, 93 per cent were abused by a family member (Giobbe, 1990, p. 73). As Giobbe puts it, prostitution is "nothing less than the commercialization of the sexual abuse and inequality that women suffer in the traditional family and can be nothing more" (*ibid.*, p. 80).

Judith Herman, in her first book about child sexual abuse, expressed succinctly the mechanism by which child sexual abuse trains women for prostitution: "The father, in effect, forces the daughter to pay with her body for affection and care which should be freely given. In so doing, he destroys the protective bond between parent and child and initiates his daughter into prostitution" (Herman, 1981, p. 4). In *Trauma and Recovery*, in which she likens women's experience of violence in childhood and in marriage to that of torture victims, she says that the sexually abused child must "develop ... an identity out of an environment which defines her as a whore and a slave" (Herman, 1994, p. 100). The possibility of becoming prostituted increases in those who have experienced such abuse, because they very often develop a sense of themselves as "bad". Herman sees this as the result of seeking to construct a system of meaning which justifies the abuse. The child concludes that her innate badness is the cause, and this, suprisingly, allows her to have some hope of change.

> Participation in forbidden sexual activity also confirms the abused child's sense of badness ... If she ever experienced sexual pleasure, enjoyed the abuser's special attention, bargained for favors, or used the sexual relationship to gain privileges, these sins are adduced as evidence of her innate wickedness. [*ibid.*, p. 104]

As the child develops the belief that she is responsible for the crimes of her abusers, she begins to describe herself as supernatural or inhuman. Children use words like "witches, vampires, whores, dogs, rats, or snakes", and abusers tell them that this is what they are (*ibid.*, p. 105). The inner sense of badness can become a stable part of a child's personality structure and persist into adult life. Perpetrators refer to the victims as sluts and whores to justify their violation, with the result that, "For some survivors, this negative identity formation results in their entry into prostitution" (*ibid.*, p. 51).

Diana Russell (1995) has analysed one of the interviews she carried out with incest victims in South Africa to show how easily such abuse can condition children for prostitution. Her analysis is called "The Making of a Whore". The 23-year-old woman interviewed identifies herself as a "whore". She was groomed by her grandfather, and, as Russell points out, this woman's experience shows how illusory the "choice" of prostitution must be for some abuse victims. The most directly effective part of the training was the way in which the grandfather paid his victim for sex: "When I did anything sexual with him, he'd give me sweets, chips, ice cream, or money. Eventually, I realised what I had to do if I wanted these things" (*ibid.*, p. 80). As she got older, she learnt to get things she wanted out of her compliance with the sexual activity.

> During the last 3 years of our relationship, I began to feel I was in charge. For example, when I saw him getting hard, I'd say, "Okay, I want to do this quickly" or "No, I'm not ready yet. Let's go to the shop first." [*ibid.*, p. 81]

There were other elements in the abuse that were direct training for prostitution. Her grandfather taught her to sit in open-leg positions and perform acts straight out of pornography magazines. The impact of such training on her adult sexual life is that she still expects "men to pay for sex". Lara concludes about her own experience: "If I had to describe myself in one sentence, I'd say, 'I'm a whore.' I can't say what whores are like, but the image I have of them is of being a woman who is totally available" (*ibid.*, pp. 85–7). She considers that,

if she had not got married, she would have become a prostitute because:

> having sex with many men doesn't faze me in the least. I am
> very good at sex, so why should it go to waste? I might as
> well give it to as many men as possible. Being good in bed has
> always been my identity ... I know all the tricks of the trade
> ... [*ibid.*, p. 81]

She feels that she "was born for it" (*ibid.*, p. 87).

Prostitution is commercial sexual violence

In the last decade, feminist activists and researchers have
begun to look rather differently at the connections between
prostitution and sexual violence. Instead of just pointing out
that very large percentages of prostituted women were sea-
soned by being sexually abused in childhood, that prostituted
women suffer from johns a great amount of rape and violence, including death, that is not paid for, some feminists are
asserting that prostitution constitutes sexual violence against
women in and of itself. Cecilie Hoigard and Liv Finstad concluded from their research that prostitution constituted a
"gross form of violence": "The impoverishment and destruction of the women's emotional lives makes it reasonable, in
our eyes, to say that customers practice gross violence against
prostitutes" (1992, p. 115). Fractured jaws would heal, they
said, but "Regaining self-respect and recreating an emotional
life is far more difficult." This discovery was a surprise to
them. It was "*new* knowledge" and the "most important discovery" they made in their research. There was a massive bibliography on prostitution, they remark, but the fact that
prostitution constituted violence was quite absent from it.

This argument is put forward most effectively in the work of
Evelina Giobbe (1991) in "Prostitution: Buying the Right to
Rape". The form of sexual violence which she considers prostitution to resemble most closely is marital rape. She sees prostitution as resembling marriage more closely than employment.

Unlike a labor contract, traditional marriage and prostitution
are both predicated on ownership and unconditional sexual
access to a woman's body. In fact, sexual harassment laws
protect laborers from this presumption of sexual access.
[*ibid.*, p. 143]

Giobbe defines traditional marriage as long-term private ownership by an individual man, and prostitution as short-term
public ownership of women by many men. Prostitution is
about "rental" rather than ownership (*ibid.*, p. 144).

In prostitution, she argues, "crimes against women and
children become a commercial enterprise". These crimes
include child sexual abuse when a man uses a juvenile prostitute, battery when a prostituted woman is used in sadomasochistic sex scenes, and sexual harassment and rape
"When a john compels a woman to submit to his sexual
demands as a condition of 'employment'". According to
Giobbe's analysis, the exchange of money does not transform
the violence of the acts involved into something else: "The
fact that a john gives money to a woman or a child for submitting to these acts does not alter the fact that he is commit-
ting child sexual abuse, rape, and battery; it merely redefines
these crimes as prostitution" (*ibid.*, p. 146).

She concludes that prostitution is the commerce of sexual
abuse and inequality, and quotes Philippa Levine, who carried
out a survey on prostitution in Florida for the Supreme Court
of that state, making the same point very clearly.

In determining the existence of prostitution as a manifestation of psycho-social and socio-economic coercion ... it
would not be mere indulgence in rhetoric to castigate prostitution as a form of collective rape, actually and symbolically.
[quoted in *ibid.*, p. 159]

Prostitution, Giobbe says, is "sexual abuse because prostitutes are subjected to any number of sexual acts that in any
other context, acted against any other woman, would be

labelled assaultive or, at the very least, unwanted and coerced" (*ibid.*, p. 159). Kathleen Barry identifies the sex that men buy in prostitution as the "same sex they take in rape— sex that is disembodied, enacted on the bodies of women who, for the men, do not exist as human beings, and the men are always in control" (1995, p. 36).

Varieties of sexual violence in prostitution

The male sexual behaviour involved in using women in prostitution includes several forms of male sexual violence. The basic male sexual practice carried out upon prostituted women is what I shall call "unwanted sexual intercourse". In heterosexual relationships, this term can be used to describe those experiences of sexual intercourse in which a woman complies with a man's demands without being willing, but also without acknowledging to herself a lack of consent. She will not call what is done to her rape because this would signify lack of consent. This experience correlates well with prostitution in which women have their bodies used in ways they cannot refuse since their livelihoods depend upon it, but which they would never tolerate otherwise. In both practices the male perpetrators inflict sexual acts upon a woman with no respect for her personhood.

Feminist work on wife rape has uncovered a vast secret world of anguish in which women are used in this way by husbands and partners. The study by Diana Russell (1990) of rape in marriage gives us some illuminating insights into women's understanding of consent to sexual intercourse. She found that rape by husbands or ex-husbands, defined conservatively as vaginal, oral or anal penetration with the threat or use of force, was reported by 14 per cent of her respondents. This might seem a high figure to those who are committed to recognising only rape which fits the police-blotter rapist model and to idealising marriage. But more interesting for our present purposes is the existence she reveals of a widespread submission to sexual intercourse which did not fall into her category of rape, and would be likely to be seen as consensual in most jurisdictions and probably by most of the men and women involved.

Women are not free and equal individuals in making marriage or relationship contracts or in giving consent (Jeffreys, 1993). The force which has operated on them all their lives and continues to operate on them within marriages and relationships remains largely invisible. This force consists partly of economic constraints. In the survey of male sexuality by Shere Hite (1981), men share their strategies for forcing an unwilling woman to submit to sexual intercourse, one of which was economic blackmail. The coercion consists of simple bad temper as well as physical violence, and all those forces which have worked upon a girl and woman in her life to persuade her that she must be attached to a man to have value and that she has little right to bodily integrity. Such forces include the massive industry of sexology, sex therapy, sex advice literature, all of which make women feel guilty and inadequate for any unwillingness to fulfil a man's sexual desires. They include sexual abuse in childhood, which can train girls to have a concept of self-worth based simply on the sexual use of their bodies, and harassment on the street and at work. They include subtler forms of harassment in the family and at school, which simply make a girl feel less important than a male. How else, apart from the use of force, are we to understand why a whole class of people, women, allow access to their bodies which can be undesired, painful, even humiliating, on a routine basis, often with no consciousness that it would be reasonable or possible to resist.

Nicola Gavey's research in New Zealand was based on interviews with women who are "articulate, educated, middle class" about what several saw as "very ordinary" experiences of sex with men. Her work shows these kinds of pressures in operation and demonstrates that these women find it hard to resist unwanted sex. One woman explained the controlling power of anger: "Things like actually being called a fucking bitch and having the door slammed. And trying always to explain that it didn't mean that I didn't care because I didn't want to have sex, but never ever succeeding" (Gavey, 1993, p. 109). Another talks of giving in simply to get some sleep. The women describe a variety of pressures that made it impossible for them to say no. Gavey concludes from her interviews that women are "sometimes not aware of consent and non-consent as distinct choices" (ibid., p. 116). The sort of men who use women in this way, it might be reasonable to surmise, are those who find it acceptable to use women in prostitution.

A good example of the level of anguish that unwanted sexual intercourse in marriage can cause comes from an anonymous writer to the Guardian newspaper in 1989:

> Sometimes I lie in bed and think of all the women who might be crying tonight. Crying because they know they'll have to "do it" tomorrow, crying because they can "feel him" coming towards them, crying because he is grunting there on top of them, crying because their bodies aren't their own any more because they promised them away 20 years ago and it doesn't seem possible to get them back. [quoted in Wilkinson and Kitzinger, 1993, p. 307]

The paper was deluged with letters thereafter from women who identified with this writer's feelings. These examples are apparently consensual in that the women generally did not say no or think that that was a possibility, but nonetheless suggest a considerable abuse of women. The unwanted sexual intercourse of prostitution is different from that which takes place in relationships because many different men are involved. It may therefore cause a different level of distress and require more effective methods of dissociation.

Sexual harassment

The other most common form of sexual violence to be paid for in prostitution is sexual harassment. Sexual harassment is one of those forms of abuse that has only been given a name and recognisable form through feminism. Catharine MacKinnon has been particularly influential in turning what feminists were beginning to define as sexual harassment into something that was actionable at law in situations, such as law or education, where it could be defined as an issue of sex discrimination. As MacKinnon explains:

> the sexually harassed have been given a name for their suffer-ing and an analysis that connects it with gender. They have been given a forum, legitimacy to speak, authority to make claims, and an avenue for possible relief. Before, what hap-pened to them was all right. Now it is not. [MacKinnon, 1987, p. 104]

Previous to this time, "The facts amounting to the harm did not socially 'exist', had no shape, no cognitive coherence; far less did they state a legal claim" (*ibid.*, p. 106).

Liz Kelly explains that in her interviews she found it was difficult to distinguish between sexual harassment and sexual assault. She defines sexual harassment as including "a vari-able combination of visual, verbal and physical forms of abuse", whereas sexual assault "always involved physical contact" (Kelly, 1989, p. 103). In detail:

> visual forms include leering, menacing, staring and sexual gestures; verbal forms include whistles, use of innuendo and gossip, sexual joking, propositioning and explicitly threaten-ing remarks; physical forms include unwanted proximity, touching, pinching, patting, deliberately brushing close, grab-bing. [*ibid.*, p. 103]

The most common sites for harassment were in the street and at work. The effect on women victims was that all these forms of harassment were "experienced as intrusive and involved assumptions of intimacy that women felt were inappropriate and/or involved men treating women as sexual objects" (*ibid.*, p. 103).

Kelly found that the work situations in which women were most likely to experience harassment were those which were most sexualised. A sex industry worker describes the abusive behaviour of the audience:

> I wish I had a pound for every time I got called a slag ... Nine times out of ten you walk onto that stage knowing you're going to be slagged off. The attention that you get is essentially hostile not flattering ... Whatever groups of men came in, irrespective of background, they would all behave in a remarkably similar way ... some of the things they would say were really disgusting. They'd do things like grab hold of a girl and try and push a bottle up her. [*ibid.*, p. 105]

Undoubtedly those who argue for the unionisation of prostituted women will explain that it is precisely this sort of problem, of poor working conditions degraded by sexual harassment, that they seek to improve. It is likely that stripping in front of a well-behaved audience of men who were silent and kept their hands to themselves would be less distressing. But there is a problem here. The job of stripping is precisely that of being a sex object so that men can ejaculate. To distinguish between what parts of the job are the sexual harassment that is paid for and therefore not harassment, and what parts are unacceptable and outside the job description, requires a belief that there can be a real difference. Women are, of course, adept at making questionable distinctions. Women are required to distinguish between, as MacKinnon puts it, sexual initiation and sexual harassment, between pornography and erotica, between ordinary sexual intercourse and rape. In the sex industry they must distinguish between paid-for sexual "attention", and sexual harassment. The problem lies in the idea that a job as a sex object is acceptable in the first place.

Work as a barmaid leads to particular problems of sexual harassment because it is traditionally sexualised work. The women in Kelly's study report that customers felt within their rights to make sexual remarks and advances.

It's part and parcel of being a barmaid, or at least that's the impression your employers give you ... Some of them [customers] were quite disgusting, the things that they would say were really, really hurtful, and you weren't supposed to show it, just get on with the job. [*ibid.*, p. 105]

At least in the case of bartending, since men can do the job too and there is an ostensible function that is not just sexual, it is possible to work towards the desexualisation of the job. Desexualisation, the assertion that being a sex object is not part of the job, may help eliminate harassment. However, the resexualisation of such work through the provision of topless barmaids, waitresses and retailing staff by sex industry agencies is likely to make the desexualisation of women's work very difficult to achieve.

Kelly comments that men have a sense of what is an acceptable level of sexual harassment to engage in, depending upon the degree of sexualisation of the woman's work and the sex ratio in the workforce. She says, "What men consider acceptable treatment of strippers would not be acceptable treatment of barmaids, and what is considered acceptable in the latter case would not be routinely acceptable in an office" (*ibid.*, p. 105). But depending upon men to be able to work out these subtle distinctions does not seem efficient. It is unlikely that men returning to the office after watching a stripper would be able to discern that their secretary was not a willing sex object. Also there is no reason to believe that from the woman's point of view sexual harassment is less distressing just because the woman is performing a more sexualised form of work.

Through different areas of the sex industry, a variety of forms of sexual harassment which cause distress to women are normalised by being paid for. Prostituted women have to accept a certain amount of hands-on sexual harassment as part of the job. They have to accept visual harassment too, in which they are reduced to sexual objects by the dominant male stare as men select the women they will use in brothels and on the street. A French prostituted woman, explaining what it felt like to be chosen as a result of this experience in a brothel, said it was "revolting, it's sickening, it's terrible for the women" (Jaget, 1980, p. 75). Visual harassment is what is purchased by men through stripping and tabletop dancing. Verbal harassment can also be bought through the sex industry's provision of phone sex lines. These sex lines institutionalise the practice of "obscene phone calls".

There has been very little feminist research on sexually harassing phonecalls. We do know that they seem to be very common (Sheffield, 1993). A US researcher found that 83 per cent of his sample of women students had received an "obscene" phone call (quoted in Kelly, 1989, p. 83). Liz Kelly reports that there are one-third of a million complaints per year to British Telecom about obscene or malicious phone calls. She found that her interviewees responded to such calls with shock, anger and/or fear. All felt "that their personal space and sense of self had been violated" (*ibid.*, p. 101). Kelly notes that the British branch of the Samaritans—a phoneline for people suffering distress and contemplating suicide—introduced a special service in the early 1980s, "Call Rita", for men wanting to make obscene phone calls. Apparently it was not successful and so women volunteers are still asked to listen to such male callers as part of their work (*ibid.*, note 5, p. 258). Clearly, the Samaritans are far from recognising such calls as a variety of male violence, or surely they would not expect their female volunteers to subject themselves to it.

The sex industry, which markets forms of sexual violence to men for a price, presents a formidable and increasingly significant obstacle to feminist efforts to eliminate sexual violence. As feminists seek to draw attention to the distress and infringement of their rights and opportunities suffered by women through practices such as unwanted sexual intercourse, sexual harassment through unwanted touch or staring or words, these practices are taught to men as exciting and acceptable through the different branches of the sex industry. The sex industry markets precisely the violence, the practices of subordination, that feminists seek to eliminate from the streets, workplaces and bedrooms.

Effects of prostitution and sexual violence

Feminist work on the effects upon women of sexual violence, such as rape, incest, sexual harassment and marital rape, can be usefully applied to the effects of prostitution. Feminist psychoanalysts and psychologists, such as Judith Herman (1994), have applied the concept of post-traumatic stress disorder, accepted by malestream psychologists as resulting from other forms of torture and imprisonment, to incest and domestic violence. In her mistressful work *Loving to Survive* (1994), Dee Graham uses the idea of the Stockholm syndrome, developed from analysing the phenomenon of hostages bonding with their captors, to describe the situation of all women who live with the fear and threat of what Graham calls "sexual terrorism".

Evelina Giobbe argues that prostitution resembles rape in the shocking similarity of its effects, as revealed in the WHISPER Oral History Project. These effects included feelings of humiliation, degradation, defilement and dirtiness. The prostituted women experienced similar difficulties in establishing intimate relationships with men. They experienced disdain and hatred towards men. They suffered negative effects on their sexuality, flashbacks and nightmares, as well as lingering fears and deep emotional pain that often resembled grieving (Giobbe, 1991, p. 155).

> I feel like I imagine people who were in concentration camps feel when they get out ... It's a real deep pain, an assault to my mind, my body, my dignity as a human being. I feel like what was taken away from me in prostitution is irretrievable. [*ibid.*, p. 156]

Some suffered from what Giobbe names "the scarlet letter syndrome", i.e. believing that people, especially men, "can 'tell' that they have been prostitutes by merely looking at them" (*ibid.*). Another effect she identifies is suicide. She reports that figures from public hospitals show that 15 per cent of all suicide victims are prostitutes and one survey of call girls revealed that 75 per cent had attempted suicide. These effects of prostitution, she points out, do not support the idea that prostitution is a victimless crime.

Prostituted women in Giobbe's study blamed themselves for the damage they suffered, assuming that they were "not doing it right", just as battered wives routinely blame themselves for the violence they suffer. Their sense of their own valuelessness was reinforced in prostitution because of the way the men treated them. The johns were so determined to treat the prostituted women they were using as nonpersons that they did not even notice when women were crying as they performed their tricks. The only parallel to this trauma, she suggests, is that found in victims of serious sexual abuse, rape and battery. No other interpersonal, social or work-related type of situation or interaction that elicits these massive traumatic effects on its "participants" would be condoned, she considers. Giobbe concludes that it is extraordinary, considering these effects, that prostituted women are seen not as victims or survivors, but as fully consenting participants.

One way in which feminists are currently seeking to show that men's use of women in prostitution constitutes sexual violence is in identifying the damage resulting from long-term prostitution abuse as post-traumatic stress disorder. Melissa Farley and Norma Hotaling gave a paper on this topic at the NGO Forum of the Fourth World Conference on Women at Beijing in 1995. They explain that their objective is to provide evidence for the harm intrinsic to prostitution.

> In the current psychological and medical literature, discussion of the harm intrinsic to the act of selling one's body for sex is rarely mentioned. We view the experience of prostitution as the experience of traumatic stress ... The experience of prostitution is the experience of being repeatedly sexually assaulted, being dominated, battered and terrorised. [Farley and Hotaling, 1995, p. 1]

They consider that prostituted women, like the victims of hostage situations and torture, suffer the multiple stressors that cause post-traumatic stress disorder.

Farley and Hotaling interviewed 130 prostituted women, transgenders and men. They found that 57 per cent had been sexually abused in childhood, and suggest that this was a low figure which might be explained by an uncertainty in respondents about what abuse was; also the fact that pimps were present while the data was collected caused the distress to be minimised. In addition, they suggest, the respondents might be in denial about their child sexual abuse. They found that, overall, 41 per cent of the 130 prostituted persons met the criteria for diagnosis of post-traumatic stress disorder. This compares with an incidence among battered women in shelters of from 45 per cent to 84 per cent and amongst Vietnam veterans of 15 per cent.

Norwegian researchers Cecilie Hoigard and Liv Finstad, in *Backstreets* (1992), are able to describe the damage done to prostituted women in Oslo in considerable detail because they conducted in-depth interviews with women over a number of years. They consider their research to be unique in concentrating on the defence mechanisms used in prostitution, and the long-term consequences of such techniques. Only one or two of their respondents did not report difficulties in maintaining separation between their public and private selves (*ibid.*, 1992, p. 107). They reported destruction of their sex lives, sometimes because sex simply became boring. One woman described her experience of seeking a sexual relationship whilst in prostitution:

> You're a piece of shit, and you make yourself sick. You get pissed off, and you get bitter. You don't see it as sex, you see it as something awful, something disgusting. I've thrown up during sex, just started throwing up without thinking that it's been awful. It's just happened. [*ibid.*, p. 109]

Others speak of losing the ability to orgasm and having to fake it. They talk of feeling they have become hard and cold. One said, "I'm only the genitals that they use." They spoke of the inability to feel anything, not necessarily because of the unpaid "violence" they experienced but because of the "regular, daily tricks" (*ibid.*, p. 112).

Two women are quoted at length on the difficulties of carrying on a life outside prostitution, such as taking exams and standing up and speaking at meetings when they feel they are still, underneath the facade, the person who was prostituted. They feel they live a double life. One wrote:

> I use tampons all the time. Even when I'm not having my period. It's because I'm afraid of stinking. I never sit too close to people. I wash my ears ten times a day because I'm afraid guck is running out of them. [*ibid.*, p. 113]

Another said that her emotional relationships failed because, when embarking on them, she starts "hating myself, my body is filthy" (*ibid.*, p. 113). Hoigard and Finstad conclude from their respondents' remarks about learning to despise their own bodies and their sexuality, seeing themselves as shit and throwing up:

> We are in our bodies—all the time. We are our bodies. When a woman prostitutes herself, her relationship to her body changes: it is as if she is moving through life inside a boil or clothed head to toe in a rash. [*ibid.*, p. 108]

Dissociation

The practice of dissociation which prostituted women employ to protect their sense of self from violation is so similar to the dissociation employed by sexually abused children that it provides good evidence that the two experiences are similarly abusive. Herman points out that all children can dissociate, but the ability is best developed in abused children.

While most survivors of childhood abuse describe a degree of proficiency in the use of trance, some develop a kind of dissociative virtuosity. They may learn to ignore severe pain, to hide their memories in complex amnesias, to alter their sense of time, place, or person, and to induce hallucinations of possession states. [Herman, 1994, p. 100]

Hoigard and Finstad asked their interviewees in some detail about the defence mechanisms they used. They wanted to know, "How do you avoid prostituting yourself when you prostitute yourself?", and considered this to be the "fundamental question for prostitutes around the world" (Hoigard and Finstad, 1992, p. 64). Prostituted women, they explain, have worked out an ingenious, complex system to protect "the real me, the self, the personality from being invaded and destroyed by customers". As they point out, literature on prostitution which has considered these mechanisms reports remarkably similar techniques (Jaget, 1980; McLeod, 1982). The women use different methods to cut off, such as thinking about something else, using alcohol, Valium or other drugs. One woman explained: "Ugh, the whole thing is sick. I close my eyes and ears. I cut out everything to do with feelings. It's never, never okay. It would be totally different with a lover. I'll stop when I get a steady boyfriend" (Hoigard and Finstad, 1992, p. 65). Another way of protecting the self, recorded by Hoigard and Finstad and other sympathetic literature, is the reservation of parts of the body for uses other than prostitution. As *Backstreets* points out, prostituted women reverse the traditional understanding of the parts that men may be allowed to touch on dates. Genitals are allowed and the mouth is taboo. One woman remarked, "Necking is gross—forget it." Another said, "I can't stand kissing either … It's revolting" (*ibid.*, p. 66).

Other techniques used include trying to make the trick as short as possible. Hoigard and Finstad explain that "the less time a john has, the less chance he has to be invasive" (*ibid.*, p. 68). One of their interviewees describes how to survive tricks and hurry them up:

If it takes more than 15 minutes, then it's a long time. A half-hour is an extremely long time. You're sitting there completely dressed—you only pull down the one pant leg. I don't call it sex. I think about other things, try to pass the time, breathe a little faster to get it to go faster. [*ibid.*, p. 69]

As another woman pointed out, "I get sore if it takes too long." Pretending excitement is a common technique to create short tricks.

Prostituted women employ various techniques of putting on new selves with wigs and new names, and shower and wash extensively after the act to protect their "civilian self" (*ibid.*, p. 70). It is disturbing that there is some evidence that the defensive mechanisms are now breaking down for some groups of women. One is that group of women who are desperate for money for drugs, particularly for crack. Where limits are dropped, then the self is reduced to the sexually exploited thing that is being used (Barry, 1995, p. 44).

Not all researchers see the technique of dissociation as a negative aspect of prostitution. Eileen McLeod, whose study of prostitution does not take a sexual violence perspective, sees this technique as demonstrating the control that prostituted women have over their work: "prostitutes have a fair degree of control over their own labour process in certain respects" (1982, p. 36). They are "negotiating from a position of strength" with the "spirit of the independent trader". As evidence of this control, she cites precisely those techniques seen by Hoigard and Finstad, for instance, as evidence of harm, such as hurrying clients up and the ability to "turn themselves off". Use of these "protective devices", she says, shows that working prostitutes are "not prepared to have their emotional beings taken over against their will any more than their bodies". But the turning off which was supposed to indicate the strength of prostitutes to control their work nonetheless had the same negative effects on her respondents as other researchers have discovered. As one of McLeod's interviewees reported, "You've got no feeling, you're a robot" (*ibid.*, pp. 40, 58).

Seeing prostitution as a form of male sexual violence enables researchers to hear and take seriously what prostituted women say about the damage they suffer, and throws light on what the consequences may be. It brings the john into view as the perpetrator, instead of just a man acting naturally. It demonstrates the serious obstacle posed by the sex industry to the success of feminist aims to eliminate violence against women. The sex industry, by encouraging men to pay for inflicting this violence, teaches that it is acceptable to treat women as sex objects, as nonpersons, unworthy of common respect. Defining prostitution as sexual violence offers a promising new approach which can be used to campaign against global prostitution, in the form of feminist human rights theory and strategy. Feminist human rights theorists, as we shall see in the next chapter, are working to incorporate into international law an awareness of men's violence against women as a violation of women's human rights.

CHAPTER 10

sexual violence, feminist human rights theory and the omission of prostitution

... homeless in her own body. [Lepa Mladjenovic, Serbian feminist anti-war activist describing effects of rape in war, quoted in Copelon, 1995, p. 202]

In October 1993 the General Assembly of the United Nations passed a resolution adopting the Declaration on the Elimination of Violence Against Women (United Nations, 1996). The Declaration is the result of the determined efforts of feminist activists to gain recognition of violence against women as a human rights violation. The general definition of violence against women it contains is well suited to the inclusion of prostitution:

any act of gender-based violence that results in, or is likely to result in, physical, sexual or psychological harm or suffering to women, including threats of such acts, coercion or arbitrary deprivation of liberty, whether occurring in public or in private life. [*ibid*, p. 475]

However, the list of the practices understood to constitute violence against women in this document specifically excludes "free" prostitution. Only "trafficking in women and forced prostitution" are included. As Kathleen Barry points out, the omission of all forms of sexual exploitation from the Declaration was "not an oversight" (Barry, 1995). Barry concluded from her conversations with those involved in the drafting that a definite decision was reached to exclude prostitution from the document. This chapter aims to show the appropriateness and importance of including prostitution in feminist human rights theory and activism against violence against women. But first I shall consider the controversy which exists within feminist theory and activism as to whether human rights are an appropriate tool for feminists to use at all. Though I consider that the language of human rights can be useful in some situations, as I will demonstrate here, this position needs to be firmly based on an understanding of the pitfalls as well as the advantages of human rights ideas.

Scepticism about rights

Scepticism about rights stems from many sources that have no relation to feminism. Jeremy Waldron explains that, though rights are being taken far more seriously at the end of the twentieth century than ever, there is still considerable controversy. Critics are concerned about:

> The abstract universalism of this sort of theory, the individualism of rights, the tension between rights and the demands of community, the use of social contract models in the theory of politics, the absolutism and apparent oversimplification of the claims that rights express, the use and abuse of reason and a priorism in political argument, and the troubled idea of natural law. [Waldron, 1987, p. 3]

The approach of Marx in his "On the Jewish Question" underlies the scepticism of many political activists and theorists including feminists, about rights. Marx argues that it is the interests of bourgeois capitalist individuals extrapolated to represent universal principles of human nature that are expressed in ideas about rights. These interests include the bourgeoisie's freedom from restriction by the state and from obligations towards social welfare so that they may pursue individual profit unhindered. From such interests spring the right to liberty, to property, to personal security.

Some human rights literature lends support to the idea that rights are in opposition to all that socialists care about. Irwin Cotler (1993) contributed a passionate chapter to *Human Rights in the Twenty-First Century*, entitled "Human Rights as the Modern Tool of Revolution". He sees what he calls the international human rights movement as the new movement of liberation which will liberate people from, among other things, socialism. He writes in a celebratory fashion about the fall of the Berlin Wall. The "power of the people" in Eastern Europe had prevailed over "the state and the party", through the human rights revolution created by the human rights movement.

> This, then, was the year of the people, the power of the powerless, the year of the revolution, the velvet revolution, "without force or lies" … And, most importantly, a revolution anchored in—and inspired by—the power of an idea—human rights—an idea emerging as the "secular religion" of our times; and of international human rights law—the internationalization of human rights and the humanization of international law—as the revolutionary change agent of the [human rights] revolution. [Cotler, 1991, p. 9]

But the sort of rights that Cotler has in mind are not those which put bread on anyone's table, and in many cases the bread is disappearing fast. It is difficult for those who care more for social justice than abstract individual rights to share with unalloyed enthusiasm in this anti-communist triumphalism.

It is not surprising that feminists from a socialist tradition have been sceptical about using rights talk. One of these is British feminist legal theorist Carol Smart, who considers that the concept of rights is too flawed to be used for social justice purposes. She explains that when women, or other less powerful groups, resort to law "structured on patriarchal precedents", they invoke a power which can work against them

(Smart, 1989, p. 138). Her examples are the *Sex Discrimination Act* and the *Race Relations Act* in Britain. Both acts can be used by the powerful, men or white Britons, to demand their rights in ways damaging to those who believed the Acts were designed to protect them. She considers that the struggles for equal rights of earlier feminists were justified because they were fighting against legally imposed impediments, whereas now the law no longer gives rights to men which it denies to women.

> I am suggesting that the rhetoric of rights has become exhausted, and may even be detrimental. This is especially the case where women are demanding rights which are not intended (in an abstract sense) to create equal rights with men, but where the demand is for a 'special" right (e.g. women's right to choose) for which there has been no masculine equivalent. [*ibid.*, p. 139]

But talk in terms of rights is attractive to feminists, she suggests, because rights constitute a "political language" through which interests can be advanced. There is a popular understanding and acceptance of rights, so that "To claim that an issue is a matter of rights is to give the claim legitimacy". Rights talk enables a claim to be taken up by trade unions, parliaments, the media. Rights talk squelches opposition, since "It is almost as hard to be against rights as it is to be against virtue" (*ibid.*, p. 143).

As an argument against using rights, she proposes that "rights oversimplify complex power relations". This can lead to the false notion that the acquisition of rights shows "that a power difference has been 'resolved'" (*ibid.*, p. 144). Legal rights, she says, do not resolve problems, but "transpose" the problem into one defined as having a legal solution. Another problem in using rights is that rights can compete with one another. This has been evident in some areas of crucial concern to women, such as the protection of women and children from male violence. "Whilst a child or a wife may have the right not to be molested, the husband also has rights that the law will uphold. For example, the right to live in "his" home, the right to see "his" children ..." (*ibid.*, p. 145). It is a problem of considerable concern for feminists that rights can be appropriated by the powerful for use against the weak. One example is the European Union *Convention on the Rights of the Child*, "which is now being used to extend the authority of unmarried men over their illegitimate children" (*ibid.*). Unmarried fathers were using the "right to a family life" to claim rights over children.

A good example of the way in which the use of rights can backfire is given by Judy Fudge in relation to the new Charter of Rights in Canada and its effect on sexual assault laws. Apparently feminists were enthusiastic about the Charter because of its commitment to equality rights, even if in a rather general form. They were appalled to discover that men could use the equality provisions of the Charter to get round the clauses of the new sexual assault laws that feminists had been instrumental in introducing. Male defendants successfully challenged two sections of the new criminal code on sexual assault by arguing that any legislation which does not apply equally to female offenders and male children is discriminatory. These sections dealt with a "male person" having sexual intercourse with a female person under fourteen or with "his stepdaughter, foster daughter or female ward" (Fudge, 1989, p. 451). This demonstrates that abstract equality rights cannot be effective in protecting members of powerless groups who start out before the law as unequal. The feminist-inspired sexual assault laws did recognise this; the Charter, which relied on notions of formal equality, could not.

Elizabeth Kingdon's *What's Wrong with Rights* is a collection of her essays put together at a time when the idea of rights is gaining some ascendancy within British political fora. There are calls for a Bill of Rights, for instance. Kingdon criticises feminist approaches to both the law and the use of rights. Marxist approaches to the law and the feminist approach associated with Catharine MacKinnon she attacks as "essentialist", "the meaning of essentialism here being the type of reductionism whereby legal relations are said to be reducible to economic relations" or, in the case of feminist theory of law, the power relations between men and women (Kingdon, 1991, p. 46). But rights are essentialist too, because they rely on essentialist theories, presumably the idea of "natural" law and innate rights. It is fashionable for post-modern and other feminists to attack any ideas they do not like as "essentialist", so that the word has lost all meaning and has become a shorthand for "I don't agree with that." It has become a word used to frighten and subdue debate. Rights do not, of course, have to rely on "natural" anything, as Attracta Ingram seeks to explain in her book *A Political Theory of Rights* (1994). Rights can be the result of a community deciding upon its values rather than seeking them in some primeval condition.

Kingdon's main reservation about feminist use of rights is the problem of competing rights. As she explains: "If feminists claim that a woman has the right to reproduce, there is no obvious reason why that right should not be claimed for men too, and on traditional liberal grounds of equality it would be difficult to oppose that claim" (Kingdon, 1991, p. 79). She suggests that feminists should not use the language of rights, but choose a language more suited to women's political situation.

> I would still make a case for reconceptualising "women's rights" in terms of capabilities, capacities and competencies, as a political working habit to help with the identification of the benefits and drawbacks for feminists which a formal declaration of rights may carry. [*ibid.*, p. 131]

She gives an example of how this could be done. In Scotland, where debate was taking place around a Bill of Rights, a women's group chose to intervene in a way which eschewed the language of rights altogether, whilst addressing the issues at stake. These women submitted an 11-point programme of recommendations for the improvement of Scottish women's political status, which included equality audits and positive discrimination. No rights were invoked, and Kingdon remarks: "it is possible to construct the materials of feminist politics of law without using rights discourse" (*ibid.*, p. 152).

The criticisms of feminist theorists of law such as Smart and Kingdon apply to regimes in which rights are not necessarily the dominating force behind the law. They are both British, and Britain does not have a Bill of Rights. US feminist theorists have a harder task of deciding how to relate to a legal system built upon the idea of rights, as Kingdon notes:

> the decision whether or not to invoke rights ... is one that must be based on calculations of likely success or failure of the campaigns so presented ... it is not always possible to choose the terrain of feminist poliltics ... The political climate of the US is not the same as that of the UK, both because in the UK there is no written constitution expressed in terms of rights ... For these reasons it would be easier for UK feminists than for US feminists to abandon the discourse of rights. [*ibid.*, p. 130]

Kingdon concludes that it is not possible to establish a "single principle, then, in terms of which it is possible to know in advance, in each and every case, whether feminist politics of law should make an appeal to rights" (*ibid.*, p. 149). The efficacy of using rights must depend on the circumstances.

The feminist enthusiasm for using international human rights law has come in for criticism from deconstructionists, too. The idea of human rights has been seen as creating a false universalism, as Western ideology imposed through colonial dominance on cultures in which it might not readily apply. Radhika Coomaraswamy considers the problem of universalism in the context of women in South Asia. She seeks to find a pathway between the "Orientalist trap", of seeing the West as ideologically superior, and the reverse of this argument, i.e. a sentimental view of the communitarianism of the East.

> It is easy to divide the world into bipolar categories: the west is progressive on women's rights and the east is barbaric and

backward. The reverse of this argument from the eastern point of view is to accept the distinction, but to say that the east is superior, more communal, and less self-centered with no place for this "adversarial" concept of rights. [Coomaraswamy, 1994, p. 40]

Coomaraswamy says she is in agreement with the "enlighten-ment" view of the human personality implicit in the feminist human rights movement, i.e. "the free independent woman as an individual endowed with rights and rational agency". But she considers that it would be wrong to assume the values contained in the *Universal Declaration of Human Rights* to be truly universal, as this would make "more than half the world the subject of ridicule" (*ibid.*, pp. 40, 41). In Sri Lanka, she explains, "Rights discourse with its notions of the empowered individual comes up against communitarian notions of the family: an ideological force far stronger than rights discourse and perhaps the most formidable obstacle women's rights activists face" (*ibid.*, p. 52). Interestingly, she concludes that it is the notion of the private sphere, which came to Sri Lanka with a colonial inheritance of personal laws, that stands in the way of women's rights.

Celina Romany stresses that a feminist critique of human rights law "needs to engage in a dialogue which forces the anti-subordination thrust of feminism through the filter of cultural diversity" (1994, p. 106). But such a project needs to "transcend any relativistic paralysis" since "relativist resigna-tion" can reinforce the status quo. She says women need to consider carefully how much authority is given to tradition because of the danger that the "challenge to the hegemony of male values" may be surrendered (*ibid.*, p. 107).

Despite these warnings by Smart, Kingdon and Fudge that rights can be appropriated by the powerful against the powerless, to members of oppressed constituencies who are just beginning to taste the language of rights, deconstruction of rights seems less urgent than the attempt to use them. The black legal theorist Patricia Williams makes this argument.

"Rights" feels so new in the mouths of most black people. It is still so deliciously empowering to say. It is a sign for and a gift of selfhood that is very hard to contemplate restructuring ... at this point in history. It is the magic wand of visibility and invisibility, of inclusion and exclusion, of power and no power. [quoted in Charlesworth, 1994, p. 61]

The feminist criticism of rights seems to relate less well, generally, to the use of international human rights law. International law is quite different from that of national jurisdictions, in that it is based specifically on rights. Any language which avoided rights would be likely to be obscure and ineffective. There is another way in which feminist criticisms could be seen as inappropriate for international law. At a one-day conference on feminism and international law at the University of Melbourne Law School in 1996, distinguished feminist legal theorists such as Hilary Charlesworth and Christine Chinkin argued that there was no choice for practitioners actually involved in seeking to use international law for women, since rights language was all that had validity. Women from the audience who worked for non-government organisations endorsed these statements by saying they had no choice other than using rights langauage. When faced with the urgent need for action, activists had to use rights language because that was the only language that worked or could set legal remedies in operation on issues such as political detainees. The *Universal Declaration of Human Rights*, for instance, could be employed in argument only by using the language of rights. The discussion of whether it was appropriate for feminists to use rights talk was characterised as an academic discussion which had little application in the malestrom of practical politics.

I have considerable sympathy with this view, and will argue that in international law it is reasonable to seek to fit women into the United Nations' understanding of rights in order to establish the unacceptability, internationally, of male violence to women. But the discussion needs to go further.

The feminist theorists of international law whom I will now consider do not spend much time on whether the concept of rights should be used or not. They mount a swingeing critique of the way in which rights have been understood and have excluded women, and particularly the problem of male violence, but they do not throw out the baby with the bathwater. They seek ways to make male violence central to the idea of rights. Elisabeth Friedman, in her description of the emergence of a women's human rights movement, explains why she sees the adoption of the language of rights as important for women. It places women's issues on the mainstream agenda; it lends legitimacy to political demands; it is accepted by most governments and has established protocols (Friedman, 1995, p. 19). Celina Romany explains that human rights discourse is "a powerful tool within international law to condemn those state acts and omissions that infringe core and basic notions of civility and citizenship" (1994, p. 85).

The feminist challenge to the concept of international human rights

Though committed to the use of human rights as a positive tool, feminist legal theorists are well aware of its masculinist and individualist roots and determined to extirpate them. Feminist legal theorists have sought to expand and change the idea of human rights so that the concerns of women might be included. This development is of fairly recent origin. Most of the critical writings have emerged since the mid-1980s, as feminist political and legal theory, which was already developing a strong critique of liberalism and the liberal state, began to apply these new understandings to the field of human rights (see Pateman, 1988; MacKinnon, 1989). Feminist theorists have shown that human rights law is clearly what Catharine MacKinnon has called law from the male point of view. This is evident even in the use of language which excludes women. Human rights have traditionally been characterised in documents as the "rights of man". The major human rights documents are written in masculine language and interpreted as applying to men, except for the 1989 *Convention on the Rights of the Child*. This masculine bias is evident still in the *Banjul Charter* or the *African Charter on Human and People's Rights* (1981) which was adopted by the Organization of African Unity (Wright, 1993). The very existence of a specialised convention on women's rights, the *Convention to Eliminate All Forms of Discrimination Against Women*, is simply an indication of the manifest failure of human rights law to deal with women's issues.

Feminist rights theorists point out that the bourgeois individuals for whom rights protections were intended were specifically male. The idea of human rights grows from civil libertarian roots in the work of Locke, Hobbes and Mill, who were concerned to protect male citizens from the egregious intrusion of the state in what were seen to be their private affairs (Abella, 1993). There was a role for the state only when one person violated the rights of another. Individuals were protected from the unwarranted interventions of the state. The men whose interests dictated the formation of the notion of rights in Western liberalism were concerned to construct "negative freedom", i.e. the "right to do or be what [he] is able to do or be, without interference from other persons" or from the state (Romany, 1994, p. 96).

Understandably, then, human rights ideas emphasise what feminist theorists have called the public/private distinction and adopt a masculine view of what is important. On the international level this is even more obvious than on a national one, because international law evolved as a system of rules to regulate relations among states, the supreme actors in public space, and remains centred on the state (Donna Sullivan, 1995). As Romany puts it, international society represents a "blown-up liberal state that legislates in accordance with liberal humanistic values". In fact, international norms call on the state to protect the institution of the family and enshrine the right of privacy in the family (Romany, 1994, p. 87). For instance, Article 16 of the *Universal Declaration of Human Rights* (1948), states: "The family is the natural and fundamental group unit of society and is entitled to protection by society and the State" (Rao, 1993, p. 73). The same formulation appears in subsequent human rights documents, such as Article 23 of the *International Convention on Civil and Political Rights* (1966) and Article 10 of the *Covenant on Economic, Social and Cultural Rights* (1966). As Arati Rao points out:

> This formal recognition of the state's role, and formal demand for the deployment of state power, in maintaining the legally-recognised heterosexual family unit is nothing short of extraordinary, given that the person who is primarily identified with the family, the woman, is not conceptually central to human rights documents or discourse. [*ibid.*, p. 74]

One difficulty that can arise from this state protection of the "family" is that a woman's "dissatisfaction with or departure from the family becomes conceptually problematic" (*ibid.*). As Catharine MacKinnon explains, the law of privacy is designed to protect "The existing distribution of power and resources within the private sphere". The concept of "privacy"

> has shielded the place of battery, marital rape, and women's exploited labor; has preserved the central institutions whereby women are *deprived* of identity, autonomy, control and self-definition; and has protected the primary activity through which male supremacy is expressed and enforced. [MacKinnon, 1987, p. 101]

The right to privacy is a right of men "'to be let alone' to oppress women one at a time", and to keep "some men out of the bedrooms of other men" (*ibid.*, p. 102).

Hilary Charlesworth explains that the Western version of the public/private distinction lies at the heart of public international law, a discipline still largely informed by Western values and structures. Therefore international law is a medium for exporting the ideology of this distinction from the developed to the developing world. Feminist concern with the distinction is twofold, she says. One concern is the way in which it has been used to exclude women from the public sphere, in areas such as the professions and the vote. Another is the problem of what has been seen to be the business of the law and what has been left unregulated. The law's absence from the supposed realm of women and the family in fact devalues women and their functions rather than signifying non-control or neutrality. As this distinction is replicated in international law, the UN Charter makes the (public) province of international law distinct from the (private) sphere of domestic jurisdiction. The law of state responsibility sorts out that which is accountable from "private" actions. "Rights", Charlesworth says, "are defined by the criteria of what men fear will happen to them". The non-regulation of the private sphere legitimates self-regulation, "which translates inevitably into male dominance" (Charlesworth, 1994, p. 71).

Charlesworth demonstrates the ways in which the three generations of rights, identified according to the chronology of their recognition, are constrained by this distinction. First-generation rights are those set out in the International *Convention on Civil and Political Rights*. These rights are designed to protect men in public life from violations by the government. This is clear from Article 6 of the *Convention on the Right to Life* which is intended, and interpreted, to be about deprivation of life through public action. It does not protect women in all those situations in which women are most at risk of losing their lives, such as botched abortion, infanticide, malnutrition, limited access to health care, and endemic violence against women. Certain of these rights specifically protect men in ways which are detrimental to women's interests. One of these is the right to privacy, which means the protection of men's power in the family. Another is the right to freedom of expression, an idea which has been used to support men's production and use of pornography despite considerable recognition of its adverse effects on women, such as incitement to violence against women (MacKinnon, 1994b).

Second-generation rights are social, economic and cultural rights. These still have a built-in public/private distinction which assumes that all effective power lies with the state. When conditions of work are considered, for instance, these are interpreted as applying to work in the public sphere. The idea of equal pay applies only to the public sphere. Women's domestic work is ignored (Waring, 1988). Moreover, the notion of cultural and religious rights can actually protect the oppression of women by protecting traditions and customs, such as female genital mutilation.

Third-generation rights are collective or group rights. These have been promoted by developing nations as a challenge to Western notions of individualism. The philosophical basis is the commitment to community over individuals. But the right to development, for instance, supports male economic domination, and the right to self-determination can be used to allow the oppression of women. An example, Charlesworth suggests, is strong US support for the Afghani resistance movement after the 1979 Soviet invasion, which showed no concern for the status of women, despite the denial of education to girls in the refugee camps. The resulting rule of the Taliban in much of Afghanistan has created a human rights emergency for women, who suffer severe violence for failing to wear regulation clothing or exercising any independent movement.

Another problem in the ideology of human rights is the reliance on the idea of equality which has serious drawbacks for women. Behind the idea of equality is the male norm, so, as Shelley Wright (1993) points out, maternity and childcare are marginalised and require special measures. Feminists seeking to fit women into a notion of human rights based on the equality principle have apparently only two directions open to them. The approach of liberal feminists has been to emphasise women's sameness to men. The difficulty with this approach is that it accepts a male norm and contradicts important material differences between the experience of women and men such as pregnancy and maternity. An alternative approach is to emphasise women's difference from men, but this contains the problem of potentially marginalising women's rights by presenting them as different from men and less worthy of resources.

There is a third possibility, which is proving difficult to achieve because it conflicts with the ideology behind human rights discourse. A new approach is required which will recognise, as Marilyn Waring puts it, that "Women suffer from social subordination, systematic abuse and deprivation of social power, resources and respect, because we are women. Owing to social inequality, women are not in the same situation as men. We cannot be treated as identical" (1997, p. 139).

MacKinnon calls the approach which recognises the structural imbalance of power between men and women, the difference that oppression creates, the "dominance approach". She opposes this to the "difference approach" which accepts a male norm.

> From the point of view of the dominance approach, it becomes clear that the difference approach adopts the point of view of male supremacy on the status of the sexes. Simply by treating the status quo as "the standard," it invisibly and uncritically accepts the arrangements under male supremacy. In this sense, the difference approach is masculinist, although it can be expressed in a female voice. The dominance approach, in that it sees the inequalities of the social world from the standpoint of the subordination of women to men, is feminist. [MacKinnon, 1987, p. 43]

As Kathleen Mahoney puts it, there needs to be "an understanding of equality in terms of socially created advantage or disadvantage instead of sameness and difference" (1994, p. 441). As she explains, the "second-class citizenship women endure ensures their difference from men, so it makes no sense to require them to be the 'same' as socially advantaged men" (ibid., p. 442).

Mahoney has been influential in Canada in gaining acceptance of these ideas. The law as it stands is inadequate to address the harms that women experience, she explains, because it is "male-defined and built on male conceptions of problems and of harms". This is particularly clear in issues concerned with sexual violence and reproduction, so that "legal treatment of sexual harassment, prostitution, sexual assault, reproductive choice, and pornography cannot be characterised or questioned as sex equality issues because the male comparators have no comparable disadvantage or need". The problem with a sameness/difference model, she says, is that it assumes that equality exists and is the norm and that from time to time autonomous individuals are discriminated against. Systemic, persistent disadvantage is not contemplated. This "Aristotelian model is incapable of proposing or restructuring or even identifying systemic discrimination in educational institutions, workplace, professions, family or the welfare system" (*ibid.*, p. 442). It assumes that these areas of public life are fine as they are and women just need the same chance as men to participate in them. In Canadian law there has been progress as a result of feminist activism. A new Canadian test determines discrimination in terms of disadvantage, i.e. whether a practice further disadvantages the already disadvantaged.

Charlotte Bunch asks the question "Why have so many degrading life experiences of women not been understood as human rights issues?", and suggests that this is because the dominant definition of human rights sees them as "ones that pertain primarily to the types of violation that the men who first articulated the concept most feared". Women, she says, are transforming the concept of human rights to "address the degradations and violations that are a fundamental threat to our human dignity and right to life, liberty, and security of person" (Bunch, 1995, pp. 11, 13). The propertied men who advanced the cause of human rights were already masters of the home. When women were denied rights in the private sphere that the men were so keen to protect, they were shut out of democracy too.

Human rights and violence against women

Feminist human rights theorists have been so thorough in their criticism of the male bias of rights ideas precisely because they want to find an effective way to employ them in a way that will help women. In the struggle against male violence, in particular, some of the sharpest critics see the human rights approach as a potentially valuable tool. Much of the most interesting, innovative and passionate work from feminist human rights theorists has been concerned with this issue. The question of violence against women must transform the basis on which human rights have been conceptualised and pursued, i.e. the models of equality and the public/private distinction which have so shaped international law. The language of human rights enables violence against women to be defined in powerful ways that the human rights community might have to take seriously. Romany describes such violence as "infringement of the core and basic notions of civility and citizenship", and says that it "assaults life, dignity and personal integrity" (1994, p. 85). Such language lifts violence against women out of the "private" realm in which it had been disregarded as "domestic" disputes, into terms which men had been accustomed to use to refer to injuries to themselves.

It is precisely because violence by husbands occurs in what liberal ideology defines as the non-political, private sphere, which should not be subject to regulation by the state, that it has been difficult within national jurisdictions to get it taken seriously. As Hilary Charlesworth puts it, "violence against women is understood ... as aberrant 'private' behaviour" when in fact it is "part of the structure of the universal subordination of women" (1995, p. 107). This problem is magnified in the international arena. To demonstrate the way in which human rights law is dedicated to protecting the interests of men but not of women against violence, feminist theorists have compared violence by husbands with torture, a practice which is taken seriously in human rights documents and fora. Catharine MacKinnon (1993) explains that torture and inequality on the basis of sex are largely recognised as core human rights violations, and asks therefore why, when these violations are combined—as in rape, battering and pornography—no violation is recognised at all. Torture is seen as taking place in the public world, and at the behest of the state. It fits the traditional understanding of human rights violations as abuses by the state of men's privileges. "Torture is regarded as politically motivated not personal; the state is involved in it" (*ibid.*, p. 25). But, MacKinnon points out, it is hard to argue that what is done to women in relationships by men is less serious as a form of violence than torture as commonly understood.

Battering, she says, is also politically motivated. It is systematic and group-based, and defines the quality of community life and the distribution of power. Violence is recognised as political only "when men control and hurt and use other men, persons who are deserving of dignity, on some basis men have decided is worthy of dignity, like political ideology" (*ibid.*, p. 26). Atrocities against women, on the other hand, do not involve acts by the state, and international instruments are seen as controlling only state action. MacKinnon points out that the state is implicated in husband violence because "the cover-up, the legitimization, and the legalization of the abuse is official" (*ibid.*, p. 29). The state can be held responsible because it acquiesces in violence against women. This approach has enabled feminist theorists to demand that men's violence against women be taken seriously and seen as actionable under human rights documents.

The definition of torture currently in use in recent human rights documents could easily include violence against women. Rhonda Copelon gives this definition as "wilful infliction of severe physical or mental pain or suffering not only to elicit information but also to punish, intimidate, discriminate, obliterate the victim's personality, or diminish her personal capacities" (1995, p. 201). Husband violence and rape, she says, have a deliberate purpose, which is to "maintain an individual woman and women as a class in an inferior, subordinate position" (Copelon, 1994b, p. 130). Her comparison of husband violence with torture on the issue of eliciting truth is most compelling. In husband violence too there are

> questions, accusations, insults, and orders: Where were you today? Who were you with? Who visited you? What do you mean you want to go out to work? Why is the coffee cold? the house a mess? this item moved? You're dumb, ugly, old ... [*ibid.*, 1994, p. 131]

Copelon defines the power structure which operates in the home, and under which battered women are forced to suffer, as a "parallel state". This parallel state is allowed to survive and not seen as a threat to the authority of the nation state because it does not disrupt, but maintains, the purposes of that nation state. Wife-beating, she explains, is "a social license, a duty or sign of masculinity, deeply engrained in culture, widely practiced, denied, and completely or largely immune from legal sanction" (*ibid.*, p. 132).

Why has prostitution been omitted?

In their consideration of violence against women as a violation of women's human rights, some feminist theorists have been careful to exclude prostitution. Kathleen Mahoney's important development of feminist rights theory to include pornography provides one example. She offers a comprehensive list of forms of male violence against women which should be seen as rights violations, with this signal omission.

> Gross human rights violations in the form of sexual violence practiced against women and children transcend cultures and national boundaries. Sexual assault, sexual harassment, wife battery, incest, marital rape and forced prostitution exist as serious social problems in all member states of the United Nations—states which, by virtue of their membership, agree to principles of inviolability of the person and gender equality. [Mahoney, 1993, p. 757]

The inclusion of "forced prostitution" suggests a distinction has been drawn between this and "free" prostitution, which is not in the list. Mahoney has been influential in arguing for the recognition of pornography as violating women's human rights because it presents "sexual degradation, sadism and violence against women as legitimate and pleasurable 'entertainment' for men" (*ibid.*). The omission of prostitution from her cogent and thorough analysis of pornography is puzzling when pornography is seen by many feminists as simply the representation of a small part of what happens in prostitution.

Mahoney's approach to pornography could apply most aptly to prostitution. She explains that the real value of pornography as freedom of expression in liberal theory has not been adequately assessed in terms of the real harms it inflicts. She goes on to argue that "a principled approach which would protect legitimate speech but also protect women's bodily security and equality rights requires a harms-based equality analysis", and according to such an analysis the production of pornography results in a loss of rights for women as a class and a gain of rights for men. She defines the harm in pornography in a way which makes the omission of prostitution from this harms-based approach seem anomalous:

> pornography subordinates and harms women in order to "entertain" men by sexually stimulating them. Because the portrayal of and actual subordination of women in pornogoraphy contributes to and exacerbates the subordination of women generally, pornography has a disparate, disadvantaging impact on all women. If women are to be recognised as full bearers of rights and if any progress toward protecting women's human rights and the elimination of violence against them is to be achieved, limits on the exploitation of women in pornography are required. [*ibid.*, p. 759]

She opposes the educative effects of pornography, but prostitution is surely educative too. She opposes the exploitation and subordination of the women in pornography so that—unless we are to assume that the real violation lies only in the fact that they were photographed—it is hard to see why the acts of prostitution involved are not violating in themselves.

Interestingly, Kathleen Mahoney has recently ceased to make this distinction between forced and free prostitution central to her thinking and activism. She is now an executive board member of the Coalition Against Trafficking in Women, which unites so-called "free" prostitution with all other forms under the category of sexual exploitation. She has explained that she thinks that the forced/free distinction is not useful to activism against trafficking. In Mahoney's view, the use of force is difficult to prove in the drive to end trafficking, as it is in rape cases, and the abolition of the distinction is likely to be the only efficacious way to proceed (personal communication).

Another anti-violence rights theorist who chooses to omit prostitution from her definition of male violence is Joan Fitzpatrick (1994). In "The Use of International Human Rights Norms to Combat Violence Against Women", she examines the way in which existing international human rights treaties could be used to combat violence against women. She considers seven areas of such violence: domestic violence and rape; female genital mutilation; violence by police and security forces, including the torture of detained women; violence against women in war; violence against women refugees and asylum seekers; and violence against women in the workplace, including sexual harassment. Her seventh category, violence associated with prostitution and pornography, clearly excludes any definition of prostitution as sexual violence in and of itself.

The passionate and powerful language and concepts used by feminist human rights theorists to describe the injury of rape could be seen to apply neatly to the injury of prostitution. Rhonda Copelon, for instance, defines rape as "against women's body, autonomy, integrity, selfhood, security and self esteem, as well as standing in the community" (1995, p. 201). Rape is, she says:

a grave violation of physical and mental integrity. Every rape has the potential to debilitate profoundly, to alienate a woman from her own body and destroy her sense of security in the world. Every rape is an expression of male domination and misogyny, a vehicle for terrorizing and subordinating women. [*ibid.*, p. 208]

The well-recognised human right not to be subjected to torture, Copelon argues, could be used to combat rape in war. Rape in war incorporates the elements which recent treaties have included in the definition of torture (*ibid.*, p. 201). In this contemporary understanding of torture, she says, degradation is either vehicle or goal or both. Does prostitution fit this definition? The prostitution of Burmese women in Thai brothels, for instance fits the definition well (Human Rights Watch/Asia, 1994). The women here suffer abrasions from the number of men they have to service, and do this in conditions of virtual slavery. Copelon defines rape as one of the most "common, terrible, and effective forms of torture against women". She quotes the Serbian feminist anti-war activist Lepa Mladjenovic as saying that rape renders a woman "homeless in her own body" (Copelon, 1995, p. 202). Now this is a phrase which could apply particularly well to prostitution, in which a woman repeatedly endures experiences which cause her to vacate her body and dissociate in order to survive.

Copelon argues that "forced prostitution" in war should be seen as a crime against humanity. She argues that, though recognising rape in wartime is the first step in seeing violence against women or "gender violence" as a human rights violation, the next step must be to explode public/private distinctions and to target rape in private and in marriage. "Gang rape in civilian life", she explains, "shares the repetitive, gleeful, and public character of rape in war" (*ibid.*, p. 208). Much of the abuse of prostituted women that takes place in brothels—such as the "slaughterhouse" brothels of Morocco, in which one French woman reported being used by one client every nine minutes for 15 hours each day—differs very little from gang rape in its dynamics (Jaget, 1980, p. 63). The use of prostituted women by parties of businessmen, who cement agreements through sharing women's bodies, as described by Linda Lovelace (1981), is likely to offer joys to the male abusers similar to other forms of gang rape.

Copelon, like other feminist rights theorists, uses the term *gender* in a way which lacks clarity. Of the Holocaust, she writes: " ... gender persecutions—the rape and forced prostitution of women as well as the extermination of gays" (Copelon, 1995, p. 206). The phrase "gender persecution" suggests that a "gender" carries out the activity, as male violence is carried out by males and father rape by fathers. In fact genders, i.e. the politically constructed differences of behaviour expected of men and women, do not persecute: only human agents do that. In the case of violence against women, it is men, not any gender, that persecutes. It may be that the phrase is meant to mean persecution on the grounds of gender, but this is equally misleading. Women are not persecuted because they exhibit the behaviour of oppression, such as deference or self-mutilation, but because they are women, and very often because they refuse subservience. The persecution of women needs to be clearly named, not disappeared by "gender". It is not helpful to characterise the extermination of gay men as a "gender persecution" either. It is not the "gender" of gay men that is attacked, but themselves. The persecution of women, of lesbians and of gay men might indeed arise from a single source, the need to maintain male supremacy and the enforcement of compulsory heterosexuality as its organising principle, but these different forms of persecution need to be separately recognised. Copelon argues that the concept of crimes against humanity needs to be expanded to include "gender". I would suggest that what needs to be included is the concept of crimes that arise from men's subordination of women. *Gender* is too vague a term and disguises the actions and suffering of real human beings.

Feminist rights theorists offer moving accounts of the suffering inflicted upon women by violent men, and the women's

298 the idea of prostitution

techniques for surviving it, to support the idea that such violence is a human rights violation. Many such descriptions apply equally to prostitution. Copelon gives an account of how a battered wife deals with marital rape: "She would just concentrate on her breathing and wait for it to be over. Jim said she wasn't feeling enough pain and hit her harder, but Molly remained silent, thinking, 'He might have my body, but I'll try not to let him have my mind'" (Copelon, 1994b, p. 119). This example of dissociation sounds very much like the sort of mind/body split that prostituted women speak of having to accomplish to deal with johns. Copelon's explanation of the way in which men's violence maintains women's subordination also has clear parallels with what is done to women in prostitution. "Violence is encouraged by and perpetuates women's dependence and her dehumanization as 'other', a servant, and a form of property. Through violence men seek and confirm the devaluation and dehumanization of women" (*ibid.*, p. 121). Certainly prostitution can be seen as being encouraged by and perpetuating women's dehumanisation as "'other', a servant, and a form of property".

Military sexual slavery

The approaches of feminist rights theorists to the issue of military sexual slavery reveal sharply the problems involved in the determination to omit prostitution from consideration as sexual violence against women. Military sexual slavery is a matter of urgent concern for feminist legal theorists because of the need to seek justice for the women who survived abuse as "comfort women" by the Japanese military. These women are old and need recompense soon. The more recent abuse of women in rape camps in Bosnia has increased the pressure to find a way to punish and discourage such violations. Whenever I read accounts of the rape and torture of these women I am struck by the similarities between what has happened to them and what happens to the women and girls imprisoned, by debt, duty or lack of alternatives, in brothels in many countries around the world. Particularly I am struck by the similarities with the experience of young women used and abused in US military prostitution in the Philippines (Sturdevant and Stoltzfus, 1992). But many in the human rights community wish to make a distinction between this latter form of prostitution, which is characterised as "free", and that which is "forced". Usually, terms such as *rape* and *military sexual slavery* are used for the prostitution which is part of wartime atrocities, so that a clear distinction can be made.

Catharine MacKinnon resists this clear distinction. She stresses the connections.

> In the camps, it is at once mass rape and serial rape in a way that is indistinguishable from prostitution. Prostitution is that part of everyday nonwar life that is closest to what we see done to women in this war. The daily life of prostituted women consists of serial rape, war or no war. The brothel-like arrangement of the rape/death camps parallels the brothels of so-called peacetime: captive women impounded to be passed from man to man in order to be raped. [MacKinnon, 1994a, p. 191]

She takes care to point out the interrelationship between ordinary peacetime prostitution and the prostitution of the rape camps. Some of the camps, she says, were "organised like the brothels of what is called peacetime", and they were "sometimes in locations that were brothels before the war" (*ibid.*, p. 187). The men who organised and took their pleasures from the military prostitution of these women were trained by the use of women in brothels before the war. They had a model. They were also geared up by the proliferation of pornography which had been occurring in Yugoslavia in recent years.

> The saturation of what was Yugoslavia with pornography upon the dissolution of communism—pornography that was largely controlled by Serbs, who had the power—has created a population of men prepared to experience sexual pleasure in torturing and killing women. [*ibid.*, p. 192]

Moreover, the Serbs created their own pornography out of the rapes and used it for propaganda purposes. They showed on television "footage of actual rapes, with the ethnicity of the victims and perpetrators switched, to inflame Serbs against Muslims and Croatians" (*ibid.*, p. 192; also Nenadic, 1996). The "peacekeepers" were not good at telling the difference between peacetime and wartime prostitution. The UN presence "increased the trafficking in women and girls through the opening of brothels, brothel-massage parlours, peep shows, and the local production of pornographic films" (MacKinnon, 1994a, p. 192). Male UN personnel were also reported to have made use of women in rape camps when offered the opportunity.

Ustinia Dolgopol writes and speaks eloquently of what was done to the "comfort women" from the Philippines and Korea. She was a member of an investigative mission sent by the International Commission of Jurists to the Philippines, Japan, the Republic of South Korea and the Democratic People's Republic of North Korea to interview government officials and victims of military sexual slavery. Dolgopol restricts herself carefully to the issue of military sexual slavery, though the language and concepts she uses seem to apply to many forms of prostitution. She says, for instance, that "Mass rape in war is the ultimate denial of a woman's humanity; it objectifies her and turns her into an item of property to be controlled by the male soldier" (Dolgopol, 1996, p. 227).

It seems clear that the Japanese military saw the abuse of women which they organised as simply a form of prostitution. One explanation for the development of the use of "comfort women" is that a system of licensed prostitution had existed in Japan since 1872, for which women were recruited in the same ways in which they were to be recruited for use by the military. The women were poor, and often sold to the brothel owners to pay off family debts. As Dologopol explains, the route for the "comfort women" was similar. They were also from poor families.

Some were kidnapped off the streets of larger cities, others had been taken during raids on their villages or their homes and in Korea some had been forced to go by district officials who would often be accompanied by recruiters claiming to be seeking women to work as nurses or to go to Japan to work in the factories. Girls and young women were promised good wages and were encouraged to believe they would be helping their family's economic situation. [*ibid.*, p. 231]

Another connection with prostitution is the fact that the Japanese military expected the setting up of military brothels to limit the degree of sexual assault carried out on the populations of occupied territories. This fits with the traditional justification for men's use of women in prostitution, that it would protect virtuous women from rape. They were concerned at the negative publicity attendant on the wholesale rapes carried out in Shanghai and Nanking.

The consequences for the women abused by the Japanese military seem to share much with what we are now beginning to understand to be the common consequences of prostitution. Dolgopol says, "These children and young adults were subjected to the most brutal horror that can befall any woman" (*ibid.*, p. 231). But the experiences of millions of women and girls across the world right now in brothel prostitution are not greatly different. She says that their

conception of themselves as human beings was shattered. Many were unable to build the lives they had dreamed for themselves in their childhood. For a great number of the girls and women their ability to trust their fellow human beings was destroyed. These women have been made to pay the price for the crimes committed against them. [*ibid.*, p. 231]

They were given disease, lost the ability to have children, or had unwanted children born of rape. "They must give birth knowing how the child was conceived and wondering about their and their child's future as it is they who will have the responsibility ..." (*ibid.*, p. 238). Many lived lives of isolation because they were so ashamed that they kept to themselves. Dolgopol found that

> It has been extraordinarily difficult for a significant number of the women to let themselves feel their own pain; they are too afraid they will be overwhelmed by their experience ... They have great difficulty seeing themselves as women in a sexual sense, they do not accept their own bodies. Many women describe feelings of numbness; others tragically have come to dislike their bodies." [*ibid.*]

This is not at all different from the experience of prostituted women.

Dolgopol is determined that what was done to the women in military sexual slavery should be seen as rape, and not prostitution. Thus she is critical of the tactic decided upon by the lawyers for the Korean survivors to bring a case before the International Labour Organisation, under the convention on forced labour. Apparently this convention, which applied to Japan during the war, only allowed for the use of males aged eighteen to forty-five as forced labour. This was a successful tactic for the lawyers because Japan was obviously in breach; it allowed for a swift and practical solution whilst the victims are still alive and able to benefit. However, the victims were not consulted on the tactic and Dolgopol considers that it glosses over the real horror of their experience.

> Leaving aside the debates about legalised prostitution, there is still an ethical dilemma in presenting an argument which would to some extent legitimise the practice of forcibly taking women and putting them into what were essentially rape camps. It is my contention that to argue that the women per-formed a "service" is to suggest that what happened to them is at some level acceptable. To suggest that this was a forced service is to deny that what was happening was rape. In the context of our domestic laws we would find it unthinkable to

argue that a rape victim should receive compensation because she performed a forced service for the perpetrator. If it is unacceptable in domestic law to raise such an argument and if we expect domestic law to develop other methods of providing compensation, then surely the same should be expected at the international level. [*ibid*., p. 4]

But presently pro-prostitution advocates make precisely this argument, that prostitution is service work and no different from any other. Thus what happened to the "comfort women" will legitimately be seen as just a variety of forced labour if this pro-prostitution analysis prevails. Notwithstanding Dolgopol's wariness of being dragged into the debate on legalised prostitution, she is already in it. Clearly she does not think that what was carried out on and in the bodies of these women is "work". Calling it rape to distinguish it from prostitution may not be a sufficient safeguard. Why is it possible for some feminist human rights activists to use a fury of passionate invective against "military sexual slavery" whilst dodging any judgements on prostitution? One explanation may be that the state is involved in military sexual slavery. The state is a much easier target to focus upon than the actions of individual men, and redress may be easier too. False distinctions, though, are odious. Connections need to be made between prostitution and rape and other forms of sexual violence.

The way forward
One way to use human rights intruments to fight violence against women is for feminists to argue for the extension of existing human rights documents to include violence against women within rights already recognised, such as the right to life. Kenneth Roth (1994), for instance, argues that domestic violence can best be dealt with through new interpretations of the articles of the *International Convention on Civil and Political Rights*. He sees this convention as being a better human rights instrument than the *Convention to Eliminate*

All Forms of Discrimination against Women. Article 6 on the right to life, Article 7 on "cruel, inhuman or degrading treatment", and Article 9 on the right to security of person, are the most suitable for using against domestic violence, he suggests.

Roth also considers that non-discrimination is a good approach for dealing with violence against women. In this approach, state inaction on violence against women could be said to be discriminatory if the state acted more effectively against violence against men. In some instances this might work, such as where quite different sentences are given to women who kill male partners from those given to men who kill female partners. There is a serious discrepancy and this could be treated as discrimination. But in many situations what happens to women does not have an exact analogy in what happens to men. Men generally are not "stalked" by women in ways which endanger their lives, for instance, and may not require the protection of a stalking law, despite the message of films such as *Basic Instinct*. Prostitution is a good example of a form of abuse which is not carried out by women against men in the same way. Examples of discrimination are hard to find, and this shows the inadequacy of any approach which starts, as does Roth's, from the standard of a male norm. Justice Elizabeth Evatt of Australia cautioned that "Clearly there is a need to lift the issue of violence out of the sphere of discrimination and private rights and to put it squarely on the mainstream human rights agenda" (quoted in Fitzpatrick, 1994, p. 560).

In the case of all kinds of violence against women, including prostitution, the balance of advantage seems clearly to lie with the adoption of a new convention which specifically outlaws such violence. Some legal theorists concerned to end violence against women argue that a separate convention is necessary because the Human Rights Commission, a UN body which meets annually, seems less than keen to acknowledge women's rights to bodily integrity and the right to life. The Commission, argues Andrew Byrnes (1992), fails to recognise that women face major, and quite different, threats to their enjoyment of these rights.

I suggest, then, that it is worth adopting the language of human rights as one means to fight sexual violence and prostitution. However, where it is possible to use different language and tactics that do not seek legitimacy in the idea of rights, this is desirable too, because I do accept the force of many of the caveats of feminist rights critics. In the international arena, human rights is the currency that is used and understood. If male violence is to be taken seriously, then let us use the powerful language and concepts that men designed mainly to identify potential injuries to themselves, such as dignity, respect and integrity, and create some embarassment by showing that women also deserve and want these precious qualities. Prostitution exactly fits this language; it needs to be considered more carefully by those feminist legal theorists who do not fetishise choice, and who wish to avoid the creation of unstable and tenuous distinctions. The distinction between "forced" and "free" prostitution is bedevilling feminist activism against the traffic in women and the possibilities for a new UN convention. Concern to maintain this distinction concentrates attention on the conditions in which the women are abused, rather than on the abusers. In the final chapter I will argue that those concerned to end the traffic in women need to shift their attention to the necessity of penalising the actions of the johns which violate the human rights of women.

CHAPTER 11

trafficking, prostitution
and human rights

> Sexual exploitation is a practice by which
> person(s) achieve sexual gratification or finan-
> cial gain or advancement through the abuse
> of a person's sexuality by abrogating that
> person's human right to dignity, equality,
> autonomy, and physical and mental well-
> being. [Proposed Convention Against Sexual
> Exploitation, in Barry, 1995, p. 326]

The traffic in women has now become the
focus of fierce international controversy within the community of scholars and activists concerned with women's human
rights. In international law there already exists a convention
that deals with trafficking in women and prostitution, the
1949 *Convention for the Suppression of the Traffic in Persons
and of the Exploitation of the Prostitution of Others*. This is
the result of the work by feminists and abolitionists through
the League of Nations that I examined in Chapter 1. Presently
there is an ideological struggle taking place between pro- and
anti-prostitution forces over the replacement of the 1949
Convention with a more effective document. One of these
groups, the Coalition Against Trafficking in Women (CATW),
represents the views of anti-violence feminists and seeks to
replace the 1949 Convention with one which defines men's
use of women in prostitution as a violation of women's
human rights. CATW's proposed convention seeks to penalise

all those who profit from or use women in prostitution, whilst decriminalising the activities of prostituted women.

A very different position is held by the Global Alliance Against Trafficking in Women (GAATW), set up at a conference in Thailand in 1994, which seeks a convention which will outlaw trafficking of anyone—men, women or children—for any purposes. GAATW makes a distinction between "trafficking", which is forced, and "free" prostitution, which is potentially a form of "work" or "self-determination" for women. It represents the pro-prostitution ideology of the prostitutes' rights movement. This ideological battle picks up the arguments developed by pro- and anti-prostitution forces that I have discussed throughout this book, and projects them onto the international stage. Before I consider in detail the arguments that are being put forward about trafficking, it is useful to look at what the globalisation of prostitution consists of currently, as well as its causes, its forms and its extent.

The traffic in women today

Trafficking is becoming a major concern of human rights organisations and feminist activists as the size of the problem and its grievous effects on the lives of women and children are becoming better known. Whereas before World War I the very existence of the so-called White Slave Traffic could be questioned, today trafficking on a world scale is unlikely to be treated with scepticism. However, the shape of the traffic in women differs in significant ways from the situation discovered in the League of Nations surveys. Kathleen Barry (1995) argues that prostitution has been "industrialised" internationally. The "industrialisation" of prostitution is linked to several developments since World War II, which have affected both the supply of women vulnerable to being trafficked into prostitution and the degree of demand from men to use such women.

The supply of women is greatly increased by mass migration resulting from destabilising economic development. Nelleke van der Vleuten explains that the world-wide traffic in women "must be analysed in terms of the structural inequality between Third World and industrialised countries" (1991, p. 5). It is a result, she says, of the increasing internationalisation of the world economy, in which local communities in the Third World become an integral part of the industrialised world, becoming dependent on social change in industrialised countries. People in the Third World lose traditional resources, such as land, paid labour or other means of income, and a permanent sub-proletariat is created with the growth of slums on the outskirts of towns and an increase in child labour. The consequences are greatest for women and girls, who have to take care of children and family because of tradition or the disappearance of male support. Women are very vulnerable because of their position in the labour market. Migration from rural areas to the cities seems one of the few possible ways for these girls and women to survive.

Another force creating the supply is warfare. Civil wars have become endemic in countries released from the rule of imperialism. In Burma, for instance, Karen refugee women and girls are vulnerable to being trafficked into prostitution in Thailand (Karen Women's Organisation, 1994, p. 10). Another force is the development of new market economies in socialist and formerly socialist countries. This has led to a dramatic expansion in prostitution as poverty has increased and old ways of life have been disrupted. Well-organised networks developed to traffic women and girls into prostitution in Vietnam after the introduction of economic reforms there (Centre for Family and Women's Studies, Hanoi, 1994, p. 23). The number of prostituted women in Ho Chi Minh City, for instance, has risen from 10,000 to 50,000 (Santos, 1995). In Europe too, the breakdown of communism has led to "professional criminal organisations" trafficking in women from Russia, Poland, Bulgaria, Rumania, the former Yugoslavia and the Czech and Slovak Republics (Foundation Against Trafficking in Women, 1994, p. 2). All these forces creating the supply of women depend upon the low status of women. In countries where the status of women is in decline, such as

Bangladesh, the problem is invariably heightened (Arn O Salish Kendar, 1994, p. 8).

Military prostitution and sex tourism have increased the global demand to use women in prostitution. Massive prostitution industries have developed in reponse to the large US military presence in Saigon, Thailand and the Philippines (Enloe, 1983; Sturdevant and Stoltzfus, 1992). This has led to increased local prostitution. A new phenomenon has developed which did not exist in earlier times, sex tourism. Affluence and leisure, the ease of communications and foreign travel, the construction of foreign prostituted women as exotic and desirable in pornography, and the deliberate policies of the governments of poor countries to develop sex tourism as a means to gain foreign exchange have contributed to this phenomenon (Truong, 1990). It is possible that the outrage of Western men confronted with changes in the status of women, resulting from the women's liberation movement in their countries, has exacerbated the desire to use foreign women in prostitution and as mail-order brides. In her interviews with British sex tourists, Julia O'Connell Davidson found "Almost all the sex tourists interviewed spoke with great bitterness about white women's power to deny them sexual access" (1994, p. 12).

A complementary trade has developed in mail-order brides, especially in Asian women from the Philippines, Thailand, South Korea, and Sri Lanka. In the Philippines in 1988–89 there was a 94 per cent increase in the number of Filipino women migrating as fiancées or spouses to Japanese, Australian, German, Taiwanese, British, and US destinations. In the late 1980s and 1990s there has been a growing dissemination and diversification of pornography through cable television, dial-a-porn, home video and computers, leading to the legimitisation of prostitution. Trafficking in women on the Internet in the form of the World Sex Guide—telling johns where and how to purchase women and girls world-wide, conversations between johns about using women and young girls, interactive pornography where men can instruct live women through the Internet to strip and perform sexual acts, and websites devoted to buying mail-order brides and to sex tourism—has aided the organisation and global scope of the sex industry (Hughes, 1996).

Examples of the size and conditions of the traffic from two regions, Europe and Asia, will help in assessing the most effective methods for reducing it. Women from Asia are trafficked into Europe as well as between countries in Asia. The Netherlands is one of the main destinations within Europe for the traffic, and this is probably why Dutch human rights activists have been particularly concerned to take action to combat it. Nelleke van der Vleuten explains that more and more non-European women are coming to work in brothels and sex-clubs in the Netherlands (1991, p. 3). In the Netherlands the proportion of non-Europeans among prostituted women is usually 30–40 per cent, and in some places at least 60 per cent. The estimated total of Dutch and foreign prostituted women is 20,000. Half of the windows used for prostitution in Amsterdam are rented out to non-European women and there are 3000 Latin-American prostituted women in Amsterdam. Prostitution, van der Vleuten says, has changed and taken on an international dimension. It is large-scale and highly industrialised. "In the past Dutch prostitution could be characterised as a local and small-scale business: now huge companies are being created while procurers with international connections obtain complete control" (*ibid.*, p. 3). The economics of prostitution is an area which needs serious research. There is little information at present on the organisation and profits of the global sex industry.

The Dutch sex industry is part of the European sex market. The majority of women travel between brothels and sex clubs in different European countries. Foreign women are the lowest in the hierarchy of prostitution. They work in insanitary conditions and are isolated both culturally and socially. They are often illegal immigrants and have no freedom of movement. Health services cannot reach them, and many work without condoms for financial reasons. A Dutch government report says many women are in a "criminal climate, where false pretexts are used to seduce women" who are "forced into prostitution and kept there" (*ibid.*, p. 4).

The Western human rights organisation, Human Rights Watch/Asia, has published two studies of the traffic in women which are useful in describing in detail the operation of the traffic in Asia (Human Rights Watch/Asia, 1994, 1995). *A Modern Form of Slavery* looks at the traffic of Burmese women into Thailand, and *Rape for Profit* at the traffic of Nepali women into India. Non-government organisations estimate Bombay's prostituted women at 100,000, of whom up to half are Nepali. One-fifth of Bombay's brothel population is thought to be girls under eighteen, and half that population may be infected with the HIV virus (*ibid.*, 1995, p. 1). The demand for Nepali girls, especially those with fair skin and Mongolian features, continues to increase. The Indian Council of Medical Research estimates the total number of prostituted women in India at about one million, of whom 200,000 are likely to be Nepali. But a voluntary organisation that serves the country's prostituted women estimates that there were more than 8 million brothel workers and 7.5 million call girls in 1992 (*ibid.*, p. 1). The age of Nepali girls is dropping, partly because fear of the HIV virus causes men to demand "clean" women. The average age of recruitment is now ten to fourteen, which means that some are younger than ten. The estimated number of prostituted women in Thailand is 800,000 to 2 million, of whom 20,000 are Burmese.

The Human Rights Watch/Asia reports explain that men's use of women in prostitution is often a death sentence for the women because they pass on the HIV virus. Far from prostituted women being a source of AIDS, they are the recipients of it. Male-to-female transmission is much more likely than female-to-male. The trafficked women in India and Thailand could not enforce condom use, even if they knew anything about the route of HIV transmission, and most do not. Brothel owners rarely supply condoms; when they do, the prostituted women are not permitted to reject johns who do not wish to use them. Trafficked women, as we have seen in the case of the Netherlands above, always experience worse conditions than local prostituted women. They are, therefore, much more likely to become infected.

Medical researchers have hypothesised that the thinner mucous membrane of the genital tract in girls is a less efficient barrier to viruses, and that young women may produce less of the mucus which has an immune function (*ibid.*, 1995, p. 66). The men's abuse of the trafficked women causes them to develop friction sores of the vagina. The rate of infection is related to the number of johns, via the rate of associated vaginal abrasion. The women are not usually permitted time off for the injuries to heal. The injuries themselves make HIV transmission easier. Condom usage makes the friction problem worse. The majority of Burmese women in closed Thai brothels who started out as young, "clean" virgins become infected about six months after entry (*ibid.*, 1994, p. 128). Of the nineteen Burmese women and girls interviewed by Human Rights Watch/Asia who had been tested for HIV, fourteen were found to be infected with the virus. The rate of infection was roughly three times higher than among non-trafficked prostituted women in Thailand.

Trafficking and prostitution in general receive the support of the state in Thailand and in India through the complicity of the police, immigration and other officials. The policemen who use the brothels receive bribes from the owners, because their activities are in fact illegal. They are the same ones who raid the brothels to arrest the trafficked women, regularly returning them later to the brothels after receiving further bribes. Often policemen are the pimps who traffic women across the borders. This total acceptance of the abuse of women's human rights destroys attempts to highlight such abuse and get it taken seriously by governments.

Trafficked women in India and Thailand are imprisoned mainly through debt bondage, which is understood to be a human rights abuse and a practice akin to slavery even in customary international law. Debt bondage is incurred when the victim's family members, "friends", or other persons who demand to be repaid for transport costs, receive payment from traffickers or brothel owners. The victim is told she must work to pay off the debt, but usually she has no idea how much the debt is, how much she earns, or how long she must work to pay it off. A sum which might have been paid off in a few months' work is usually, through this ruse, employed to keep a victim in brothels for years. Sometimes the women and girls are simply kidnapped and sold.

> A ten-year-old girl from Shan State ... whose kidnapper received 35,000 baht, said she was given to a farang (Westerner) who paid 5000 baht ($200) for her virginity. It hurt so much she passed out, and the brothel owner later beat her with a stick. [*ibid.*, p. 65]

The trafficked women are forcibly contracepted by the brothel owners, usually by injections or pills of chemical contraceptives considered dangerous to health by Western women's health activists, such as Depo-provera, and without any medical supervision. The women and girls are given no choice of which contraceptives they take and do not understand how they work. In at least one case, the brothel owner kept the girls from menstruating by giving them improper instructions about using the pills, so that they had no excuse to stop work. For young girls, these dangerous practices can be particularly damaging. One girl of twelve was given pills and "started haemorraghing shortly thereafter, but the brothel owner would not take her to a doctor" (*ibid.*, p. 69).

There are countries which have serious problems with sexual exploitation in the form of sex tourism and local prostitution exacerbated by military prostitution, but which are not significant destinations for trafficking. The Philippines is a good example. The Philippines is more significant as a sending than as a receiving country as far as trafficking is concerned, but still there are many concerned women in the Philippines in organisations like Women's Education, Development, Productivity and Research Organisation (WEDPRO) and

Coalition against Trafficking in Women, Asia/Pacific, who want to ameliorate what they see as the grievous and damaging effects of men's use of Filipino women in prostitution in the Philippines itself. As Aida Santos of WEDPRO explains, prostituted women are found "in bars, nightclubs, massage parlors, karaoke joints, beer houses or the equivalent of pubs, and other establishments which are fronted as diners, restaurants, among others, and those who walk the streets, the 'hookers' or 'streetwalkers'" (1995, p. 12).

Brothel prostitution is found in the Philippines too, but is hidden and not easy to research. The brothels are called *casas* and women in them are subject to debt bondage. Santos gives one example of a girl just fifteen years old "and already diseased", who was "sold by her mother for a measly five thousand pesos—a little more than a month's salary of a public school teacher—after she was raped by her stepfather". To illustrate the dire conditions of brothel prostitution, Santos gives an example of a woman interviewed by WEDPRO who "acceded to a client without money in return for a pail of water that he would fetch for her" (*ibid.*, p. 13).

Santos (1992) provides estimated figures for the extent of prostitution in other Asian countries. In South Korea there are estimated to be 18,000 registered prostituted women employed in bars around the US bases, with about 9000 unregistered ones. The rough estimate for Indonesia is 500,000, including unregistered women. Bangladeshi young women and children trafficked into Pakistan are estimated at 200–300 per month. In Japan between 65,000 and 70,000 Filipinos are working, more than 80 per cent of them reportedly as "entertainers", a euphemism for use in prostitution. Hundreds of these Filipino women "entertainers" have reportedly returned home "suffering from mental disorders due to the distressing situation they found themselves in, with a number reporting cases of rape and other sexual abuse" (Santos, 1995, p. 25). The total number of prostituted women in the Philippines is estimated conservatively at 500,000. Australian men are particularly prominent as organisers and as johns in sex tourism in the Philippines. Australian proprietors, for instance, have taken over the hotels and bars that service sex tourism in Angeles City (Distor and Hunt, 1996). The prostitution industry was developed there to service the US Clark Airforce Base and might have decreased dramatically but for Australian involvement.

Explanation of the globalisation of prostitution tends to focus on economics, and certainly women and children impoverished by the forces of economic development are under immense pressure to enter prostitution. But economics alone cannot be a sufficient explanation. The poverty of Western countries is much less extreme but prostitution thrives there too, and is presently changing form as it becomes integrated into a world prostitution system. Feminist analysis emphasises the ways in which the maintenance of masculinity as a foundation for male supremacy interacts with economic forces to construct global prostitution. Cynthia Enloe describes how the use of women in military prostitution constructs the masculinity of the abusers:

Among these different men there may be diverse masculinities. Women in Okinawa, Korea, and the Philippines describe how they had to learn what made American men feel that they were manly during sex; it was not always what they had learned made their Korean, Japanese, or Filipino sexual partners feel manly ... Tourists, colonial officials, international technocrats and businessmen, and soldiers have long been the internationalisers of sexualised masculinity. [Enloe, 1992, p. 25]

Aida Santos explains that the economic argument is simply not sufficient.

In all the studies conducted in the past, prostitution was analyzed in the context of poverty ... Patriarchal culture in the Philippines, or anywhere else, has produced men who think it absolutely correct—even proper!—to exercise what they perceive and hold as their right to the full expression of the range

of their sexual needs, both within and outside of marriage ...
[Santos, 1992, p. 39]

Military prostitution can be seen as a result of the "heightened
integration" of "racism, sexism, and imperialism". This is well
illustrated by a popular T-shirt sold in Olongapo in the
Philippines, with the message "Little Brown Fucking Machines
Powered with Rice". Santos describes this as "one of the most
disgusting racist concoctions imaginable ..." (*ibid.*, p. 40).

1949 Convention

The changing scale and shape of the problem of the traffic in
women has caused a reconsideration of the effectiveness of
the 1949 *Convention for the Suppression of the Traffic in
Persons and of the Exploitation of the Prostitution of Others*.
The signing of the Convention was delayed by World War II.
Despite the continued work of feminists and abolitionists to
get governments to sign, the Convention was signed and ratified by a small number of countries. Only sixty-seven ratified
the Convention compared with 126 for the *International
Convention on Social, Economic and Cultural Rights* and 125
for the *International Convention on Civil and Political
Rights*. This low rate of ratification has had an influence on
the effectiveness of the Convention and the respect in which it
is held. It is significant that countries like Australia, Sweden,
the Netherlands, Britain, which have a good record of signing
other Conventions relevant to women's rights, have not
signed or ratified this one. The United States has a poor
record on Conventions related to women in general. Besides
the low rate of signing, the Convention has weaker monitor-
ing and implementation procedures than other conventions.

The Convention draws together and fills in the gaps of the
previous agreements and conventions on trafficking. Parties
to the Convention agree to punish any persons who procure
women for the purposes of prostitution or make a profit from
prostituting others. The most controversial part of the
Convention in terms of the current debate is that it outlaws

such actions even when the prostituted persons are consenting. There is no distinction between "forced" and "free" prostitution. Persons who keep or manage brothels, or let or rent buildings "for the purpose of the prostitution of others", are also to be punished. Article 6 of the Convention outlaws state regulation of prostitution by the abolition of laws which subject prostituted women to registration or possession of a special document.

The Convention sought to end the exploitation of prostitution rather than prostitution itself, but many of those who had campaigned for it *did* wish to end prostitution. They saw the penalising of all those who trafficked in, or profited from, prostitution as the best means towards the goal of decreasing prostitution, since they were most anxious not to penalise the women. The anti-prostitution sentiments are clear in the preamble, which states: "Whereas prostitution and the accompanying evil of the traffic in persons for the purpose of prostitution are incompatible with the dignity and worth of the human person and endanger the welfare of the individual, the family and the community" (*The Shield*, October 1950, p. 7). This is an anti-prostitution convention which sought to attack prostitution by cutting off the routes by which women entered it and the business forces which promoted it.

The pro-prostitution position on trafficking

The pro-prostitution lobby sees the 1949 Convention as unworkable and requiring replacement by a new anti-trafficking Convention, simply because it is anti-prostitution. The ideas and practice of the Bangkok-based Global Alliance Against Trafficking in Women depend upon the theoretical perspective developed by feminist human rights lawyers and activists in the Netherlands. According to Nelleke van der Vleuten (1991) of Utrecht, the Netherlands did not sign the 1949 Convention because of the "even with consent" clause. She gives a picture of the Netherlands government as always libertarian in its approach and determined to prioritise consent. The Netherlands government of the time considered that the criminal law should be used only if the exploitation of prostitution included coercion. It saw the 1949 Convention as being concerned with the promotion of morality. The Netherlands subsequently became the focus of the "sexual revolution" in Europe. Public prostitution from windows on the street became part of the liberal face of that country along with a liberal climate for drug use. It is not surprising, therefore, that a campaigning group which takes an extremely liberal position on prostitution should emerge in that country. The Netherlands government and Dutch human rights activists and academics have developed a detailed and concerted position on trafficking and prostitution, which is having considerable influence within the international human rights community.

This position was expounded at a conference on Combatting the Traffic in Persons in Utrecht and Maastricht in November 1994. Exponents argued that the "right to prostitute" needed to be acknowledged. Yvonne Klerk from the University of Utrecht explained: "It would be a violation of the principle of self-determination of individuals to forbid to prostitute. Moreover, a prostitute has the right to let another person exploit her, and she might have good reasons for that" (1995, p. 16). The argument that the rights issue involved in prostitution is the "right to prostitute" rather than a violation of the prostituted, is frequently made in the pro-prostitution literature. It is an example of the problem of competing rights which has exercised critics of the efficacy of rights approaches. It might appear to contradict the idea that prostitution is a human rights violation. The "right to prostitute" argument could mean that we should look upon the johns as helpful agents enabling the woman to exercise her right to prostitute herself. But for those who consider that the men who use prostituted women are abusive and violate the woman's human rights, her "right to prostitute" does not cancel out their abuse. For a violation of human rights, two parties are required, and the violation does not become transmogrified into a kindness just because the victim asks for the abuse. Feminists seeking an anti-prostitution convention do not accept the validity of this "right". Kathleen Barry wrote up the final report of the International Meeting of Experts on Sexual Exploitation, Violence and Prostitution, hereinafter called the *Penn State Report* in 1992. The report explains: "Does the 'right to prostitute' exist? Clearly prostitution cannot exist as a right because it negates already established human rights of the prostitute woman to human dignity, bodily integrity, physical and mental well-being" (UNESCO, 1992, p. 6).

It is written into the fundamental human rights instrument, Article 30 of the *Universal Declaration of Human Rights*, that:

> Nothing in this Declaration may be interpreted as implying for any State, group, or person any right to engage in any activity or to perform any act aimed at the destruction of any of the rights and freedoms set forth herein. [*ibid.*]

The "right to prostitute" could be seen as nullifying "all other protections of women's human rights, both for the woman prostituted and ultimately for all women" (*ibid.*, p. 6). As human rights are universal and inalienable, *The Penn State Report* asserts, they "cannot be reduced to the instrumentality of individual choice alone because individual choice can and does include the right to harm or propagate harm on others or to inflict harm on oneself" (*ibid.*).

The establishment of a "right to prostitute" transforms the right of some men to abuse women in prostitution and of others to make a profit from that use—interests which arguably provide the real fuel for the pro-prostitution posi-tion—into a woman's right to have her human rights violated. Men's rights to use women need to be concealed behind the ostensible rights of women as a public relations strategy. The "right to prostitute" is not a challenging demand in societies where the selling of her body is always seen as woman's last resort, and considered to sum up her very nature. Far from the "right to prostitute" being under threat, it has historically and in the present been protected by the forces of the state in most countries.

Since the Dutch lobby wishes to continue the protection of the "right to prostitute" and sees prostitution as unproblematic, it wishes to redefine trafficking to leave out all mention of prostitution. The Netherlands Advisory Committee on Human Rights, for instance, considers that there should be a broader definition of traffic. It says it is "not logical to restrict the concept of traffic in persons to prostitution" when it accepts prostitution as a "normal job" (Klerk, 1995, p. 17). What should be fought, it suggests, is "the coercion of people to do something against their wishes", and that could be anything at all. Nonetheless, whilst supporting this argument, Yvonne Klerk asserts that 99 per cent of trafficking is in women and the vast majority is for the purposes of prostitution. Other advantages which the Dutch lobby puts forward for broadening the definition include covering forms of the traffic not now covered, such as other workers in the sex industry like dancers, pornography models, domestics and mail-order brides.

The Foundation Against Trafficking in Women, based in Utrecht, also makes a clear distinction between trafficking, which it sees as a human rights violation, and prostitution which it sees simply as a profession. It prefers a definition of trafficking which does not refer specifically to prostitution but covers all carriage of persons by force over state boundaries for financial gain. It defines trafficking as:

> "brokering" accompanied by coercion, deception, material exploitation, physical, psychological and emotional abuse which constitutes the crime of trafficking, be it brokering for marriage, domestic or industrial work or for prostitution. [Lap-Chew, 1995a, p. 2]

This group is chary of seeming to harbour any hostility to prostitution in practice or theory. It has eliminated the core offence of the 1949 Convention, trafficking for the purposes of prostitution. Its definition of trafficking requires evidence of explicit force, and trafficking can be for any purpose.

The trafficking of women, men and children for purposes other than prostitution constitutes a serious crime in its own right, and appropriate human rights instruments are required to deal with it. In Bangladesh, for instance, women, men and children are being trafficked for forced labour and for their organs, as well as for the purposes of sexual slavery. As one newspaper report in 1993 explained, in relation to forty-nine people who were rescued:

> the middle aged men and women would be taken to some hospitals, in Bombay and Madras. The blood, bones, kidney, eyes, skin and their hair would be sold to these hospitals. The young girls would be sold to the brothels in Pakistan and India. [UBINIG, 1995, p. 33]

A determination explicitly to maintain the crime of trafficking for prostitution does not represent a failure to understand the seriousness of these other varieties. It does mean that this crime, which is specific to the power relations between the sexes and has particular consequences as a crime of *sexual* violence, will be made visible and specifically targeted.

Young girls constitute the most valuable cargo in the traffic in Bangladesh. They are most often sold into individual slavery as the result of fake marriages, accepted by families in dire poverty who have no money to support a daughter or give her a dowry. The girls are often never heard of again. Girls sold into individual sexual slavery in India frequently end up in brothels because they have no alternative.

> Here the Bangladeshi girls are compelled to live a sub-human life like a slave with her so-called husband … generally these girls are kicked out of the house and soon they become commodity in the hands of others. Thus their ownership continues to change one after another … She has to go to brothel to

earn livelihood as the last means. [Association for Community Development, 1995, p. 15]

Using the approach taken by the Foundation Against Trafficking in Women, which wants to separate "free" trafficking from that which is "forced", it might be possible to argue that women in a situation like that above are exercising free "choice". No obvious force is applied here, but there is no alternative.

The Foundation Against Trafficking in Women justifies the decision to "discuss trafficking ... separately from the issue of prostitution" with the argument that prostitution should just be seen as legitimate work. "It would be useful to consider placing prostitution, since we are referring, in these times, to 'commercial sex workers' under labour issues, and not as an issue of violence against women" (Lap-Chew, 1995a, p. 2). It considers that prostitution needs to be professionalised.

> The more "professional" the sex worker, the more care she takes of herself. The more "legal" or "legitimate" she feels, the less she will be afraid to report abuse and exploitation, the more she will seek health and other kinds of care for herself and be able to develop a degree of professionalism in her work. Is this not an argument in favour of recognition of prostitution as a form of legitimate work? [*ibid.*, p. 3]

According to such an argument, those who campaign against men's abuse of women in prostitution can be seen as precisely those who want to make life more difficult for prostituted women. Feminist anti-prostitution activists rather than the sexual exploiters can be seen as the problem, for creating a stigma around prostitution and preventing the prostituted woman from feeling good enough about herself to look after her health and well-being.

Janice Raymond, on behalf of CATW, specifically rejects these attempts to separate "trafficking" from prostitution. She points out that such distinctions are used to create permissible forms of sexual exploitation and that CATW is concerned that "these distinctions will create remedies only for 'deserving victims'—for children, or for women who can prove that they were overtly coerced—if they survive and have the means to demonstrate coercion". She says it will "legitimise practices of sexual exploitation not involving overt and demonstrable coercion" (Raymond, 1995, p. 2). She sees little sense in seeking to separate trafficking from prostitution when "Prostitution, of course, is the goal of sex trafficking and builds the base for the trafficking in women and children." As she explains, "When prostitution is accepted by a society, sex trafficking and sex tourism inevitably follow."

Van der Vleuten points out one of the difficulties of separating out trafficking from "free" prostitution: "In fact national and international trafficking in women are not separate processes and possibly intertwine." In Thailand, girls are recruited directly for the international traffic in rural areas.

> The situation in Third World countries is not the only explanation for traffic in women. The situation at the "demand" end, in the countries of destination, is of major importance as well. These are, the changing character of prostitution in Western countries, the attitude of procurers and the prevailing image of foreign women in general and prostitutes in particular. [*ibid.*, pp. 10–11]

Distinguishing between trafficking and prostitution is difficult when both women trafficked from outside a country and ones from within it end up in the same conditions of brothel slavery.

A further advantage of defining trafficking in a way which does not include the phrase "for the purposes of prostitution", according to lobbyists for a new trafficking convention, is that a new definition would make the legal process easier. It would alleviate the necessity of finding the burden of proof needed to show that prostitution was the object of the trafficking. Klerk argues that removing the "for prostitution" clause would make the legal process easier for the victim because, when prostitution has to be proved, "He [sic] would have to be obliged to recall all kinds of awful events that he would prefer to forget", and the victim's country of origin might find out and be prejudiced against "him" (1995, p. 18-19). Interestingly, Klerk uses the masculine pronoun in her article, which seems retrogressive considering feminist advances in challenging this kind of sexist bias in language. The masculine pronoun in a piece on prostitution seems a particularly inappropriate choice and adds a surreal note. Such an argument appears to acknowledge that there might be something about being trafficked for prostitution that is different from being trafficked for carpet-making, if the details would be so distressing to recall.

Even those who disagree with the position of CATW on trafficking and prostitution are not necessarily willing to sub-scribe to a trafficking convention which omits the idea of prostitution entirely, because they do see that there is some-thing different about prostitution. Liesbeth Lijnzaad, after criticising the "abolitionists", states:

> The idea to omit the element of forced prostitution altogether is based on misunderstood liberalism that ignores the reality and the relevance of shame, humiliation and physical vulner-ability specifically relevant to working in the sex industry. [Lijnzaad, 1995, p. 24]

Clearly she does not consider prostitution to be just a job like any other. Another feminist scholar from the Netherlands has indicated her anxiety at the way in which this new analysis sidelines feminism entirely. In a paper on public policy towards the trafficking of women in the Netherlands, Joyce Outshoorn says that "all actors have come more or less to agree to the construction of prostitution as work" (1996, p. 16). As the traffic is defined more broadly to disappear the link between prostitution and trafficking, this has led to "the undoing of an old feminist construction". Somehow, in this view, male sexual dominance has dropped out of the picture altogether.

> This link helped to sustain the idea that women were trafficked for sex for men, and thus that both issues are about sexual domination. Male sexuality was therefore always an issue for these feminists. The question is what has got lost in this process. [*ibid.*, p. 16]

Prostitution and the
international human rights community

Until the late 1980s it does seem to have been the case that the international human rights community considered prostitution inconsistent with certain basic human rights, such as the right to dignity and integrity of the person, though they may not have been in favour of establishing this understanding in a convention. The report of the UN Rapporteur, J. Fernand-Laurent, in 1983 stated that prostitution was a form of slavery, and recommended that national authorities seek co-operation with social organisations, including organisations of prostituted women, "but only when they do not call for prostitution to be recognised as a profession" (Haveman, 1995, p. 140). The 1986 Meeting of Experts organised by UNESCO on the causes of prostitution and sexual exploitation stated in its conclusions:

> we depart from the traditional understanding of prostitution by refusing to make a distinction between forced and voluntary prostitution. Consequently, we refuse to recognise prostitution as a profession ... The "sex" that the customer purchases requires that the body of the woman becomes an instrument for men to use ... this constitutes an assault against the dignity of women and a form of sexual violence. [UNESCO, 1992, p. 33]

But this common understanding has begun to change. One of the forces responsible may be the AIDS epidemic. Justice

Elizabeth Evatt of Australia commented at the Dutch conference in 1994, apparently with approval, that "One can witness a rather slowly growing tolerance towards prostitution in Australia", as combating the marginalisation of prostituted women and men was seen as necessary for safe sex education (1995, p. 95). Certainly it has been argued in some Western nations that tolerance of prostitution is necessary to successful AIDS prevention, but accepting prostituted women is not the same as tolerating their abusers' behaviour.

Anti-Slavery International (ASI) provides a good example of how an important human rights organisation has changed its position on prostitution under the influence of the pro-prostitution lobby. In the 1960s and 1970s Patrick Montgomery was the director of what was then called the Anti-Slavery Society. He was associated with the Josephine Butler Society and its strong anti-prostitution position. His efforts resulted in getting the Working Group on Slavery to accept in 1974 that the traffic in women was a form of slavery (van der Vleuten, 1991). The position of the ASI under a new, female director, Lesley Rogers, in the 1990s, is one that Montgomery would have found hard to accept. The ASI issued in 1995 a statement of its position entitled, "Redefining Prostitution as Commercial Sex Work on the International Agenda".

> ASI believes that the definition of prostitution as commercial sex work has more scope than an exclusively abolitionist approach for enhancing the welfare of women and men whose sexual services are sold. By looking at commercial sex as work, in terms of labour conditions, those involved can be included and protected under the existing instruments which aim to protect all workers and, where appropriate, forced labour and migrant workers; all persons from violence; and women from discrimination. [ASI, 1995]

Rogers considers that the redefinition of prostitution as commercial sex work is necessary to deal with trafficking, because the slavery of trafficking can only be tackled when the work done in slavery is subject to ordinary labour contracts (personal communication, August 1995).

Rogers attended the conference on Combatting the Traffic in Persons in the Netherlands in November 1994, one of the few non-Dutch people to do so, and it is the Dutch position which her organisation in London has now adopted. It may be a problem for human rights organisations as they begin to work on the issue of trafficking that they do not have the understanding of sexual violence necessary to address the issue of prostitution. An inability to see the injury of prostitution in adult women, though they will usually see it as an injury in children, suggests a lack of familiarity with feminist theory and activism against rape, sexual abuse and pornography.

Anti-Slavery International has a strong commitment to working with organisations such as the international End Child Prostitution in Asian Tourism against the prostitution of children, which it counts as slavery with or without evidence of force. However the ASI newsletter of October 1993 states an argument of cultural relativism for prostitution which it does not accept for human rights generally: "Indeed, in some parts of the world, being a prostitute is not seen as a demeaning occupation but as a legitimate choice of work" (ASI, October 1993, p. 4). "ASI's mandate is limited to two areas: child prostitution (under 18 years of age); and forced prostitution." Both of these evils were difficult to prevent whilst prostitutes were "not clearly protected by employment or criminal law". Declaring prostitution a violation of human rights will "leave large numbers of women even more marginalised socially than they are now". This position on prostitution seems to contradict the strong position on the universality of human rights. Quoting the Vienna Declaration on Human Rights (1993), "The universal nature of [all human rights and fundamental freedoms] is beyond question", ASI states in its newsletter that, "Were ASI to consider many practices as cultural relativism, slavery would never be abolished" (ASI, 1993, June, p. 1). But apparently the sexual abuse of women in prostitution constitutes an exception to this principle.

Human Rights Watch/Asia seems also unwilling to take any position on prostitution. The study of the traffic of Nepali women raises two problems involved in seeing only trafficking, and not prostitution, as the problem. One is apparent in the title *Rape for Profit*. This emotive title depends for its effect on the expectation that readers will see the prostitution that women end up in as particularly violating. Trafficking for the carpet trade, which is common in the areas concerned, would not be seen as so heinous. This suggests that the authors, though they focus exclusively on trafficking as the problem, do recognise that there is something different about the "work" of prostitution. Another difficulty of this approach is that in the destination brothels there are also Indian women. There is no discussion as to whether they have been trafficked, though it is likely that they suffer the same extreme conditions of abuse as the Nepali women. The authors seem to have experienced some contradiction in restricting themselves to condemning trafficking rather than prostitution, because they clearly see the connections. In the concluding section of the study on the trafficking of Nepali women, Human Rights Watch/Asia states:

> The demand for Nepali girls and women in India's brothels drives the trafficking from Nepal. This demand is fueled by a fear of AIDS and the tastes of the consumer and is made possible by the active support of Indian police. It is essential therefore that India take immediate steps to curb this demand. [Human Rights Watch/Asia, 1995, p. 86]

This conclusion echoes that reached by the trafficking committee of the League of Nations between the world wars, that it is impossible to eliminate trafficking without tackling prostitution and curbing men's demand. But Human Rights Watch/Asia is very guarded in what it is prepared to say about prostitution. It asks for reform of Indian prostitution laws to make them less discriminatory, but says it "takes no position on prostitution per se" (Human Rights Watch/Asia, 1994,

p. 154). It may be that it is time for human rights organisations to take a position on prostitution, since their determination to treat trafficking separately, whilst knowing that it is not separate, undermines the strength of their arguments.

The position taken on trafficking and prostitution in the final document of the Fourth UN Conference on Women 1995 in Beijing could be seen as evidence of the extent to which the libertarian Dutch position on trafficking has advanced its influence. Lin Lap-Chew, co-ordinator of the Foundation Against Trafficking in Women in the Netherlands, certainly sees it that way. She considers that the Global Alliance Against Trafficking in Women, of which her organisation is a member, won the day. The formulation eventually adopted in the Platform for Action makes a distinction between "forced" and "free" prostitution. GAATW, she says, "supported by members of prostitutes' organizations", placed trafficking in a "broader and human rights context, and attempted to avoid focussing on prostitution as the issue to be addressed" (Lap-Chew, 1995, p. 2).

The wording of the Platform for Action, however, includes considerable concern with trafficking specifically for prostitution: "The effective suppression of trafficking in women and girls for the sex trade is a matter of pressing international concern" (Lap-Chew, 1995b, p. 5). No definition of trafficking is given which specifies that it must be the result of force. But the distinction between forced and free is recognised in statements such as "trafficking in women and forced prostitution" in the definition of violence against women. The force behind the document, however, does not seem to be the position, advanced by the GAATW, that trafficking can be of men or women, for any purpose, and is quite distinct from prostitution. In the section outlining the violence against women which "violates and impairs or nullifies the enjoyment by women of human rights and fundamental freedoms", "trafficking" is of women and children, and it is surrounded in the list by forms of specifically sexual violence: "sexual abuse, sexual slavery and exploitation, and international trafficking

in women and children, forced prostitution and sexual harassment" (*ibid.*). It seems there has been an uneasy compromise,
with the idea that trafficking is connected to prostitution, and
that there is something different about prostitution which is
related to sexual violence, winning the day. But a most vigor-
ous campaign is required to ensure that the anti-prostitution
position is not completely overwhelmed in international
conferences and documents.

The anti-prostitution position on trafficking

Western non-government organisations approach prostitution
in Asia from the standpoint of sexual liberalism. They may feel
under pressure to make a distinction between "trafficking",
which is seen to be forced, and "free" prostitution. Feminist
non-government organisations in Asia do not necessarily take
this position, partly because sexual liberalism is not the dominant sexual philosophy, and partly because the obvious and
brutal poverty of the situations from which women move into
prostitution do not so easily allow for arguments of "choice"
about any women in those cultures. Independent "sex
worker" entrepreneurs do not seem to be common in Asia.

The anti-prostitution position on trafficking is prevalent in
the Philippines, for instance, where feminists are very concerned about the effects of the history of military prostitution
and contemporary sex tourism on the women victims and
on the status of women in the Philippines in general. Anti-
prostitution campaigners use the term *prostituted women*
instead of *prostitutes*. This is a deliberate political decision
and is meant to symbolise the lack of choice women have over
being used in prostitution. It is adopted to

> provide a political context, where the great majority of the
> women had been prostituted by society's unjust social and
> economic structures, pushing them to poverty and prostitu-
> tion. Of the terms, this one is the most political, posing a
> direct critique against existing socio-economic structures and
> policies. [Santos, 1995, p. 14]

Aida Santos from WEDPRO describes the pro-prostitution position, such as that of GAATW, as a philosophy from "some developed countries in the North [with a] few adherents in the South", which differentiates between "forced" and "voluntary" prostitution and does not really apply to Asia. Santos characterises this position as one which supports the "sexual objectification of women as sexual objects" (*ibid.*, pp. 31, 34). Those who accept that prostitution is "an inevitable social institution" accept that:

> sex, however it is obtained, either by coercion, commercialization or even seduction, is a male right, and that bodies of women and children, and men too, can be and should be packaged and sold as a commodity because there is a buyer and there is a seller. [*ibid.*, p. 38]

She sees the idea of "voluntary" prostitution as inappropriate for the Asian context which is one of "material deprivation and political marginalisation of the masses of people". In Asia, she says, "the question of 'voluntary' prostitution seems to be superfluous" (*ibid.*).

CATW Asia/Pacific, which is based in the Philippines, has developed a language for talking about prostitution which factors in the men who use and profit from women, a language which avoids the concentration on women as the source and problem of prostitution which is found in most academic and political discussion. Chat Garcia explains: "When we say prostitution, we think of women, and it is women who are constantly described, analyzed, condemned and 'saved'. But prostitution is not about women. It is not the story of individual women selling their bodies" (1994, p. 2). To avoid this bias, the new language emphasises the three components of prostitution:

> the Business, the Buyer and the Bought and while traditionalists and the pro-prostitution lobby have invariably focused on the bought, it is the business and the buyers that should be

examined, for it is these two that build up and benefit from the trade in women and children. [*ibid.*, p. 3]

Prostitution, Chat Garcia, explains, is a "highly organised and highly profitable, multinational and multi-billion dollar industry" which is linked to trafficking, tourism and pornography internationally and often organised by crime syndicates that are supported by the local police. The word *bought* for prostituted women avoids the false trails provided by "choice" arguments. She argues that the "choice" of women to enter prostitution in this context is irrelevant because it is not women's willingness to prostitute themselves which creates prostitution. It is profiteers and johns who create the need for prostituted women, and where none are "willing" they will always acquire women by force.

> The industry is propelled by its own demands, and the so-called needs of male customers. The horrific and widespread stories of women and children abducted, tricked and sold into prostitution make it very clear that the industry will get women through any means. [*ibid.*]

The distinction between "forced" trafficking and "free" prostitution is blurred in the conditions of Asian prostitution. Where women are sold into prostitution "willingly" because the money will help their family, a common situation in Thailand, there is no "force" in the Western understanding of that word. Moreover, force would be difficult to prove in a court of law, as it is in rape trials. In Burma, the situation is complicated by the fact that Burmese women rescued from prostitution to be returned to Burma will often slip back into Thailand to prostitution. This is because no reasonable future awaits them in Burma, where they are seen as damaged goods and will not necessarily be welcomed by their family. Would their return to prostitution be considered "forced"? Legislation based upon the "forced" versus "free" distinction would offer little help to women. An approach which makes no distinction and sees women's entry to being prostituted as always entailing some coercion—sometimes very brutal, sometimes less obviously so—is more effective and realistic. Western free-market individualism, depending on the expression of free will, is even less suited to the situation of women in Asia than it is to women in Oslo or New York.

The Convention Against Sexual Exploitation

The fruit of the anti-prostitution feminist position has been the drawing up of a proposed new convention to deal with prostitution in all its forms. The 1949 Convention is seen as inadequate and not going far enough. *The Penn State Report* sees it as implicitly acknowledging that some prostitution is "voluntary". It sees the Convention as implying a distinction between coerced and "voluntary" prostitution by targeting "pimping, procuring, and brothels because they constitute coercion" (UNESCO, 1992, p. 1). Such a focus, it says, suggests that prostitution is freely chosen if exploitation by pimps is absent. The offence that is penalised is the exploitation of prostitution, not the perpetration of the act itself. So the Convention effectively decriminalises the john, legitimising his sexual exploitation of the prostituted woman. The Convention obscures how prostitution violates human rights in and of itself, not just through force or trafficking, and it ignores the role of prostitution in the overall subordination of women in society.

The International Meeting of Experts on Sexual Exploitation, Violence, and Prostitution in 1991, organised through the Coalition Against Trafficking in Women and UNESCO, was called to draft a new convention. It is entitled the *Convention Against Sexual Exploitation*. This Convention answers the need, which feminist human rights theorists have been demonstrating, for a convention specifically penalising violence against women. But whereas other discussions of how to proceed have excluded prostitution, this proposal has both trafficking and prostitution as central to its concerns. Sexual exploitation is defined as:

a practice by which person(s) achieve sexual gratification or financial gain or advancement through the abuse of a person's sexuality by abrogating that person's human right to dignity, equality, autonomy, and physical and mental well-being. [Barry, 1995, p. 326]

It is defined as including, but not being limited to, female infanticide, wife and widow murder, battering, pornography, prostitution, genital mutilation, female seclusion, dowry and bride price, forced sterilisation and forced child-bearing, sexual harassment, rape, incest, sexual abuse and trafficking, temporary marriage, and sex predetermination. Prostitution is defined as "the use of a woman's body as a commodity to be bought, sold, exchanged not always for money", and includes "casual prostitution, street prostitution, prostitution sanctioned by socio-cultural practices, brothels, military prostitution, development prostitution, pornography, sex tourism, and mail-order bride markets" (ibid., p. 327). The new Convention incorporates Articles 1 and 2 of the 1949 Convention in relation to pimping, procuring and brothels, but includes an important new clause which penalises johns, whilst rejecting any form of penalisation of the prostituted woman. It also includes the penalising of the "producers, sellers, and distributors of pornography", who are seen to be promoting and engaging in sexual exploitation.

The new Convention pays detailed attention to what The Penn State Report analyses as the causes of prostitution. Article 7 deals with rejecting economic development policies which channel women into sexual exploitation, via the economic development of women. It prohibits sex tourism in sending and receiving countries, and requires educational programmes to change social and cultural patterns that promote sexual exploitation. Articles 8 and 9 incorporate the kind of measures that anti-trafficking conventions and agreements had been concerned with since the beginning of the twentieth-century, protection of immigrant and emigrant women and children, publicity about the dangers of trafficking, supervision of transit points. There are guarantees of retention of passports and travel documents, and protection of the freedom to travel. Article 11 is concerned with putting in place provisions and observers to protect against sexual exploitation of women in wartime. Articles 12 and 13 seek to help women to leave prostitution and to provide alternatives through educational programmes and work, shelters and other social and health services.

This proposed Convention is strongly opposed by the pro-prostitution lobby. The philosophy of the draft Convention tends to be either misunderstood or misrepresented in the literature of the pro-prostitution theorists. Nelleke van der Vleuten (1991) describes two positions, abolitionists and decriminalisers. The abolitionists are described as seeing prostitution as a "moral evil and an undermining of the family". Their position is damaging to prostitutes because "By defining prostitutes and trafficked women simply as victims, they are also stigmatised" (ibid., p. 21). The opposite position, to which van der Vleuten subscribes, is that of decriminalisation which requires the legitimisation of prostitution. This characterisation of two positions leaves out the feminist politics of groups like CATW entirely. CATW does intend to abolish men's abuse of women in prostitution, but also intends the decriminalisation of the abused women. This sort of anti-prostitution position which emerges from feminist anti-violence politics has little in common with the old-fashioned Christian conservatism that Dutch pro-prostitution activists attribute to CATW. Anti-prostitution feminists are concerned to end violence, not to shore up the family which is often the very seat of male power and common site of male violence. But Liesbeth Lijnzaad sees the abolitionist position as having "moralist implications" as well as being unrealistic and "whimsical" (1995, p. 130).

Van der Vleuten accuses the anti-prostitution position, which she sees as dominant, of cultural imperialism. She argues that the attitude to the traffic in women in the international community is "dominated by an abolitionist and also Western attitude *vis-à-vis* prostitution. It is considered an ethical problem and not a survival strategy" (van der Vleuten, 1991, p. 34). In fact, it could be argued that it is the sexual libertarian position which is culturally imperialist. The sexual libertarian position which regards the sex industry as offering good and reasonable jobs for women is a product of the 1960s sexual revolution which is specifically Western. This Western sexual revolution sold women the idea that their liberation consisted of performing as better sex objects for men, and the notion that liberation could indeed lie in sex (Jeffreys, 1990). In a country like the Philippines, controlled by Spain and the Catholic Church for centuries, the moralistic approach has been dominant. A Western-style sexual revolution has not occurred, and the sexual liberalism represented by the Dutch position is clearly an imported philosophy. Sexual libertarian arguments, such as the idea that being prostituted could represent fulfilment for women, developed in an alien cultural and economic context, hold less sway with human rights activists in Asian countries.

Penalising the perpetrators

The most controversial aspect of the proposed Convention might be expected to be the penalising of johns, since that has not been suggested in previous trafficking instruments. The idea of penalising the john is entirely reasonable if prostitution is recognised as a violation of women's human rights. The perpetrator, or violator, should be subject to penalty. Interestingly, this idea seems to have made some headway in Scandinavia, according to Sven-Axel Mansson's contribution to the 1994 Netherlands conference. Mansson indicts the conference for neglecting even to mention the role of men in prostitution, the johns in particular. He asserts that the "traffic in women can only exist because there is emotional and sexual demand amongst the male population" (Mansson, 1995, p. 120). Very little research had been done on the demand side, and the john's role was rarely challenged. He argues that "one of the central questions for understanding prostitution must deal with what is purchased, that is to say, it must deal with men's motives and need for sexuality" (*ibid.*).

Mansson explains that the pro-prostitution lobby has had less influence in Sweden than in Germany and the Netherlands. In Sweden, for instance, the Working Group for the Role of the Male argues that the john "can no longer be allowed to escape responsibility for his actions" (*ibid.*, p. 122). The group proposed a law to prohibit the buying of sexual services. Its purpose would be to discourage potential sex buyers, lessen the number of prostituted women through decreasing demand, and "thus the extensive human suffering and social damage that prostitution entails for the persons involved". Such a law would have the useful effect of focusing attention on the double standard of morality which has authorised men's use of women, and forcing the public debate to

> pay attention to those elements of the sexual socialization of men that predispose for the role as a sex-buyer ... The key message of penalizing the client is that society cannot any longer accept the escape from human and social responsibility that prostitution in all times has offered men. [*ibid.*, p. 122]

Mansson demands that men take responsibility for their role in prostitution. To decrease men's demand for prostitution, there must be serious education to challenge the construction of masculinity. Such education must "influence and change the social learning processes in which boys are made men and girls women". If prostitution is unacceptable, he argues, "all further efforts of the international pro-prostitution lobby to legalise prostitution" must be counteracted (*ibid.*, p. 123).

An attack on men's demand is crucial to any strategy to combat the abuse of women in prostitution, whether they are trafficked or not. A convention against trafficking in women which fails to target men's abuse of women in prostitution is doomed to be ineffective. The trafficking in women for prostitution, which is the vast majority of trafficking that takes place, requires specific penalty because the purpose of the trafficking does affect the nature of the injury. The "forced" versus "free" distinction must be abandoned, since the outlawing of "forced" trafficking alone would require difficult adjudications of "consent" which would make trafficking almost impossible to combat. It is prostitution which creates trafficking, rather than the other way around. If nothing is done to decrease the demand from men to use prostituted women, then the demand will be supplied by means which include trafficking.

CONCLUSION
universalising prostitution

This book has been written to challenge the idea of prostitution, both the idea in the heads of the johns that enables them to contemplate the abuse of women in prostitution, and the idea proposed by pro-prostitution activists and theorists that prostitution is just work, and sex, and choice. I have suggested a rather different idea of prostitution: that it is a form of male sexual violence and a violation of women's human rights. By saying that men's prostitution behaviour is abusive whether carried out in the East or in the West, on children or adults, in exclusive brothels or in alleyways, I am universalising. This practice of creating universal understandings has become contentious amongst feminist theorists in recent years.

Some feminist theorists in the 1980s adopted a body of masculine and bourgeois theory—much of it coming from gay men—called post-structuralism. They manipulated feminist concern with recognising the diversity of women's experience to create the idea that it is always wrong to "universalise" about the condition of women, and presumably, about the behaviour of men. Linda Nicholson is one of those who has adopted the ideas of a group of male thinkers who criticise Enlightenment certainties, to attack feminist theorising. She explains that all feminist theory from the late 1960s to the mid-1980s "tended to reflect the viewpoints of white, middle-class women of North America and Western Europe" (Nicholson, 1990, p. 1). Their scholarship was limited because they "falsely universalised on the basis of limited perspectives". Universalising, Nicholson said, was indeed the most serious fault of feminist theorists:

> not only did feminist scholars replicate the problematic universalizing tendencies of academic scholarship in general but, even more strikingly, they tended to repeat the specific types of questionable universalizing moves found in the particular schools of thought to which their work was most closely allied. [ibid.]

Universalising was a particular problem of feminists in regard to sexuality, argue Fraser and Nicolson whilst criticising the work of Catharine MacKinnon:

> to construct a universalistic social theory is to risk projecting the socially dominant conjunctions and dispersions of her own society onto others, thereby distorting important features of both. Social theorists would do better first to construct genealogies of the categories of sexuality, reproduction, and mothering before assuming their universal significance. [quoted in Yeatman, 1990, p. 291]

The implication seems to be that the construction of a "genealogy" of sexuality would facilitate a culturally relativist view of behaviours, such as that of men in prostitution as benign in some cultures though abusive in others.

The determination of post-modern feminist thinkers to avoid anything definite arose from the fashion for a masculine theory which threw into question in this period any idea of "truth", and defined any categorisation as "essentialist". The male masters whose work was adopted did not share the oppressed status that required a liberationist philosophy, and of course liberationist philosophy can be envisioned only if categories of persons and "oppression" are recognised as existing. The new post-structuralist ideology, when carried to extremes, made any political theory or action almost impossible.

Post-structuralist feminists never minded universalising about the impossibility of being definite, of course. Universal definites, rather than universal indefinites, were seen as the problem.

In the 1990s radical feminist theorists have embarked on a thoroughgoing critique of post-modern "feminism". Australian Katja Mikhailovitch points out that post-modernism is "no less masculinist than its predecessor" (1996, p. 344). There has been a strong masculine tradition of doubting "truth" in philosophy, she explains. The post-modern turn is just the latest version. She quotes Nietzsche as saying, "there are many kinds of 'truths', and consequently there is no truth", and the Buddha saying, "We are what we think. All that we are, arises from our thoughts. With our thoughts we make our world" (*ibid.*, p. 345).

The question of whether it is reasonable to universalise bedevils feminist theorising of prostitution. Feminist theorists and activists involved in campaigning against the abuse of women in prostitution in Asian countries tend to be wary of universalising. Some see it as important to make distinctions between prostitution East and West. The language in which prostitution is thought about is very different in these different contexts. Whilst women in pro-prostitution groups in the West talk of prostitution as "choice" and "work" and "sex", prostituted women in the Philippines and those who campaign with and for them, see their experience as exploitation, do not like the idea that it is just work, do not see themselves as having choice, and certainly do not see their use by men as having anything to do with their sexuality.

Saundra Sturdevant and Brenda Stoltzfus, in their powerful indictment of the American military's abuse of women in prostitution in the Philippines, Korea and Okinawa, *Let the Good Times Roll* (1992), are well aware of the troubling contradiction these conflicting arguments present. They quote a Filipino activist who had attended a US conference remarking:

Brenda, when you return to the States, you will have a hard time with the women's movement there. They spend all their time arguing about whether or not prostitution can be a free choice. We women from Third World countries got really bored with their fighting. Our issues around prostitution are different. [Sturdevant and Stoltzfus, 1992, p. 300]

They sidestep the issue of the difficulties the pro-prostitution position creates for universalising prostitution by stressing the differences between prostitution East and West. "The voices of prostituted women from Third World countries may not echo the voices of prostitutes from industrialised countries. Their voices and agendas may be very different" (*ibid.*, p. 302).

Sturdevant and Stoltzfus reject both sides of what they see as a purely Western debate; they refute the arguments both of anti-prostitution theorists such as Kathleen Barry and of pro-prostitution "choice" activists. Barry, they say, "tries to extend an analysis based on her work to all forms of sexual labor, without including the voices and issues of prostitute groups" (*ibid.*). But including the voices of prostitute groups is not an easy answer when groups such as WHISPER, for instance, disagree so radically with COYOTE. A principled decision has to be made on whom to believe. Sturdevant and Stoltzfus also criticise Western pro-prostitution groups for generalising. They "have wrongly generalised their experience to all prostituted women, without taking up the issues of prostituted women working in Third World countries or as migrant women in industrialised countries" (*ibid.*). They point out that the perspective of prostituted women from the East can be a thorn in the side of such a universalising pro-prostitution position, and quote the migrant Filipino woman at the Second Whores' Congress, who spoke about "the right to choose not to be a prostitute" (*ibid.*, p. 94).

Is it reasonable, then, to resolve the contradiction by simply stressing the differences between prostitution East and West and being determined not to generalise? Sometimes the perpetrators of the abuse in the East, the johns, are from the West as in military prostitution and sex tourism. Western men with Western expectations, exacerbated by racism, can be involved in great brutality. The perpetrators of the abuse described so starkly in *Let the Good Times Roll* are American servicemen. These men are likely to provide the clientele of prostituted women in the United States on their return, having learnt the commerical use of women. This makes it difficult to separate prostitution in the United States from that in the Philippines. Filipino women describe the brutal abuse by their American johns, such as the favourite practice of "three holes". This connotes the use of a woman as an object with three convenient orifices which can all be used sexually. Women and bars were advertised to Americans as three-holers. The cruelty of this practice is described by Madelin, who explains that she went with an American because she was pregnant and needed money: "'He wanted to do things to me that I didn't like, such as three holes.' She fought ... 'He was choking me ... I was getting weak. I was having difficulty breathing'" (*ibid.*, pp. 61–2). This woman was rescued because hotel employees heard the noise of the struggle. Another American behaved in a similar way: "He turned me over and was entering my ass. I lost it then. I fought ... I had taken part in the wrestling in the bar before" (*ibid.*, p. 62). The Americans demanded the institution of the practice of boxing and wrestling between women in the bars. They found the spectacle of women hurting each other exciting.

Another woman, Lita, describes her first time in prostitution with an American when she was fourteen and a virgin. "I really didn't want to, but he forced me. It was very painful. He tried to undress me but I wouldn't get undressed. There was a lot of blood on my clothes". Her third American behaved in the same way: "He had already had sex with me. His penis couldn't enter because it was too large. I cried ... He pushed my head into the pillow so I wouldn't be able to yell ... He did all kinds of things to me. I cried" (*ibid.*, p. 80).

Glenda, aged thirty, reports of her experience in being used by Americans: "I didn't know about blow jobs and three holes ... It was anal sex that made me cry." When another of her "three holes" was used, it was equally distressing: "The first time I gave a blow job, I threw up outside. I didn't know that throwing up outside is banned. I carried a small towel with me after that" (*ibid.*, pp. 121, 122). Glenda also had to take part in floor shows to excite the American clients:

> There were only three of us doing the floor show. We were completely nude. I put an egg in my vagina ... I didn't know that some of the shell was left inside ... I began earning more money by giving blow jobs under the table. I would give blow jobs to five men at the same time under the table, one right after the other. [*ibid.*, p. 122]

Glenda considers that the Americans thought of the Filipino women as "pigs". "What I felt about the Americans when I did floor shows is that they seemed brutal. It seemed they didn't respect Filipinos—like they saw us as pigs" (*ibid.*, p. 124). Other women in the book drew the same reasonable conclusion about American attitudes. All of the above would be classified as "free" prostitution, since the women "chose" what was done to them. If the perpetrators also abuse women in prostitution in the United States, as seems likely, what is the difference between this and United States prostitution that would discourage generalisation? Young women of fourteen and younger are increasingly used in Western countries in prostitution. An article in the *Far Eastern Economic Review* estimates the number of children under eighteen used in prostitution in the United States at 300,000, in India at 450,000, and in Thailand at 100,000 (Vatikiotis *et al.*, 1995). Such estimates are very difficult to make, but it does seem that use of children in the West is as endemic as in the East. The activities do not seem to be very different, and the violence faced can be similarly cruel.

It is possible that feminists who make such a distinction do so because they see women in poorer countries as having much less "choice". Filipino women are clearly in a much worse position financially than those in the United States or Australia or Norway. However, financial need is the primary

motive of women in Western countries for entering prostitution too, so the distinction is hard to make and must depend
on relative poverty.

The determination to oppose generalisation about prostitution has become fashionable amongst European academics theorising prostitution presently, just at the moment when the
legalisation of prostitution is becoming a burning issue in the
European Union. A 1997 British collection, entitled *Rethinking
Prostitution*, suggests that the aim of such "rethinking" should
be the realisation that prostitution takes many different forms,
only some of which may be oppressive. Graham and Annette
Scambler explain in their introduction:

> Certainly nobody who has observed a homeless 15-year-old
> girl high on drugs touting for business on the streets ... can be
> in any way sanguine. But a distinction has to be drawn
> between female sex work per se, and female sex work in a
> society characterised by patriarchal institutions and ideolo-
> gies and capitalist economic relations. Too often these are
> conflated. However counter-intuitive it may seem, the link
> between female sex work and the use and abuse of women by
> men is contingent rather than necessary. [Scambler and
> Scambler, 1997, p. xv]

They consider that there can be a "good" prostitution, once
the disadvantages laid on the profession by patriarchal prejudice and discrimination are overcome. Thus the solution is to
"empower" prostituted women. Men's hands and penises
would remain on and in the bodies of prostituted women, but
the women would feel quite differently about it. If they dis-
liked the new and benign sex industry, it would be their own
fault. But this cheerful liberal paternalism is not convincing
for many.

Confrontation with what happens in prostitution on the
streets in Britain was shocking to two British researchers in the
same way in which Sturdevant and Stoltzfus were disturbed by
prostitution around United States bases in the Philippines. Neil

McKeganey and Marina Barnard researched prostitution on the streets of Glasgow from the perspective of encouraging safe sex. As they point out, much prostitution research is now being done with money from AIDS-prevention sources. But their research had to cover much more ground than simply condom usage because they discovered what was happening to the women on the streets and how that impacted on their lives and relationships. Their book, *Sex Work on the Streets*, provides a grim picture of the women's experience, even though the foreword is by the pro-prostitution activist Priscilla Alexander, who says, "I was struck by how clearly the women described their methods of establishing their control of the situation in the first negotiations with the client" (McKeganey and Barnard, 1996, p. x). The researchers' findings are in fact far from representing this relentlessly positive approach. One evening they went into the alleys where prostituted women took their johns. They came across women running away from violence, women injured by men, and saw the acts of prostitution take place.

> This was the first occasion that the reality of what being a prostitute entails has been made starkly apparent—alone, on your knees, with a client's penis in your mouth. It is difficult to say why but it was incredibly shocking to see that reality. It also brought home just how vulnerable the women are with a client standing over them. (*ibid.*, p. 11)

They realised that, when they talked with the prostituted women about their "work", "the routinised manner in which relations with clients tended to be discussed did in a sense belie the actual reality of the nature of the work they were doing ..." [*ibid.*, p. 12]

McKeganey and Barnard were honest enough to admit they were shocked. Many researchers on prostitution write as if they are trying to overcome their prejudices at seeing another human being reduced to a spittoon. They take a determinedly neutral position. But in fact the implication of

pro-prostitution work by researchers is that the women in
prostitution must somehow be different from themselves, possessed of a more accepting attitude, or less sensitive, since it is
most unlikely they could envisage themselves being able to
engage in the "work" of prostitution. Failing to recognise the
abuse in prostitution may betray a determined paternalism
towards those who are "different", and is certainly the opposite of the feminist project of making connections.

Those who recognise the abuse of street prostitution may
argue that all that is needed is better conditions that will transform the basic acts of prostitution into an ordinary kind of
work. Such a view is not supported by reports from survivors
of brothel prostitution. Marianne Wood has written a novel
based upon her lifetime of experience in such prostitution in
Melbourne. She gives details that more sanitised accounts omit
of the realities of being used by men in brothels.

> During the massage he parts his legs and raises his buttocks.
> It is going to be a difficult booking. There is an odour of his
> genitals and anus. I turn him over and he begins pawing me.
> It is so difficult for me to be pleasant. I can smell his breath ...
> Then he brushes his hands over my breasts. I tell him no, but
> he continues ... his eyes occasionally darting to the porno-
> graphic video above the bed ... [Wood, 1995, p. 140]

Wood's central character remarks, "not even Dettol can take
away the smell or wipe away the memory. Because it is more
than just a job" (*ibid.*, p. 110). If women can lean over a massage table to do a blow job it may certainly feel a little better
than being on their knees in an alley. But the experience does
not change in fundamentals, only in degree of damage and distress. The severity of other human rights violations may vary
too, such as a distinction between being a political prisoner
who is tortured and one who is not, but they remain violations.

Andrea Dworkin, who has experience of being abused in
prostitution, argues powerfully that it is not useful to make
distinctions:

from the perspective of a woman in prostitution or a woman who has been in prostitution—the distinctions other people make between whether the event took place in the Plaza Hotel or somewhere more inelegant are not the distinctions that matter. These are irreconcilable perceptions, with irreconcilable premises. Of course the circumstances must matter, you say. No, they do not, because we are talking about the use of the mouth, the vagina, and the rectum. The circumstances don't mitigate or modify what prostitution is. [Dworkin, 1997, p. 141]

What is being done to prostituted women is the same regardless of the venue, she says, and it consists of "the mouth, the vagina, the rectum, penetrated usually by a penis, sometimes hands, sometimes objects, by one man and then another and then another and then another and then another. That's what it is …" (ibid., p. 140).

The determination by pro-prostitution activists and theorists to make distinctions between "forced" and "free", between adult and child, and between East and West, merely reinforces the idea that there can be a good and reasonable form of men's abuse of women in prostitution. The creation of such distinctions disappears the male abusers once again. The johns do not agonise over distinctions. The prostitution abuse by the johns is becoming more and more universalised. Western sex tourists use both adult and child prostitutes in the East with little concern for whether their victims are "forced" or "free". Women and children are trafficked together and held in the same brothels. Johns in the West are likely to be able to use young teenage girls on the streets and trafficked Asian women in brothels. Men's abuse of women, children and other men in prostitution internationally stems from the idea that such abuse is natural, inevitable, and justified. In response, it is important to create an even more powerful idea amongst those concerned with the abuse of women's human rights: that prostitution is a form of brutal cruelty on the part of men that constitutes a violation of women's human rights, wherever and however it takes place.

BIBLIOGRAPHY

ABC Radio National. (1996, February 11). You Can Touch Me. I'm Part of the Union, *Radio Eye.*

Abella, Rosalie. (1993). From Civil Liberties to Human Rights: Acknowledging the Differences. In Mahoney and Mahoney (1993).

Abelove, H. *et al.* (1993). *The Lesbian and Gay Studies Reader.* New York: Routledge.

Abramson, Jeffrey. (Ed.). (1996). *Postmortem: The O. J. Simpson Case.* New York: Basic Books.

Acton, William. (1987a /1870). Prostitution Considered in its Social and Sanitary Aspects. In Jeffreys (1987).

Acton, William. (1987b / 1875). The Functions and Disorders of the Reproductive Organs. In Jeffreys (1987).

Adkins, Lisa, and Vicki Merchant. (Eds.). 1996. *Sexualizing the Social: Power and the Organization of Sexuality.* Basingstoke, Hants: Macmillan.

Alexander, Priscilla. (1988a). Prostitution: A Difficult Issue for Feminists. In Delacoste and Alexander (1988).

Alexander, Priscilla. (1988b). Why This Book? In Delacoste and Alexander (1988).

Allen, Sheila, and Diana Leonard. (1996). From Sexual Divisions to Sexualities: Changing Sociological Agendas. In Weeks and Holland (1996).

Altman, Dennis. (1994). *Power and Community: Organizational and Cultural Responses to AIDS.* London: Taylor and Francis.

Anon. (n.d., a). *In the Grip of the White Slave Trader.* London: M.A.P.

Anon. (n.d., b). (c.1912–14) *Pitfalls for Women.* London: Success Publishing Company.

Anon. (1995, May 21). Dances with Wolves, *Sunday Age*, Melbourne.

Anthony, Jane. (1986, January–February). Prostitution as Choice, *Ms*, 86–7.

Anti-Slavery International. (1993, June and October). *Newsletter*. London: Anti-Slavery International.

Anti-Slavery International. (1995). *Redefining Prostitution as Commercial Sex Work on the International Agenda*. London: Anti-Slavery International.

Armstrong, Louise. (1978). *Kiss Daddy Goodnight: A Speak-Out on Incest*. New York: Pocket Books, Simon and Schuster.

Armstrong, Louise. (1994). *Rocking the Cradle of Sexual Politics: What Happened When Women Said Incest*. Reading, Massachusetts: Addison-Wesley.

Ashby, Dame Margery Corbett. (1968). Fifty Years of Women's Suffrage, *The Shield*. London: Josephine Butler Society.

Association for Community Development. (1995). *International Migration of Women: A Study on Causes and Consequences*. Rajshari, Bangladesh: ACD.

Bailey, Eleanor. (1995, December). Emotional Issues: When Wife Meets Prostitute, *Marie Claire*, 4.

Barnett, Ola W., and Alyce D. LaViolette. (1993). *It Could Happen to Anyone*. Newbury Park, California: Sage.

Barry, Kathleen. (1979). *Female Sexual Slavery*. Englewood Cliffs, New Jersey: Prentice-Hall.

Barry, Kathleen. (1995). *The Prostitution of Sexuality*. New York: NYU Press.

Bart, Pauline, and Eileen Moran. (Eds.). (1993). *Violence Against Women: The Bloody Footprints*. Newbury Park, California: Sage.

Basserman, Lujo. (1967). *The Oldest Profession: A History of Prostitution*. London: Arthur Barker.

Bell, Alan P., and Martin S. Weinberg. (1978). *Homosexualities: A Study of Diversity among Men and Women*. New York: Simon and Schuster.

Bell, Diane, and Renate Klein. (Eds.). (1996). *Radically Speaking: Feminism Reclaimed*. Melbourne: Spinifex Press; London: Zed Books.

Bell, Laurie. (Ed.). (1987a). *Good Girls, Bad Girls: Sex Trade Workers and Feminists Face to Face*. Toronto: Women's Press.

Bell, Laurie. (1987b). Realistic Feminists: An Interview with Valerie Scott, Peggy Miller, and Ryan Hotchkiss of the Canadian Organization for the Rights of Prostitutes (CORP). In Bell (1987a).

Bell, Shannon. (1994). *Reading, Writing and Rewriting the Prostitute Body*. Bloomington, Indiana: Indiana University Press.

Benjamin, Harry, and R. E. L. Masters. (1965). *Prostitution and Sexual Morality*. London: Souvenir Press.

Billington-Greig, Teresa. (1913, June). The Truth about White Slavery, *Englishwoman's Review, 14*.

Blake, Elissa. (1996, February 21). What They Do in Men's Clubs ... And Why Business is Booming, *Age*, Melbourne.

Bland, Lucy. (1995). *Banishing the Beast: English Feminism and Sexual Morality, 1885–1914*. London: Penguin.

Bloch, Iwan. (1919 / 1908). *The Sexual Life of Our Time*. London: William Heinemann.

Boyle, Nina. (1931). What is Slavery? An Appeal to Women, *The Shield, 7*, 3rd series.

Brecher, Bob. (1987). Surrogacy, Liberal Individualism, and the Moral Climate. In Evans (1987).

Brecher, Bob. (1990). The Kidney Trade: or, The Customer is Always Wrong, *Journal of Medical Ethics, 16*, 120–3.

Brecher, Edward. (1972). *The Sex Researchers*. London: Panther.

Brownmiller, Susan. (1975). *Against Our Will: Men, Women and Rape*. London: Secker and Warburg.

Bristow, Edward. (1982). *Prostitution and Prejudice: The Jewish Fight Against White Slavery, 1870–1939*. Oxford: Clarendon Press.

British Commonwealth League. (1925–38). *Conference Reports*.

Bullough, Vern, and Bonnie Bullough. (1987 / 1978). *Women and Prostitution: A Social History*. New York: Prometheus Books.

Bunch, Charlotte. (1995). Transforming Human Rights from a Feminist Perspective. In Peters and Wolper (1995).

Butler, Josephine E. (1881). *A Call to Action. Being a Letter to the Ladies of Birmingham. Supplementary to an Address Given in Birmingham. November*. Birmingham: Hudson and Son.

Butler, Judith. (1990). Gender Trouble, Feminist Theory, and Psychoanalytic Discourse. In Nicholson (1990a).

Byrnes, Andrew. (1992). Women, Feminism and International Human Rights Law—Methodological Myopia, Fundamental Flaws or Meaningful Marginalisation?, *Australian Year Book of International Law, 12*.

Caine, Barbara, and Rosemary Pringle. (Eds.). 1995. *Transitions: New Australian Feminisms*. St Leonards, New South Wales: Allen and Unwin.

Califia, Pat. (1981). Feminism and Sadomasochism, *Heresies, 12*.

Califia, Pat. (1982). A Personal View. In Samois (1982).

Califia, Pat. (1988). *Sapphistry: The Book of Lesbian Sexuality*. Tallahassee, Florida: Naiad.

Califia, Pat. (1989). *Macho Sluts*. Boston: Alyson Publications.

Califia, Pat. (1994). *Public Sex: The Culture of Radical Sex*. Pittsburgh: Cleis Press.

Calkin, Jeremy. (1994, September 10). The Third Sex, *Age*, Melbourne. Reprinted from *The Independent on Sunday*.

Caprio, Frank. (1963). *The Sexually Adequate Female*. New York: Citadel Press.

Caputi, Jane. (1993). The Sexual Politics of Murder. In Bart and Moran (1993).

Carole. (1988a). Interview with Barbara. In Delacoste and Alexander (1988).

Carole. (1988b). Interview with Debra. In Delacoste and Alexander (1988).

Catterall, Dr R. D. (1968). Prostitution and the Venereal Diseases (10th Alison Neilans Memorial Lecture), *The Shield*.

Centre for Family and Women's Studies, Hanoi. (1994). Country Report: Vietnam. In *Foundation for Women*, Thailand (1994).

Charlesworth, Hilary. (1994). What Are "Women's International Human Rights?". In Cook (1994a).

Charlesworth, Hilary. (1995). Human Rights as Men's Rights. In Peters and Wolper (1995).

Chesler, Phyllis. (1990). Mothers on Trial: Custody and the "Baby M" Case. In Leidholdt and Raymond (1990).

Comfort, Alex. (1979 / 1973). *The Joy of Sex*. London: Quartet.

Comfort, Alex. (Ed.). (1984 / 1977). *More Joy of Sex: A Lovemaker's Companion*. London: Quartet.

Connell, Robert. (1995). *Masculinities*. St Leonards, New South Wales: Allen and Unwin.

Cook, Rebecca J. (Ed.). (1994a). *Human Rights of Women: National and International Perspectives*. Philadelphia: University of Pennsylvania Press.

Cook, Rebecca J. (1994b). Women's International Human Rights Law: The Way Forward. In Cook (1994a).

Cooke, Amber. (1987). Sex Trade Workers and Feminists: Myths and Illusions. In Bell (1987a).

Coomaraswamy, Radhika. (1994). To Bellow like a Cow: Women, Ethnicity, and the Discourse of Rights. In Cook (1994a).

Copelon, Rhonda. (1994a). Surfacing Gender: Reconceptualizing Crimes against Women in Time of War. In Stiglmayer (1994).

Copelon, Rhonda. (1994b). Intimate Terror: Understanding Domestic Violence as Torture. In Cook (1994a).

Copelon, Rhonda. (1995). Gendered War Crimes: Reconceptualising Rape in Time of War. In Peters and Wolper (1995).

Corbin, Alain. (1990). *Women For Hire: Prostitution and Sexuality in France after 1850*. Cambridge, Massachusetts: Harvard University Press.

Cotler, Irwin. (1993). Human Rights as the Modern Tool of Revolution. In Mahoney and Mahoney (1993).

Coveney, Lal, *et al.* (1984). *The Sexuality Papers*. London: Hutchinson.

Crowdy, Rachel. (1949). Past Achievements: The Present Task. In International Bureau for the Suppression of the Traffic in Women and Children, *Traffic in Women and Children*. London.

Cullen, Bernard. (1987). The Right to Work. In Evans (1987)

Daly, Mary. (1979 / 1978). *Gyn/Ecology: The Metaethics of Radical Feminism*. London: Women's Press.

Daly, Mary. (1984). *Pure Lust: Elemental Feminist Philosophy*. London: Women's Press.

Davidson, Julia O'Connell. (1994, July 8–10). British Sex Tourists in Thailand. Paper presented to the Women's Studies Network Annual Conference, Portsmouth. Reprinted in M. Maynard and J. Purvis. (Eds.). (1995). *(Hetero)Sexual Politics*, London: Taylor and Francis.

Davidson, Julia O'Connell. 1996. Prostitution and the Contours of Control. In Weeks and Holland (1996).

Davis, Kathy. (1995). *Reshaping the Female Body: The Dilemma of Cosmetic Surgery*. New York: Routledge.

Davis, Kingsley. (1937). The Sociology of Prostitution, *American Sociological Review*, *II, 744–55.*

Davis, Nanette J. (Ed.). (1993). *Prostitution: An International Handbook on Trends, Problems, and Policies*. Westport, Connecticut: Greenwood Press.

Day, Sophie, and Helen Ward. (1996). The Praed Street Project: A Cohort of Prostitute Women in London. In Jackson and Scott (1996).

de Beauvoir, Simone. (1972 / 1953). *The Second Sex*. London: Penguin.

Delacoste, Frederique, and Priscilla Alexander. (Eds.). (1988). *Sex Work: Writings by Women in the Sex Industry*. London: Women's Press.

Delphy, Christine. (1993). Rethinking Sex and Gender. *Women's Studies International Forum, 16* (1), 1–9.

Delphy, Christine, and Diana Leonard. (1992). *Familiar Exploitation*. Cambridge: Polity Press.

Denfeld, Rene. (1995). *The New Victorians: A Young Woman's Challenge to the Old Feminist Order*. St Leonards, New South Wales: Allen and Unwin.

Deutchman, Iva. (Forthcoming). It's (Not) Just the Victim in Me: Sexuality and Power in the 1990s, *Women and Politics*.

Distor, Emere, and Dee Hunt. (Eds.). (1996). *Confronting Sexual Exploitation: Campaign Against Sex Tourism and Trafficking in Filipino Women*. Justice Place, 84 Park Road, Woolloongabba, Qld, 4102: Centre for Philippine Concerns.

Dolgopol, Ustinia. (1995). Women's Voices, Women's Pain, *Human Rights Quarterly*, 17 (1), 127–54.

Dolgopol, Ustinia. (1996). Pragmatism, International Law and Women's Bodies. *Australian Feminist Studies*, II (24).

Duberman, Martin *et al.* (Eds.). (1991). *Hidden from History*. London: Penguin.

Duggan, Lisa, and Nan D. Hunter. (1995). *Sex Wars: Sexual Dissent and Political Culture*. New York and London: Routledge.

Dumble, Lynette. (1995, October 6). When Dismissal Amounts to Scandal: The Medical Response to Silicone Implant-Related Disorders. Plenary address to the North American Congress on Women's Health Issues, Galverston, Texas.

Dworkin, Andrea. (1981). *Pornography: Men Possessing Women*. New York: Perigree.

Dworkin, Andrea. (1983). *Right-Wing Women: The Politics of Domesticated Females*. London: Women's Press.

Dworkin, Andrea. (1987). *Intercourse*. London: Secker and Warburg.

Dworkin, Andrea. (1988). *Letters from a War Zone*. London: Secker and Warburg.

Dworkin, Andrea. (1997). *Life and Death*. New York: Free Press.

Dworkin, Andrea, and Catharine MacKinnon. (1993). Questions and Answers. In Russell (1993).

Dworkin, Ronald. (1977). *Taking Rights Seriously*. London: Duckworth.

Easteal, Patricia. (1994). *Voices of the Survivors*. Melbourne: Spinifex Press.

Edelstein, Judy. (1988). In the Massage Parlor. In Delacoste and Alexander (1988).

Ellis, Henry Havelock. (1946 / 1937). *Sex in Relation to Society*. London: W. M. Heinemann.

Enloe, Cynthia. (1983). *Does Khaki Become You? The*

Militarisation of Women's Lives. London: Pluto Press.

Enloe, Cynthia. (1992). It Takes Two. In Sturdevant and Stoltzfus (1992).

Evans, David T. (1993). *Sexual Citizenship: The Material Construction of Sexualities*. London: Routledge.

Evans, J. D. G. (1987). *Moral Philosophy and Contemporary Problems*. Cambridge: Cambridge University Press.

Evatt, Elizabeth. (1995). Women in Australia. In Klap *et al*. (1995).

Everywoman. (1988). *Pornography and Sexual Violence: Evidence of Harm*. London: Everywoman Ltd.

Faderman, Lillian. (1985). *Surpassing the Love of Men*. London: Women's Press.

Farley, Melissa, and Hotaling, Norma. (1995, September 4). *Prostitution, Violence and Posttraumatic Stress Disorder*. NGO Forum, Fourth World Conference on Women Beijing.

Faust, Beatrice. (1994). *Backlash? Balderdash!* Sydney: University of New South Wales Press.

Fitzpatrick, Joan. (1994). The Use of International Human Rights Norms to Combat Violence Against Women. In Cook (1994a).

Flexner, Abraham. (1964 / 1914). *Prostitution in Europe*. Montclair, New Jersey: Patterson Smith.

Forel, August. (n.d., c.1910). *The Sexual Question: A Scientific, Psychological, Hygienic and Sociological Study*. New York: Rebman Company.

Foucault, Michel (1978). *The History of Sexuality, 1*. London: Allen Lane.

Foundation Against Trafficking in Women. (1994). Country Report: Netherlands/Central and Eastern Europe. In *Foundation for Women,* Thailand, (1994).

Foundation for Women, Thailand. (1994, October 17–21). *International Workshop on International Migration and Traffic in Women*. Chiangmai. Foundation for Women, Thailand; Women's Study Centre, Chiangmai; Women and Autonomy Centre, Leider University.

Friedman, Elisabeth. (1995). Women's Human Rights: The Emergence of a Movement. In Peters and Wolper (1995).

Friedman, Milton, and Rose Friedman. 1980. *Free to Choose: A Personal Statement*. New York and London: Harcourt Brace Jovanovich.

Fudge, Judy. (1989). The Effect of Entrenching a Bill of Rights upon Political Discourse: Feminist Demands and Sexual Violence in Canada, *International Journal of the Sociology of Law, 17,* 445–63.

Fryer, Peter. (1988). *Black People in the British Empire: An Introduction*. London: Pluto Press.

Gagnon, John H., and William Simon. (1974). *Sexual Conduct*. London: Hutchinson.

Garcia, Chat. (1994, October 6–7). Sex Trade: A Multinational Industry. Paper presented to a conference on Stopping Violence Against Filipino Women: A Government and Community Responsibility, Melbourne.

Garner, Helen. (1995). *The First Stone: Some Questions about Sex and Power*. Sydney: Picador.

Gavey, Nicola. (1993). Technologies and Effects of Heterosexual Coercion. In Wilkinson and Kitzinger (1993).

Gerrull, Sally-Anne, and Boronia Halstead. (1992). *Sex Industry and Public Policy*. Canberra: Australian Institute of Criminology.

Gibson, Barbara. (1996). *Male Order: Life Stories from Boys Who Sell Sex*. London: Cassell.

Giddens, Anthony. (1992). *The Transformation of Intimacy: Sexuality, Love and Eroticism in Modern Societies*. Cambridge: Polity Press.

Giobbe, Evelina. (1990). Confronting the Liberal Lies about Prostitution. In Leidholdt and Raymond (1990).

Giobbe, Evelina. (1991). Prostitution: Buying the Right to Rape. In Ann Wolpert Burgess (Ed.). *Rape and Sexual Assault III. A Research Handbook*. New York: Garland Publishing, Inc.

Giobbe, Evelina. (1992). Juvenile Prostitution: Profile of Recruitment. In Ann Wolpert Burgess (Ed.). *Child Trauma: Issues and Research*. New York: Garland Publishing, Inc.

Glover, Edward. (1943). The Medical Arguments (With Special Reference to Pathology). In International Bureau for the Suppression of the Traffic in Women and Children (1943).

Glover, Edward. (1969 / 1943). *The Psychopathology of Prostitution*. London: Institute for the Study and Treatment of Delinquency.

Goffman, Erving. (1974 / 1963). *Stigma: Notes on the Management of Spoiled Identity*. Harmondsworth, Middlesex: Pelican.

Goodley, Steven. (1994). A Male Sex Worker's View. In Perkins *et al*. (1994).

Graham, D. L. R., with E. Rawlings, and R. Rigsby. (1994). *Loving to Survive: Sexual Terror, Men's Violence, and Women's Lives*. New York: NYU Press.

Grauerholz, Elizabeth, and Mary A. Koraliwski. (Eds.). (1991).

Sexual Coercion: A Sourcebook on Its Nature, Causes, and Prevention. Lexington, Massachusetts: Lexington Books.

Greenwald, Harold. (1964 / 1958). *The Call Girl.* New York: Ballantine Books.

Halberstam, Judith. (1994). F2M: The Making of Female Masculinity. In Laura Doan (Ed.). *The Lesbian Postmodern.* New York: Columbia University Press.

Hall, Gladys Mary. (1933). *Prostitution: A Survey and a Challenge.* London: Williams and Norgate.

Harding, Sandra. (1987). The Instability of the Anaytical Categories of Feminist Theory. In Sandra Harding and Jean F. O'Barr, *Sex and Scientific Inquiry.* Chicago: University of Chicago Press.

Harding, Sandra. (1991). *Whose Science? Whose Knowledge? Thinking from Women's Lives.* Milton Keynes: Open University Press.

Harding, Sandra, and Merrill B. Hintikka. (Eds.). (1983). *Discovering Reality: Feminist Perspectives on Epistemology, Metaphysics, Methodology, and Philosophy of Science.* Boston: D. Reidel Publishing Co.

Hartley, Nina. (1988). Confessions of a Feminist Porno Star. In Delacoste and Alexander (1988).

Hartsock, Nancy. (1983). The Feminist Standpoint: Developing the Ground for a Specifically Feminist Historical Materialism. In Harding and Hintikka (1983).

Hatty, Suzanne. (1992). The Desired Object: Prostitution in Canada, United States and Australia. In Gerrull and Halstead (1992).

Haveman, Roelof. (1995). Traffic in Persons as a Problem. In Klap *et al.* (1995).

Hauptmann, Emily. (1996). *Putting Choice Before Democracy: A Critique of Rational Choice Theory.* Albany, New York: State University of New York.

Hawthorne, Susan. (1991). What do Lesbians Want? Towards a Feminist Sexual Ethics, *Journal of Australian Lesbian Feminist Studies,* 1 (2).

Heidenry, John. (1997). *What Wild Ecstasy: The Rise and Fall of the Sexual Revolution.* Melbourne: William Heinemann Australia.

Heise, Lori L. (1995). Freedom Close to Home: The Impact of Violence Against Women on Reproductive Rights. In Peters and Wolper (1995).

Henriques, Fernando. (1965 / 1962). *The Pretence of Love: Prostitution and Society,* 1: *Primitive, Classical and Oriental.* London: Panther.

358   bibliography

Henriques, Fernando. (1968). *Modern Sexuality, III* of *Prostitution and Society*. London: MacGibbon and Kee.
Henley, Nancy. (1977). *Body Politics: Sex, Power and Nonverbal Communication*. Englewood Cliffs, New Jersey: Prentice-Hall.
Henslin, James M. (Ed.). (1971). *Studies in the Sociology of Sex*. New York: Appleton-Century-Crofts.
Henslin, James M., and Edward Sagarin. (1971). Towards a Sociology of Sex. In Henslin (1971).
Herman, Judith Lewis. 1981. *Father–Daughter Incest*. Cambridge, Massachusetts: Harvard University Press.
Herman, Judith Lewis. 1994. *Trauma and Recovery: From Domestic Abuse to Political Terror*. London: Pandora.
Hester, Marianne, Liz Kelly, and Jill Radford. (Eds.). 1996. *Women, Violence and Male Power*. Buckingham: Open University Press.
Hite, Shere. (1977). *The Hite Report: A Nationwide Study of Female Sexuality*. Sydney: Summit Books, Paul Hamlyn.
Hite, Shere. (1981). *The Hite Report on Male Sexuality*. London: Macdonald.
Hoagland, Sarah Lucia, and Julie Penelope. (Eds.). (1988). *For Lesbians Only*. London: Onlywomen Press.
Hochschild, Arlie. (1983). *The Managed Heart: Commercialization of Human Feeling*. Berkeley: University of California Press.
Hoffman, Barry. (1994). Editorial Meanderings, *Gauntlet* (Springfield, Pennsylvania), *1*.
Hogan, Christopher J. 1996. What We Write About When We Write About Porn. In Michael Bronski (Ed.). *Taking Liberties: Gay Men's Essays on Politics, Culture and Sex*. New York: Masquerade Books.
Hoigard, Cecilie, and Liv Finstad. (1992). *Backstreets: Prostitution, Money and Love*. Cambridge: Polity Press.
Hoigard, Cecilie, and Liv Finstad. (1993). Prostitution in Norway. In Davis (1993).
hooks, bell. 1994. *Outlaw Culture: Resisting Representations*. New York and London: Routledge.
Howard, Rhoda. (1993). Health Costs of Social Degradation and Female Self-Mutilation in North America. In Mahoney and Mahoney (1993).
Hughes, Donna. (1996). Sex Tours via the Internet, *Agenda: Empowering Women for Gender Equity*, *28*, 71–6.
Human Rights Watch/Asia. (1994). *A Modern Form of Slavery*. New York: Human Rights Watch.
Human Rights Watch/Asia. (1995). *Rape for Profit*. New York: Human Rights Watch.

Hunt, Mary. (1990, Spring). The De-eroticization of Women's Liberation: Social Purity Movements and the Revolutionary Feminism of Sheila Jeffreys, *Feminist Review, 4*.

Hunter, Andrew. (1992). The Development of Theoretical Approaches to Sex Work in Australian Sex-Worker Rights Groups. In Gerrull and Halstead (1992).

Hunter, Susan Kay. (1994). Prostitution is Cruelty and Abuse to Women and Children. *Michigan Journal of Gender and Law, 1*, 1–14.

Ingram, Attracta. (1994). *A Political Theory of Rights*. Oxford: Clarendon Press.

International Bureau for the Suppression of the Traffic in Women and Children. (1930, 1937). *Congress Reports*. London: International Bureau.

International Bureau for the Suppression of the Traffic in Women and Children. (1943, October). *The Abolition of Tolerated Houses*. Lectures nos 22–3.

Isherwood, Charles. (1996). *Wonder Bread and Ecstasy: The Life and Death of Joey Stefano*. Los Angeles: Alyson Publications.

Jackson, Margaret. (1984). Sexology and the Universalization of Male Sexuality. In Coveney *et al.* (1984).

Jackson, Margaret. (1994). *The Real Facts of Life: Feminism and the Politics of Sexuality, c.1850–1940*. London: Taylor and Francis.

Jackson, Stevi. (1978). *On the Social Construction of Female Sexuality*. London: Women's Research and Resources Centre Publications.

Jackson, Stevi. (1996a). Heterosexuality and Feminist Theory. In Richardson (1996).

Jackson, Stevi. (1996b). Heterosexuality as a Problem for Feminist Theory. In Adkins and Merchant (1996).

Jackson, Stevi, and Sue Scott. (Eds.). 1996. *Feminism and Sexuality: A Reader*. Edinburgh: Edinburgh University Press.

Jacobs, Janet Liebman. (1994). *Victimized Daughters: Incest and the Development of the Female Self*. New York: Routledge.

Jaget, Claude. (Ed.). (1980). *Prostitutes Our Life*. Bristol: Falling Wall Press.

Jaggar, Alison M. (1988 / 1983). *Feminist Politics and Human Nature*. Totowa, New Jersey: Rowman and Littlefield.

James, J., and J. Meyerding. (1977). Early Sexual Experiences and Prostitution, *American Journal of Psychiatry, 134*, 1381–5.

James, Jackie. (1996). Excuse Me, Madam, Are You Looking for a

Good Time? In Nicola Godwin, Belinda Hollows and Sheridan Nye (Eds.) *Assaults on Convention: Essays on Lesbian Transgressors*. London: Cassell.

Jaschok, Maria. (1988). *Concubines and Bondservants: The Social History of a Chinese Custom*. London: Zed Books.

Jeffreys, Sheila. (1982). The Sexual Abuse of Children in the Home. In Scarlet Friedman and Elizabeth Sarah (Eds.) *On the Problem of Men*. London: Women's Press.

Jeffreys, Sheila. (1985). Prostitution. In McNeil and Rhodes (1985).

Jeffreys, Sheila. (Ed.). (1987). *The Sexuality Debates*. London: Routledge.

Jeffreys, Sheila. (1991 / 1990). *Anticlimax: A Feminist Perspective on the Sexual Revolution*. London: Women's Press; New York: NYU Press.

Jeffreys, Sheila. (1993a). *The Lesbian Heresy: A Feminist Perspective on the Lesbian Sexual Revolution*. Melbourne: Spinifex; (1994) London: Women's Press; (1995) Munich: Frauenoffensive; (1996) Valencia: Caixsa, University of Valencia.

Jeffreys, Sheila. (1993b). Consent and the Politics of Sexuality, *Current Issues in Criminal Justice* (Australian Institute of Criminology, Sydney), 173–83.

Jeffreys, Sheila. (1994). The Queer Disappearance of Lesbians, *Women's Studies International Forum*, 17 (5), 459–72.

Jeffreys, Sheila. (1995). Women and Sexuality. In June Purvis (Ed.). *Women in Britain, 1870–1945*. London: University College Press.

Jeffreys, Sheila. (1997 / 1985). *The Spinster and Her Enemies: Feminism and Sexuality, 1880–1930*. Melbourne: Spinifex.

Jeness, Valerie. (1993). *Making It Work: The Prostitutes' Rights Movement in Perspective*. New York: Aldine De Gruyter.

Jones, Ann. (1994). *Next Time She'll Be Dead: Battering and How to Stop It*. Boston: Beacon Press.

Juno, Andrea. (1991a). Interview with Susie Bright, *Angry Women. RE/SEARCH, 13*. San Francisco: Re/Search Publications.

Juno, Andrea. (1991b). Interview with Annie Sprinkle, *Angry Women. RE/SEARCH, 13*. San Francisco: Re/Search Publications.

Kappeler, Susanne. (1990). Liberals, Libertarianism, and the Liberal Arts Establishment. In Leidholdt and Raymond (1990).

Kappeler, Susanne. (1995). *The Will to Violence: The Politics of Personal Behaviour*. Melbourne: Spinifex.

Karen Women's Organisation. (1994). Country Report: Burma

(Karen). In *Foundation for Women,* Thailand (1994).

Kelly, Liz. (1989 / 1988). *Surviving Sexual Violence.* Cambridge: Polity Press.

Kelly, Liz, Sheila Burton, and Linda Regan. (1996). Beyond Victim or Survivor: Sexual Violence, Identity and Feminist Theory and Practice. In Adkins and Merchant (1996).

Kendar, Arn O Salish. (1994). Country Report: Bangladesh. In *Foundation for Women,* Thailand (1994).

Kerr, Joanna. (Ed.). (1993). *Ours By Right: Women's Rights as Human Rights.* London: Zed Books.

Keuls, Eva. (1993 / 1986). *The Reign of the Phallus: Sexual Politics in Ancient Athens.* Berkeley: University of California Press.

King, Amanda. (1994). Speaking the Ineffable: New Directions in Performance Art. Linda Sproul's Liaten and Barbara Campbell's Backwash, *Artlink: Australian Contemporary Art Quarterly, 14* (1).

Kingdon, Elizabeth. (1991). *What's Wrong with Rights? Problems for Feminist Politics of Law.* Edinburgh: Edinburgh University Press.

Kinsey, Alfred C., Wardell B. Pomeroy, and Clyde E. Martin. (1949). *Sexual Behaviour in the Human Male.* Philadelphia and London: W. B. Saunders Co.

Kirp, David L., Mark G. Yudof, and Marlene Strong Franks. (1986). *Gender Justice.* Chicago: University of Chicago Press.

Klap, Marieke, Yvonne Klerk, and Jacqueline Smith. (Eds.). (1995). *Combatting Traffic in Persons.* SIM Special No 17. Studie - en Informatiecentrum Mensenrechten, Janskerhof 16, 3512 BM, Utrecht.

Klein, Renate. (1996). (Dead) Bodies Floating in Cyberspace: Postmodernism and the Dismemberment of Women. In Bell and Klein (1996).

Klerk, Yvonne. (1995). Definition of 'Traffic in Persons'. In Klap *et al.* (1995).

Kronhausen, Dr Eberhard, and Dr Phyllis Kronhausen. (Eds.). (1967). *"My Secret Life", by Walter.* London: Polybooks.

Krum, Sharon. (1996 February 24–25). Cervix with a Smile, *Weekend Australian Magazine.*

Lahey, Kathleen A. (1990). Women and Civil Liberties. In Leidholdt and Raymond (1990).

Lap-Chew, Lin. (1995a, March). Letter to the Special Rapporteur, *Foundation Against Trafficking in Women: News Bulletin, 2.* Utrecht: Foundation Against Trafficking in Women.

Lap-Chew, Lin. (1995b, November). The Significance of the Women's Conference in Beijing for Work on the Issue of Trafficking in Women, *Foundation Against Trafficking in Women: News Bulletin, 4*. Utrecht: Foundation Against Trafficking in Women.

League of Nations. (1921). *International Conference on Traffic in Women and Children: Provisional Verbatim Report*. Geneva: League of Nations.

League of Nations. (1922–36). Minutes of Advisory Committee on the Traffic in Women and Children. Geneva: League of Nations.

League of Nations. (1927). *Report of the Special Body of Experts on the Traffic in Women and Children*. C.52.M.52.1927.IV. Geneva: League of Nations.

League of Nations. (1933). *Commission of Enquiry into Traffic in Women and Children in the East*. Report to the Council. C.26.M26. Geneva: League of Nations.

League of Nations. (1939). Advisory Committee on Social Questions. *Enquiry into Measures for the Rehabilitation of Prostitutes*. Parts 1–4. Geneva: League of Nations.

League of Nations. (1943). Advisory Committee on Social Questions. *Prevention of Prostitution*. C.26.M.26. Geneva: League of Nations.

Leidholdt, Dorchen, and Janice G. Raymond. (Eds.). (1990). *The Sexual Liberals and the Attack on Feminism*. New York: Pergamon Press.

Leigh, Carol. (1994). Thanks, Ma. In Sappington and Stallings (1994).

Lerner, Gerda. (1987). *The Creation of Patriarchy*. New York: Oxford University Press.

Liazos, Alexander. (1972). The Poverty of Sociology of Deviance: Nuts, Sluts, and Perverts, *Social Problems, 20, 103–20*.

Lijnzaad, Liesbeth. (1995). Women of No Consequence: The Inadequacy of the International Protection against Trafficking. In Klap *et al.* (1995).

Lovelace, Linda. (1981). *Ordeal: An Autobiography*. London: W. H. Allen.

Lumby, Catharine. (1997). *Bad Girls: The Media, Sex and Feminism in the 90s*. St Leonards, NSW: Allen and Unwin.

Macik, Donna. (n.d.) *A Qualitative Study of the Victorian Sex Industry*. Melbourne: ACV.

MacKinnon, Catharine A. (1979). *The Sexual Harassment of*

Working Women: A Case of Sex Discrimination. New Haven: Yale University Press.

MacKinnon, Catharine A. (1987). *Feminism Unmodified.* Cambridge, Massachusetts: Harvard University Press.

MacKinnon, Catharine A. (1989). *Towards a Feminist Theory of the State.* Cambridge, Massachusetts: Harvard University Press.

MacKinnon, Catharine A. (1993). On Torture: A Feminist Perspective on Human Rights. In Mahoney and Mahoney (1993).

MacKinnon, Catharine A. (1994a). Rape, Genocide, and Women's Human Rights. In Stiglmayer (1994).

MacKinnon, Catharine A. (1994b). *Only Words.* London: HarperCollins.

McKeganey, Neil, and Marian Barnard. (1996). *Sex Work on the Streets: Prostitutes and Their Clients.* Buckingham: Open University Press.

McLeod, Eileen. (1982). *Women Working: Prostitution Now.* London: Croom Helm.

McLintock, Anne. (1992). Gonad the Barbarian and the Venus Flytrap. In Segal and McIntosh (1992).

McNeil, Sandra, and Dusty Rhodes. (Eds.). (1985). *Women Against Violence Against Women.* London: Onlywomen Press.

Mahoney, Kathleen. (1993). Destruction of Women's Rights through Mass Media Proliferation of Pornography. In Mahoney and Mahoney (1993).

Mahoney, Kathleen. (1994). Canadian Approaches to Equality Rights and Gender Equity in the Courts. In Cook (1994a).

Mahoney, Kathleen and Paul Mahoney. (1993). *Human Rights in the Twenty-First Century: A Global Challenge.* Dordrecht, Boston, London: Martinus Nijhoff.

Mansson, Sven-Axel. (1995). International Prostitution and Traffic in Persons from a Swedish Perspective. In Klap *et al.* (1995).

Marcus, Steven. (1970 / 1964). *The Other Victorians: A Study of Sexuality and Pornography in Mid-Nineteenth Century England.* London: Book Club Associates with Weidenfeld and Nicolson.

Masters, William H., and Virginia E. Johnson. (1970). *Human Sexual Inadequacy.* Boston: Bantam Books.

Maynall, Alice, and Diana E. H. Russell. (1993). Racism in Pornography. In Russell (1993).

Mies, Maria, Veronica Bennholdt-Thomsen, and Claudia von Werlhof. (1988). *Women: The Last Colony.* London: Zed Books.

Mikhailovitch, Katja. (1996). Post-modernism and its "Contribution" to Ending Violence Against Women. In Bell and Klein (1996).

Miller, Carol. (1994). "Geneva the Key to Equality": Interwar Feminists and the League of Nations, *Women's History Review*, 3 (2).

Miller, Elaine, and Lynn Harne. (Eds.). (1996). *All the Rage*. London: Women's Press.

Miller, JoAnn. (1991). Prostitution in Contemporary American Society. In Elizabeth Grauerholz and Mary A. Koraliwski (Eds.). (1991).

Millett, Kate. (1972). *Sexual Politics*. London: Abacus, Sphere Books.

Millett, Kate. (1975 / 1971). *The Prostitution Papers*. St Albans, Herts: Paladin Books.

Miner, Maude E. (1916). *The Slavery of Prostitution: A Plea for Emancipation*. New York: Macmillan Co.

Morgan, Peggy. (1988). Living on the Edge. In Delacoste and Alexander (1988).

Nenadic, Natalie. (1996). Femicide: A Framework for Understanding Genocide. In Bell and Klein (1996).

Nestle, Joan. (1988). *A Restricted Country*. London: Sheba.

Nicholson, Linda J. (Ed.). (1990a). *Feminism/Postmodernism*. New York: Routledge.

Nicholson, Linda J. (1990b). Introduction. In Nicholson (1990a).

Nozick, Robert. (1974). *Anarchy, State and Utopia*. Oxford: Blackwell.

O'Neill, Maggie. (1996). Researching Prostitution and Violence: Towards a Feminist Praxis. In Hester *et al.* (1996).

Outshoorn, Joyce. (1996, March 29–April 3). Dealing in Sex: The Trafficking of Women in the Netherlands. Paper presented to the European Centre for Political Research Joint Sessions of Workshops, Oslo.

Overall, Christine. (1992, Summer). What's Wrong with Prostitution? Evaluating Sex Work, *Signs*, 705–24.

Parker, Tony. (1970 / 1969). *The Twisting Lane: Some Sex Offenders*. London: Panther.

Pateman, Carole. (1988). *The Sexual Contract*. Cambridge: Polity Press.

Patterson, Orlando. (1982). *Slavery and Social Death*. Cambridge, Massachusetts: Harvard University Press.

Pearl, Cyril. (1980 / 1955). *The Girl with the Swansdown Seat: An Informal Report on Some Aspects of Mid-Victorian Morality.* London: Robin Clark.

Pearsall, Ronald. (1971 / 1969). *The Worm in the Bud: The World of Victorian Sexuality.* London: Penguin.

Penelope, Julia, and Susan Wolfe. (Eds.). (1993). *Lesbian Culture: An Anthology.* Freedom, California: Crossing Press.

Perkins, Roberta. (1994). Female Prostitution. In Perkins *et al.* (1994).

Perkins, Roberta, and Gary Bennett. (1985). *Being a Prostitute.* St Leonards, New South Wales: Allen and Unwin.

Perkins, Roberta Sharp Prestage, Rachel Garrett, and Francis Lovejoy. (Eds.). 1994. *Sex Work and Sex Workers in Australia.* Sydney: University of New South Wales Press.

Person, Ethel Spector. (1980). Sexuality as the Mainstay of Identity: Psychoanalytic Perspectives. In Catharine R. Stimpson and Ethel Spector Person (1980).

Peters, Julie, and Andrea Wolper. (Eds.). (1995). *Women's Rights, Human Rights: International Feminist Perspectives.* New York: Routledge.

Pheterson, Gail. (Ed.). (1989a). *A Vindication of the Rights of Whores.* Seattle: Seal Press.

Pheterson, Gail. (1989b). Not Repeating History. In Pheterson (1989a).

Pheterson, Gail. (1996). *The Prostitution Prism.* Amsterdam: Amsterdam University Press:

Plummer, Ken. (1975). *Sexual Stigma: An Interactionist Account.* London: Routledge and Kegan Paul.

Plummer, Ken. (1996). Intimate Citizenship and the Culture of Sexual Storytelling. In Weeks and Holland (1996).

Plummer, Ken and Roberta Perkins. (1994). Introduction. In Perkins *et al.* (1994).

Prestage, Garrett. (1994). Male and Transsexual Prostitution. In Perkins *et al.* (1994).

Radford, Jill, and Diana E. H. Russell. (Eds.). (1992). *Femicide: The Politics of Woman Killing.* Buckingham: Open University Press.

Radicalesbians. (1988). The Woman Identified Woman. In Sarah Lucia Hoagland and Julia Penelope.

Rao, Arati. (1993). Right in the Home: Feminist Theoretical Perspective on International Human Rights, *National Law School Journal, 1,* Special Issue: Feminism and the Law, 62-81. National Law School of India University, Nagarbhavi, Bangalore (1982).

Raymond, Janice G. (1990). Sexual and Reproductive Liberalism. In Leidholdt and Raymond (1990).

Raymond, Janice G. (1994a). *Women as Wombs*. Melbourne: Spinifex Press.

Raymond, Janice G. (1994b / 1982). *The Transsexual Empire*. London: Women's Press; (1994) New York: Teachers' College Press.

Raymond, Janice G. (1995). *Report to the Special Rapporteur on Violence Against Women. The United Nations, Geneva, Switzerland*. North Amherst, Massachusetts: Coalition Against Trafficking in Women.

Rawls, John. (1973 / 1972). *A Theory of Justice*. Oxford: Oxford University Press.

Rich, Adrienne. (1984). Compulsory Heterosexuality and Lesbian Existence. In Ann Snitow (1984).

Richardson, Diane (Ed.). (1996). *Theorizing Heterosexuality*. Buckingham: Open University Press.

Roberts, Nickie. (1992). *Whores in History*. London: HarperCollins.

Rodmell, Sue. (1981). Men, Women and Sexuality: A Feminist Critique of the Sociology of Deviance, *Women's Studies International Quarterly*, 4 (2), 143–55.

Roiphe, Katie. (1993). *The Morning After: Sex, Fear and Feminism on Campus*. Boston, New York, Toronto, London: Little, Brown and Co.

Romany, Celina. (1994). State Responsibility Goes Private: A Feminist Critique of the Public/Private Distinction in International Human Rights Law. In Cook (1994a).

Roth, Kenneth. (1994). Domestic Violence as an International Human Rights Issue. In Cook (1994a).

Rubin, Gayle. (1982). A Personal History of the Lesbian S/M Community and Movement in San Francisco. In Samois (1982).

Rubin, Gayle. (1984). Thinking Sex. In Carole Vance (1984).

Rubin, Gayle. (1993). Thinking Sex. In H. Abelove *et al.* (1993).

Rush, Florence. (1980). *The Best Kept Secret: Sexual Abuse of Children*. New York: McGraw-Hill.

Russell, Bertrand. (1972 / 1929). *Marriage and Morals*. London: Allen and Unwin.

Russell, Diana. (1975). *The Politics of Rape*. New York: Stein and Day.

Russell, Diana. (1990). *Rape in Marriage*. Bloomington: Indiana University Press.

Russell, Diana. (1993a). *Against Pornography: The Evidence of Harm*. Berkeley, California: Russell Publications.

Russell, Diana. (Ed.). (1993b). *Making Violence Sexy: Feminist Views on Pornography*. Buckingham: Open University Press.

Russell, Diana. (1995, March). The Making of a Whore, *Violence Against Women, 1*, 77–98.

Ryan, William. (1971). *Blaming the Victim*. New York: Pantheon Books.

St James, Margo. (1989). Preface. In Pheterson (1989a).

Samois. (Eds.). (1982). *Coming to Power: Writings and Graphics on Lesbian S/M*. Boston: Alyson Publications.

Santos, Aida F. (1992). Gathering the Dust: The Bases Issue in the Philippines. In Sturdevant and Stoltzfus (1992).

Santos, Aida F. (1995, May). Picking Up the Pieces of Women's Lives: Prostitution and Sexual Exploitation in Asia-Pacific. Paper submitted to WHO, May.

Sappington, Rodney, and Tyler Stallings. (Eds.). (1994). *Uncontrollable Bodies: Testimonies of Identity and Culture*. Seattle: Bay Press.

Scambler, Graham, and Annette Scambler. (Eds.). (1997). *Rethinking Prostitution: Purchasing Sex in the 1990s*. London: Routledge.

Schneider, Elizabeth M. (1996). What Happened to Public Education about Domestic Violence? In Jeffrey Abramson (1996).

Segal, Lynne, and Mary McIntosh. (Eds.). (1992). *Sex Exposed: Sexuality and the Pornography Debate*. London: Virago.

Sheffield, Carole J. (1993). The Invisible Intruder: Women's Experiences of Obscene Phone Calls. In Bart and Moran (1993).

The Shield: Journal of the Association for Moral and Social Hygiene. 1918–68. London: AMSH.

Shrage, Laurie. (1994). *Moral Dilemmas of Feminism: Prostitution, Adultery and Abortion*. London: Routledge.

Silbert, Mimi, and Ayala Pines. (1984). Pornography and Sexual Abuse of Children. In Russell (1993).

Sinclair, Amanda. (1994). *Trials at the Top: Chief Executives Talk about Men, Women and the Australian Executive Culture*. Melbourne: Australian Centre, University of Melbourne.

Smart, Carol. (1989). *Feminism and the Power of Law*. London and New York: Routledge.

Snell, Cudore L. (1995). *Young Men in the Street: Help-Seeking Behaviour of Young Male Prostitutes*. Westport, Connecticut: Praeger.

Snitow, Ann. (Ed.). (1984). *Desire: The Politics of Female Sexuality*. London: Virago.

Stanko, Betsy. (1993). Ordinary Fear: Women, Violence, and Personal Safety. In Bart and Moran (1993).

Sternberg, David. (1983). Prostitutes as Victimizers. In Donal E. J. Macnamara and Andrew Karmen (1983).

Stiglmayer, Alexandra. (Ed.). (1994). *Mass Rape: The War Against Women in Bosnia-Herzegovina.* Lincoln: University of Nebraska Press.

Stimpson, Catharine R., and Ethel Spencer Parsons. (Eds.). (1980). *Women, Sex and Sexuality.* Chicago: University of Chicago Press.

Stoltenberg, John. (1990). *Refusing to be a Man.* London: Fontana.

Stretton, Hugh, and Lionel Orchard. (1994). *Public Goods, Public Enterprise, Public Choice: Theoretical Foundations of the Contemporary Attack on Government.* Basingstoke: Macmillan.

Sturdevant, Saundra Pollock, and Brenda Stoltzfus. (1992). *Let the Good Times Roll: Prostitution and the U.S. Military in Asia.* New York: New Press.

Stychin, Carl F. (1995). *Law's Desire: Sexuality and the Limits of Justice.* London and New York: Routledge.

Sullivan, Barbara. (1992). Feminist Approaches to the Sex Industry. In Gerrull and Halstead (1992).

Sullivan, Barbara. (1994). Feminism and Female Prostitution. In Perkins *et al.* (1994).

Sullivan, Barbara. (1995). Rethinking Prostitution. In Caine and Pringle (1995).

Sullivan, Donna. (1995). The Public/Private Distinction in International Human Rights Law. In Peters and Wolper (1995).

Summer, Toby. (1993). A Working-class Dyke Speaks Out Against Buying Women for Sex. In Penelope and Wolfe (1993).

Summers, Rosie. (1988). Prostitution. In Delacoste and Alexander (1988).

Sumner, Colin. (1994). *The Sociology of Deviance: An Obituary.* Buckingham: Open University Press.

Sundahl, Debbie. (1988). Stripper. In Delacoste and Alexander (1988).

Sykes, Gresham M., and David Matza. (1957, December). Techniques of Neutralization: A Theory of Delinquency, *American Sociological Review*, 22, 664–70.

Szasz, Thomas. (1980). *Sex: Facts, Frauds and Follies.* Oxford: Basil Blackwell.

Truong, Thanh-Dan. (1990). *Sex, Money and Morality: Prostitution and Tourism in Southeast Asia.* London: Zed Books.

Truong, Thanh-Dan. (1996). Serving the Tourist Market: Female Labour in International Tourism. In Jackson and Scott (1996).

UBINIG. (1995). *Trafficking in Women and Children: The Case of*

Bangladesh. Pamphlet produced for Fourth World Conference on Women. Dhaka, Bangladesh: Narigrantha Prabartana (The Feminist Bookstore).

Ullerstam, Lars. (1964). *The Erotic Minorities*. New York: Grove Press.

UNESCO and Coalition Against Trafficking in Women. (1992). *The Penn State Report: International Meeting of Experts on Sexual Exploitation, Violence and Prostitution*. State College, Pennsylvannia.

United Nations. (1996). *The United Nations and the Advancement of Women 1945–46*. New York: United Nations Department of Public Information.

Valentino, Margaret, and Mavis Johnson. (1980). On the Game and On the Move. In Jaget (1980).

Vance, Carole (Ed.). (1984). *Pleasure and Danger: Exploring Female Sexuality*. London: Routledge Kegan Paul.

van der Vleuten, Nelleke. (1991). *Survey on "Traffic in Women": Policies and Policy—Research in an International Context*. Vena Working Paper No 91/1, Research and Documentation Centre. Leiden: Women and Autonomy Centre, Leiden University.

Vatikiotis, Michael, Sachiko Sakamadi, and Gary Silverman. (1995, December 14). On the Margin: Organized Crime Profits from the Flesh Trade, *Far Eastern Economic Review*.

Vigilance Record: Journal of the National Vigilance Association. 1910–12. London.

Waldron, Jeremy. (Ed.). (1984). *Theories of Rights*. Oxford: Oxford University Press.

Waldron, Jeremy. (Ed.). (1987). *Nonsense upon Stilts: Bentham, Burke and Marx on the Rights of Man*. London and New York: Methuen.

Waring, Marilyn. (1988). *Counting for Nothing: What Men Value and What Women are Worth*. Wellington: Allen and Unwin.

Waring, Marilyn. (1997). *Three Masquerades*. Auckland: Auckland University Press.

Weeks, Jeffrey. (1981). *Sex, Politics and Society*. London: Longman.

Weeks, Jeffrey. (1985). *Sexuality and its Discontents*. London: Routledge Kegan Paul.

Weeks, Jeffrey. (1991). Inverts, Perverts and Mary-Annes: Male Prostitution and the Regulation of Homosexuality in England in the Nineteenth and early Twentieth Century. In Martin Duberman *et al.* (1991).

Weeks, Jeffrey and Janet Holland. (Eds.). (1996). *Sexual Cultures: Communities, Values and Intimacy*. Basingstoke: MacMillan Press.

West, D. J. (in association with Buz de Villiers). (1992). *Male Prostitution: Gay Sex Services in London*. London: Duckworth.

Wijers, Marjan. (1995). Supporting Victims of Trafficking. In Klap et al. (1995).

Wilkinson, Sue, and Celia Kitzinger. (Eds.). (1993). *Heterosexuality: A Feminist and Psychology Reader*. London: Sage.

Williams, Linda. (1989). *Hard Core: Power, Pleasure, and the "Frenzy of the Visible"*. Berkeley: University of California Press.

Williams, Linda. (1992). Pornographies On/scene. Or Diff'rent Strokes for Diff'rent Folks. In Segal and McIntosh. (1992).

Wilson, Elizabeth. (1983). *What Is to be Done about Violence against Women?* Harmondsworth: Penguin.

Wittig, Monique. (1992). *The Straight Mind and Other Essays*. Boston: Beacon Press.

Wolf, Naomi. (1993). *Fire with Fire: The New Female Power and How It Will Change the 21st Century*. New York: Random House.

Wood, Marianne. (1995). *Just a Prostitute*. St Lucia: University of Queensland Press.

Working Girl. (1995, Spring). Melbourne: Prostitutes Collective of Victoria.

Wright, Shelley. (1993). Human Rights and Women's Rights: An Analysis of the United Nations CEDAW. In Mahoney and Mahoney (1993).

Yeatman, Anna. (1990). A Feminist Theory of Social Differentiation. In Nicholson (1990a).

Young, Wayland. (1968 / 1965). *Eros Denied*. London: Corgi Books.

INDEX

abolitionists, 13–17, 19, 31, 32, 68, 316, 324, 335–6
abortion, 287
abuse, 3, 6, 37, 51, 69, 71, 78–9, 81, 84, 87–8, 90, 105, 108–16, 120–1, 126, 140–1, 153, 157, 164, 195, 212, 222–3, 225–7, 249, 253, 263, 265, 339, 348
    children, 18, 94
    consent, 135–7
    effects, 268–71
    racism, 113
    sex industry, 265
    see also child sexual abuse; children, abuse; choice; sexual harassment; violence; woman-hating
abuse identification
    see naming
adoption, 18–19, 20
advertising, 125
affection, 108, 109
Africa, 177
age of protection, 13
agency, 128–9, 145–8
aggression, 36, 40, 59
    see also domination; violence

Alexander, Priscilla, 73, 78, 163, 174, 220, 224, 346
Allen, Sheila, 202–4
American Civil Liberties Union, 71
Americans
    see United States
Amsterdam
    see Netherlands
anal sex, 44, 51, 109, 234–5, 261
Anthony, Jane, 152–3
anti-civil libertarian
    see civil libertarianism
anti-pornography feminists, 74, 94, 235–6
    see also pornography
anti-prostitution, 112–13, 317
    activists, 322, 342
    campaigns, 1–2, 7–9, 25, 31–4, 38, 80
    feminists, 7–10, 31–4, 37–8, 58, 65–6, 74, 79–84, 235–6
    movement, 306–7, 317, 322, 336
    trafficking, 330–3
anti-slavery movement, 20, 326–8
    see also League of Nations; trafficking
apologists, 75

Armstrong, Eliza, 10
Armstrong, Louise, 151
art
  see performance art
Artlink (journal), 89
Ashby, Mrs Marjorie Corbett, 20, 330–4
Asia region, 17–19, 341
  child prostitution, 327
  international human rights, 281–2
  prostitution comparison with West, 341–3, 348
  sex industry, 327–33
  trafficking, 308–16, 327–33, 336
assault
  see abuse; battery; rape; sexual harassment; violence
Association of Hindu Women, 22
Association for Moral and Social Hygiene, 19–20, 23, 31–3
auletrides, 50, 123
Australia, brothels, 347
Australian Liquor, Hospitality and Miscellaneous Workers' Union, 191–2
Australian men, 314
Australian prostitutes' collectives, 74–5, 164

Bangladesh, 308–9, 321–2
barmaids, 265–6
Barnard, Marina, 346
Barry, Kathleen, 6, 9–10, 74, 135–7, 151, 177, 213–14, 261, 275–6, 307, 319, 342
bars, 314
Basserman, Lujo, 36, 42–3, 48–9
battery, 245, 247, 255, 256, 260, 270, 286, 291–3, 334
  see also abuse; violence
Bell, Shannon, 52, 90, 191

Benjamin, Harry, 37–9, 40, 162–3, 215–16
Bennett, Gary
  see Prestage, Garrett
Billington-Greig, Teresa, 10
bills of rights, 278–81
biological determinism, 28–9
bisexuals, 95
black males, 109, 113
blame (for prostitution), 25–32
  medical model, 27–32
  woman-blaming, 27–32
blow jobs, 88, 343–4, 347
body and self, 186–91, 220, 221, 223, 254, 263, 267, 270–1, 301–2
  dissociation, 271–4
  identity, 256–9
  oppression, 189–91
  self-esteem, 259, 262, 295
  self-mutilation, 89–90
  see also effects; identity; self and self-esteem
bondage (for debts), 312–14
bottoms, 118, 120–1
Boyle, Nina, 20–1
boys
  prostitution, 92–3, 108–13
  see also paedophilia
Brazil, 115
"breaking-in" system, 26
breast implants 146–7
Brecher, Bob, 180, 186–7
Brecher, Edward, 42
brides, mail-order, 309
Bright, Susie, 80, 125
Britain, prostitution 345, 346
  White Slave Traffic, 8–11
British Commonwealth League, 19–21
British Dominions Women Citizens' Union, 20
British India, 18
British Malaya, 18

British Overseas Committee
International Woman Suffrage
Alliance, 20
brothels, 50, 112, 266–7, 300
Asia region, 321
Australia, 347
Bangladesh, 321–2
Germany, 112
India, 321, 328
Japan, 300–1
licensed, 9, 14, 16, 22, 35, 39
military, 275, 298–301
mobile, 63
Morocco, 296–7
Netherlands, 112, 310
Philippines, 314
punishment, 317
rape camps, 298–300
sexologists, 36, 39
Thailand, 311-13, 296
violence, 256
watching, 44–5
see also state regulation
Brownmiller, Susan, 140–1
Buenos Aires, 15
Bulgaria, 308
Burger, John, 117
Bunch, Charlotte, 290
Burma and Burmese women, 177,
308, 311, 312, 332
Thai brothels, 296
Burt, Cyril, 29, 31
businessmen, 44, 193–4, 296–7
Butler, Josephine, 8–10, 19, 33
see also Josephine Butler Society
Byrnes, Andrew, 304–5

Califia, Pat, 95–6, 99, 102, 122, 126
call girls, 269, 311
Canada, 78–9, 289–90
Canadian Organisation for the Rights
of Prostitutes, 78

capitalism, 185, 276–8, 333
sexual liberation, 119
see also patriarchy; sex industry
CATW Asia/Pacific, 324, 331–2, 335
causes (of prostitution), 26–32
woman-blaming, 27–32
celebration (of prostitution), 35–6, 70,
71, 79
see also sexology; sexual revolution
celibacy, 228
censorship, 54, 76, 209
gay pornography, 117
cervixes, 85
"charities", 107
Charlesworth, Hilary, 283, 286–8, 291
Chesser, Eustace, 229
child abuse, 94, 255, 256
child marriage, 17, 20
child prostitution, 108–9, 256–9, 327,
344
see also trafficking
child protection, 278–9
child sexual abuse, 242, 243, 247,
260, 262, 270, 278–9
childcare, 288
children
girls, Afghanistan, 288
identity, 256–9
rights, 284
trafficking, 12, 13, 15, 20–1, 323
China, 18–19, 177
Chinkin, Christine, 283
choice (in prostitution), 7, 8, 70, 73,
78, 91, 100, 128–60, 242, 247,
253, 258, 263, 305, 322, 332
abuse, 153
consent, 135–9
liberal theory, 130–5
prostitution, 128–60
sexual liberalism, 129, 142–6
victim blaming, 139–42
women's agency, 145–8

choice (in prostitution) *contd*
  see also "forced prostitution"; "free
    prostitution"
circumcision, female, 20, 288, 295
citizenship rights, 134–5, 291
  see also choice; rights and liberties
civil libertarianism, 285
  choice, 129
  discrimination, 24
  equality, 22, 24, 25
  see also libertarianism; rights and
    liberties
class, 104, 106, 108, 120, 126, 153,
    154, 157, 158, 181, 185–6, 189,
    194–5, 202–4, 206, 209, 211,
    240, 250, 262, 292
classical liberalism, 132
clients, 3, 4–5, 37, 39, 59, 99, 103,
    109–11, 187–8, 231, 256, 274
  control, 123–4
  male and female prostitution, 103–6
  punishment, 40, 336–8
  transsexuals, 113–15
  see also brothels; johns
Coalition Against Trafficking in
  Women, 7, 306–7
coercion, 152, 260–1, 262, 318, 323
  see also choice; consent; "forced"
    prostitution; "free" prostitution
Collison, Miss M. Chave, 19
Comfort, Alex, 36, 37–9, 41–8, 63,
    228–9
comfort women, 275, 300–1, 303
  Japan, 275, 298, 300–1
  Korea, South, 300–1
  Philippines, 300
commercial sex industry
commercial sexual violence, 259–61
  see also pornography;
    violence
communism, 39
compulsory repatriation, 23–4

condoms, 310, 311–12
congresses, 1930s, 23–4
  see also League of Nations; United
    Nations
Connell, R. W. (Bob), 206
consent, 211, 247, 252, 261, 263,
    269, 276, 317–18, 338
  abuse, 135–87
  choice, 135–9
Contagious Diseases Acts, 8, 83, 84
contraception, 313
  see also condoms
contracts
  equality, 173–6
  ethics, 144
  theory, 130
control, 123–4, 273
conventions
  see international conventions;
    League of Nations
Coomaraswamy, Radhika, 281–2
Copelon, Rhonda, 292–3,
    295–6, 298
CORP, 79, 82, 65, 165–6
cosmetic surgery, 146–8
Cotler, Irwin, 271–2, 277
Council for Prostitution Alternatives,
    256
COYOTE, 66, 69–74, 77, 78, 135,
    163–4, 174, 342
crime and criminalisation, 166, 269
  prostitution, 260–1
  rape, 243–5
  see also violence
criminal violence, 243–4
  see also violence
Crowdy, Rachel, 12–14
cruelty, 94
  see also abuse; sadomasochism;
    violence
cruising, 106, 107
Cullen, Bernard, 168–9

cultural rights
  see traditions and customs
customers
  see clients; johns
customs
  see traditions and customs

Daly, Mary, 149
dancers, 50, 252, 266–7, 320
Davis, Kathy, 146–8
Davidson, Julia O'Connell, 181–3, 309
De Graaf, A., 17
de Sainte-Croix, Madame Avril, 7, 21
debt bondage, 312–14
Declaration on the Elimination of Violence Against Women, 275
decriminalisation, 335
defence mechanisms
  see dissociation
degradation, 89
  see also abuse; body and self
Delphy, Christine, 189
demand
  see men's demand
democracy, 134
  morality, 97
  private sphere, 290
  see also choice
Denfeld, Rene, 149, 150
Denmark, sterilisation, 30
desexualisation, 266
devadasi, 17, 20
deviancy, 76, 93, 103, 106, 242
  sociologists and sociology, 36–7, 40, 59–62
dicks, "chick with a dick", 10–11
"difference approach", 289
dignity, 22, 306, 317, 319
  work, 168–73
  see also body and self

dikteriades, 50
discrimination, 23–4, 67, 71, 76, 304
  civil libertarian notions, 24
  sex industry, 99
dissociation, 271–4, 298
Dolgopol, Ustinia, 300–3
domestic slavery, 20–1
  see also child marriage; marriage
domestic violence, 243, 268, 275, 291, 295, 303–4
  gender-neutral term, 141
  see also abuse; child sexual abuse; marital rape; rape; violence
domestic work, 288
dominance and domination, 3, 48, 100, 115, 127, 141, 185, 193–4, 206–7, 213–14, 218, 228–30, 235, 270, 289, 295, 325
  pornography, 117–18
  see also male sexuality; men's demand; slavery
dominatrixes, 96
drugs, 110, 112, 154, 272, 273
Dutch brothels
  see Netherlands
Dutch East Indies, 18
Dworkin, Andrea, 80, 81, 194, 209, 227–9, 234–6, 347–8
Dyer, Richard, 117

East, the
  see Asia region
economic analyses (of prostitution), 65, 67–8, 74–5, 82, 108, 111, 113, 120, 262, 288, 300–1, 315–16
economic status, 104, 330
  see also choice; class
economy, world
  trafficking, 307–16
Edelstein, Judy, 221–2
education, 337–8

education *contd*
 see also sex education
effects
 prostitution and violence, 268–71
Ellis, Havelock, 48, 215, 223, 228
Elmy, Elizabeth Wolstenholme, 1
emotional life, 268, 2509
 see also identity; self and self-esteem
employment
 see work
employment agencies, 12, 13, 26
empowerment, 345
End Child Prostitution in Asian
 Tourism, 327
English Collective of Prostitutes, 67–8,
 74, 82
equal pay, 288
equal rights
 see equality and inequality; rights
 and liberties
equality and inequality, 20–1, 102,
 126, 159, 175, 184, 185, 189,
 193, 208–9, 212, 238, 240, 257,
 260–2, 277–80, 288–90, 293–4,
 306
 civil libertarian notions, 22
 contracts, 173–6
 feminism, 208–12
 moral standards, 32–4
 see also rights and liberties
erotic groupings
 see sexual minorities
erotica and eroticism, 244, 265
 hierarchy, 207–8, 217
 see also sexuality
escort services, 83
essentialism, 198–9, 279–80
ethics
 contracts, 144
eugenics, 30
Evans, David, 134
Evatt, Elizabeth, 326

executive culture, 193–4
exploitation
 see sexual exploitation

false consciousness, 128–9
family and home, 256–9, 262, 282,
 285–6, 292–3, 335
 see also child sexual abuse; incest;
 marital rape;
 marriage; private sphere; traditions and customs
Farley, Melissa, 255–6, 269–70
father rape, 151
 see also child sexual abuse; incest
Faust, Beatrice, 149
Federation of National Unions for the
 Protection of Girls, 9
fellatio, 52
 see also oral sex
female genital mutilation, 20, 288,
 295
female genitals, 227, 229
female seclusion, 334
femicide, 246–7, 251–2
 see also murder
feminism, 37–8, 197–8, 264, 324
 1920s and 1930s, 7–10
 anti-pornography, 74, 94, 235–6
 anti-prostitution, 7–9,
 19–27, 31–4, 38, 58, 65–6, 74,
 79–84
 anti-violence, 151–2
 choice and oppression, 128–9, 143,
 159–60
 economic arguments
 (for prostitution), 65
 equality, 208–12
 gender, 98–9
 human rights theory, 274, 275–305
 international human rights, 281–2,
 284–90
 League of Nations, 12–13, 38

liberal, 143, 149–50, 160, 189, 210, 250, 254, 288
libertarian, 208–10, 241
male supremacy, 126
naming abuse, 251
oppression, 249
pornography, 74, 119–20, 122, 235–6
post-modernism, 128–9, 190–1, 340, 341
prevention (of prostitution), 19–27
prostitutes' rights movement, 65–6, 77–84
prostitution, 35, 37–8, 79–84, 90–1, 98–9, 101–13, 121–2, 128, 224–5
radical, 2, 4, 66, 68, 80, 143, 156–7, 189–91, 196–7, 205–12, 226, 341
rights and liberties 276–93
sex reform, 236–7
sexual violence, 248
sexuality theories, 96–9, 196–212
social purity, 25
socialist, 68–9, 156–7, 186, 189, 207, 277–8
trafficking, 19–24
United Nations, 38
victimism, 148–52
violence analyses, 242–3
White Slave Traffic, 10, 12
woman-blaming, 30
work, 169–70
see also women's organisations
feminism and law
see human rights theory
Feminist Anti-Censorship Task Force, 209
feminist historians, 53–4
sexology, 37
feminist sociologists, 62

fetishists, 95
Filipino women, 18
Japan, 314
see also Philippines
financial need, 344–5
Finley, Karen, 89
Finstad, Liv, 153–5, 179, 252–3, 255, 259, 270–4
Fitzpatrick, Joan, 295
Flexner, Abraham, 4, 41
flight attendants, 171–3
folklore (of prostitution), 49
see also history; myths
"forced" prostitution, 7–11, 15, 23, 26, 276, 294–6, 299, 305, 307, 317, 322, 324, 332, 338, 348
foreign women, 18, 310–11, 323
licensed brothels, 23–4
trafficking, 15–16
see also international trafficking; refugees
Forel, August, 198–9
Forum magazine, 125
Foucault, Michel, 93, 196, 197, 201, 202, 203, 205
Foundation Against Trafficking in Women, 320, 322
Franks, Marlene Strong, 131
free choice
see choice
"free" prostitution, 7, 10, 11, 23, 276, 294–5, 299, 305, 307, 317, 322, 332, 338, 344, 348
free speech
pornography, 232–3
free market and free-market liberalism, 2, 119–21, 187–8
see also capitalism; sex
freedom, 95, 126, 127, 210–11, 221, 254, 262
sexual, 208–9
see also choice; personal;

freedom *contd*
    rights and liberties; sexual freedom
freedom of expression, 287
    liberalism, 294
French, Dolores, 163–4
French prostitutes, Lyons, 67
Frenzell, Ruth, 191–2
Freud, 199, 200–1, 229
Friedman, Elizabeth, 284
Friedman, Milton and Rose, 134
frigidity, 110, 237
Fudge, Judy, 279, 282
Furse, Katharine, 12

Gagnon, John, 60, 199–201, 214–15
gang rape, 47, 51, 296–7
gangsta rap, 230–1
Garcia, Chat, 331–2
Gauntlet (journal), 129
Gavey, Nicola, 262–3
gay and lesbian movement, 69
    sexual libertarianism and prostitu-
        tion, 102–13
    see also lesbians
gay culture
    sex industry, 106
gay liberation movement, 120, 202
gay males
    pornography, 116–21
    sex work, 107
    see homosexuality
gay male prostitution, 76, 92–3, 95
    see also queer politics
gay sociologists, 200–1
gays
    persecution, 297
gender, 102, 206–7, 211, 217, 218,
        264, 297
    choice, 131
    feminism, 98–9
    justice, 131–2
    policy, 132–3

    sexuality, 98–9
gender hierarchy, 228
gender persecution, 297
gender violence, 296–7
    see also violence
genital mutilation
    see female genital mutilation
genitalia, 227, 229, 271, 272
Germany, 177, 337
    brothels, 112
    sterilisation, 30
Ghandi, 39
Gibson, Barbara, 109
Giddens, Anthony, 202
Giobbe, Evelina, 72, 257,
        259–61, 268–9
girls, 321–2
    adoption, 20
    Afghanistan, 288
    marriage, 17, 20–1
    temple prostitution, 17
    Thailand, 323
    trafficking, 20–1, 311–14
    see also child marriage; child sexual
        abuse; incest
glamour, 107
Global Alliance Against Trafficking in
        Women, 307, 329–31
Glover, William, 29
"good" prostitution, 345
Grabinska, Madame Wanda, 31
Graham, Dee, 268
Greece, classical, 36, 49–52, 123
Greenwald, Harold, 142

Hall, Gladys Mary, 33
harassment
    see abuse; sexual
        harassment
Harding, Sandra, 156–7, 158
Hardwick, Miss K. B., 31
Hartsock, Nancy, 156–7

hatred, 246
  see also racism; woman-hating
Hatty, Susanne, 225
head shaving, 177–8
health, 28, 83, 112–13, 120–1, 287,
  310–12, 313, 322
  cosmetic surgery, 146–8
  see also body and self;
    HIV-AIDS; identity;
    medical; risk
Hefner, Hugh, 234–5
Heidenry, John, 88
Hellfire club, 88–9, 96
Henriques, Fernando, 36, 49
Henslin, James, 59–60
Herman, Judith, 252, 268
hetaerae, 49–51
heterosexuality, 206
  patriarchy, 184
  see also men's demand
hierarchy, 207–8, 217, 228
  see also dominance and domination;
    subordination; supremacy
HIRE, 164
historians and histories, 36, 48–54
  1960s, 42–3
  feminist, 53–4
Hite, Shere, 237–8, 262
HIV-AIDS, 76, 109, 113, 120, 311–12,
  326
Hochschild, Arlie, 170–2
Hoffman, Barry, 129
Hogan, Christopher, 116
Hoigard, Cecilie, 153–5, 179, 252–3,
  255, 259, 270–4
homelessness, 108, 109
  male prostitutes, 93
  see also economic status
homosexuality, 39, 40
  identity, 116–17
  prostitution, 92–127
  see also gay males; lesbians; "queer"

perspective and politics
Hong Kong, 20
Hotaling, Norma, 255–6,
  269–70
Hotchkiss, Ryan, 82
human rights, 347, 348
  activists, 7
  language, 305
  liberalism, 284
  omission of prostitution, 293–8
  prostitution, 325–30
  trafficking, 306–38
  violence, 290–3
  see also body and self;
    dignity; rights and liberties
Human Rights Commission, 304–5
human rights theory
  feminism, 274, 275–305
Human Rights Watch/Asia, 311–12,
  328–9
Hunter, Andrew, 74–7
Hunter, Susan Kay, 256
husband violence, 291–3
  see also marital rape;
    marriage; violence
Hustler, magazine, 125
hydraulic model, 199

identity, 190, 194, 209, 221, 256–9,
  270–1, 301–2, 319
  children, 256–9
  dissociation, 271–4
  homosexuals, 116–17
  see also body and self; effects
ideology
  legitimising of homosexual prostitu-
    tion, 105
  pro-prostitution, 8
  ruling class, 157
  see also capitalism;
    patriarchy; traditions
    and customs

imperialism, 316
imprisonment
  see criminalisation; institutionalisa-
    tion; punishment; reformatories
incest, 151, 258–9, 268, 278–9, 293,
  334
  see also child sexual abuse
India, 17–19, 22, 39, 115, 311, 321
  brothels, 311, 312–13,
    321–2, 328
  child marriage, 20
  girls, 321
  trafficking, 312–13, 328
individualism, 156, 288, 333
Indo-China, 18
industrialisation of prostitution
  see sex industry
inequality
  see discrimination; equality and
    inequality
infanticide, 247, 287, 334
Ingram, Attracta, 280
Institute of Public and Urban Affairs
  (US), 71
institutionalisation, 153, 155
  see also family and home
intercourse, sexual, 226–31
International Abolitionist Federation,
  19, 31, 32
International Bureau for the
  Suppression of the Traffic in
  Women and Children, 14, 19,
  23–4, 30
international campaigns
  see League of Nations
International Committee for
  Prostitutes' Rights, 73–8
international conventions, 2, 242,
  284–7, 303–4, 306, 307, 316,
  333–6
  trafficking, 316–18
  see also League of Nations

International Council of Women, 22
international human rights, 275, 277,
  325–30
  Asia region, 281–2
  feminism, 281–90
  see also human rights theory; rights
    and liberties
International Labour Organisation,
  302–3
international law, 274, 283–4, 306–87
  public/private distinction, 285–8
  trafficking, 11–12
  violence, 283–4
International Suffrage Alliance, 22
international trafficking
  see trafficking
International Woman Suffrage
  Alliance, 20
international women's associations,
  1920s and 1930s, 21–2
Internet
  World Sex Guide, 309–10
Iraqi women, 18
Italian Committee against Trafficking
  in Women, 30
Isherwood, Charles, 116

Jackson, Stevi, 205–6
Jaggar, Alison, 156, 157
James, Jackie, 125–6
Japan
  brothels, 300–1
  comfort women, 275, 298, 300–1
  Filipinos, 314
  Kwantung, 18
  military sexual slavery, 298, 341
  slavery, 21
Jeness, Valerie, 66, 69, 71,
  72–3, 163
jobs, 104
  prostitution, 64, 65–6
  see also prostitution; sex work;

work
johns, 3, 4, 55, 74, 82, 105, 126, 179,
    221, 235, 239–40, 241, 274, 348
  class, 157
  as heroes, 226–7
  lesbians, 122
  punishment, 305, 336–8
  sexual revolution, 35–6
  sexuality, 214–19
  transsexuals, 113–15
  violence, 255–6
  see also clients; violence
Johnson, Mavis, 67–8
Jones, Ann, 138–9
Josephine Butler Society, 33, 326–7
  see also Butler, Josephine

Kantian liberalism, 130–1
Kappeler, Susanne, 210–11
Karen refugees, 308
  see also Burmese women
Kelly, Liz, 243, 247–8, 250–4, 264–6
Kemp, Dr Tage, 27–9
kidney trade, 186–8
killing
  see murder
King, Amanda, 90
Kingdon, Elizabeth, 279–82
Kinsey, Alfred, 39, 199
Kirp, David, 131
kissing, 272
Klein, Renate, 190–1
Klerk, Yvonne, 318, 320, 324
Korea, South, 309
  comfort women, 300–2, 341
Korean women, 18
Kronhausen, Drs Phyllis and
    Eberhard, 54, 56–8

labour market
  slavery, 20–1
  see also prostitution; sex

work; work
Lacan, 196, 197
Ladies National Association for the
    Repeal of the Contagious Diseases
    Acts, 1, 19
Lady Chatterley's Lover, 56
Lahey, Kathleen, 209–10
language
  rights and liberties, 280, 283–5, 305
Lap-Chew, Lin, 329
law
  gay pornography, 117
  partriarchy, 277
  power, 277–8
  privacy, 286–7
  rights, 277–9
  see also international law; rights and
    liberties
League of Nations, 7–8, 11–12, 306
  1920s, 15–17, 20, 22, 23
  1930s, 16–19, 24–6, 30–2
  1940s, 25–7
  feminists, 12–13, 38
  international conventions, 12–14,
    17, 20, 35
  report on prevention, 27–32
  sexual slavery, 20, 21
  trafficking, 12–20
legal discrimination, 67
  see also discrimination
legalisation, 191, 345
  see also brothels, licensed; state reg-
    ulation
legitimisation (of prostitution), 35
  see also brothels, licensed; historians
    and histories; sexual revolution;
    state regulation
Leigh, Carol, 84
Leonard, Diana, 189, 202–4
Leppington, Miss Blanche, 22
Lerner, Gerder, 53–4, 180–1
lesbian persecution, 297

lesbian movement
  see gay and lesbian movement
lesbian separatists
  sadomasochism, 125
  see also feminism, radical
lesbians, 228
  johns, 122
  politics, 121–7
  pornography, 80, 117
  prostitution, 92–3, 106, 122, 222–3
  sadomasochism, 95, 150
  sex industry, 124–6
  see also feminism; homosexuality
Levine, Philippa, 260
Liazos, Alexander, 61
liberal democracy, 250
liberal theory
  choice, 130–5
liberalism, 48, 70, 94, 152, 159, 288, 324
  choice, 146
  classical, 132
  contractualism, 173
  freedom of expression, 294
  human rights, 284
  Netherlands, 73–4
  sexual, 99, 121, 127, 196
  state, 285–6
  trafficking, 330
  see also feminism; sexual liberalism; women's liberation
liberation ideologies, 82, 93, 96, 117, 120
  see also feminism
libertarianism, 96, 100, 122, 129, 156, 208, 241
  sex industry, 336
  theory of prostitution, 102–13
  see also liberal; sexual libertarianism
liberties

see rights and liberties
licensed brothels, 9, 14, 16, 22
  foreign women, 23–4
  see also brothels; state regulation
Lijnzaad, Liesbeth, 335
local customs
  see traditions and customs
Lovelace, Linda, 234–5, 2987

Macao, 18
Macik, Donna, 81
McKeganey, Neil, 345–6
MacKinnon, Catharine, 150–1, 156, 159–60, 197–8, 205, 207, 209, 217–18, 231–5, 243–7, 264, 279–80, 284, 286, 291–2, 340
MacLeod, Eileen, 68, 84, 216, 238–9, 256, 273–4
Mahoney, Kathleen, 289–90, 293–5
mail-order brides, 309–10
Malaya, 18
male abuse
  see abuse; discrimination; sexual harassment; murder; rape; violence
male dominance
  feminism, 126
  see also dominance and domination; slavery; subordination; supremacy
male novelists, 226–7
male power
  see power
male prostitution, 92–127
  class, 104
male sexual violence
  see violence
male sexuality, 198–9, 226–8
  customers, 103
  prostitution, 213–19
  subordination of women, 37

see also clients; johns; sexology;
    sexual revolution
male supremacy, 81, 183–4
see also supremacy
malnutrition, 287
Manchuria, 18
Mansson, Sven-Axel, 336–7
Marchiano, Linda
    see Lovelace, Linda
Marcus, Stephen, 37, 57
marketplace
    pornography, 119
    see also capitalism; free-market and
        free market liberalism
marital rape, 243, 260, 261–2, 268,
    286, 293, 296, 298
marriage, 158, 174–5, 257, 260, 263,
    316
    child marriage, 17, 20–1
    procuration, 26
    slavery, 20–1
    see also marital rape
marriage customs
    see traditions and customs
Marxism, 152, 156–7, 170, 207, 276–7
masculine language, 284
    see also language
masculinity, 315, 337
massage parlours, 45, 87, 222, 300
Masters and Johnson, 36, 42, 47, 167
Masters, R. E. L., 37–9, 40, 162–3,
    215–16
Masters, William H., 37–9
masturbation, 40
maternity, 288
    see also pregnancy
media
    COYOTE, 73
medical model of blame
    (for prostitution), 27–32
men, 2, 7, 20
    anti-slavery convention, 20

battery, 140–1
    Australian, 315
    liberal, 70
    rights and choice, 129
    see also abuse; clients; dominance
        and domination; johns; men's
        demand; rape; sexology; subordi-
        nation; violence
Men Against Pornography, 218
men and boys
    prostitution, 92–127
Menachim, Amir, 139
men's demand (for prostitution), 25–7,
    31, 336–8
men's rights, 278–9
mental well-being, 112–13, 120–1
    see also body and self; health
migration, 308–9
    see also refugee women
Mikhailovitch, Katja, 341
military
    prostitution and brothels, 300–1,
        309, 313, 341, 342–3
    rape, 298–300
    sexual slavery, 298–303
    see also comfort women; rape; rape
        camps; war and wartime atrocities
Miller, Henry, 226–7
Miller, JoAnn, 152
Miller, Peggy, 79, 82
Millett, Kate, 66–7, 173, 226–7, 229,
    249
Mills, C. Wright, 170
Miner, Maude E., 26
"minimising", 252–3
misogynous killing, 246–7
    see also murder
misogyny, 227–31, 295
    see also abuse; supremacy; violence;
        women-hating
Mladjenovic, Lepa, 295
mobile brothels, 63

money
gay sexual practice, 106–7
moral standards and morality, 19,
    318, 337
    democratic, 97
    equality, 32–4
    johns, 74
    see also ethics
Morocco
    brothels, 296
mui-tsai system, 18, 20
murder, 67, 242, 246–7, 249, 251–2,
    255–6
    see also abuse; supremacy; violence
mythology
    prostitution, 36, 53, 77–8
    rape, 243–5

naming, 178, 250–4
National Vigilance Association, 11, 19
Neilans, Alison, 19–20, 32–3
neo-regulationism, 31
Nepali women, 311, 328
Nestle, Joan, 122, 126
Netherlands, 112, 220–1, 310,
    317–18, 320, 329, 335, 336, 337
    liberalism, 73–4
neutralising techniques, 137–8
    see also dissociation
Neville Rolfe, Sybil, 25
New York, 26
Nicholson, Linda, 339–40
North China, 18
Norway, 153–5, 179, 270–1
novelists, 226–7
Nozick, Robert, 130–2
Nussbaum, Hedda, 140–1

objectification, 100, 117,
    121, 125, 147, 173, 182, 192,
    206–19, 264–6, 274, 300, 331
    subjecthood, 209–12

O'Connell Davidson, Julia, 181–3,
    309
O'Neill, Maggie, 155
oppression, 77–9, 91, 211, 225, 246
    body, 189–91
    choice, 159–60
    feminism and feminist theorists,
        249–50
    political, 194–5
    see also abuse; class; gender; sexual
        harassment; power; violence
oral sex, 44, 221, 238–9, 240, 261
Orchard, Lionel, 133
orgasm, 104, 213, 219, 222, 223,
    228, 237, 238, 271
Oriental women, 17
    see also Asia region
Oslo, 153–5, 179, 270–1
outlawry, 122, 126, 127
Outshoorn, Joyce, 324–5
Overall, Christine, 183–6
Overs, Cheryl, 75–6

paedophilia, 94, 95, 98–9, 129
Pakistan, 321
Parker, Lisa, 148
Parker, Tony, 61
Pass the Bill Committee, 10, 11
Pateman, Carole, 130, 173–6, 183
paternalism, 345
    protection of women, 23
patriarchy, 143, 149, 183–5, 230,
    277, 315–16
    heterosexuality, 184
Patterson, Orlando, 176–80
Pearl, Cora, 123
Pearl, Cyril, 54–5
Pearsall, Ronald, 54–5, 55–6
penalisation
    see punishment
Penn State Report, 319, 333–5
Penthouse magazine, 234

performance art, 84–91, 164
Perkins, Roberta, 103, 104, 106–8,
      114, 126, 164
persecution
   gays, 297
Persian women, 18
Person, Ethel Spector, 217–18
personal choice
   see choice
personal freedom, 20, 20–1
   see also choice; freedom; rights and
   liberties
personality and personhood, 261, 292
   see also effects; emotional life; identity; body and self; self and self-
   esteem; social relations
perversions, 93–5, 99, 209–10
   see also sexual minorities
Pheterson, Gail, 73–4, 78
Philippines, 18, 309, 330–1, 341
   brothels, 314
   CATW, 331–2
   comfort women, 300
   sex tourism, 315
   trafficking, 313–15
   US military prostitution, 298–9,
      341, 343–4
phone sex lines, 267
pimps, 11, 16, 177, 178, 234–5, 255,
      270, 312
Pines, Ayala, 232
Playboy magazine, 234–5
Playboy Foundation, 69
pleasure, 104, 110, 197, 220, 221,
      223, 228–9, 238, 246, 257, 299
Plummer, Ken, 200
pluralism
   see sexual pluralism
police, 67, 312
policy
   gender, 132–3
political oppression, 194–5

politics
   choice and liberal theory, 130–5
   queer, 74–7
   sexual, 206–7
   see also liberal democracy
PONY, 85
pornography, 37, 41, 48, 58, 64, 65,
      74, 78, 85, 97, 99, 124, 125,
      129, 143, 144, 150, 180, 209–10,
      218, 230, 244, 247–8, 258, 265,
      287, 291, 293–5, 309, 320
   campaigns against, 235–6
   censorship, 54
   dominance and submission, 117–18
   feminism, 74, 119–20, 122, 190–1,
      235–6
   free speech, 232–3
   gay and women's liberation, 117–18
   gay male defence, 116–21
   industry, 120–1
   interactive, 309–10
   lesbians, 80, 117, 150
   prostitution, 231–6
   post-modernism, 118–19, 121,
      190–1
   revolutionary, 118
   sadomasochism, 95–6, 118, 119
   stars, 120–1
post-modernism, 205, 279–80, 340
   pornography, 118–19, 121
   prostitution, 127
Post-Porn Modernists, 86
   see also Sprinkle, Annie
post-traumatic stress disorder, 269–70
post-structuralism, 201–5, 339, 340–1
poverty, 315–16
   see also economic status
power, 66, 93, 103, 108, 111, 121,
      174, 178–83, 189, 197, 202–9,
      225, 226, 244, 247, 282–3,
      286–9, 293, 321
   law, 277–8

power *contd*
see also dominance and domination;
   slavery; state; subordination;
power *contd*
   supremacy; violence
pregnancy, 188–9, 288
prejudice
   see woman-hating; stigma
Prestage, Garrett, 102–4, 108,
   114–15, 164
prevention (of prostitution), 24–7, 31
   feminist approaches, 19–27
   public education, 27
privacy and law, 286–7
private sphere, 282, 291, 304
   democracy, 290
   private/public distinction, 285–90
pro-prostitution
   feminist movement, 2, 65–6, 79–84
   ideology, 8
   lobbyists 1970s, 79–84, 163, 306–7
   trafficking, 317–25
   see also choice; prostitutes' rights
      movement
procuration, 11, 13, 15, 26, 316–17,
   323
professional standards, 166–7
promiscuity, 33–4
PROS, 68–9
prostituted women, 5
   punishment, 40–1
   sexual minority, 92
   slaves, 50–1
   see also choice; prostitution
Prostitutes' Collective of Victoria, 81
prostitutes' rights movement, 2, 5, 7,
   50, 65–91, 92, 122, 224
   beginnings, 67–73
   choice, 128–9, 135
   feminists, 77–84
   international organising, 73–4
   work, 161–2

prostitution, 1, 10, 33–4, 309, 348
   boys, 92–3, 108–13
   child sexual abuse, 256–9
   choice, 128–60
   crime, 260–1
   definitions, 4, 275, 334
   effects, 268–71
   feminism, 1, 35, 37–8, 79–84, 90–1,
      98–9, 101, 121–2, 127, 224–5
   free-market, 187–8
   gay men, 92–3, 95
   history, 48–54
   homosexuality, 92–127
   international human rights, 325–30
   lesbian and gay sexual libertarian-
      ism, 102–13
   lesbian politics, 121–7
   lesbianism, 92–3, 106
   male and female, 102–13
   male sexuality, 213–19
   male supremacy, 183–6
   pornography, 231–6
   post-modernism, 127
   queer perspective, 74–7, 127
   liberation, 62–5, 84, 91
   sexual revolution, 35–64
   sexuality, 35–6, 41–8, 236–41
   slavery, 176–83
   sociology, 59–64
   transsexuals, 111–15
   universalising, 339–48
   unpaid violence, 255–6
   violence, 5, 242–74, 343
   work, 161–95
   see also "forced" prostitution,
      "free" prostitution, trafficking
prostitution abuser, 3, 4
prostitution performance art, 84–91
protection
   age of, 13
   paternalism, 23
psychiatry

see health
psychoanalysis, 29, 118, 216–18, 268
psychology, 25, 31, 33, 210–11, 268
public choice theory, 133
   see also choice
public education
   prevention of prostitution, 27
   see also education; sex education
public health, 22, 71
   see also health
public/private spheres, 285–91
pudendum, 229
punishment, 123, 227, 253, 306–7,
   316–17
   johns, 40, 336–8
   prostituted women, 40–1
punters, 112

"queer" perspective and
   politics, 74–7, 118–19
   homosexuality and prostitution,
   92–127
   prostitution, 74–7
   sexual minorities, 93–102

racism, 109, 113, 159, 233–4, 316
Radford, Jill, 246–9, 251–2
radical feminism
   see feminism, radical
Rao, Arati, 286
rape, 44, 56, 115, 135, 151, 158, 234,
   242–5, 247, 249, 252, 256,
   259–61, 265, 268–9, 291, 292,
   295, 298–303, 314, 334
   definition, 243–5, 295–6
   gang, 296–7
   marriage, 243, 261–2
   military, 275
   myths, 139, 243–5
   torture, 295–6
   war, 206–7, 275, 298–303
   see also marital rape; violence

rape camps, 275, 298–303
Rawls, John, 130–1, 133–4
Raymond, Janice, 142–5, 152, 322–3
recruitment for brothels, 11, 13
   see also procuration;
    trafficking; White Slave Traffic
Red Thread, 73–4
reformatories, 30–1
refugee women, 18, 295, 308
regulation
   see state regulation
rehabilitation, 26–7, 31, 32, 54–9
Reich, Wilhelm, 216
religious rights, 288
   see also traditions and customs
repatriation, compulsory, 23–4
reproductive liberalism, 142–6
"rescue" work, 25–7, 32
researchers, attitudes to prostitution,
   346–7
"revolutionary activity", 95, 118
Rich, Adrienne, 160
Richards, David, 132
rights and liberties, 19–21, 70–1,
   316–17, 347
   equal rights, 20
   feminism, 119–20, 276–93
   feminist human rights theory,
    275–305
   language, 280, 283–5
   men's rights, 278–9
   omission of prostitution, 293–8
   pornography, 119–20
   protection of women and children,
    278–9
   right to prostitute, 318–20
   scepticism, 276–84
   trafficking, 306–38
   violence, 250–1, 290–3
   woman-blaming, 25–32
   see also choice; prostitutes' rights
    movement

risks, 104–5
  pregnancy, 188–9
Roberts, Nickie, 50–4, 77, 80, 84,
  129–30
Rogers, Lesley, 326–7
Roiphe, Katie, 149, 150
role play, 11, 122, 125, 127
Romany, Celina, 282, 284, 285, 291
Rome, ancient, 51
Ross, Andrew, 98
Rosta, Eva, 164
Roth, Kenneth, 303–4
Royalle, Candida, 90
Rubin, Gayle, 95–9, 102, 205
ruling-class ideology, 157
  see also class
Rumania, 308
Russell, Diana, 232, 234, 243, 251–2,
  258, 261–2
Russia, 177, 308
Russian refugee women, 18
Ryan, William, 159

sacred healers, 90
sacred prostitution, 52–4
Sacred Slutism, 86
sadomasochism, 94–5, 99, 100, 117,
  125, 135, 150, 205, 208, 223,
  260
  lesbian separatists, 125
  pornography, 118, 119
sadomasochist clubs, 88–9
safe sex, 346
Sagarin, 59–60
SAGE, 72
Saint James, Margo, 69, 70, 72–4,
  163, 220
Saint Joan's Social and Political
  Alliance, 22
Samaritans, phonelines, 267
Samois, 95
San Francisco, 95

sandwiches, 44
Santos, Aida, 314, 331
Save the Children Fund,
  1930s, 20
Scambler, Graham and Annette, 145,
  345
Scarlet Alliance, 74, 75–6
scarlet letter syndrome, 268–9
"scientific knowledge"
  see sexology
Scott, Valerie, 82
self and self-esteem, 120
  self-mutilation, 110, 111
  see also body and self;
    transsexuals
selling, children, 20–1
semen swallowing, 109
sensuality, 237
service work, 163, 165, 170, 224,
  302–3
sex
  prostitution, 213–41
  violence, 244–5
sex education, 27, 41, 48, 84, 86, 95,
  124
  see also sexology;
    surrogacy
sex equality
  see equality and inequality
sex industry, 5–6, 81, 95–9, 106,
  121–2, 124–6, 175, 193–4, 241,
  248, 266, 307–16, 324, 336, 345
  abuse, 265
  Asia region, 327–33, 343–5
  performance art, 84–91
  public relations and performance
    art, 84–91
  queer perspective, 74–7
  sexual harassment, 248, 263–8
  USA, 1970s, 48
  violence, 267–8, 274
  see also COYOTE

sex reform, 236–7
sex slavery, 20, 21, 296
sex therapy
  see sexology; surrogacy
sex tourism, 18, 309, 313, 323, 327,
    330, 334, 342, 348
  Philippines, 315
sex trafficking
  see trafficking
sex work, 1, 3, 5, 65–6, 70, 75, 77–9,
    84, 101–2, 163, 183, 191–2, 345,
    346
  gay males, 107
  murder, 255–6
  see also prostitution; sex industry;
    work
sexism, 97, 231, 316
sexology, 25, 33–43, 47, 64, 93, 95,
    141–2, 162–3, 167, 197, 198–9,
    214–16, 228–9, 237, 242, 262
  brothels, 36, 39
  feminist historians, 37
  sex industry, 37
  surrogates, 45–7
  transsexuals, 114
  see also sexual revolution
sexual abuse
  see abuse; child sexual abuse; rape;
    violence
sexual behaviour, 3, 4–5
  changes, 33
  see also abuse; aggression; domi-
    nance and domination; subordina-
    tion; violence
sexual "deviation", 29–31
sexual exploitation
  definition, 306, 334
sexual freedom, 62–4, 77, 208–11
sexual harassment, 71, 171, 192, 225,
    234, 244, 249, 252–4, 260–8,
    293, 334
  feminist naming, 251

sex industry, 248, 263–8
sexual intercourse, 226–31
sexual liberalism, 36, 48, 63, 64, 129,
    142–6, 210, 211, 254
  see also sexual liberation
sexual liberals
  see liberalism
sexual liberation, 8, 34, 41, 65, 84,
    86, 91, 119, 220–2
  see also liberation ideologies
sexual libertarianism, 81, 150, 208
  see also libertarianism
sexual minorities, 76–7, 92, 104, 110
  "queer" theory, 93–102
sexual objectification
  see objectification
sexual performance art
  see performance art
sexual pleasure
  see pleasure
sexual pluralism, 202, 212
sexual politics, 206–7
  see also Millett, Kate
sexual revolution, 14, 34–64, 197, 336
  johns, 35–6
sexual slavery, 20–1, 29, 74, 126, 235,
    321
  military, 298–303
  see also brothels; comfort women
sexual terrorism, 268–9
sexual violence, 6, 246–8
  see also child sexual abuse; rape;
    violence
sexuality
  choice, 128–60
  feminists, 98–9
  gender, 98–9
  johns, 214–19
  perversion, 209–10
  prostitution, 35–6, 36, 41–8, 64,
    236–41
  radical feminism, 205–8

sexuality *contd*
  theory, 196–212
  see also dominance and domination;
    subordination
sexuality theories
  feminism, 196–212
shaving of heads, 177–8
shelters
  see battered women
The Shield, 19, 20–23, 25–6, 30, 31,
    32, 33, 34
  trafficking, 20, 22, 23
Shrage, Laurie, 166, 185–6
Silbert, Mimi, 232
Simon, William, 60, 199–201, 214–15
Sinclair, Amanda, 194
skills, 163, 166–7, 171
slavery, 6, 9, 20–1, 26, 50–1, 54, 74,
    112, 113, 126, 312, 325
  Japan, 21
  prostitution, 50, 176–83
  sexual, 19, 235, 296
  trafficking, 326–8
  see also sexual slavery;
    trafficking; war and wartime
    atrocities
Smart, Carol, 277–8, 280–1
Smith, Dorothy, 156–7
Snell, Cudmore, 108–9
Snow, Dr, 23
social constructionism, 197–8,
    199–201, 205
Social Hygiene Council, 25
social justice, 277
  see also rights and liberties
social purity feminists, 25
social relations, 158, 206, 255
  see also child sexual abuse; class;
    dominance and domination; eco-
    nomic status; marriage; subordi-
    nation; traditions and customs
social skills

  see skills
social theorists, 340
socialism, 276–8
  feminists, 68–9, 156–7, 186
  work, 168–9
  see also feminism
sociologists, 214–15
  gay, 200–1
sociology and sociologists,
    36–7, 59–64, 214–15, 242
  choice, 137–8
  deviancy sociologists, 59–62
  gay, 200–1
  sexuality, 197, 199–201, 203–4
  victim-blaming, 142
Solken, Anna, 11
souteneurs
  see pimps
South Africa, 21
specula, 85
Sprinkle, Annie, 52, 84–9, 96, 124
Sproule, Linda, 89
Sri Lanka, 309
standpoint theorists, 158–9
Stanko, Betsy, 249
state, 292–3
  liberalism, 285–6
  military sexual slavery, 303
state regulation, 9, 13–14, 16–17, 19,
    21–2, 191–2
  Japan, 300–1
  punishment, 317
  Thailand, 312–13
Stead, W. T., 10
Stefano, Joey, 116, 120–1
Steinberg, Joel, 140–1
sterilisation, 30, 344
Stern, William, 144
Sternberg, David, 63
"stiff standers", 57
stigma, 223–31, 255, 322
Stockholm syndrome, 268

Stoltenberg, John, 218
Stoltzfus, Brenda, 341–2
Stratten, Dorothy, 235
street hustlers, Sydney, 106–7
street prostitution, 108
Streetwise Youth, 109
stress disorder, 269–70
Stretton, Hugh, 133
strippers and stripping, 124, 125, 193, 252, 265–6, 310
Sturdevant, Saundra, 341–2
Stychin, Carl, 117, 119–20
subjecthood, 209–12, 228
subjugation, 228, 230
submission, 100, 194, 206, 206–7, 228–9
subordination, 22, 27, 37, 102, 107, 173, 175, 194–5, 209, 229, 240, 268, 289, 291, 292, 294, 295, 297–8
see also slavery
suffragists, 10, 19–20, 20, 22, 33
suicide, 269
Sullivan, Barbara, 81, 224–5
Summer, Toby, 150, 222, 225, 254
Sundahl, Debbie, 124
Sundquist, Madame, 30
supremacy, 194–5, 207, 217, 230, 286, 315
see also dominance and domination; subordination
surrogacy, 45–7, 144, 180
survivors, 151, 168, 195, 213, 243–4, 251, 302
Sweden, 30, 337
swinging, 43
Sydney, 106–7
symbolic interactionism, 201–5
Syrian women, 18
Szasz, Thomas, 37, 58

tabletop dancing, 193, 252, 266–7
telephone calls, 267
telephone sex, 267
temple prostitution, 20, 36, 52–3
girl children, 17
Thailand, 115, 309, 311
brothels, 311, 312–13
girls, 323
Karen and Burmese women, 297, 308
trafficking, 312–13, 332
"three holes", 343–4
Tite, Constance, 25
topless barmaids, 266
torture, 291–2
rape, 295–6
see also violence
tourism
see sex tourism
trade unions, 191–2, 265
traditions and customs, 17–18, 20–1, 282
sexual slavery, 20–1
Traffic in Women Committee, 13, 19, 25
trafficking, 7–24, 11–19, 106, 177, 295, 330
AMSH, 23
anti-prostitution position, 330–3
Asia region, 17–18, 308–16, 327–33
children, 12, 13, 15, 20–1, 323
contemporary, 307–16
definition, 320–1, 323–4
demand, sexual, 336–8
economy, world, 307–16
Europe, 15–18
feminist analysis, 19–24
foreign women, 15–16
girls, 20–1, 311–14
human rights, 306–38
international conventions, 316–18
kidneys, 186–8

trafficking *contd*
 League of Nations, 12–19, 30
 Philippines, 313–15
 pro-prostitution position, 317–25
 The Shield, 19, 20
 slavery, 326–8
 see also choice; "forced" prostitution; "free" prostitution; League
   of Nations; rape camps; war and
   wartime atrocities
training, 26, 30
 see also "rescue" work
transgressive sexualities, 93
 see also sexual minorities
transsexuals, 95, 99, 102, 103, 111,
   127
 abuse, 164
 clients, 113–15
 johns, 113–15
 prostitution, 111–15, 164
 sexology, 114
transvestites, 94, 95
trauma
 see emotional life; identity; self and
   self-esteem; violence
traumatic stress disorder, 269
truth-telling, 128–9

Ulfbeck, Mademoiselle, 30
Ullerstam, Lars, 63
underwear, 42–3
UNESCO, 325
unions, 191–2, 265
United Nations, 14, 38, 283, 304–5,
   325
 Beijing conference, 329
 Declaration of the Elimination of
   Violence Against Women, 275
 Human Rights Commission, 71
 rape camps and UN
   personnel, 300
 see also international law

United States
 Institute of Public and Urban
   Affairs, 71
 military prostitution, Philippines,
   298–9,341, 343–4
 sterilisation, 30
universalising prostitution, 339–48
unpaid violence, 255–6
unprotected sex, 120
 see also condoms; health; HIV-AIDS
uterus, 229

Valentino, Margaret, 67–8
van der Vleuten, Nelleke, 307–8,
   317–18
van der Zijden, Terry, 220–1
Vance, Carole, 209
Vera, Veronica, 52, 84, 90, 224
verbal harassment, 267
victim-blaming, 139–43
victimism, 148–52
victimologists, 139
Victorian England, 54–9
Victorian era, johns, 55
Vietnam, 308, 309
Vietnam veterans, stress, 270
Vigilance Record (journal), 11
violence, 11, 26, 40, 51, 56–7, 62, 67,
   71, 91, 97, 105, 115, 125, 132,
   149, 195, 224, 225, 227, 230,
   232–6, 259, 242–74
 definition, 247
 domestic, 303–4
 effects, 268–71
 human rights, 290–3
 international law, 283–4
 prostitution, 5, 242–74, 259–61,
   343
 rights and liberties, 250–1, 290–3
 sex, 244–5
 sex industry, 267–8, 274
 subordination, 297–8

unpaid, 225–6
White Slave Traffic, 8
see also abuse; pornography; rape;
    sexual harassment
violence identification
    see naming
visual harassment, 266–7
voluntary prostitution
    see choice; "forced" prostitution;
    "free" prostitution
vulnerability, 346

wage-earners
    anti-slavery convention, 20
Waldron, Jeremy, 276
"Walter", 56–9
war and wartime atrocities, 295,
    308–9
    forced prostitution, 296
    see also military; rape; rape camps
Waring, Marilyn, 169, 289
"watching", 44–5
WEDPRO, 313–14, 331
Weeks, Jeffrey, 8, 93–5, 102, 105–7,
    201–3, 211–12
the West, prostitution
    comparison with the East 341–3,
    348
WHISPER, 72, 77–8, 91, 257, 268–9,
    342
White Slave Traffic, 8, 11–12, 23, 307
    campaign against, 8–14
    feminists, 10, 12
Whitehead, Mary Beth, 144
whore stigma
    see stigma
wife murder, 334
wife rape
    see marital rape
Williams, Linda, 209
Williams, Patricia, 282–3
Wilson, Elizabeth, 49–50

Wittig, Monique, 206
Wolf, Naomi, 149, 150
woman-battering, 245–6
    see also abuse; violence
woman-blaming, 25–32, 139–42
    causes (of prostitution),
    27–32
woman-hating, 227–31, 233–4
woman's body
    see body and self
women
    advertising, 125
    prostituted sex, 219–23
    users of prostitutes, 99
Women Against Violence Against
    Women, 125
women's agency, 128–9
    choice, 145–8
Women's International League for
    Peace and Freedom, 22
women's liberation, 69–70, 85, 309
women's liberation movement
    1970s, 65–6
    see also feminism
women's organisations, 19, 31–2
    see also names of organisations
women's rights, 19, 316–17
    see also rights and liberties
Women's Social and Political Union,
    10
Wood, Marianne, 347
work, 99, 179–80, 194–5, 242, 307,
    324, 328
    dignity, 168–73
    idea of prostitution as, 8, 65–6, 70,
    73–6, 78–9
    prostitution, 161–95, 191–4
    rape camps and ILO, 302–3
    slavery, 20–1
    see also service work
work, service
    see service work

World Charter for Prostitutes' Rights, 73–4
World Health Organisation, 71
World Sex Guide, Internet, 309–10
Wright, Shelley, 288

YWCA, 22
Yudof, Mark, 131
Yugoslavia, former Republic of, 308
  rape camps, 298–300